An Atlas of ANGLO-SAXON ENGLAND

For Thomas Hardin of Withycombe
in the county of Somerset

An Atlas of ANGLO-SAXON ENGLAND

David Hill

Basil Blackwell

First published 1981
Paperback edition (with corrections) first published 1984
Basil Blackwell, 108 Cowley Road, Oxford OX4 1JF, England

Maps 1, 3 and 18 are reproduced by kind permission of the British Library.

British Library Cataloguing in Publication Data

Hill, David, 1937—
An atlas of Anglo-Saxon England 700–1066.
1. England — Historical geography — Maps
2. Great Britain — History — Anglo-Saxon period, 449–1066
I. Title
911'.42 G1815

ISBN 0–631–11181–6
0–631–13684–3 pbk

Phototypesetting by Oxford Publishing Services

Printed in Great Britain

Contents

The Events

Administration

The Economy

The Church

Preface and Acknowledgements

This work is an attempt to display all the evidence on later Anglo-Saxon England that can be placed in a topographic or chronological framework. It covers the period from 700 to 1066 and attempts to cut across many of the narrow specialisms and draw on the fields of history, archaeology, charter studies and all other disciplines which throw light on the period. As such, it tends to be a personal view which reflects the way that I see the evidence and so, unfortunately, also contains my prejudices and shortcomings. What it cannot convey is the great pleasure I have known over many years in the study of the period. That pleasure has been enhanced by the many kindnesses I have received from others in the field.

My principal thanks are due to John Bosanko who introduced me to the subject, to Martin Biddle who fired my enthusiasm for research and to Peter Addyman whose help was unstinting in the years when I first attempted serious work, and whose understanding saw me through university.

Great assistance has been rendered by many people, either in advice or in allowing me to use work in advance of publication: F. Aldsworth, D. Austin, M. Dolley, V. Fearn, A. Goodier, J. Hassall, G. Harling, D. Hooke, H. R. Loyn, D. M. Metcalf, J. Parkhouse, D. Powlesland, and F. Shepherd and many others.

Patrick Wormald has been particularly generous in the time he has spent weaning me away from prejudice and error; faults that remain bear witness to my stubborness.

Caveat and General Note

These maps are an illustration and a starting point. Interest in Anglo-Saxon England is growing apace and serious students will need to validate for themselves the particular items that make up the maps. This is especially true of anything arising out of charter evidence.

A continuous narrative is provided by Stenton (1971) who is an indispensable companion; an introduction to the documents is provided by Whitelock (1955). Current bibliographies are provided by **Anglo-Saxon England** on a yearly basis whilst archaeological work is reported in advance of publication in **Medieval Archaeology**.

Except where otherwise indicated, the maps show present day shorelines and courses of rivers.

For those who work on a basis of measurement which rests on a sub-division of an inaccurate estimate of the girth of the world it may be as well to know that one mile, the unit used on these maps, equals 1.6093 kilometres. The furlong is the eighth part of a mile.

Introduction

Bede began his *Ecclesiastical History of the English Nation* (completed in AD 731) with a chapter entitled 'Of the Situation of Britain and Ireland, and of their Ancient Inhabitants', in which he attempted to sketch the physical background to his historical and ecclesiastical account. Unfortunately, the chapter is brief, and draws heavily on Classical authorities. Other descriptions exist from the period, the latest, largest and most helpful being the massive record of Domesday Book, which attempts to record the state of England in January 1066. All the major recent historians of pre-Conquest England have appended a few maps to their works, as an aid to the student.

This volume is an attempt to illustrate those historians' work. It is not a continuous record but an aid, in which those things which can be looked at spatially have been recorded. It has been said elsewhere that our surest record is the landscape itself and this is an attempt to set various strands against that landscape. It may not be possible for a modern historian to spend a lifetime roaming the face of England, but it is possible to recognize the geographic framework in which our predecessors lived and the constraints it laid upon them. These maps are an attempt to assist towards those insights.

An Anglo-Saxon atlas should begin with an Anglo-Saxon map. The Cotton Tiberius map is a multicolour map of the world, based, like so much Anglo-Saxon learning, on late Antique exemplars. Ker dates the manuscript from which it comes to the first half of the eleventh century (Ker 1957, 255). It was probably produced at Winchester.

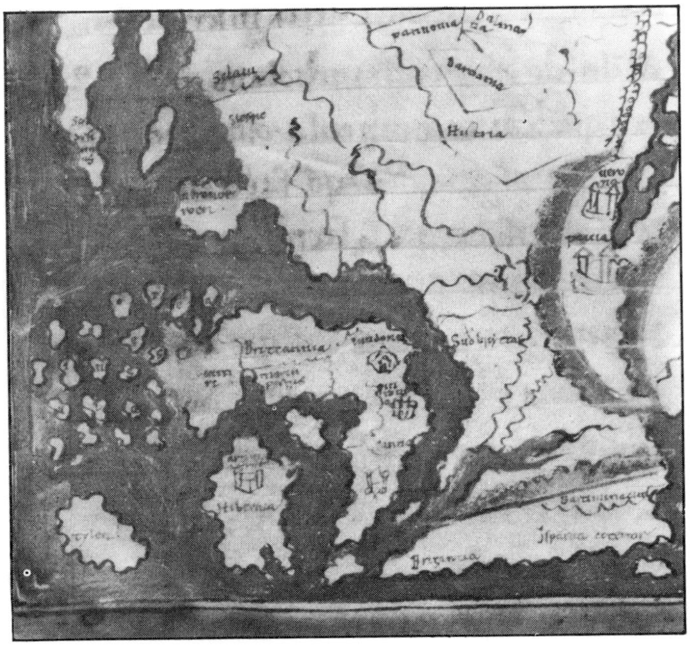

1 The British Isles from the world map, Cotton Tiberius B.V. f. 56v.

The shape of the British Isles on the Cotton Tiberius map (**1**) is reasonably good when compared with other maps of the time, most of which were influenced by the Frankish 'Saint Sever' map (**2**), and made no attempt to describe the shape of Britain. The Cotton Tiberius map, however, is quite unlike the formalized maps that were beginning to appear. England is seen as a country with important towns, sharing the island with other races and surrounded by other, smaller islands, including Ireland, with its monastery at Armagh, and the Orkney Islands. Although the divisions of England appear arbitrary and anachronistic — **Cantiae, Brittaniae** and **Marin Pergis** — the map as a whole provides an interesting comparison with the earlier account in Bede:

Britain, an island in the Ocean, formerly called Albion, is situated between the north and the west, facing, though at a considerable distance, the coasts of Germany, France and Spain, which form the greatest part of Europe. It extends 800 miles in length towards the north, and is 200 miles in breadth, except where several promontories extend further in breadth, by which its compass is made 3675 miles. To the south, as you pass along the nearest shore of the Belgic Gaul, the first place in Britain which opens to the eye is the city of **Rutubi Portus**, *by the English corrupted into* **Reptacestir**. *The distance from hence across the sea to* **Gessoriacum**, *the nearest shore of* **the Morini**, *is fifty miles, or as some writers say, 450 furlongs. On the back of the island, where it opens upon the boundless ocean it has the islands called the* **Orcades**. *Britain excels for grain and trees, and is well adapted for feeding cattle and beasts of burden. It also produces vines in some places, and has plenty of*

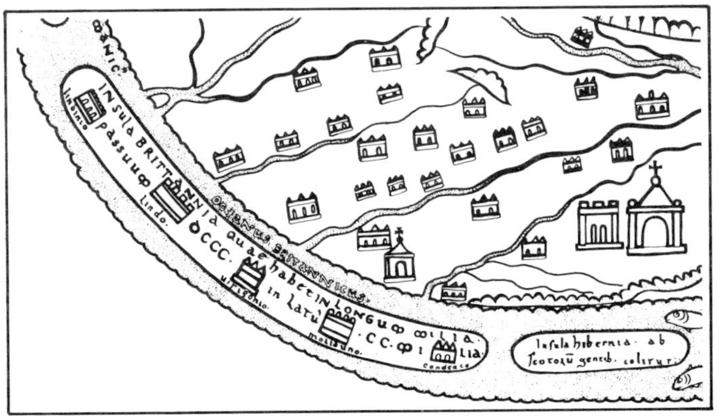

2 The British Isles from the St Sever world map (1028–72)

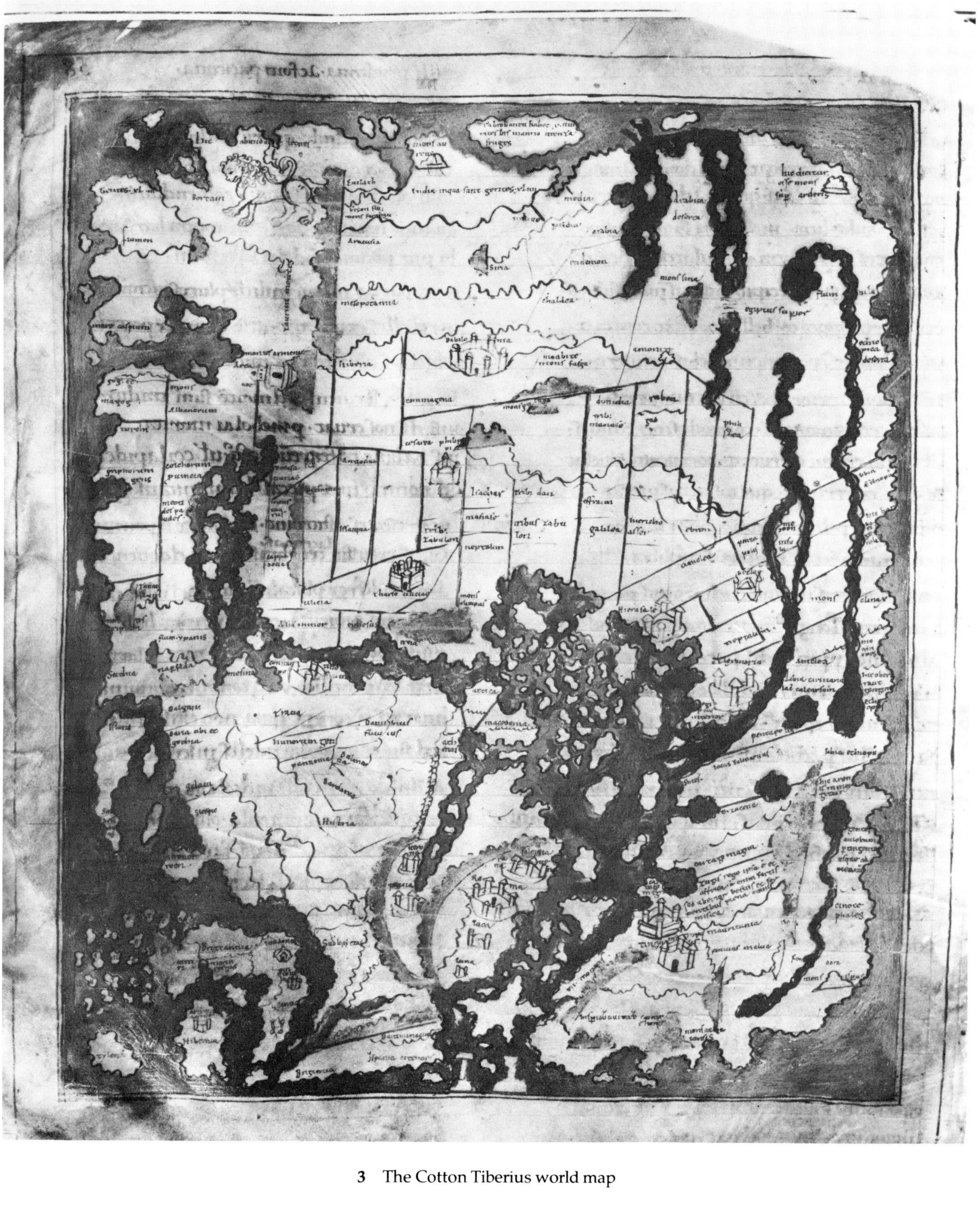

3 The Cotton Tiberius world map

land and water-fowls of several sorts; it is remarkable also for rivers abounding in fish, and plentiful springs. It has the greatest plenty of salmon and eels, seals are frequently taken, and dolphins, as also whales; besides many sorts of shell-fish, such as mussels, in which are often found excellent pearls of all colours, red, purple, violet and green, but mostly white. There is also a great abundance of cockles, of which the scarlet dye is made; a most beautiful colour, which never fades with the heat of the sun or the washing of the rain; but the older it is, the more beautiful it becomes. It has both salt and hot springs, and from them flow rivers which furnish hot baths, proper for all ages and sexes and arranged accordingly. . . Britain has also many veins of metals, as copper, iron, lead and silver; it has much and excellent jet. . . The island was formerly embellished with twenty-eight noble cities, besides innumerable castles, which were strongly secured with walls, towers, gates and locks. And, from its lying almost under the North Pole, the nights are light in summer, so that at midnight the beholders are often in doubt whether the evening twilight still continues or that the morning is coming on; . . . This island at present, following the number of the books in which the Divine law was written, contains five nations, the English, Britons, Scots, Picts and Latins. . . (Knowles 1965, 4–5)

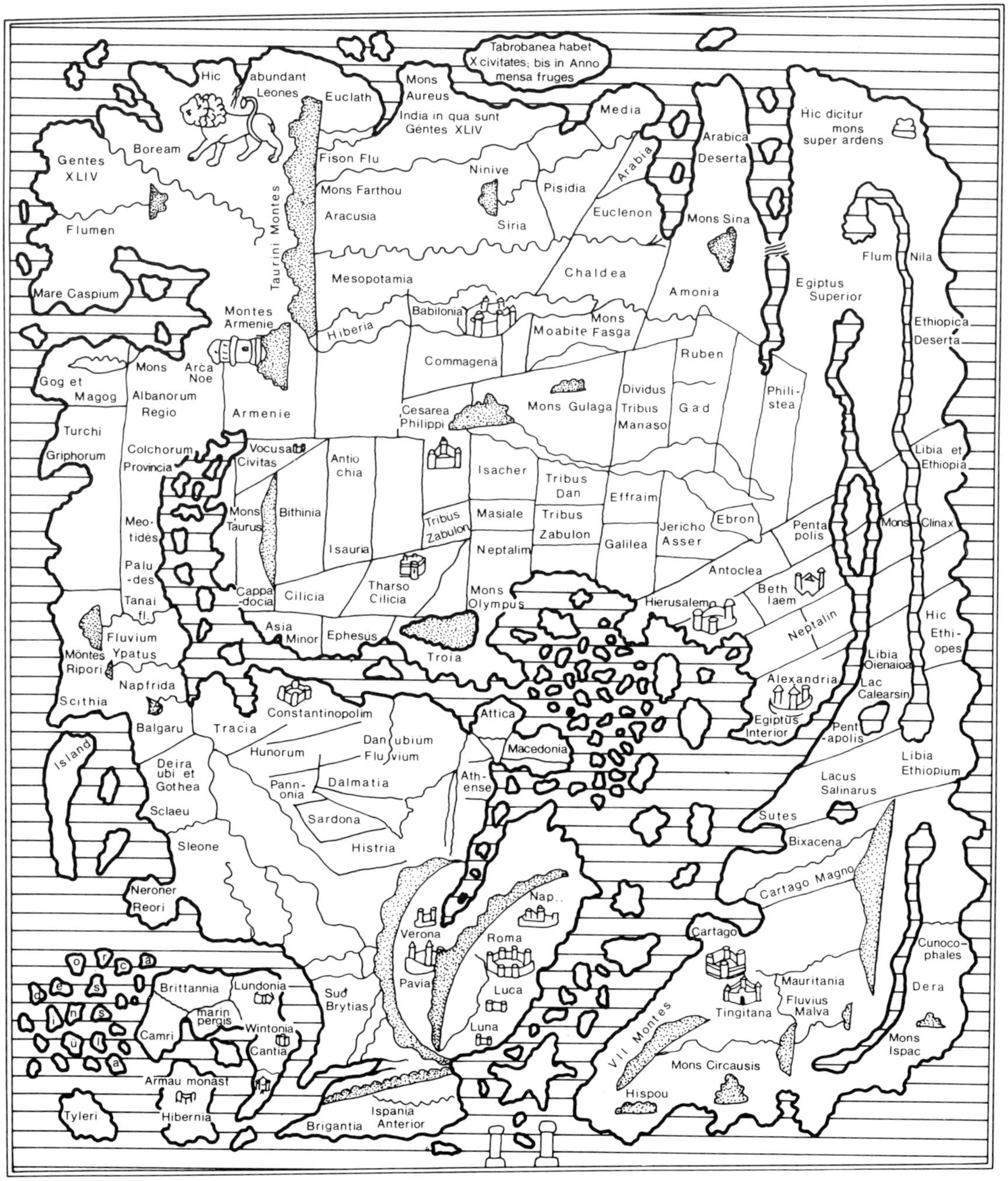

4 Diagram of the Cotton Tiberius world map

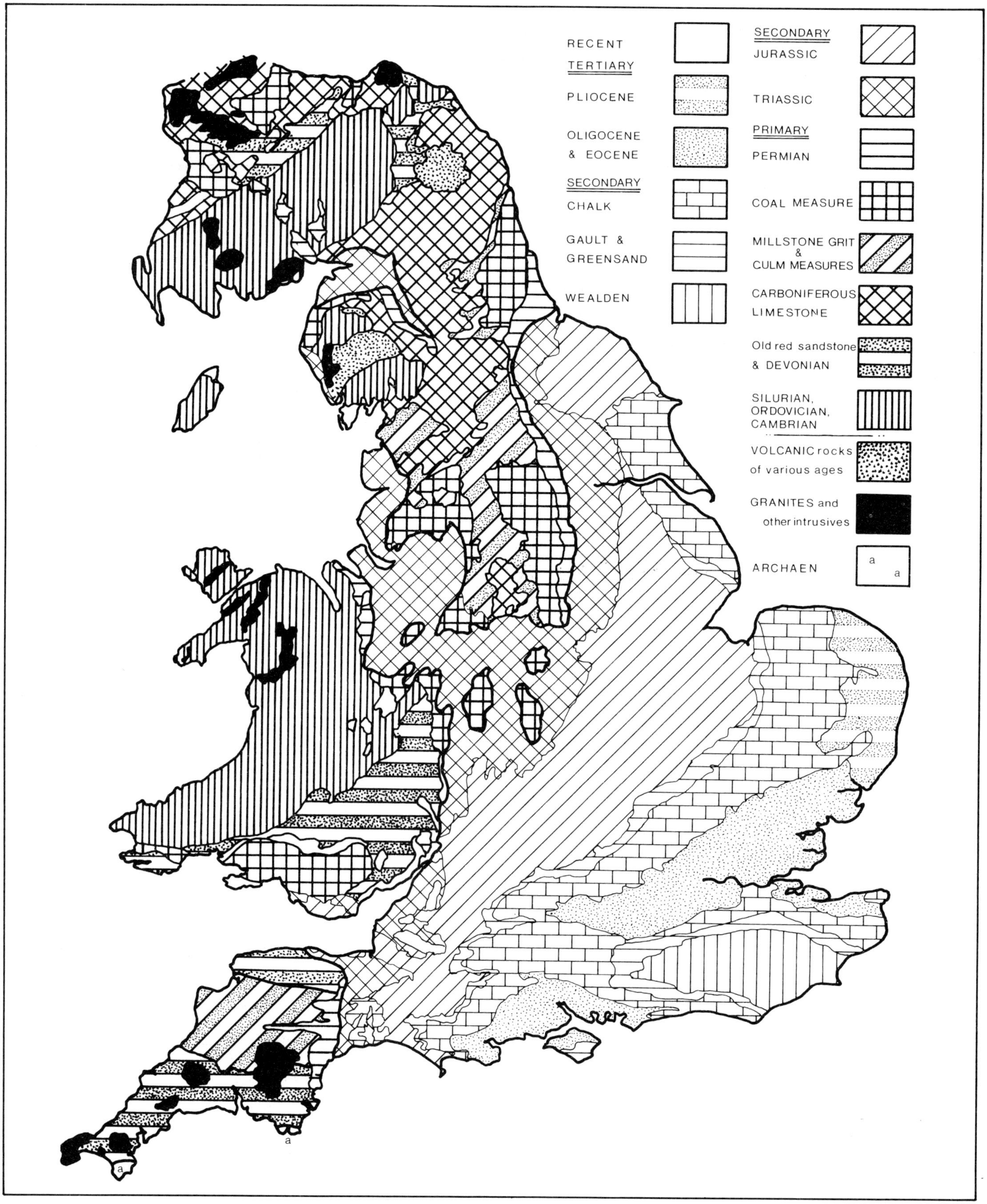

5 Simplified solid geology

The Background

Geology, Relief and Soil (5–9)

The picture revealed in the mapping of Anglo-Saxon England is often distorted, a distortion to which two factors have contributed: first, the distortion imposed by physical and geographic factors, for England was not a flat plain, uniformly vegetated, watered and peopled; and secondly, the bias that comes from the available evidence. Thus, an apparently significant distribution of an artefact or an event may only reveal the survival pattern or the retrieval pattern of the evidence.

The geographical constraints that affect all settlement in England are interrelated and often interact. Geology supplies the bare bones: in general, the older hard rocks are to the west and the softer sedimentary rocks to the east (map **5**). Patterns of erosion affect soil and relief, available minerals affect trade, and ridges such as the great Jurassic scarp control the routeways and also the provision of good building stone (maps **199** and **200**). However, there are large areas of England where the solid geology is unimportant, as it is overlaid by vast areas of fluvial or glacial drift (map **6**), often to a considerable depth.

The archaeology of Britain has typically been divided for all periods into that of highland and lowland zones (map **7**). But although this is as true for the Anglo-Saxon period as for any other, with the Celts holding the highland zone and the centres of Anglo-Saxon population in the lowland zone, it is clear that there are great differences not only within zones of relief (map **8**) but also in the configuration of the landscape. It remains true, nevertheless, that the economy and life of the highland zone marked out its settlement and later history from the more desirable lowland zone because of its high relief, hard rocks, poor soils, heavy rainfall and more extreme climate.

Map **9** is a simplification of the results of the Land Utilization Survey (1941) and shows the soils in broad categories. The quality of the land is the product of drift, solid geology, relief and rainfall: these soils are a key to settlement. Although map **9** indicates soil quality, it must be remembered that it is the result of **modern** research and therefore reflects those soils of most use for today's agricultural practices.

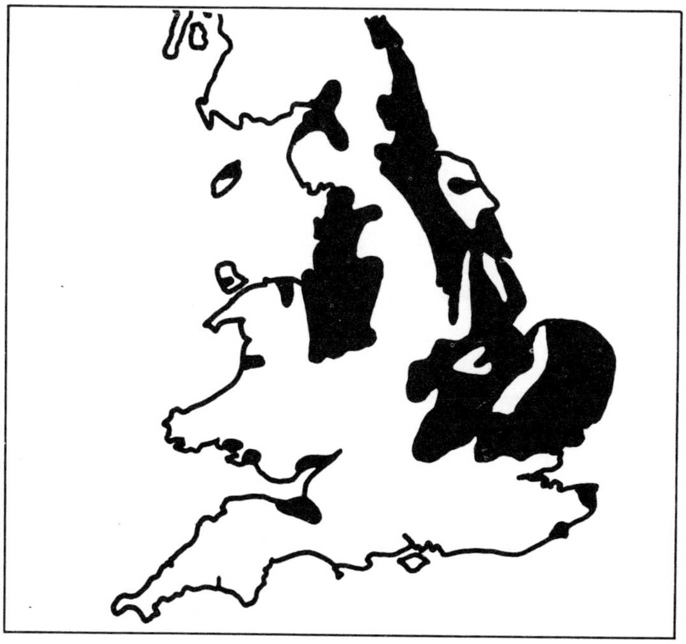

6 Drift-covered areas

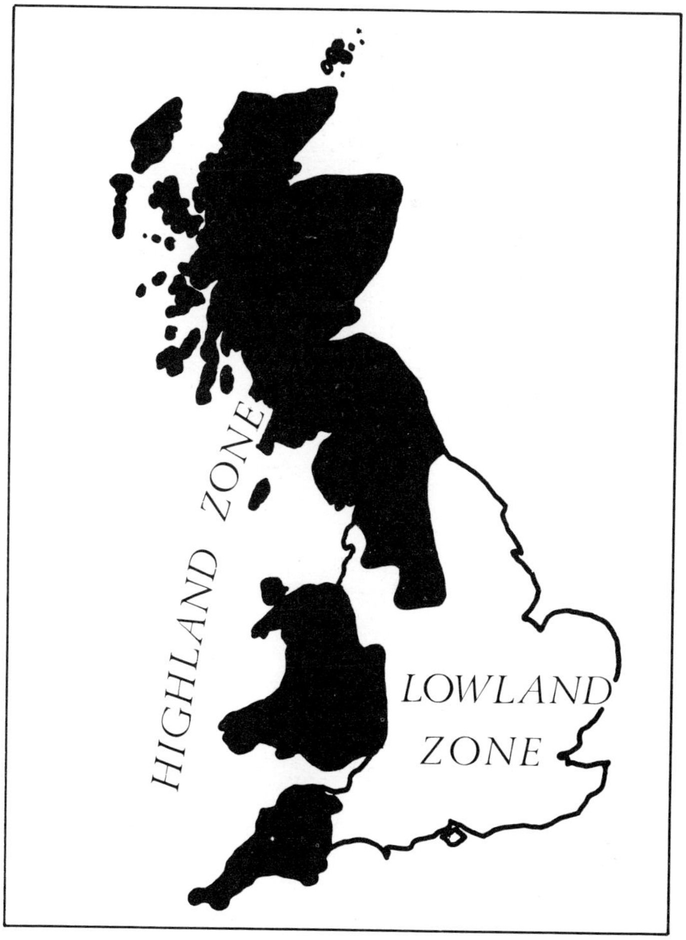

7 Highland and lowland zones

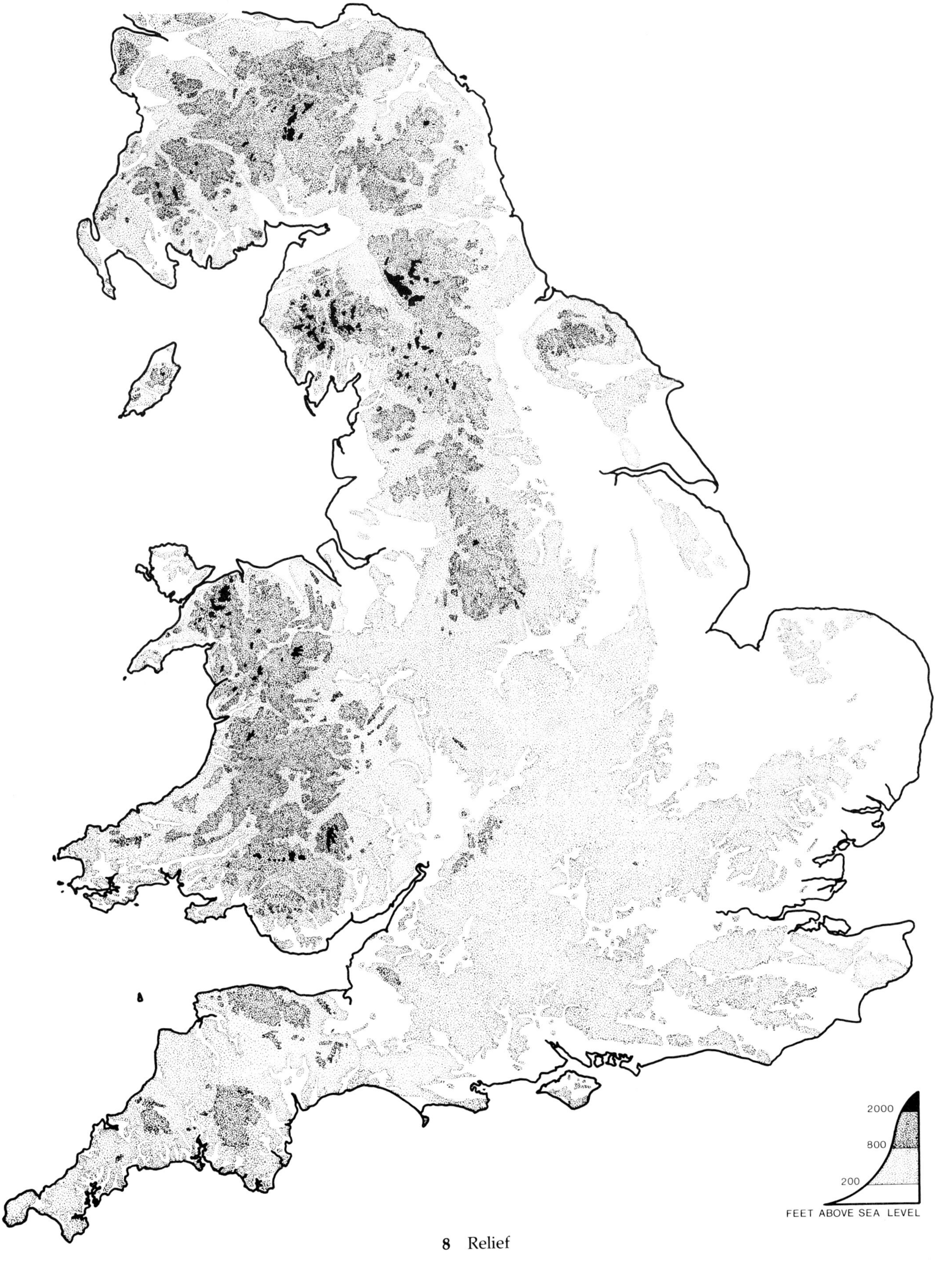

8 Relief

9 Land quality

10–13 Modern Climate

Modern Climate (10–14)

It is now accepted that there have been major fluctuations in the climate both on a world scale and on a more local level in historic times. These changes have many important effects, and it should be understood by all those interested in the period that these variations have numerous ramifications. The Viking movements, agriculture, diet, coastline and trade, the early history of Greenland and the bone skates from York, the cultivation of the vine and the distribution of the sceatta coinage are all linked and modified by climatic development.

Interest in the subject is growing rapidly, and the present state of knowledge has recently been reviewed (Lamb 1978). Unfortunately for us, the comparison with the present state of British climate (maps **10–13**) is neither straightforward nor confined to one simple statement such as 'it was warmer', although it is possible to find statistics of one type that appear to summarize the overall trend for our period (AD 700–1066) and which demonstrate that it **was** warmer. The recovery of the Oxygen 18 isotopes from the Greenland icecap (**14**) provides further evidence. Because the layers in the ice can be dated, the isotope can be measured and related to specific years. It is believed that the production of Oxygen 18 is related to long-term trends in temperature and thus is a useful indicator of those trends. The physics may be beyond us, but the implications of this, and much else, in Lamb's latest work should be noted by everyone interested in the period.

In general, the pattern that emerges can be seen as building up to a period known as the medieval warm epoch, or 'Little Optimum', which took place from perhaps AD 950 to 1300, with variations around the world within those broad limits. There was then a shift of climate in the later Middle Ages towards the 'Little Ice Age', which controlled the entire early Modern period from Tudor times until the last century.

If we take it that the general trend from perhaps the sixth or seventh centuries was towards a drier and less stormy climate, we may see several climatic changes in the period c. AD 550 to c. 1180.

1 It was warmer: summer temperatures may have been one degree centigrade higher.
2 A Continental effect, with the depression track further to the north of the British Isles, meant that Britain was affected by Continental weather patterns — warmer in summer, much colder in winter — but the average for the year would have been higher than present-day averages.
3 Bog growth can be taken as an index of wetness. The Tregaron series shows a standstill or very slow growth between AD 900 and 1200, followed by rapid growth indicating a return to wet conditions.
4 There is some evidence for an increase in storminess in the North Sea after AD 1000.

'In general we can say that for a few centuries in the Middle Ages the climate regained something approaching the warmth of the warmest postglacial times' (Lamb 1978, 435).

The effects were numerous and included a higher tree line and the growth of crops and forests further north than either after 1300 or in the present day. Map **196**, showing the vineyards in England in the pre-Conquest period, provides a good illustration of the point.

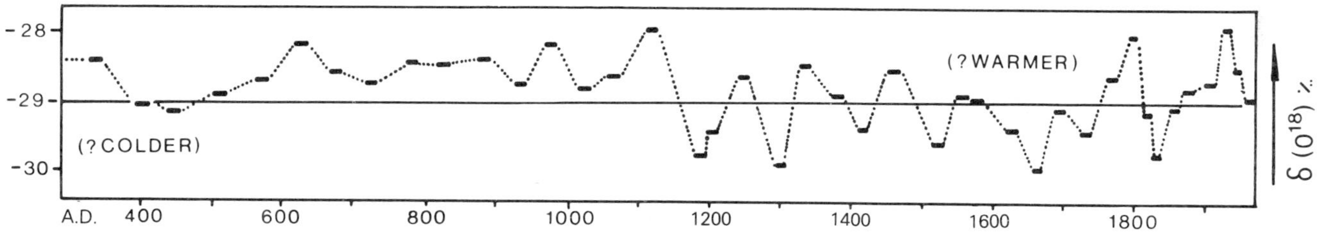

14 Oxygen isotope variations in the north-west Greenland icecap which are believed to represent broadly the course of temperature variations (from W. Dansgaard in Lamb 1978)

15 Coastline changes and navigable rivers

Coastline Changes and Navigable Rivers (15–16)

Widespread coastline changes (map **15**) have occurred between the Anglo-Saxon period and the present day, but they were very much a continuous process within the period, as may perhaps be demonstrated by the annal for 1014:

. . . and in this year on Michaelmas Eve [28 September] the great tide of the sea flooded widely over this country, coming up higher than it had ever done before, and submerging many villages and a countless number of people.

Although the 'coast' is simply that line along which the sea intersects the land, the causes of coastline changes can be complicated. In the Anglo-Saxon period there was a worldwide, eustatic rise in sea level as water from the icecaps and glaciers returned to the sea. This, of course, was also linked to the general rise in long-term averages in temperature discussed earlier. At the moment, water levels are rising at about 2 mm a year, and it can be seen that rises have been important at some earlier stages, leading to flooding of the land ('submergence' or 'marine transgression'). A lowering of the mean sea level ('emergence') is associated with the drying out of certain coastal flats. The subject is complex, as it also involves the questions of silting and man's interference with the shorelines. The data in **16** follow Fairbridge, as quoted in Bruce-Mitford (1975). Coupled to these changes in sea level are the tectonic changes in the land masses, with the southern part of the North Sea area tending to fall, whilst the North British area, centred on the West Grampians, tended to rise.

The navigable river pattern is fairly simple to reconstruct but it can lead to endless argument. What is navigable now may not have been so a millennium ago, and there is a problem in supplying an acceptable definition of 'navigable'. Minor streams in West Somerset may float a punt somewhere along their lengths after a wet February, but the navigable rivers in question are those thought to have been used regularly for the transport of goods and passengers.

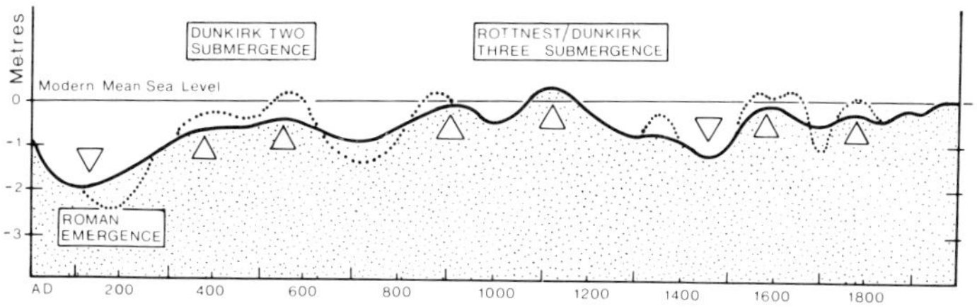

16 Sea level changes in the North Sea area. The possible extremes are shown by the dotted line

The Fens and the Wash (17–18)

There is in the Midland district of Britain a most dismal fen of immense size, which begins at the banks of the river Granta not far from the camp (**castello**) *which is called Cambridge* (**Gronte**) *and stretches from the south as far north as the sea. It is a very long tract, now consisting of marshes, now of bogs, sometimes of black waters overhung by fog, sometimes studded with wooded islands and traversed by the windings of tortuous streams. (Felix's* **Life of St Guthlac**, *early eighth century, quoted in Colgrave 1956, 87)*

The changes that have taken place in this area are enormous and mostly post-medieval, although the Anglo-Saxons were increasingly active here throughout the period (map **17**). The Fens themselves included great stretches of water (for example Whittlesea Mere in map **18** which, although shallow, was the largest body of fresh water in lowland Britain), which figure prominently in charters of the fenland monasteries because they represented an important resource for fish and fowl. The pattern of the coastline, but more particularly of the river systems, has changed greatly from that shown in Saxton's 1576 map (**18**). (It should be noted that present-day shorelines and river lines are shown throughout this atlas.)

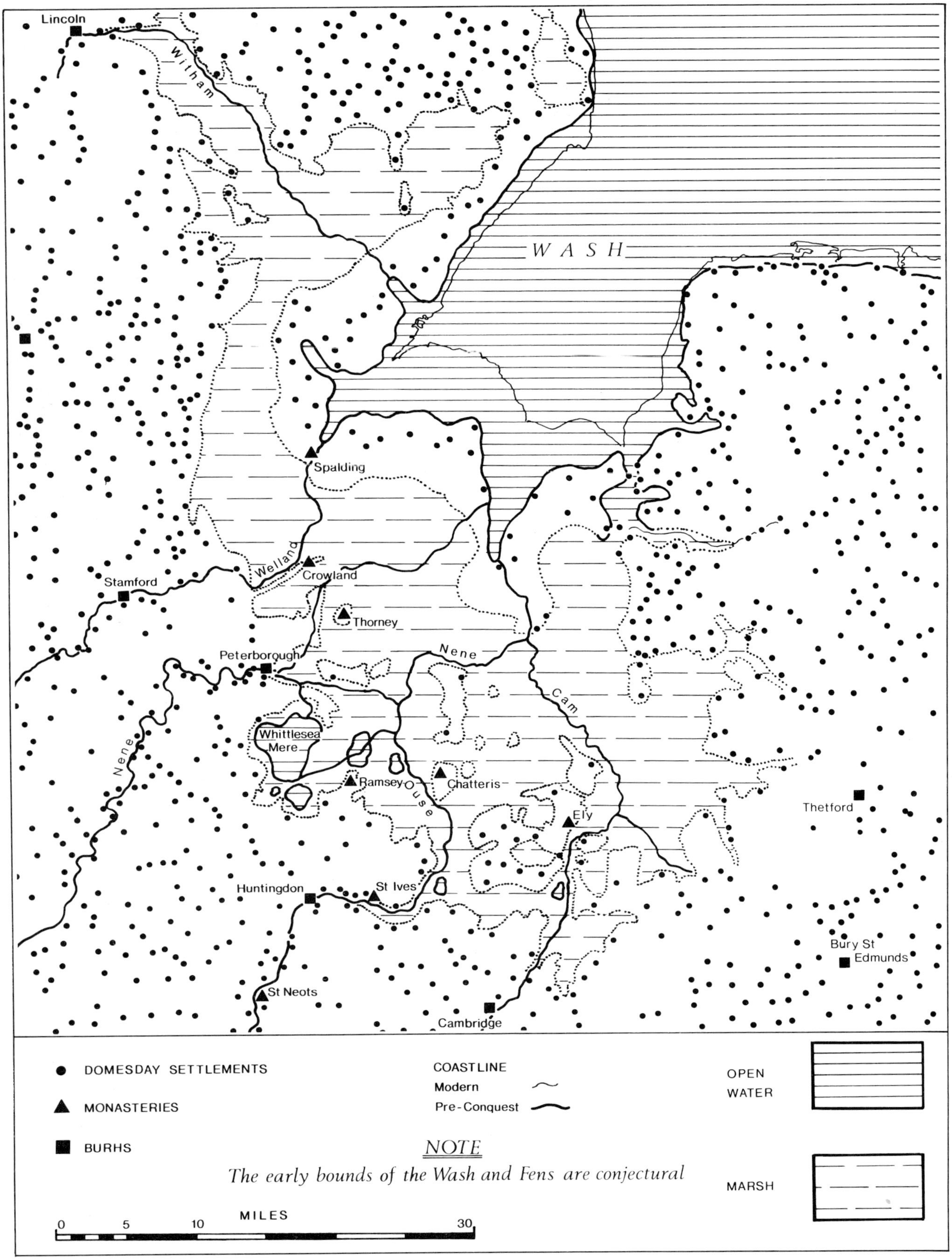
Lincoln
Witham
WASH
Spalding
Welland
Crowland
Stamford
Thorney
Peterborough
Nene
Whittlesea Mere
Ramsey
Ouse
Chatteris
Cam
Ely
Thetford
Nene
Huntingdon
St Ives
St Neots
Cambridge
Bury St Edmunds
DOMESDAY SETTLEMENTS
MONASTERIES
BURHS
COASTLINE
Modern
Pre-Conquest
OPEN WATER
MARSH
NOTE
The early bounds of the Wash and Fens are conjectural
MILES
0 5 10 30

17 The Wash

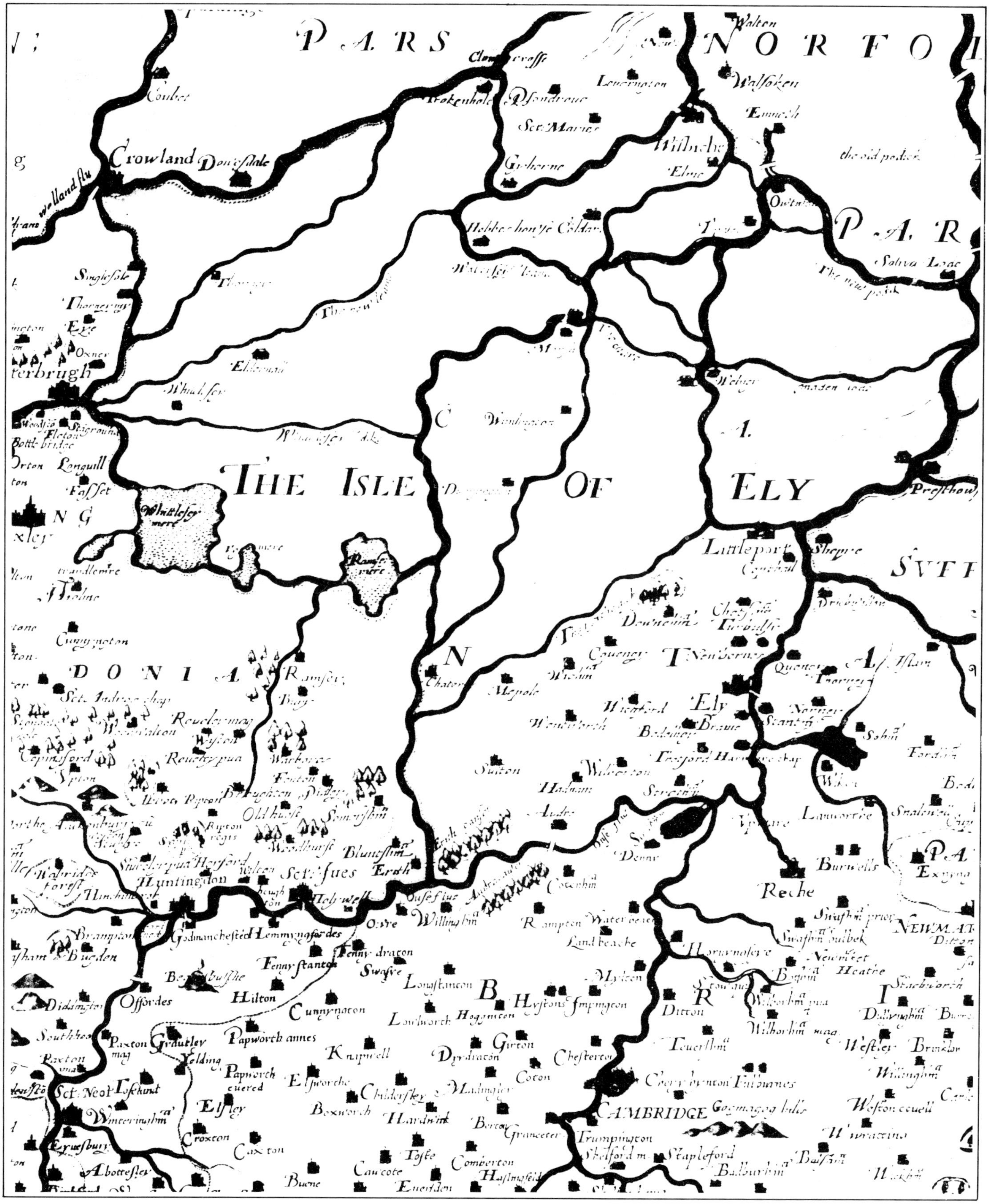

18 Whittlesea Mere and the rivers of the southern Fens according to Saxton (1576)

The Wantsum Channel (19–22)

On the east of Kent is the large Isle of Thanet containing according to the English way of reckoning, 600 families, divided from the other land by the river Wantsum, which is about three furlongs over, and fordable only in two places, for both ends of it run into the sea. (Bede's Ecclesiastical History, Book I, Cap. 25)

The Wantsum Channel (map **19**) would appear to have been an important part of the sheltered waterway system that ran from Ribe in Denmark to Quentovic in northern Gaul, and from the Alps to the Thames. The toll stations reflect this importance as does the concentration of finds of sceattas seen in maps **203** and **205**. Apart from the fact that this channel led to the important markets of Canterbury and into the Thames mouth, it may have avoided the dangers of the North Foreland. It can be assumed that the passage was made as the shipping was carried from the Downs and Sandwich up the Wantsum by the tide until they reached Sarre, where they waited until the tide fell and carried them north to the North Mouth.

Two important ports — Richborough at the early period and Sandwich at the later period — were situated to the south of the Wantsum Channel. Sandwich is described in the **Encomium Emmae Reginae** (c. 1041) as 'Sandwich which is the most famous of all the ports of the English'.

The dating of the closure of the channel as a passage for shipping is unclear, but the North Mouth is mentioned in connection with shipping and with Sandwich in the annal for 1052 (from the Anglo-Saxon Chronicle).

There are other cases of channels silting during this period: the important Limfiord in Jutland appears to have closed at this time, and there were major changes in the coastline of Frisia. The ninth century changes in the Rhine, which led to the abandonment of Dorestadt, are recorded in 864 (Brøndsted 1965, 47) as follows:

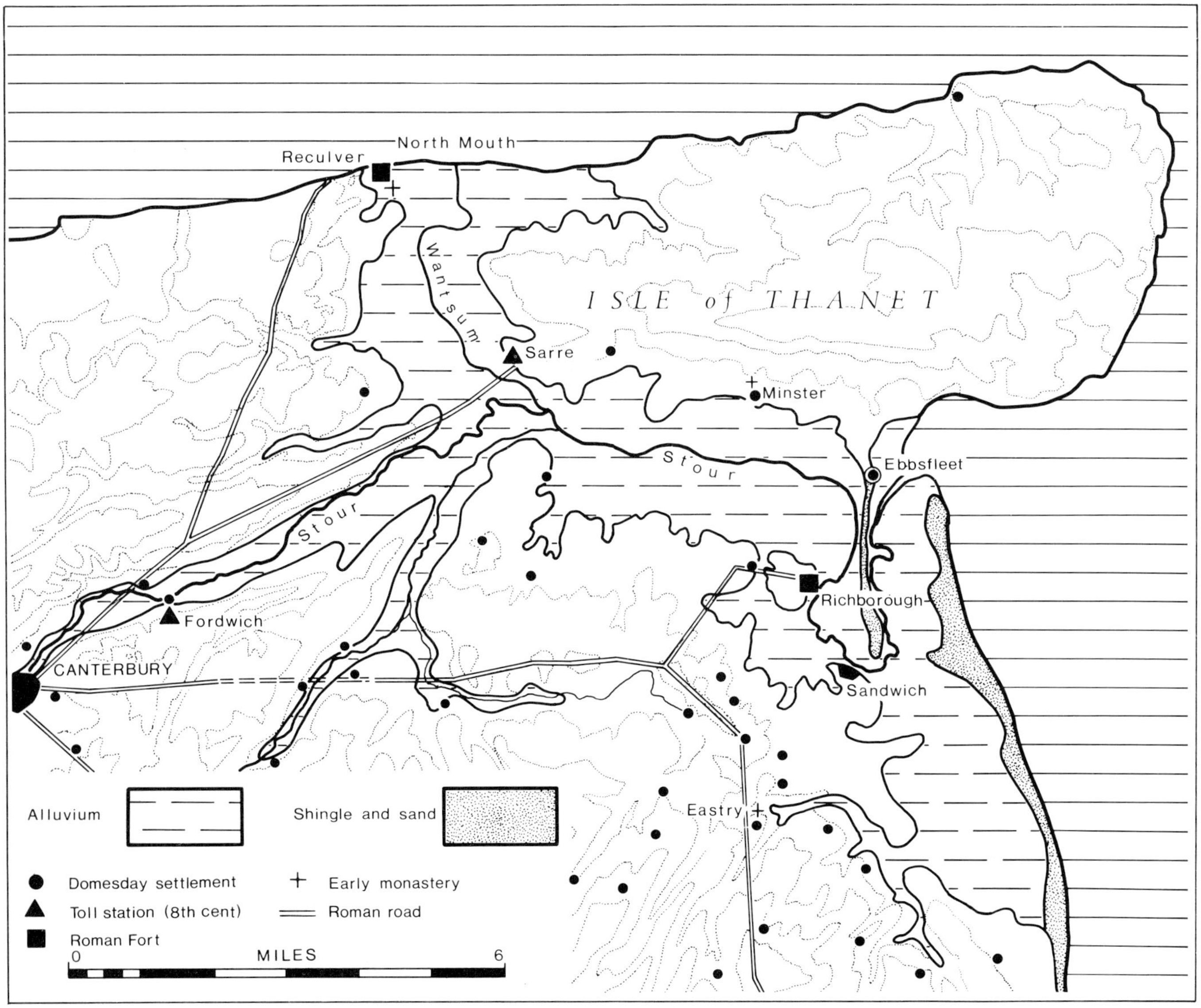

19 The Wantsum Channel. The earlier importance of the Channel is marked by the siting of the Roman forts at Richborough and Reculver

Strange portents were observed in the sky, and these were followed by plagues, gales, tidal waves, and floods. The waters of the Rhine were forced back by the sudden rush of the sea, drowning masses of people and animals in Utrecht and all over Holland. From then on, the River Lek was embanked with dikes, and the Rhine changed its course towards Utrecht, while at Katwijk it completely silted.

As yet there is no definitive work on the changes affecting much of the coast of South-east England, in the areas around Romney and Hastings, although there have been some brave attempts. To assist future work on the subject — and to indicate the nature of the problem maps **20** and **21** show two only partially successful efforts to reconstitute the pre-Conquest shoreline in the Rye area.

Great changes in the Dungeness area make it difficult to understand the early history of Appledore and Romney without some reconstruction of the coastline (map **21**). A model of the early course of the River Rother is also necessary when reading the annal for 892 and considering the site of Eorpeburnan (Davison 1972) (see map **150**).

The central part of Somerset was as waterlogged and marshy an area as the Fens. It was on the borders of these marshes that Alfred found refuge in 878, and the Somerset Levels (map **22**) were probably used by hunting parties from Cheddar in the tenth century. Early attempts at reclamation were made by the monastery at Glastonbury.

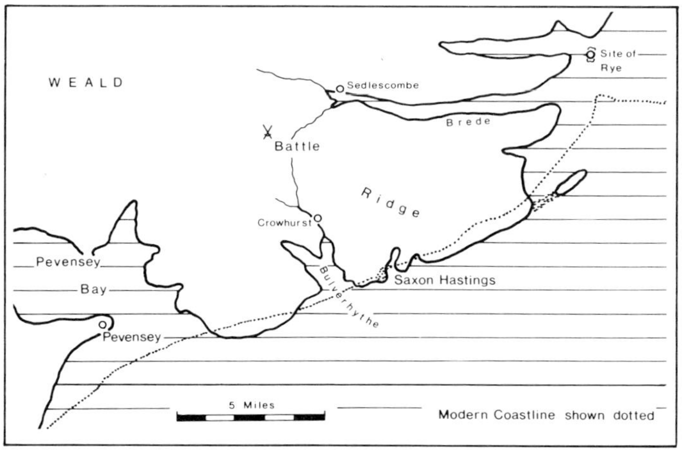

20 A reconstruction of the Hastings coastline in 1066 (Williamson 1959)

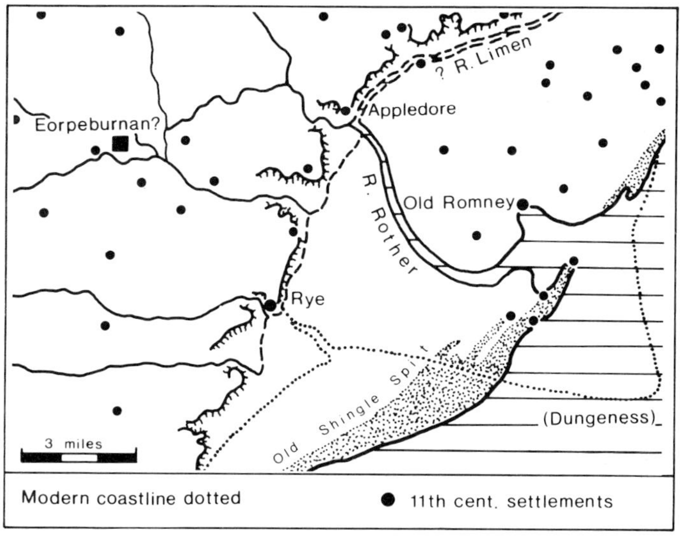

21 Early Dungeness (after Davison)

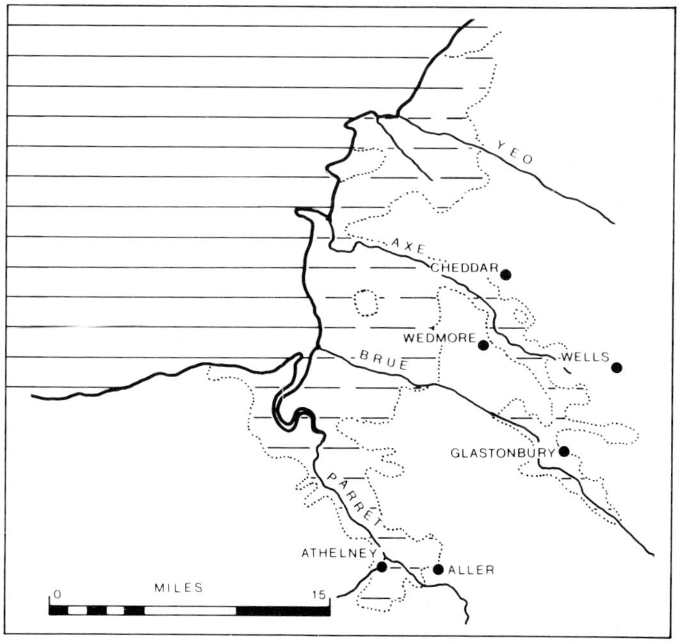

22 The Somerset Levels showing early medieval marine transgression (after Fowler 1972)

23 Alternative views of forest cover in Anglo-Saxon times (Stenton 1971 and Ordnance Survey 1935)

Forest (23–24)

No topographical feature of Anglo-Saxon England has come and gone with such rapidity as the great forest charted on many maps and influencing many interpretations of the events of the period. In 1935 the Ordnance Survey maps of Dark Age Britain and of Roman Britain were liberally covered with tracts of forest; in the latest version of the Ordnance Survey Map of Dark Age Britain (1966) this forest has apparently vanished:

The change . . . is seen in the abandonment of any attempt to restore natural woodlands on a geological basis. No apology is due for this. It has already been done on the third edition of the map of Roman Britain because wider knowledge of human distribution in that period shows that most of the natural wooded areas carried much larger populations than was thought possible thirty years ago. . . In any case the ancient equipment for cutting and removing timber was not greatly different from that which was commonly used in this country until as late as the 18th. century. . . .

Both approaches present problems: the first fill the map with tracts of impassable land, which deflected the reasoning of historians and archaeologists, while the second approach avoids the problem altogether. Map **23** therefore juxtaposes the 1935 view, which was most influential, and the Stenton view, which is milder. It should be noted that the two often bear little relation to one another. The matter should be treated as an open question and one which is not resolved here. The Domesday settlement evidence (maps **25–26**) is helpful and further evidence will come from the detailed place name work now being carried on

It is worth noting that the distribution of woodland in England today (map **24**) is unexpected and it is equally likely that actuality may belie our preconceptions for the Anglo-Saxon period. It is true that there were then important forests in England, that the country was more heavily wooded than in later periods, that the degree of forest cover decreased throughout the period. Our view of the nature of that forest has, however, changed from an impassable, damp oak forest to a canopy forest through which passage was possible and in which foraging animals provided a useful resource for man. The means do not yet exist to delineate many of these areas more closely, although there are signs that advances are being made (Sawyer 1978, 148).

Settlements and Population shown in Domesday Book (25–26)

One of the achievements of recent historical geography has been the compilation of **The Domesday Geographies of England** from Domesday Book. This work, edited by H.C. Darby, offers a view of the last days of Anglo-Saxon England as it was recalled by the jurors of 1086.

Most of England south of the Tees was covered and the majority of the settlements are included, although minor settlements are often considered under the name of the main estate (map **25**). We are given some idea of the true matrix into which we can fit our scraps from the charters and the Chronicle, and the calculated population distribution (map **26**) allows us to adjust our views of earlier periods and their settlements accordingly.

It is clear from these two maps that the constraints outlined in the preceding maps — those of geology, relief, land quality, highland and lowland zones, climate and coastline — combine to highlight the 1066 distributions. In map **25** the Wash, the Weald and Dartmoor can be identified as can the settlements following the streams in chalk areas of Wiltshire. It is a little more difficult to account for the areas of high population in map **26**.

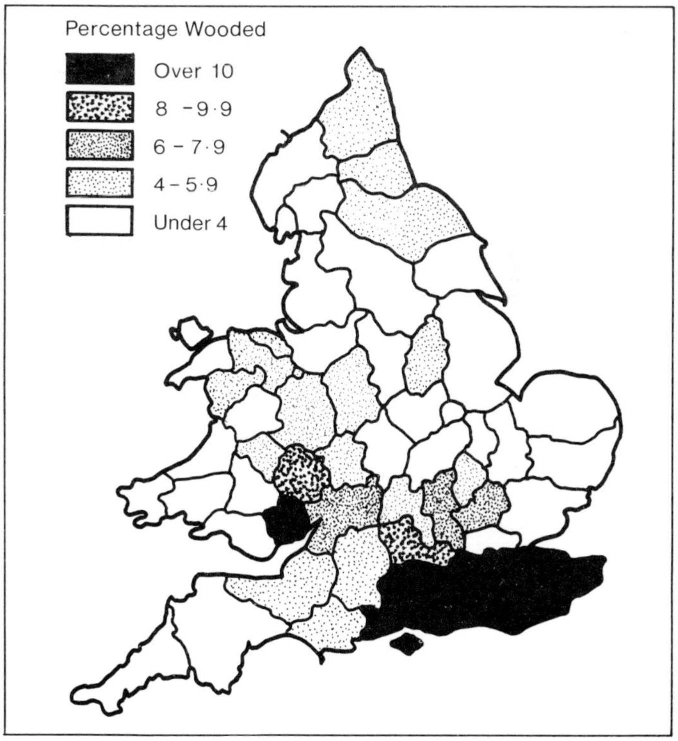

24 Proportion of shires wooded in 1947

25 Settlements in Domesday Book

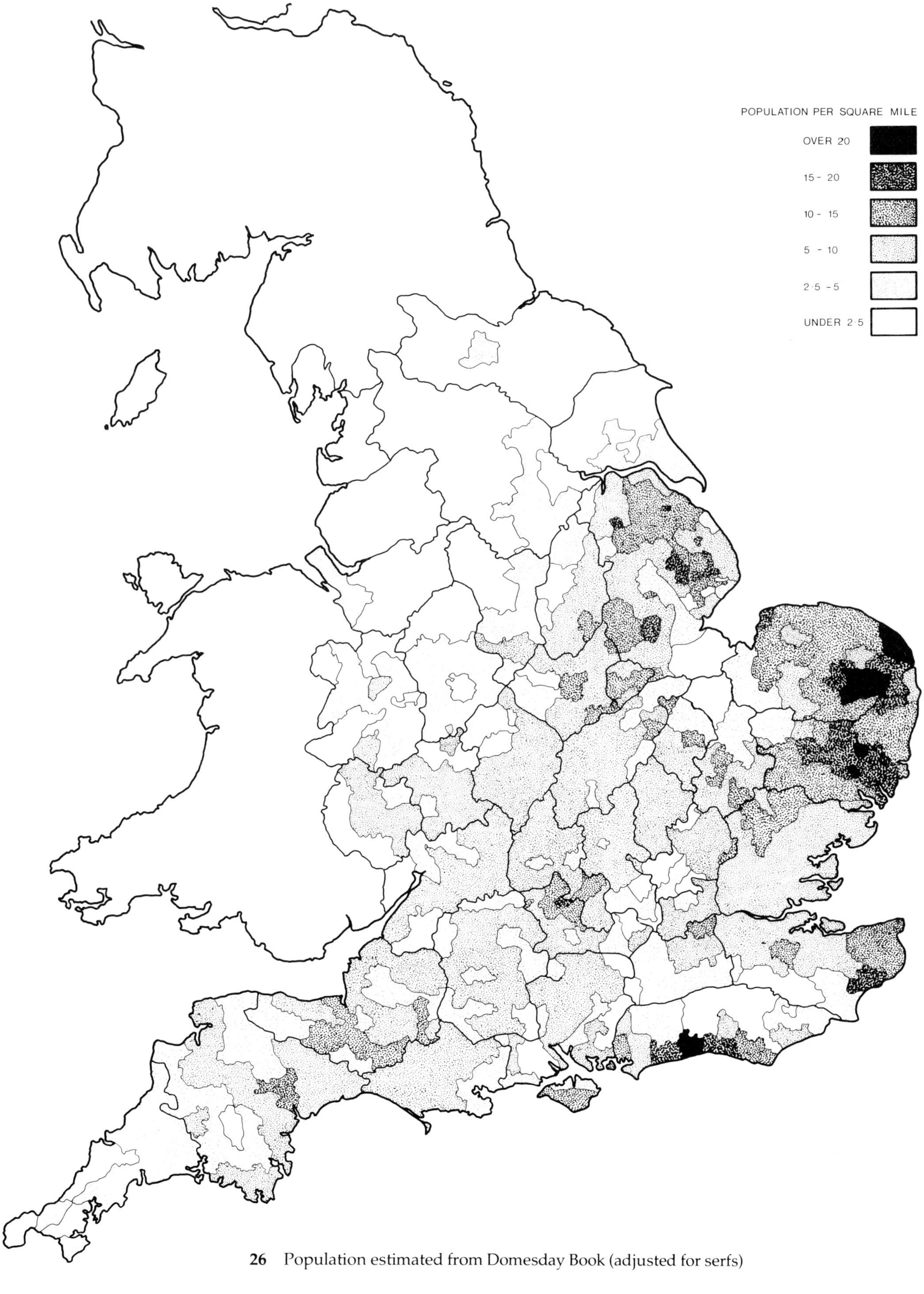

26 Population estimated from Domesday Book (adjusted for serfs)

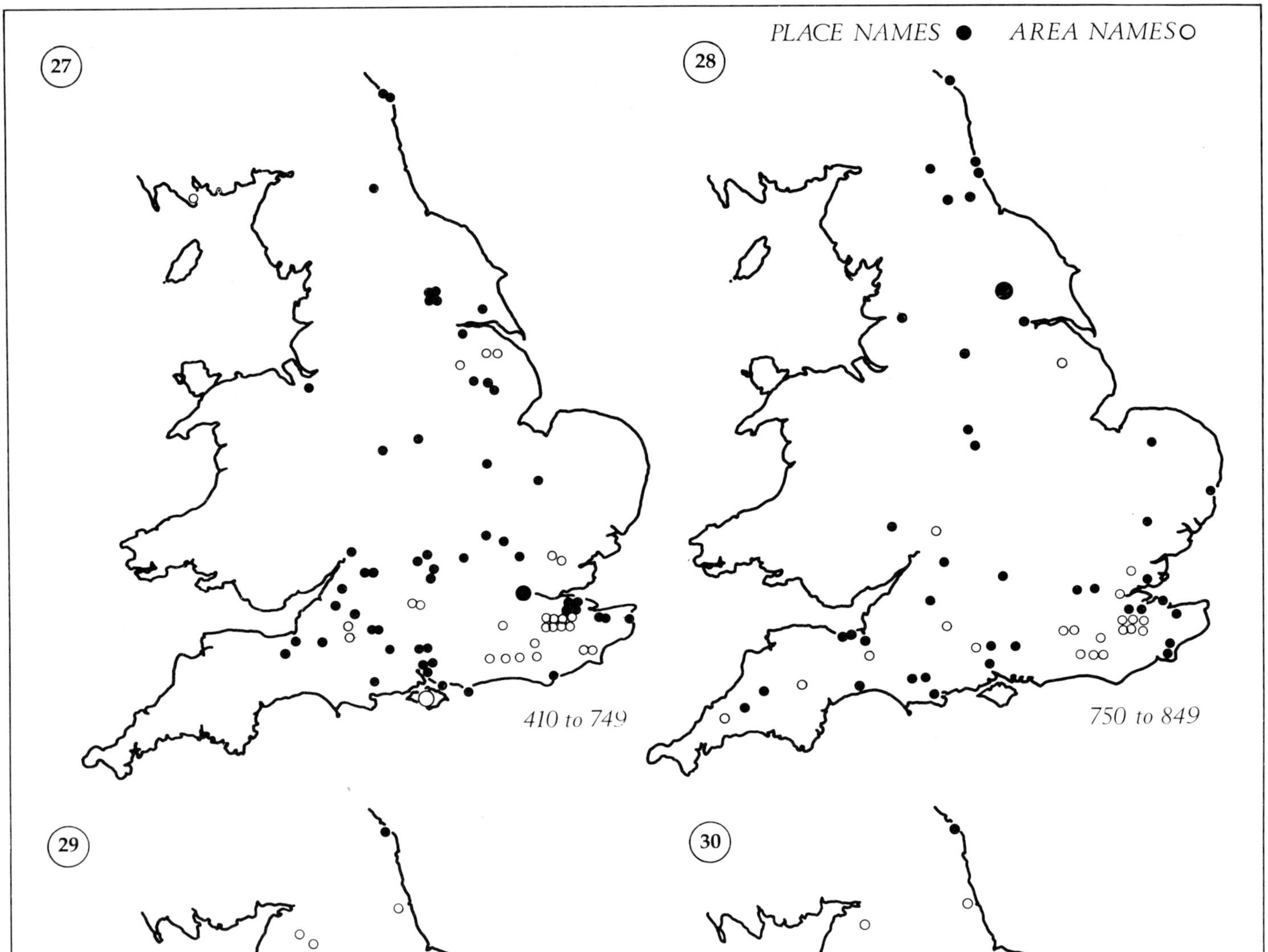

27–30 Places mentioned in the Anglo-Saxon Chronicle

Regional Bias in the Anglo-Saxon Chronicle (27–30)

The preceding set of maps has attempted to show some of the parameters within which the development and the life of Anglo-Saxon England took place. In particular it should have become apparent that there were vast differences between one part of the country and another. To ignore these differences and to treat the country as an homogeneous entity leads to serious misunderstandings.

The ensuing series of maps makes a similar point. It attempts to underline the range that the surviving evidence spans; it shows that the most important evidence is, not surprisingly, documentary but there are other valuable bodies of evidence; and that all these sources are subject to distortions. The major source for the history of the whole period is the Anglo-Saxon Chronicle and maps **27–30** show the geographical bias from period to period within the dates covered by this atlas. These maps are intended to elucidate points on the primary source for Anglo-Saxon studies from the end of the Age of Bede until the Conquest. The best introduction to these sources (for the Chronicle is a collection of parallel and complimentary documents drawn together from earlier materials in the reign of King Alfred and then developing separately in its several manuscripts) is in the foreword to **The Anglo-Saxon Chronicles: A Revised Translation,** edited by Dorothy Whitelock (1965).

Stenton has already pointed to the south-western bias at the early part of the era within the Chronicle and a southern, particularly a south-easterly, drift is visible in the later part of the period. It is clear from these maps that we cannot be certain that the omission of events or places from the record has any significance other than the interest of the author of a particular annal. These maps should also be viewed in conjunction with map **41**, the England of Bede, whose information affects map **27**, and is itself distorted, containing only places from the east of the country. Finally, these maps together with **31** and **35** should go some way to explaining why this atlas has so little to say about England north of the Humber.

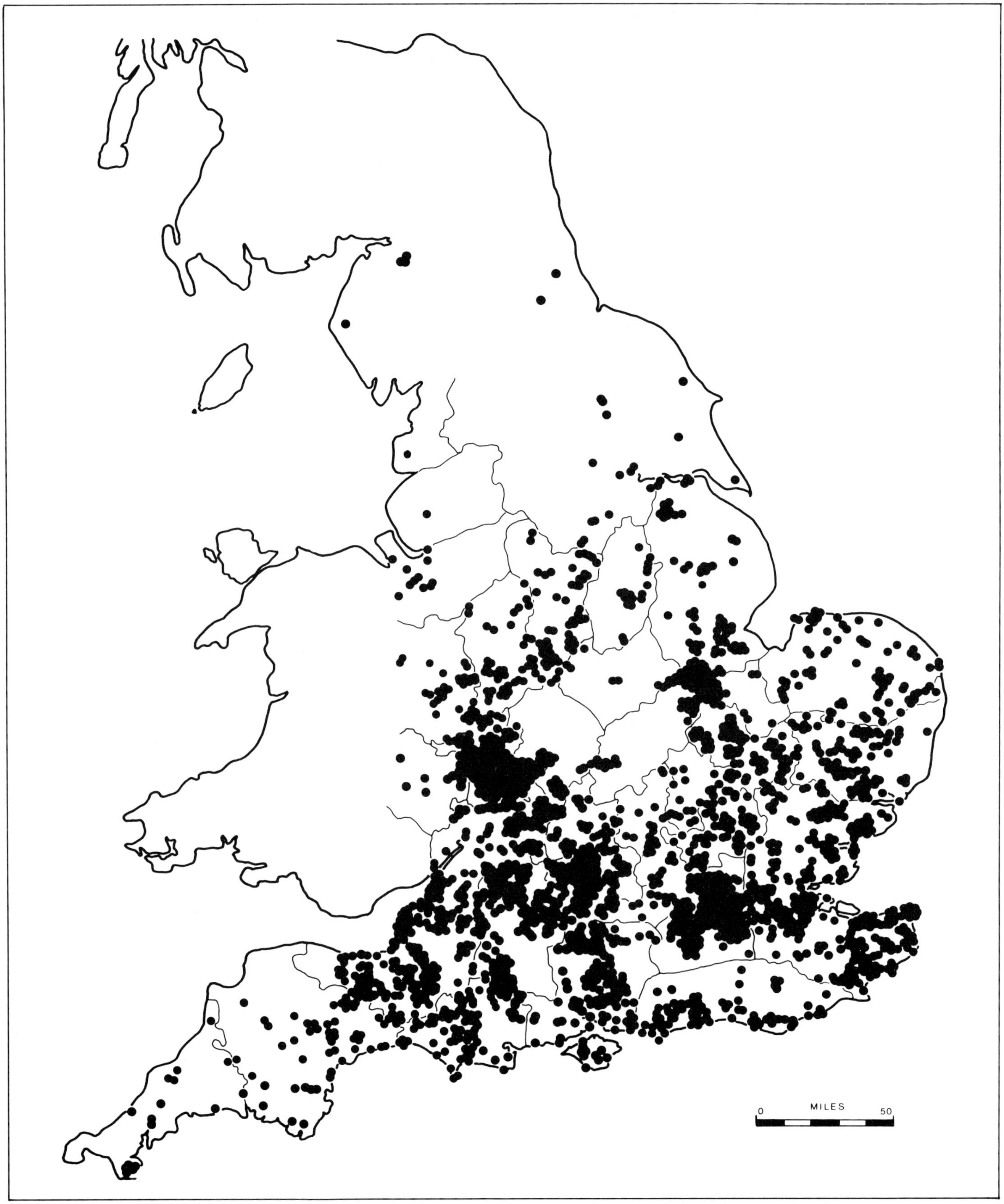

31 Distribution of estates mentioned in charters (after Goodier (unpublished)). All reputed charters, writs, leases and wills have been included

Charters as a Source of Evidence (31–35)

The land documents, wills, leases and writs, known collectively as charters, form the second most important Anglo-Saxon documentary source after the Chronicle, although the class of information is completely different. The Chronicle paints on a wide canvas whilst the charters deal with the particular: one talks of kings and battles, the other of fields and meadows.

The preponderance of the charters from a few houses is clearly reflected in map **31**. Worcester, the Canterbury and Winchester houses and Abingdon provide so many charters that the counties around them are well represented. Kent has the best coverage, whereas shires such as Lancashire or Herefordshire have practically none.

In map **31** the mention of a settlement is reflected by one dot, no matter how often that settlement is mentioned in subsequent charters. The map also includes all charters mentioned in Sawyer (1968) without any attempt to validate individual charters.

The general problem of the distribution of charters is reflected in the distribution of various categories of charters. Leases, for example, tend to be grouped around Worcester and lost and incomplete charters around Glastonbury. The problem is equally illustrated by the writs (map **32**), which replaced charters. Only a knowledge of the churches receiving the lands or rights makes any sense of an otherwise random distribution.

As a very large proportion of charters were in favour of, or granted by, the Church (see **33**), the vast majority of all documents come to us through the hands of the Church. When using documentary evidence we are in danger of seeing Anglo-Saxon England through stained glass windows.

One of the most interesting features of the charters is the whole category of intensely topographical information locked in the bounds. It is only recently that work has once again started on boundary clauses, which are such a rich source of every kind of evidence. In some areas the estate bounds interlock, allowing detailed work on the Anglo-Saxon landscape of several shires, for example Worcestershire (map **34**). Map **35** shows the distribution of all charter bounds, whether still attached to charters or not.

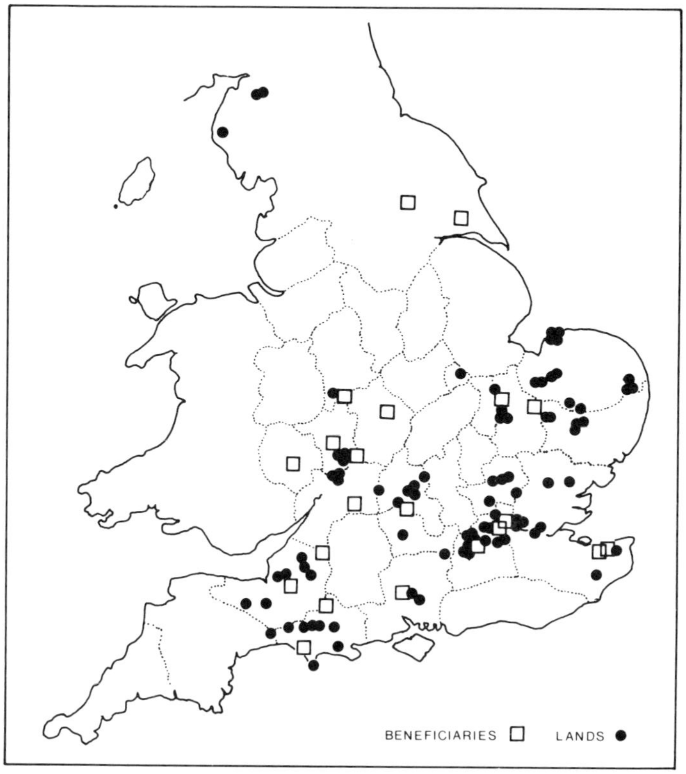

32 Distribution of beneficiaries and lands mentioned in alleged Anglo-Saxon writs

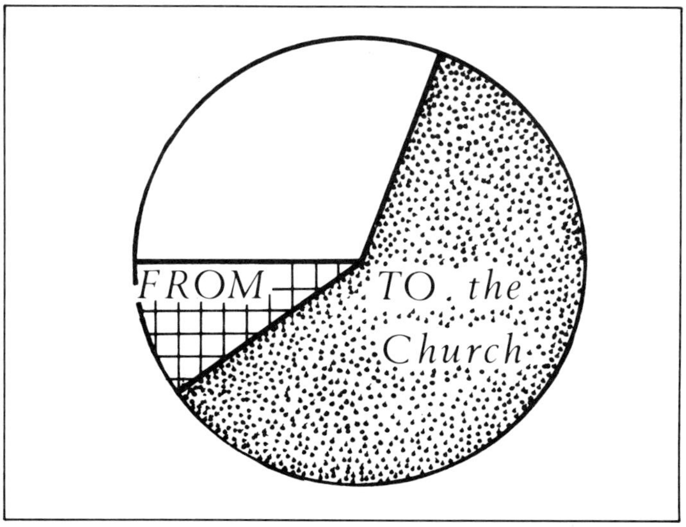

33 Proportion of charters issued by and to the Church

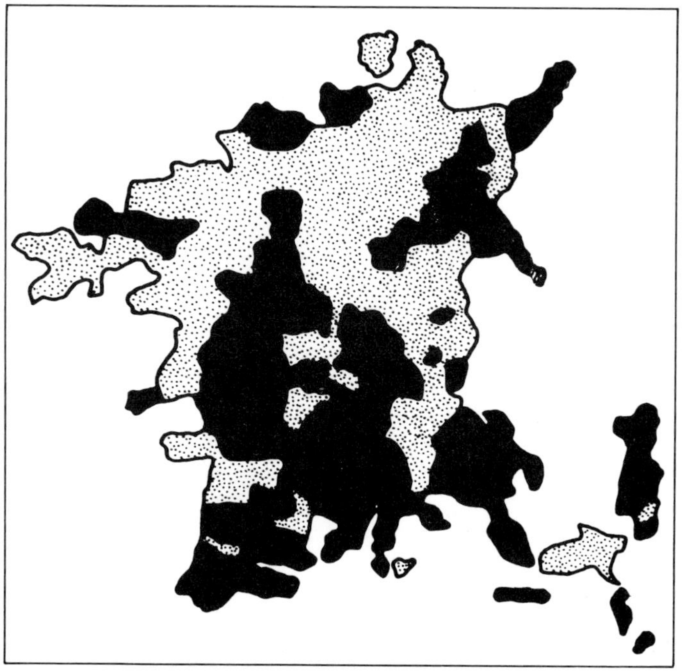

34 Worcestershire estates with detailed charter bounds shown solid (after Hooke (unpublished))

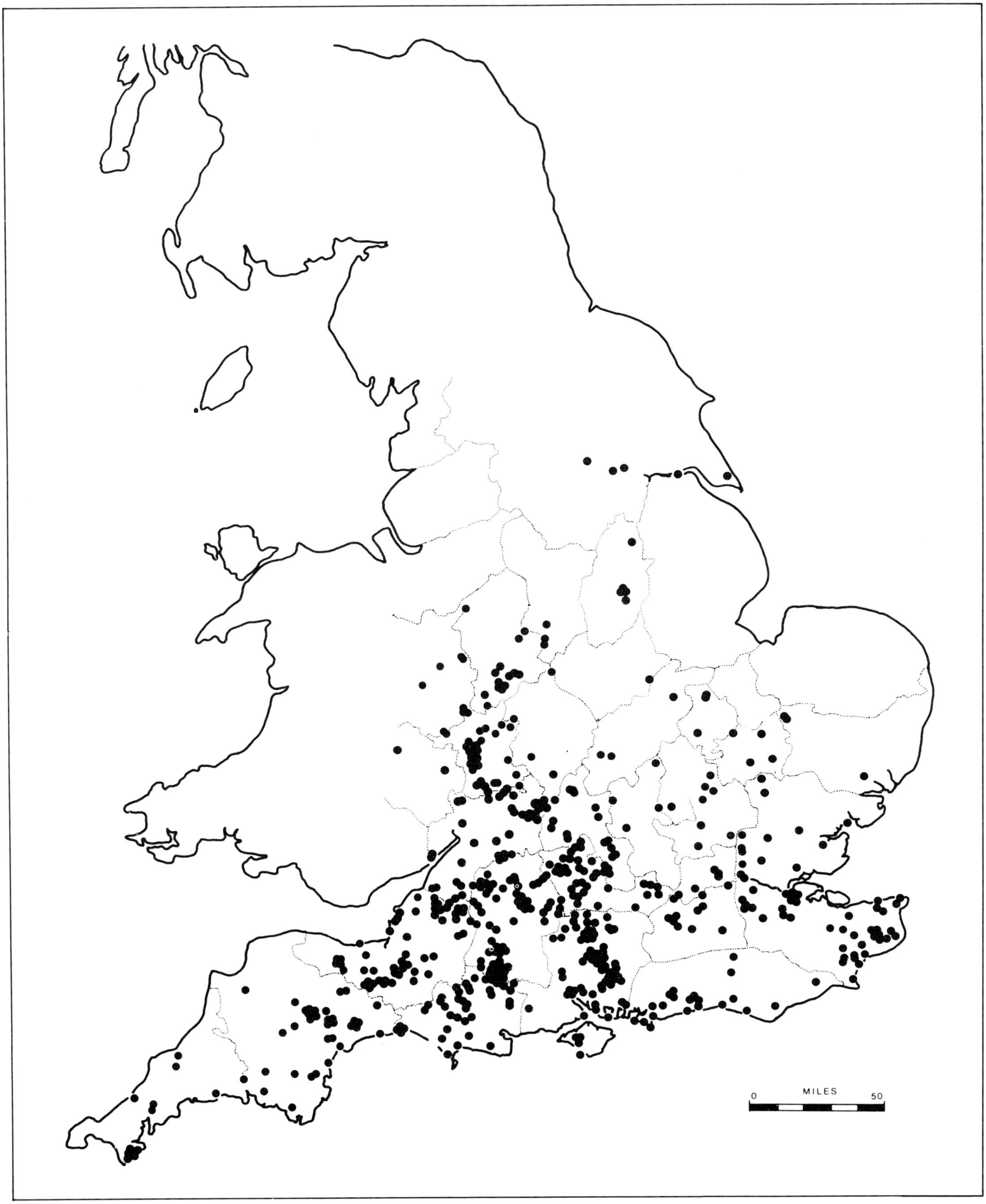

35 Distribution of charter bounds including detached bounds (after Goodier (unpublished))

Chronological Bias: Charters and Anglo-Saxon Chronicle (36–37)

Geographical factors are not the only distortion in the major sources — there is also a chronological distortion. It would be reasonable to suppose either that all years are roughly equally represented by the charters or, rather more likely, that the later charters have survived better. The actual pattern (**36**) is therefore surprising: an enormous proportion of the charters was produced in the mid-tenth century, while the earlier period has a fairly uniform proportion of the charters produced, with a tailing off before the great wave of tenth-century charters. In the last years of the Anglo-Saxon monarchy there is a revival in the number of documents, particularly when writs are included.

This means that when we quote charter evidence on practically any subject we are probably quoting a tenth-century charter, and, from the evidence given above, a charter from a particularly limited part of the country. An awareness of the bias in the evidence will help to offset it.

If the number of words in the longest versions of the annals in the Anglo-Saxon Chronicle for a particular year are counted and then plotted in blocks of ten years it is possible to illustrate the very wide range of available evidence (**37**). This portrays the Chronicle as consisting of a steady background of annals with four enlarged portions which are, in effect, the 'Deeds of Alfred', the 'Deeds of Edward the Elder', 'The fall of Ethelred the Unready' and 'The reign of Edward the Confessor'. This severely restricts, for example, the available evidence for a discussion of the merits of kings such as Offa and Eadred. It is essential to remember that the Chronicle deals with a very narrow band of evidence, usually told from a fixed standpoint and often in a much abbreviated form.

Archaeology (38)

There has been an enormous expansion in the amount of money spent on archaeological excavations in Britain. Although much is to be hoped for from the growth of the subject, considerable care must be exercised when using archaeological evidence. Despite the discipline's claims to be 'scientific', map **38** shows how uneven is the spread of archaeological evidence which, in a most unscientific way, tends to leave large areas untested. Nevertheless it is cheering to note how much influence individual and group commitment has on the pattern. The map merely charts all Anglo-Saxon excavations, field-work and chance finds reported to **Medieval Archaeology** in the twenty-one years of its summaries.

What the map does not show is the large proportion of all funds spent on urban archaeology: town excavations form the bulk of all work that has been carried on in the last two decades.

Kings and Princes (39–40)

It is a rare individual who can recite the names of all the kings of Mercia, Wessex and England before the Conquest, yet on the names of kings we tend to hang our history. The charts in **39** and **40** may be of some assistance in this respect, but they have the more useful function of allowing us to see what kings and princes were contemporaries. The charts also show some trends in the development of Anglo-Saxon history: first, the extinction of the minor kingdoms and the supremacy of Mercia; followed by the rise of Wessex, so that by 860 there were only five kingdoms to be reckoned with (Mercia, Wessex, Northumbria, East Anglia and the Wales of Rhodri Mawr). Then come the Viking invasions; and the eventual union of the entire Anglo-Saxon kingdom.

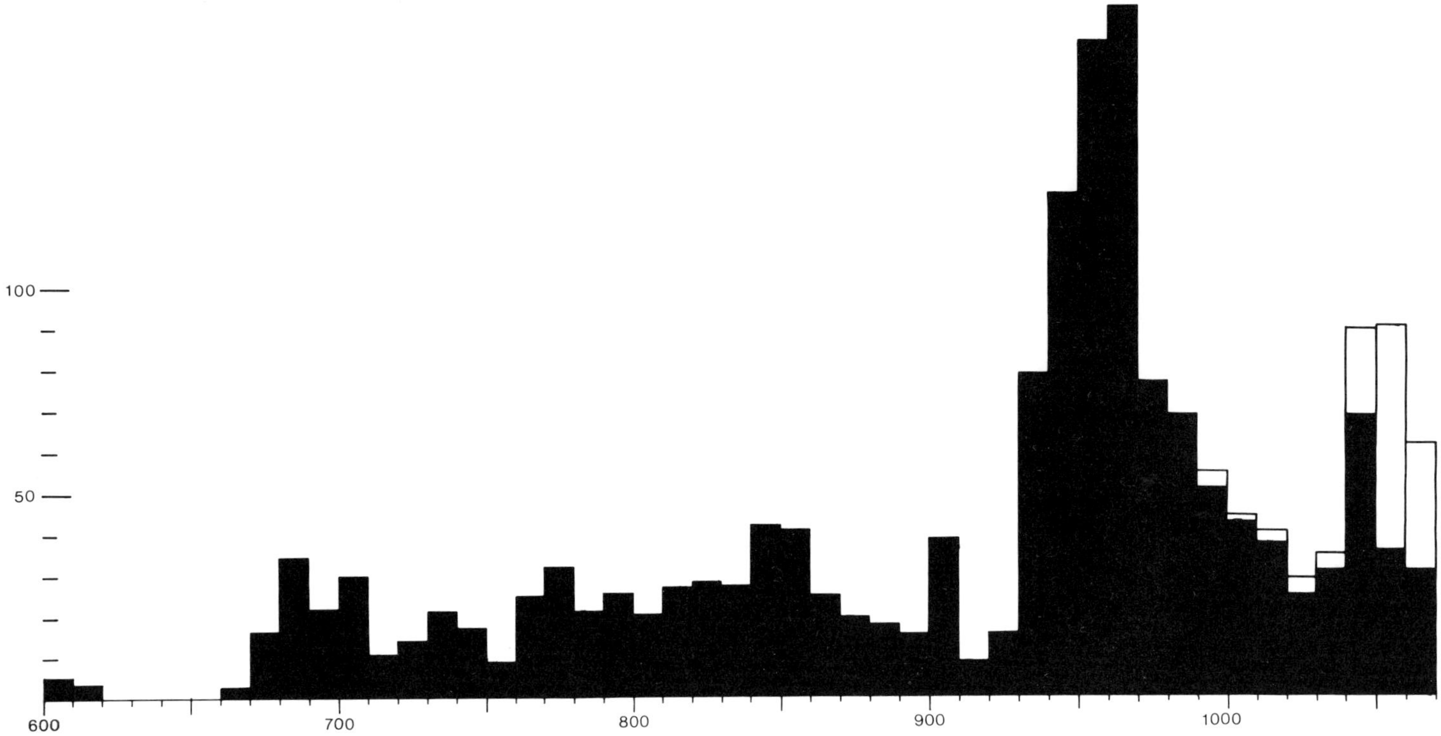

36 Anglo-Saxon charters: distribution by decades. Writs are shown in outline

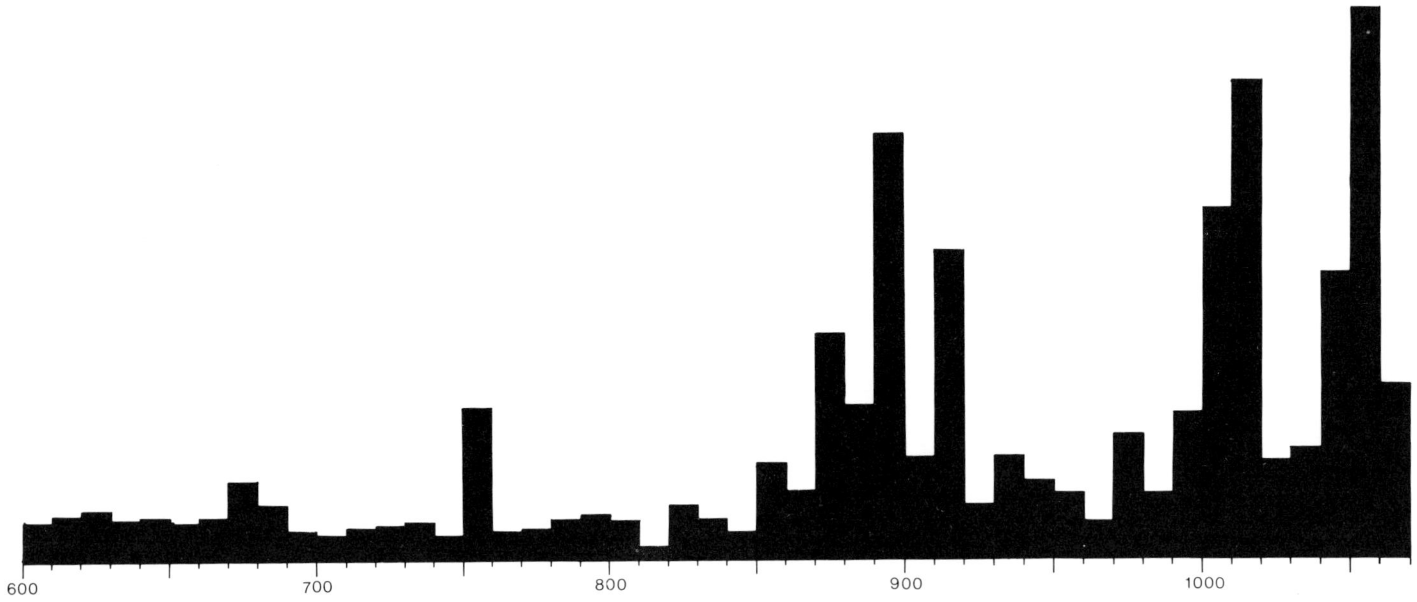

37 Comparative lengths of annals in the Anglo-Saxon Chronicle by decades

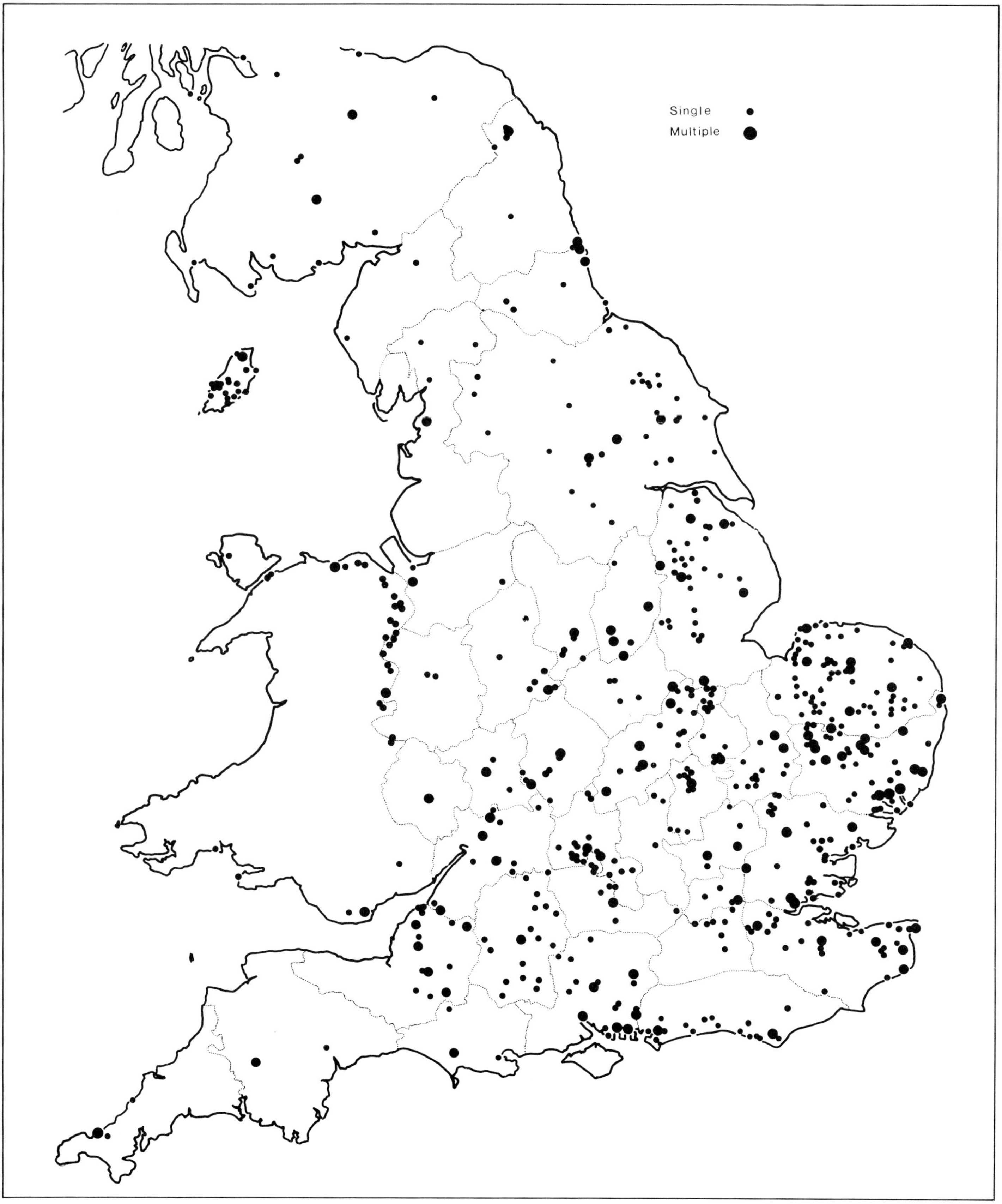

38 Archaeology of the Anglo-Saxon period. Excavations, field-work and chance finds reported in **Medieval Archaeology** 1957 to 1977

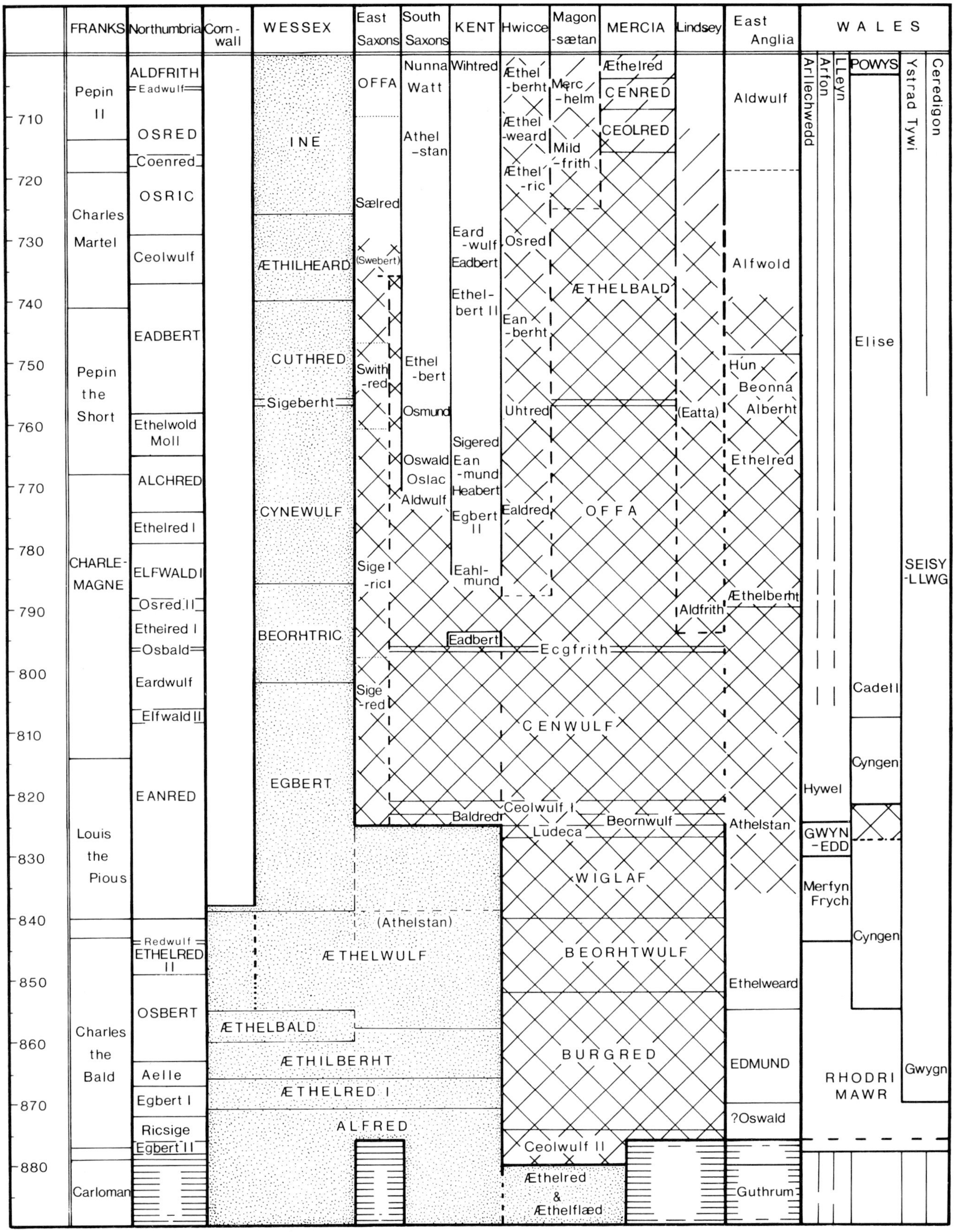

39 Kings and princes: chronology 700–880

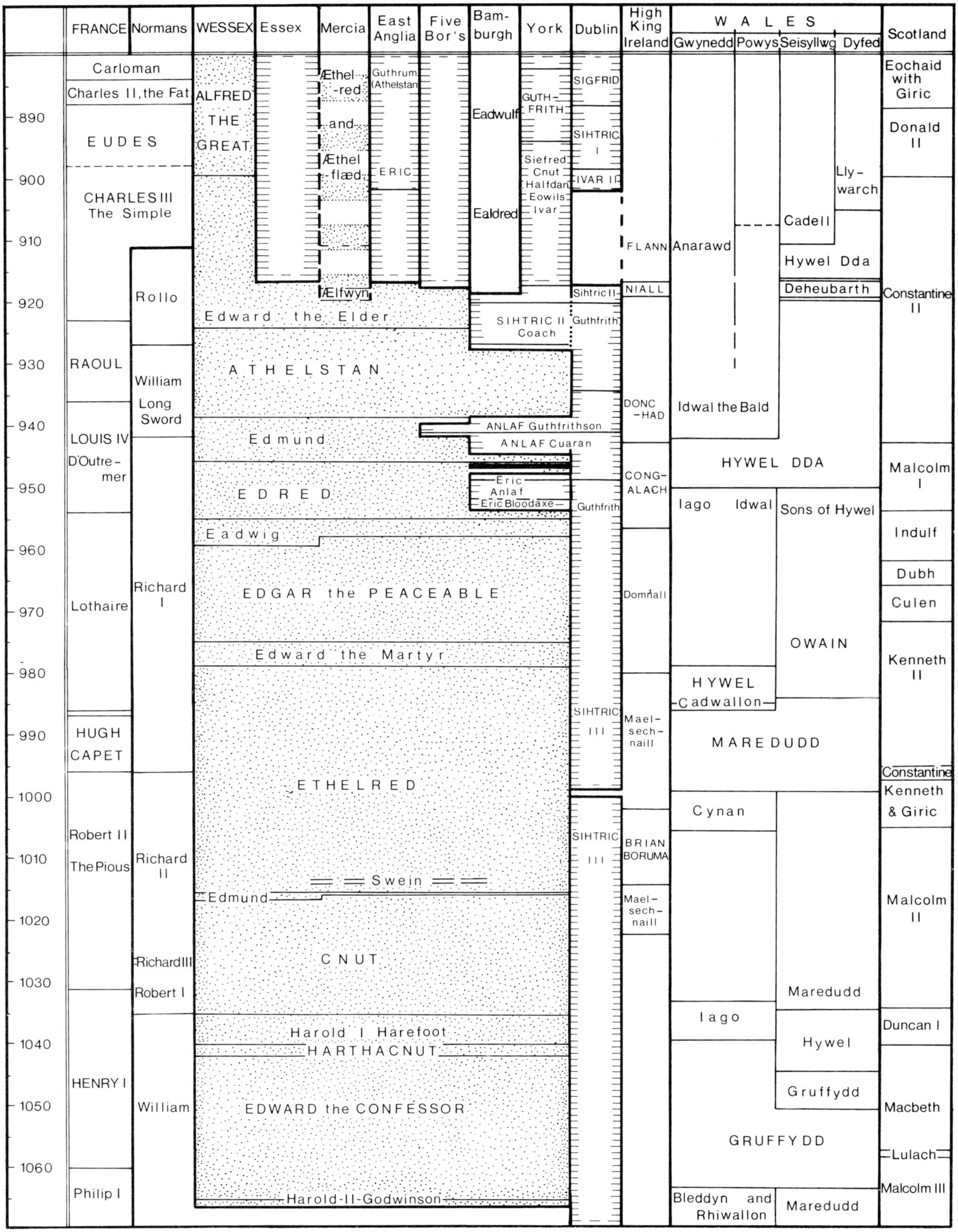

40 Kings and princes: chronology 880–1066

41 The England of Bede c.731. Places names from the **Ecclesiastical History**

The Events

From Bede to the Rise of Wessex (41–43)

The first century of the period covered by this atlas gives an appearance of great stability. Bede talks of an island in which the Anglo-Saxon portion was divided between a series of kingdoms, often referred to as the 'Heptarchy' under the sway or **imperium** of one kingdom (map **41**). The situation was by no means static but can overall be seen as the era of 'the supremacy of Mercia', the dominant kingdom (map **42**). The period does not lend itself to mapping but the itinerary of the Mercian kings is shown in map **145**; the disappearance of the minor kingdoms can be traced in outline in **39**; and places associated with the various campaigns can be found on maps **226–234**.

Essentially Anglo-Saxon England was divided between Northumbria and the area of Mercian domination, Southumbria, up until the reversal of Mercian fortunes following the battle of Ellendun in 825. There is still some dispute as to whether the collapse of Mercia was influenced by overcommitment to the campaigns and the final occupation of north Wales, but it cannot have been easy to conduct a war on two fronts nor to find the men both to hold down north Wales and to fight the West Saxons. The battle of Ellendun was to prove decisive as far as south-eastern England was concerned, as this became a permanent part of Wessex (map **43**). The submission of Mercia and of Northumbria, however, proved to be transitory. The final occupation by Wessex of Cornwall probably came with Athelstan but after the battle of Hingston Down in 838 the kings of Cornwall appear to have lost any freedom of action.

Two points should be made in relation to map **41** which shows England c. 731. First, in common with maps **27–30**, it reflects restrictions on the information available, or of interest to, Bede: the northern and eastern lands are well covered whilst the western and Celtic lands are ignored. The cluster of place names in Hampshire could, perhaps, be the result of the efforts of some particular correspondent of Bede's. Secondly, it is of interest for the study of the development of towns, to find that the nomenclature adopted for places was in the eighth century influenced more by their history than by their status. The appellation **civitas** was used for places with a known Roman ancestry, **urbs** for non-Roman towns. For a more accurate and extensive treatment see Campbell (1979, 52–3).

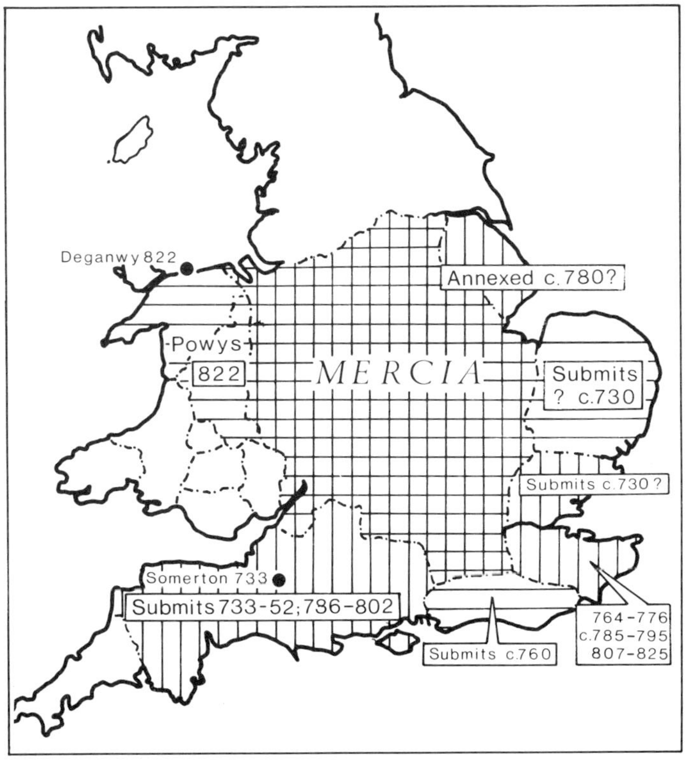

42 The supremacy of Mercia

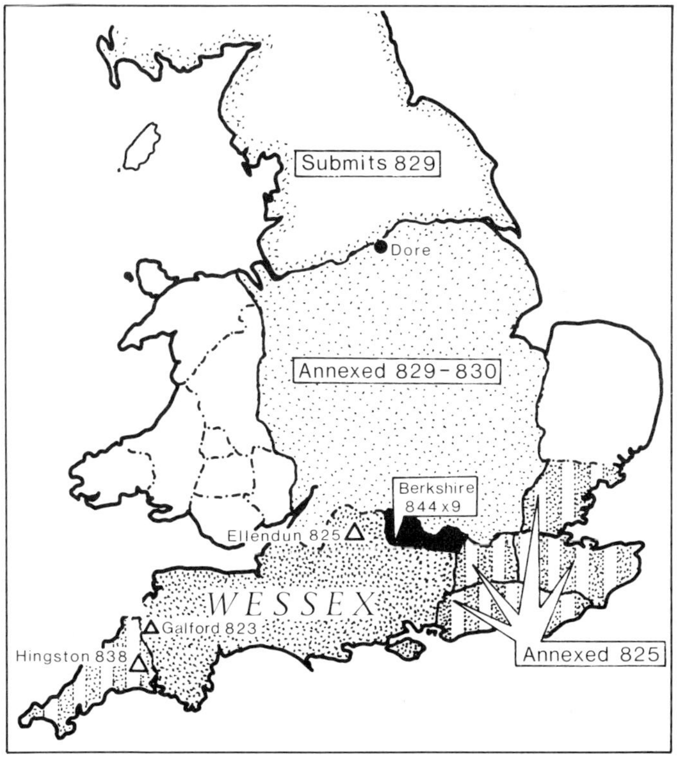

43 The rise of Wessex

The Vikings: Introduction (44–47)

It must be emphasized that this text makes no attempt to compete with the many excellent works dealing with the Vikings in Britain (Stenton 1971: Loyn 1977, etc.) or the large numbers of detailed studies of various aspects of their culture and impact (conveniently summarized in Wilson 1976, 393–404). These maps are a companion to such works, both insular and continental. Serious students should also consult, and evaluate, the series of important studies by A. P. Smyth (1975; 1977).

There were three Germanic groups in Europe — the Anglo-Saxons, the Continental Germans and the Scandinavians (map **44**). It was the latter group of Germanic peoples that expanded in this period and came to dominate Ango-Saxon history for more than two centuries. The Scandinavian expansion, loosely referred to as the 'Viking Age', had a great impact on the West and constitutes the dominant theme for the period 860 to 950 in England. The ramifications of the Viking impact cannot really be studied in isolation for England — even the British Isles is too limited an area. In fact, this study of the West European context could be criticized as too limited, for while the Vikings in eastern England were learning to come to terms with Edward the Elder, other Vikings were active on the shores of the Caspian. It is only possible to cover so much, and these Vikings have had to be left out, although, like Constantinople or Rome, they cannot be ignored by a student of Anglo-Saxon England.

During the whole of the period it is essential to bear in mind two factors. The first is the geographical separation of the Norse (Norwegian) areas of impact from the Danish areas. Dolley (1966) has illustrated their different areas of influence in the British Isles using coin finds (map **45**). Although there are areas of overlap on occasion (for example the early Norse expeditions to France before 820, or the Danish adventure linked with the name of Turgeis in Ireland in the 840s) the areas remain distinct. The same could be said for the Continent, for the line drawn by Dolley could be extended southwards so that mainland France is split, with the Loire and Brittany being, in the main, Norse and the Seine, Somme and Low Countries regions being Danish.

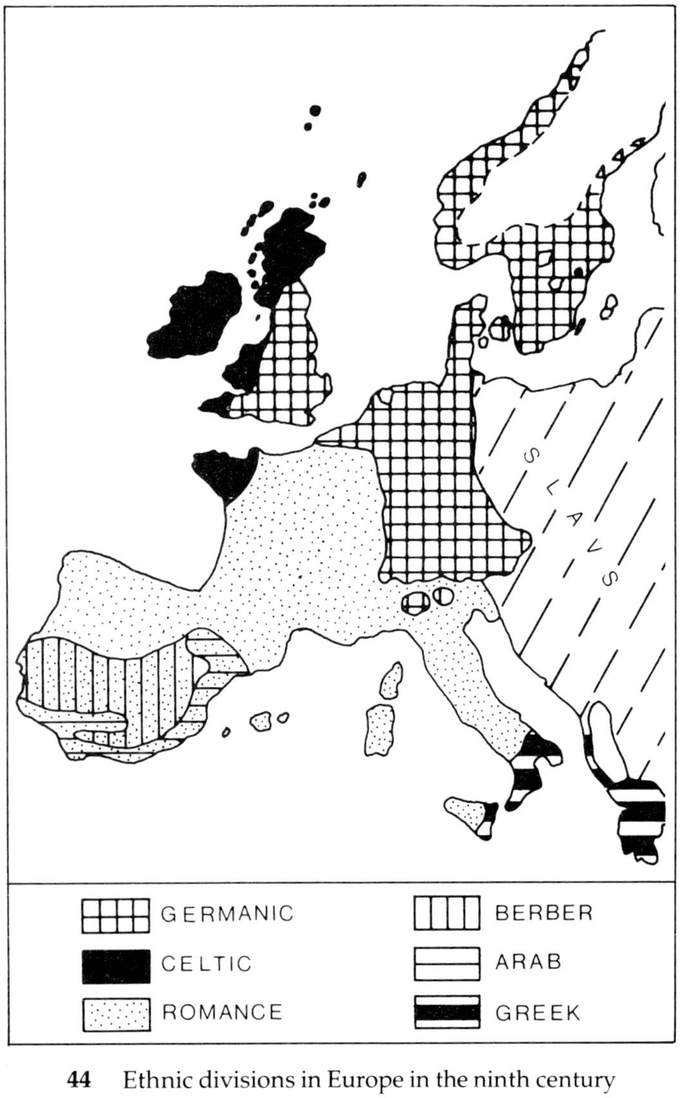

44 Ethnic divisions in Europe in the ninth century

45 Zones of Norse and Danish influence according to coin finds (after Dolley 1966)

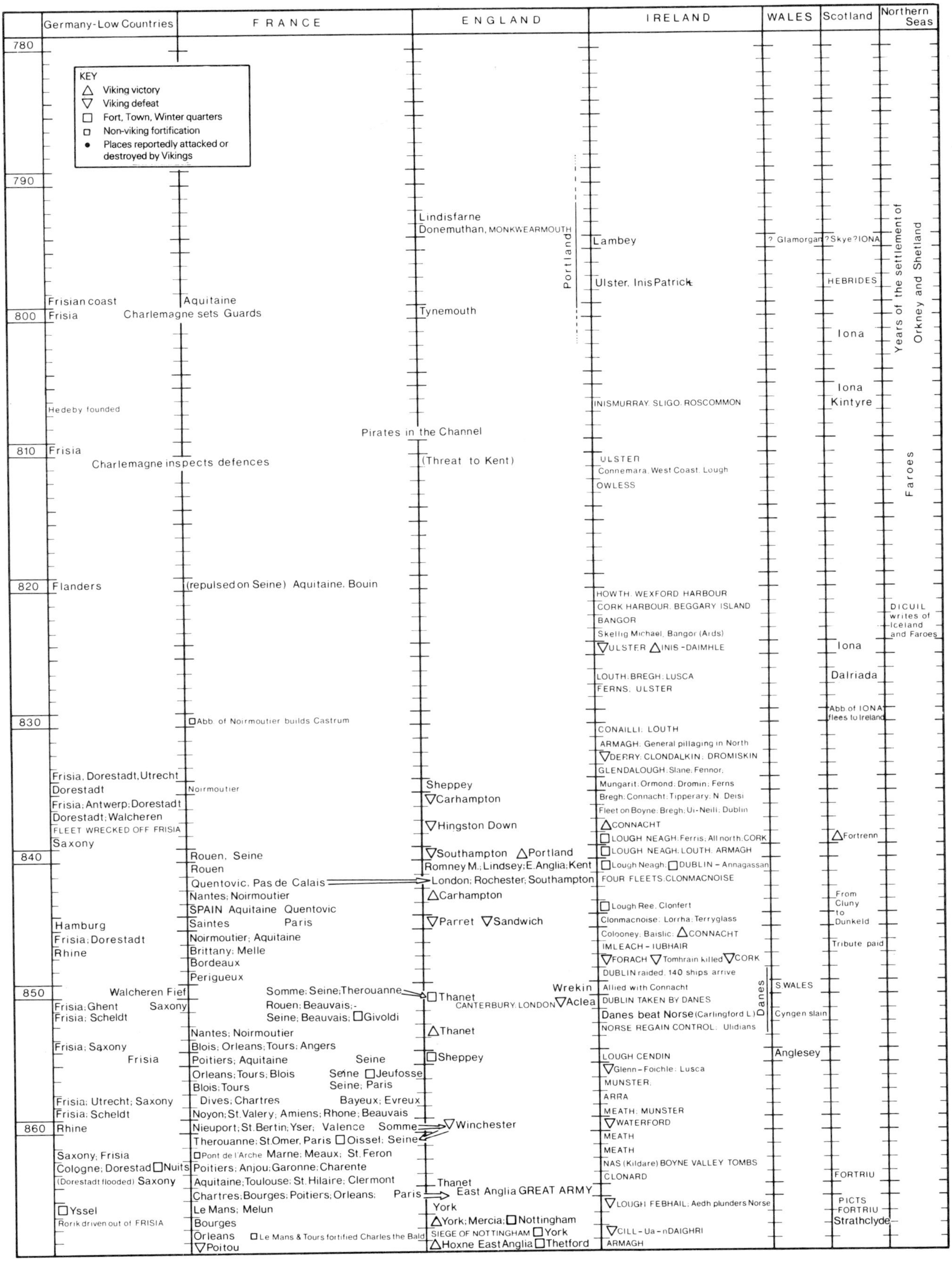

46 The Vikings in the West: chronology 780–869

The second factor is that many enterprises are linked together under the name **Viking**. To quote Brøndsted (1965, 31):

The Viking raids were inspired by several motives. On that account a mere chronological account of them would produce an obscure and contradictory pattern, and an attempt must therefore be made to classify them according to their varying motives and objectives. The Swedish scholar, Fritz Askeberg, has proposed a fourfold classification:

(1) Pirate raids conducted by individuals
(2) Political expeditions
(3) Colonizing ventures
(4) Commercial penetration

Such a division, as Askeberg himself points out, cannot be universally applicable, and many of the raids doubtless proceeded from mixed motives. But, so long as it is remembered that this classification is in no sense a chronological one, it serves to put the Viking period into perspective.

To some extent at least, these categories are modified by the Norse/Danish division: the scale of the Danish raids appears to have been larger, the raids involved greater numbers of participants, and more often than not the Danes when settling appeared to aim to take over as a ruling class. The Danes apparently attempted to gain some form of title to their lands, in the case of the Continent by taking the lands as fiefs from the emperor or king, in England by setting up, at least initially, a puppet king through whom they ruled.

The charts showing the chronology of the Vikings in the West (**46** and **47**) are, of necessity, simplified but together with the maps that follow they attempt to give some general picture of the ebb and flow of events in the West. What emerges very strongly is the interrelation of events in one country with events in another. For the Norse sphere of influence, the **Landnama** is closely linked to the 'forty years' rest' in Ireland, and periods of activity in France are periods of comparative rest in England. Thus the Great Army which comes together about 835 with the attacks on Frisia, moves to France and then to England, in each case leaving a period of rest behind it. Sometimes, as in the period 878 to 895, each move can be linked with a reverse in one country leading the Great Army to move on to fresh, and possibly easier, pastures. Although there is little evidence that the Great Army was used as an official title, on a par with Napoleon's **Grande Armée**, it is a useful concept for the principal conjunction of Danish forces, greater than the armies on the Seine, Somme or Loire. It is important to note that the army drew recruits from Scandinavian or Viking settlements, and that reinforcements, not being centrally directed, tended to follow success. Thus the Reconquest of the Danelaw made that area unpalatable to fresh Vikings just at the time that the settlement and expansion of Normandy drew recruits. The whole region was interlocked.

The army usually stayed in the West: it did not return home but consisted of groups who found their way West, joined, fought, made money, left and settled. The 'summer army' was a different, and rarer, phenomenon of lesser import. Although it did occasionally emerge, presumably largely though not exclusively from a Scandinavian base, the general weight of attack, certainly from 860, was from the army in the West. It is unlikely that armies of the size active at this time would have been welcome if they had returned **en bloc** to Scandinavia, several hundred ship-loads strong, practised in war, rich with booty, and led by men with royal pretensions. A returning army could be a most disruptive influence on the kingdoms of Scandinavia.

In the classic phase of Viking attacks on England, 830–95, the armies sailed not from Scandinavia but from France, Frisia or Ireland, and they can be recognized as groups operating there.

In the charts it should be noted that the right-hand side — covering Ireland, Wales, Scotland and the Northern Seas — deals in the main, with the area of Norse activity. The same symbols are used on both maps and charts in the following sections.

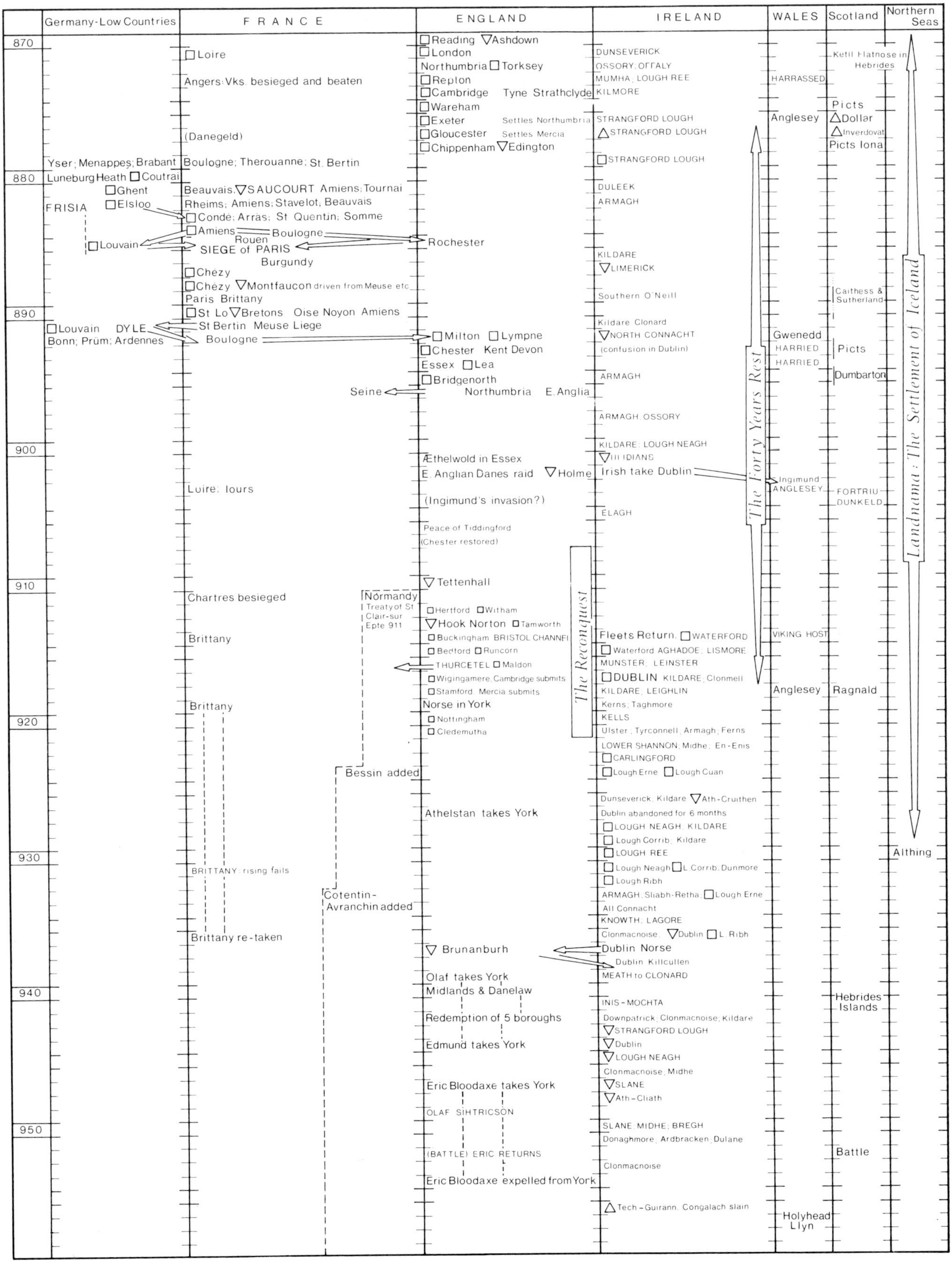

47 The Vikings in the West: chronology 870–959

The Vikings in the West c. 789–850 (48–53)

The Viking Age opened with the contact of the Norse with the West. It seems apparent that they were using two routes, the most important being from Norway to Faroes, Shetland, Orkney, Western Isles and the western seaway. Although they occasionally probed the coasts of Frisia, England and France, the brunt of the attacks was taken by Ireland. It is quite possible that the Norse/Norwegian interest in the Loire area stemmed from their discovery that Irish trade was moving from southern Ireland to the saltpans around the coast of Aquitaine and the Vikings followed that established route which led them circuitously to France. The following of established paths and possibly using guides, as well as collecting sailing instructions, accounts for several 'discoveries', including, perhaps, Iceland.

The distribution of the raids in England at this period, together with the lesser problem of those in Wales, gives the impression that for the first forty years of the Danish and Norse raids England was a calm centre in a storm. This may well be a mistaken impression. The evidence from the chronicles is slim for the decades of Viking activity to 850 (compare **37**). The evidence from the one or two existing charters of the period does indicate threats to Kent in the first decades of the ninth century, as well as piracy in the Channel. There is a later record of heathens in the area of the Wrekin. These references alone should warn us of the sketchy nature of the Chronicle record.

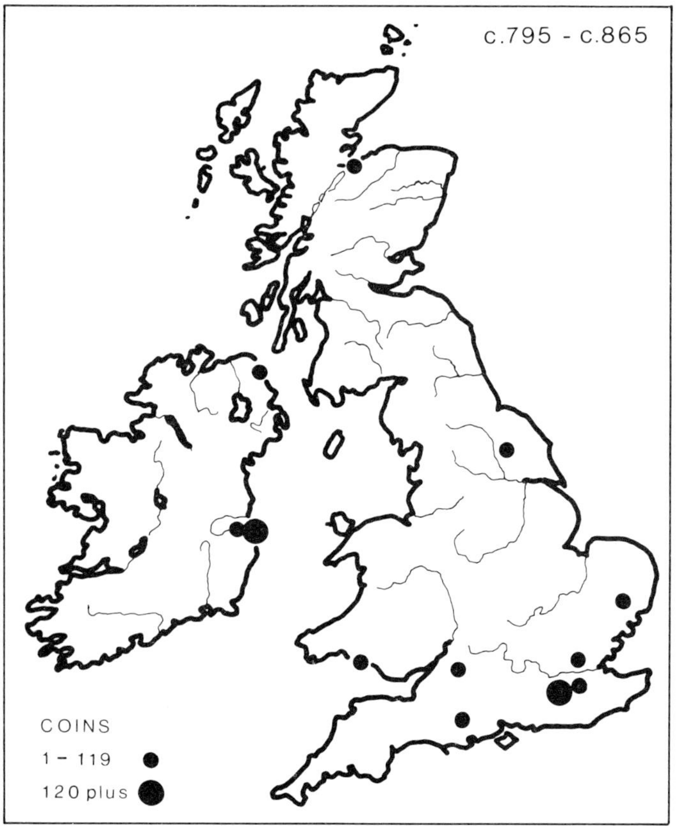

48 Hoards of coins deposited c.795–c.865

There is another form of evidence for the effect of the Vikings: the hoards of coins deposited, and not subsequently recovered by their owners, in the ninth and tenth centuries (map **48**). The deposition of these hoards may not always be linked to threats of war, for hoards are certainly also deposited in times of peace, but their increase is linked to times of uncertainty. Michael Dolley (1966) has carried out some very interesting research on these coin hoards and the patterns revealed certainly show that the general shape of the Chronicle account is right. It should be remembered that there is an increase in coin use during the whole of this period, resulting in more coin being available to hoard, and an increase in the areas (particularly in Ireland) using coin. Therefore we must expect more hoards at the end of the period than at the beginning.

The response of Charlemagne to the Vikings was vigorous: two of his tours of inspection are shown on map **49**, indicating that he saw the narrow seas as the point of greater danger. His use of coastal defence (beacons, fleets and forts) was to be followed fitfully by many Western rulers in the ensuing years.

Although the Danes had figured largely in the politics and diplomacy of Charlemagne and of Louis the Pious and although to read the chronicles of their reigns it would seem that the extensive coastal defences and fleets were built against them it is clear that the bulk of the campaigning in the West was Norse until about 834. The campaigns in Ireland increased in the 830s and it is to these campaigns we must look for a context to Hingston Down and Carhampton (map **50**). The attack on Sheppey on the other hand was an overspill from Frisia. The Frisian campaigns were a new departure and the defences were clearly overrun. The raids moved through the Straits of Dover.

The new era in Viking raids began with the sacking of Rouen in 840 (map **51**), and from this date we can detect a change in the character of Viking attack, with a pattern of widespread raiding on major centres, of considerable forays inland and of bases in the West either on islands or on rivers (map **52**). It should be noted that this new phase came after fifty years of very minor activity on the part of the Vikings, except in Ireland — and even there the raids had been minor compared with what was to follow.

For the British Isles the interaction of Viking raids in the West as a whole is vital. Some of the Viking adventures are of great interest, and invested with romance but of no significance for the Anglo-Saxons. The Greenland/Vinland expeditions, for example, are justly famous — but of no import to our studies. The well-known episodes in the Mediterranean may in fact only consist of three expeditions. That of 858–59 was the famous raid that continued into southern France and to Luna in Italy. The greatest impact of the Mediterranean adventures was in Moorish Spain (map **53**) where the Arabs reacted by founding a series of fortifications which have been identified by their **rapita** place names.

With the sacking of Paris in 845 the second phase of Viking raids was firmly under way (map **52**). The Norse were still active in the Western Isles and Ireland but it

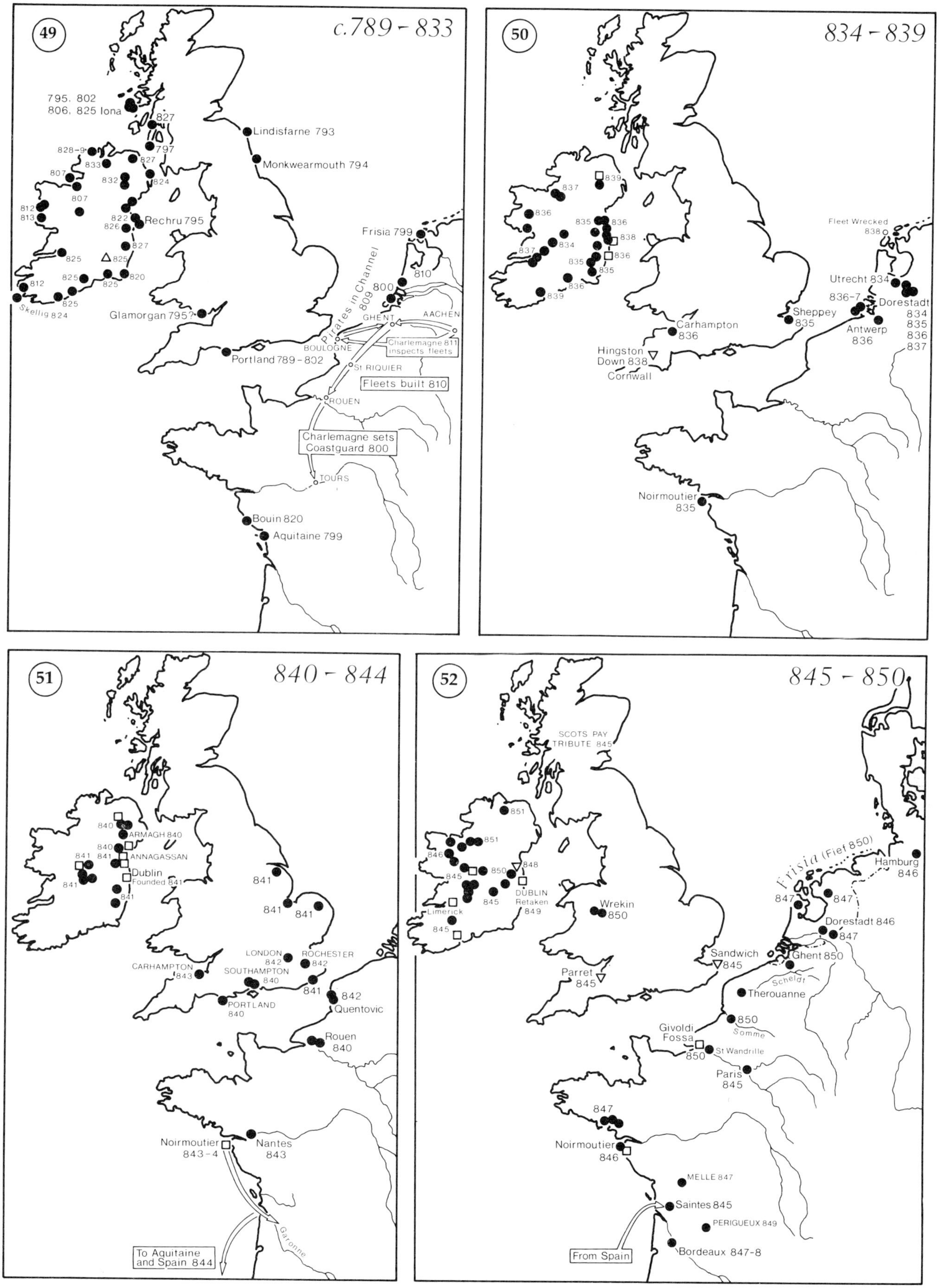

49–52 The Vikings in the West c.789–850. For key to symbols on these and later Viking maps, see **46**

was the Danish semi-permanent armies operating from bases that were typical of this phase. There were also a number of armies in the Seine and Loire (and in the Somme a little later) which, together with the lack of fixed purpose on the part of the Carolingians, gave the second phase its character.

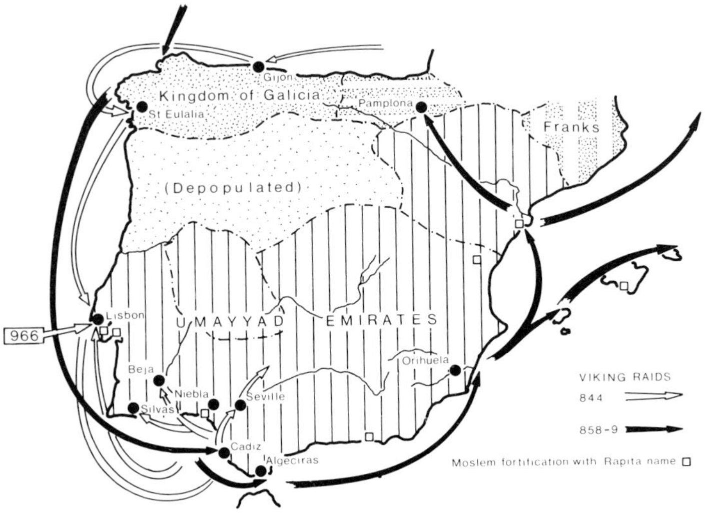

53 The Vikings in Spain

The Vikings in the West 851–878 (54–57)

The Danish armies roamed widely over the West and finally came into conflict with the Norse in Ireland in 851 (map **54**). Here the Vikings were distinguished as the 'black foreigners' (the Danes) and the 'white foreigners' (the Norse). At this stage it is already possible to discern the beginning of a process that was to absorb the Vikings into Irish life as the 'Hiberno-Norse', Vikings who had never seen Scandinavia and who came to dominate Irish commercial life. In the battles between Dane and Norwegian the native Irish came to take part as allies and to raid their Celtic neighbours for a share of the booty.

There had already been some raids into England by the Danes but they appear to have led to reverses which helped to keep England clear of the armies. The activities of the Norse are probably in evidence in the west of England. Yet it is possible that the full tally of raids has not been passed down to us. For the latter half of the 850s (map **55**) attention was concentrated on the campaigns in the Seine and the Somme where Carolingian resistance was at its most feeble. Although the bases at Jeufosse and Oissel were deep inside Carolingian territory, there seems to have been no concerted effort to dislodge them. This failure is usually attributed to the internecine struggles of the Carolingian Royal House: it has been said that to Charles the Bald, fighting for his throne against his brothers, the attacks of the Danes were like the buzzing of a wasp in the hair of a man being strangled. Yet the effects on trade, the towns, the peasantry, tax returns, in fact on every form of life in this, the richest part of France (compare map **211**) must have been considerable.

The overspill of Danes into England is shown by the raid of 860 when the Danes on the Somme were paid to attack and remove those on the Seine. Instead they sailed for England and attacked Winchester before sailing to the Seine. The northern armies were drawn off in 866 to England (map **56**), the result for France being a period of eleven years during which northern France had a respite and only the mainly Norse Loire army was active (map **57**). A significant factor accounting for these movements was Charles the Bald's vigorous defence of his realm before the fleets sailed for England. The series of bridge works at Pont de l'Arche, les Ponts de Cé and elsewhere were only part of his efforts — efforts which often failed but which certainly contributed to the increasing difficulties facing the Danes.

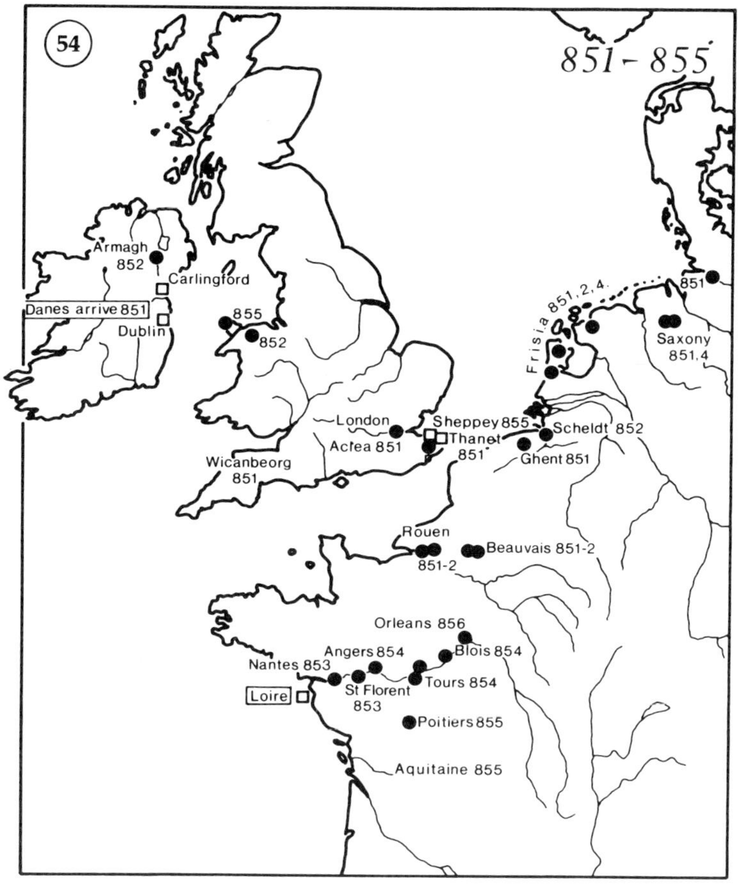

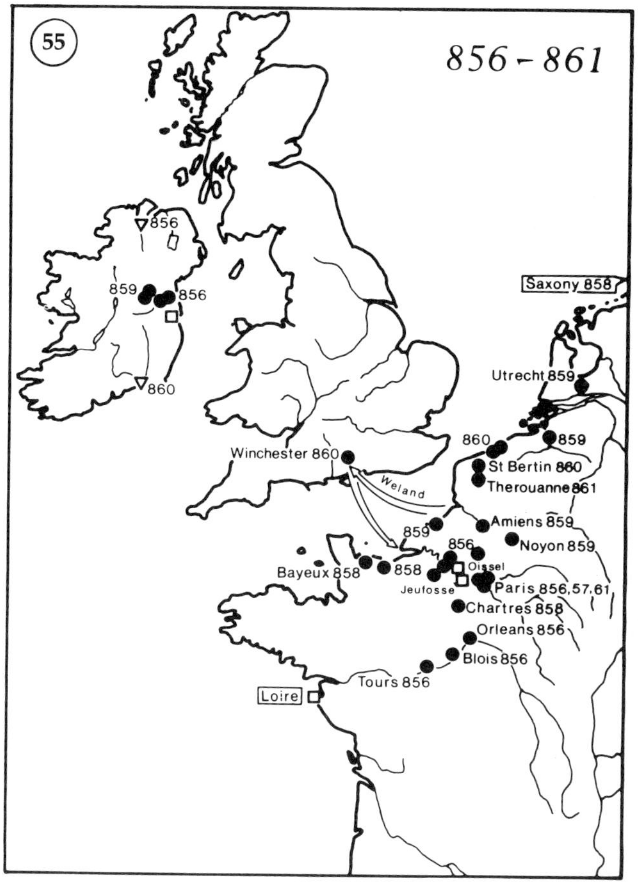

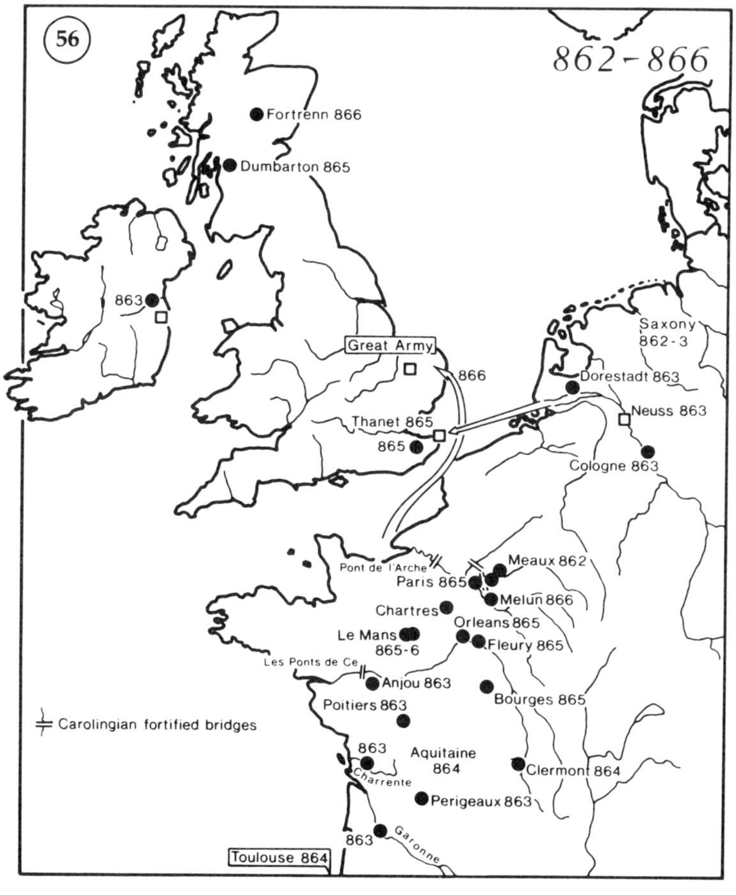

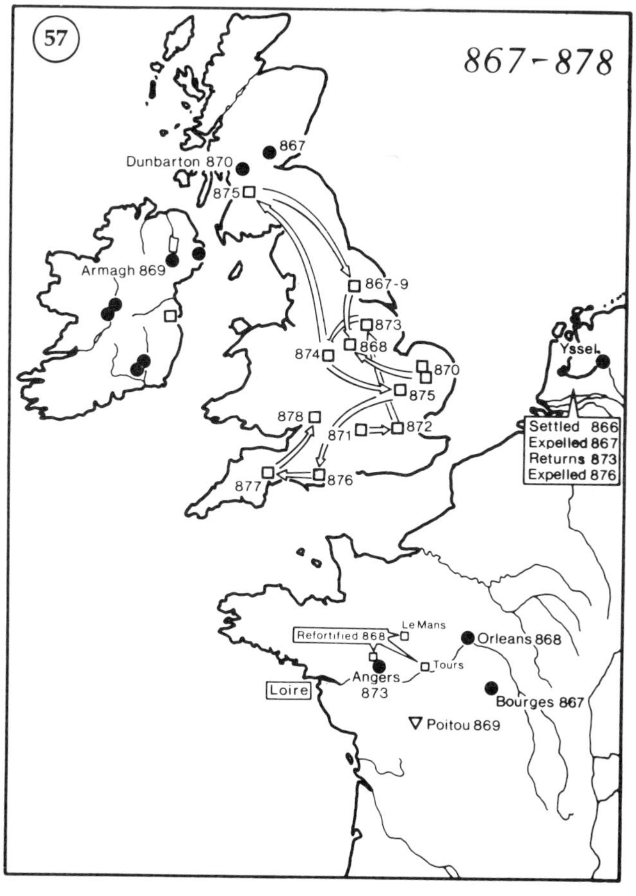

54–57 The Vikings in the West 851–878

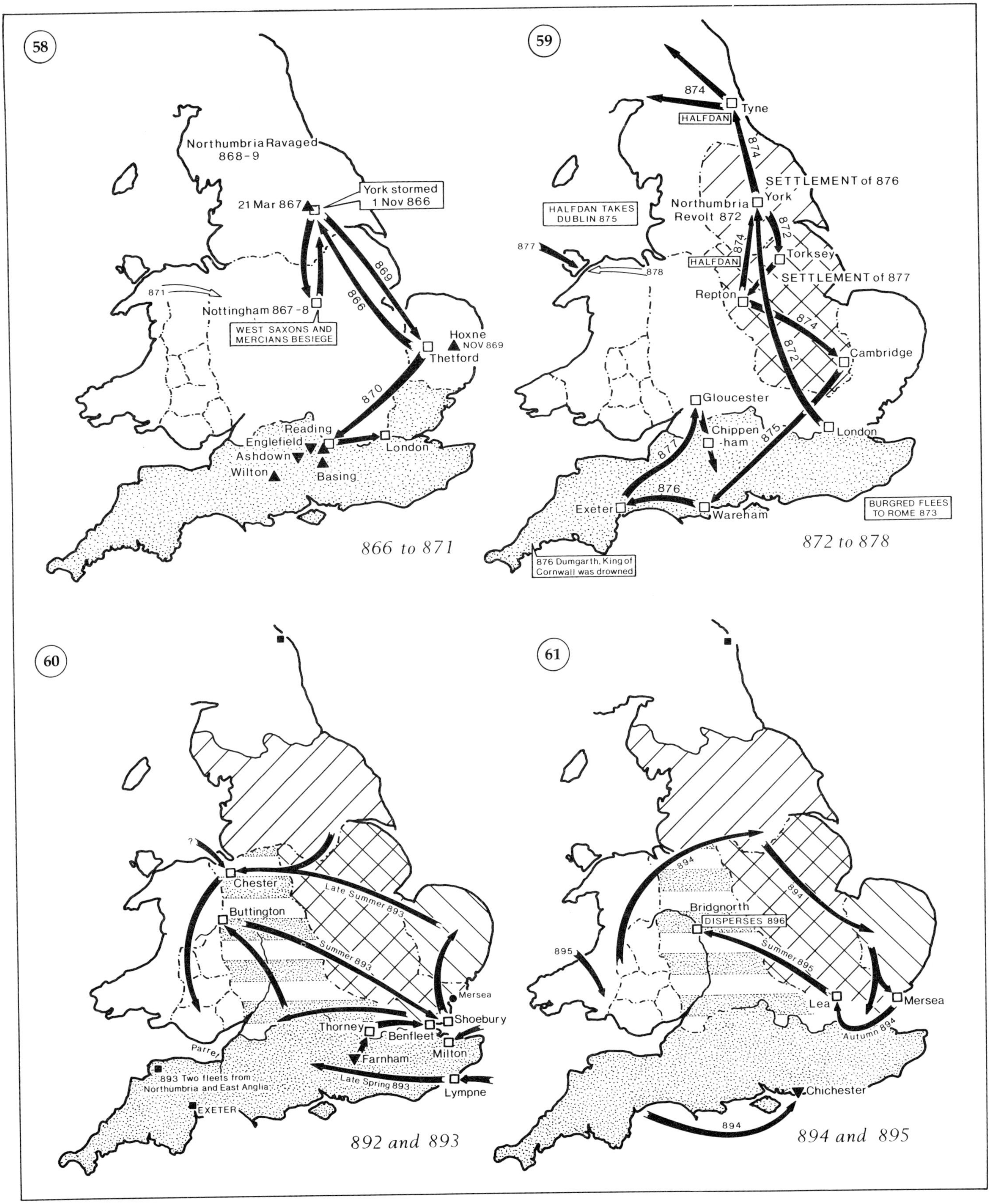

58–61 The Vikings in England 866–895

The Vikings in England 866–895 (58–61)

No part of the Anglo-Saxon story is better known than the epic of Alfred the Great and the Danes: it is well covered in Stenton and in most other general works, and most of the evidence is contained in Asser and the Chronicle which can be read easily and consecutively. While it is not necessary to recount the events here, certain points need to be stressed. The account we have is Wessex based and throws little light on the role of Mercia, particularly in the early stages, nor on the transfer of power in Mercia to the West Saxons. The Danes' intention of becoming the ruling elite is shown by their appointment of puppet rulers in at least three kingdoms: only later did they start to farm the land. Even then the role of Danish peasant farmers may have been limited, unlike the Norse whose peasant farming can be detected in the north and west at a later date.

The political impact of the Danish wars (maps **58** and **59**) was immense. By the close of 879 the map of England had been transformed: the south and west were Saxon; soon (probably by 880, certainly soon after) to be West Saxon was the protected state of the Ealdormanry of Mercia; the east and central northern areas were a series of Danish states, namely East Anglia, Danish Mercia and York; and in the far north the rump of the Kingdom of Northumbria, known to the Irish at least as being ruled by the King of the North Saxons, known to the West Saxons (and through their writings to posterity) as ruled by the Ealdorman of Bamburgh.

The final set of raids (maps **60** and **61**) was more spectacular than damaging. Close investigation shows them to be the raids of an army that had split many times, lost many men to the new settlements and been defeated in a series of battles from Ethandun to Saucourt and the Dyle. The campaigns consisted of armies operating in the marginal land of Essex, where their bases were built after moving from the south-east. The raids then swept across the whole of middle England. The apparent ease with which the raiders moved is deceptive for they were always travelling along the no-man's-land between the new Danish settlements and the lands controlled by the West Saxons. The West Saxon heartland had already been fortified by a series of **burhs** (fortified centres) and the army of King Alfred had been reorganized. Although the process of **burh**-building is not well documented for these years, it was certainly going on. Charles the Bald had similarly been re-fortifying towns in 868 and indeed this had been a general response against the Vikings throughout the area: the **rapitas** in Spain, the **burhs** in Wessex, the fortified bridges and towns in the lands of Charles the Bald are all evidence of the same trend. It may well be that the obsession of the Chronicle with the movements of the Danish army in France from 878 to 892 stemmed from anxiety as the West Saxons raced to complete their fortifications before the next blow fell.

The Vikings in the West 879–896 (62–64)

The Vikings who left for France in 879 were only part of the Danish armies and they had suffered a serious reverse in England. The movements of this army in the next twelve years were those of a body of men now known to be fallible (map **62**). Although they devastated large parts of the north of France and a new army in 880 and in 883 had successes in the lands of the East Franks, they also received disastrous checks at Saucourt and the Dyle, from the Bretons and in front of Paris (map **63**). When they finally re-entered England they were a very battered force and even the arrival of an army from the Loire to assist them was less hopeful than at first appeared for they too were defeated before they set out (map **64**).

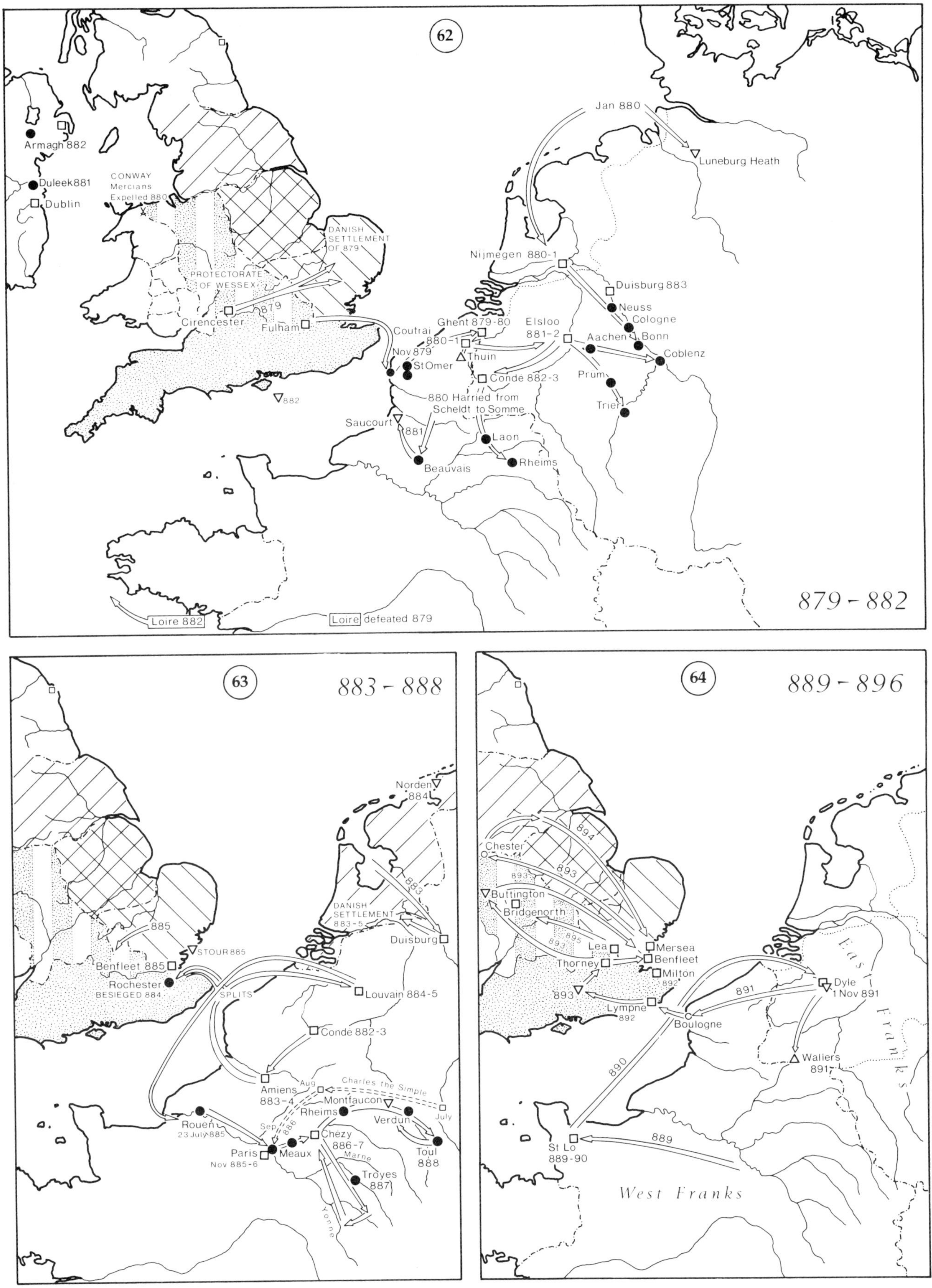

62–64 The Vikings in the West 879–896

Scandinavian Coins and Graves (65–67)

The Scandinavian settlement of large parts of England was in general a short-lived phenomenon. Nevertheless, when the last Viking kingdom disappeared in 954, real and long-lasting effects were to be seen, not in independent Danish kingdoms, but in the settlement of peoples with language, laws and a separate form of organization loosely referred to as the Danelaw. The limits of the Danelaw are very hard to fix (see maps **174–177**) but some of the results of the settlement can be charted.

The northern settlements do show quite well on the map of coin hoards listed by Dolley (map **65**), the Yorkshire area being particularly well represented. The strangest point to emerge from Dolley's listings is the lack of material from Ireland, from which one can only deduce that the 'forty years' rest' was a time of limited activity in the area. (For a full discussion of the hoard material see Dolley (1966) and several more recent articles by the same author.)

When the comparative material from the Continent is considered (map **66**) the number of graves in Britain looks more impressive. There are only two inhumations (a man at Antum and a woman at Pitres) and a cremated ship-burial in the Cruguel mound on the Ile de Groix.

The distribution of Scandinavian artefacts is surprisingly limited and consists of very few finds; the number of burials (map **67**) is small, particularly for the area of Danelaw, although the small number of pagan burials of the Viking Age may suggest the swift adoption of Christian practices or at least of Christian burial places by the Viking settlers (Wilson 1976, 394).

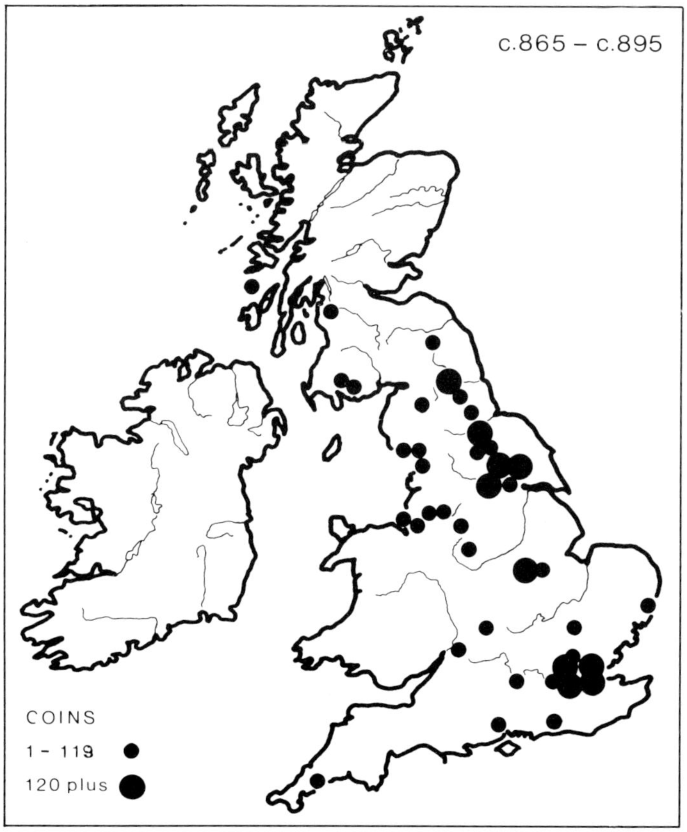

65 Hoards of coins deposited c.865–c.895

66 Viking graves in western Europe

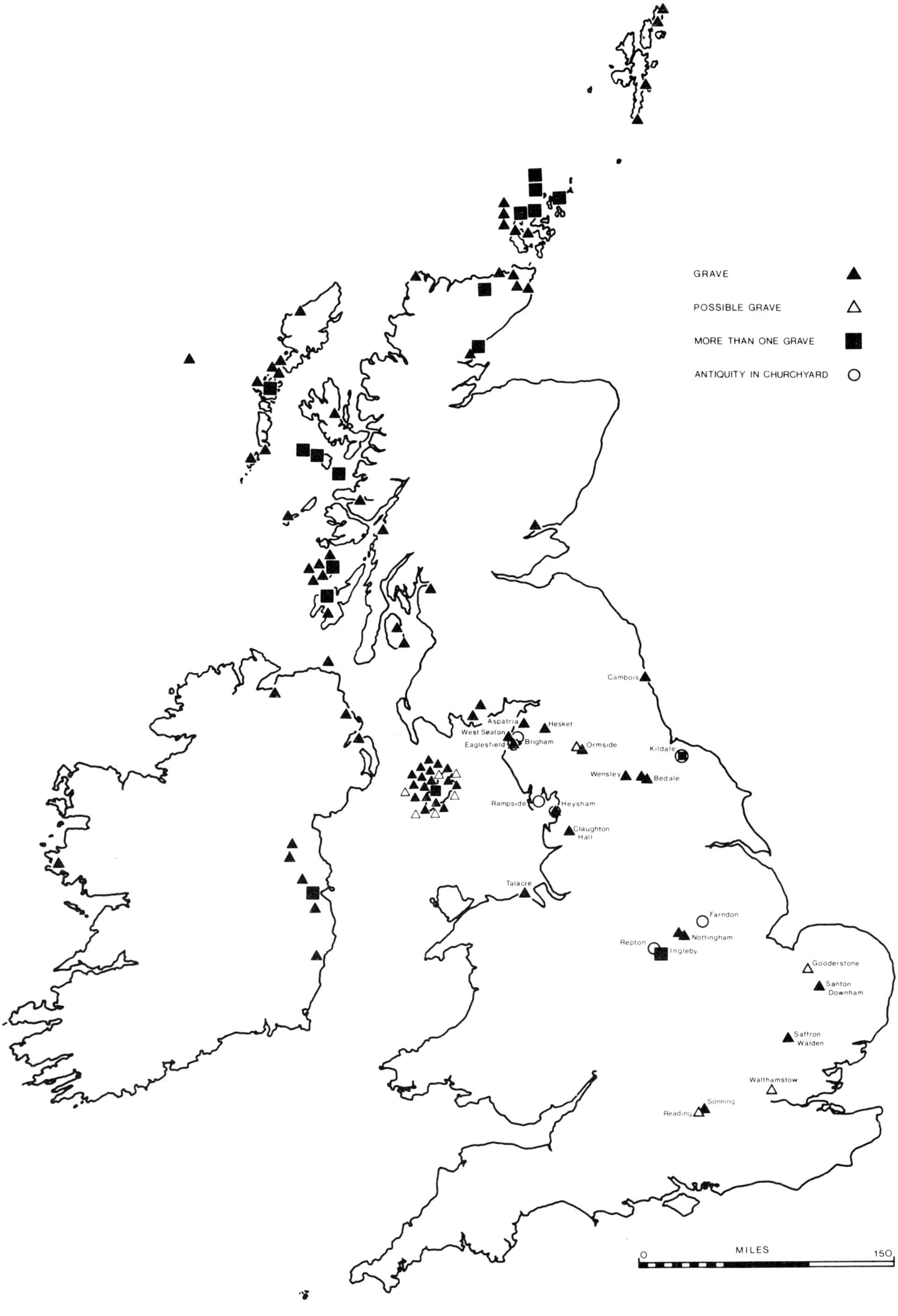

67 Scandinavian graves of the Viking age (after Wilson 1976)

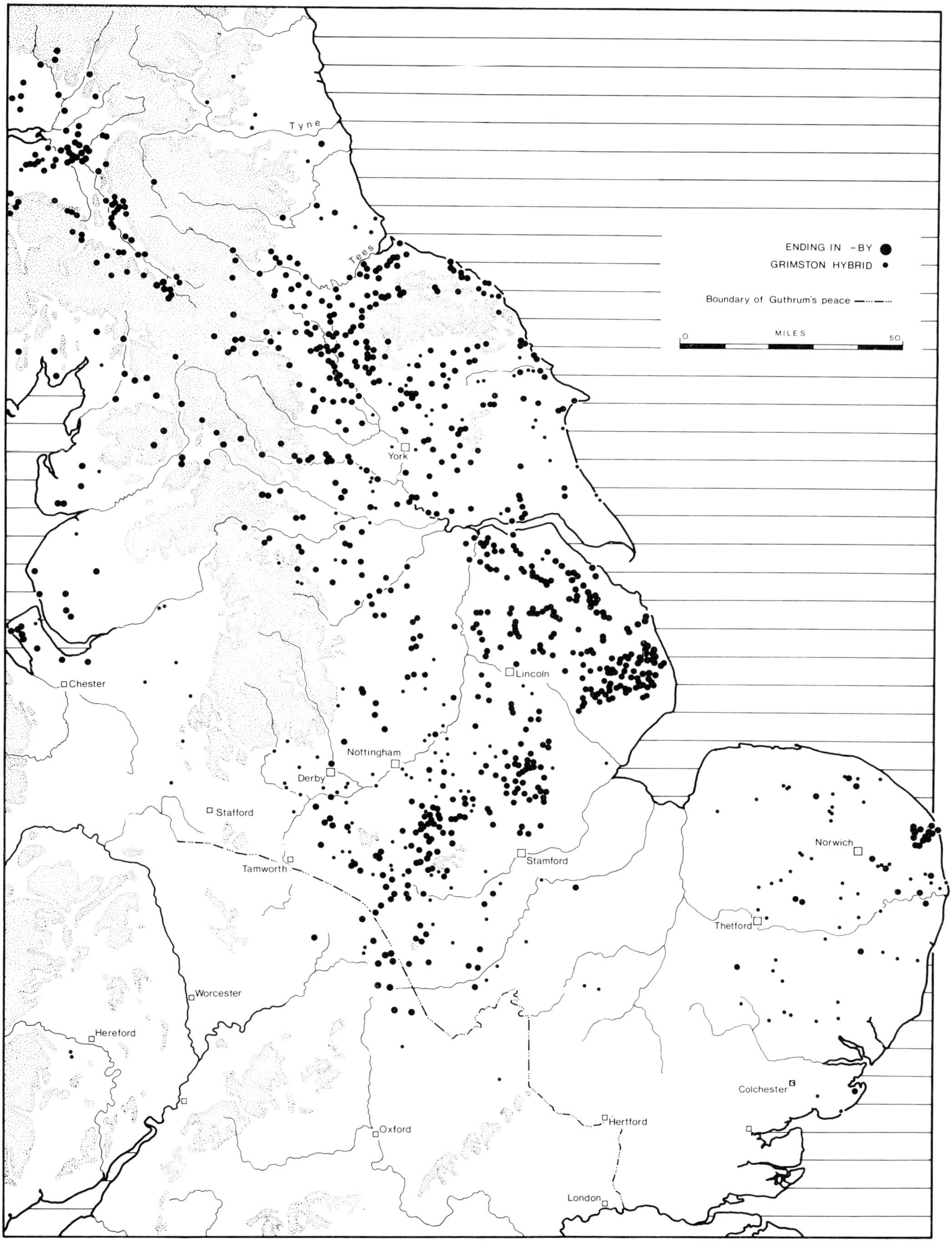

68 Scandinavian place names of eastern England

Scandinavian Place Names (68–69)

The place name evidence for Anglo-Saxon England is extensive but not well represented in this volume for, in general, it tends to illustrate themes not touched on here. It should also be noted that the English Place Name Society volumes have yet to cover the whole country.

The evidence (map **68**) does illustrate the Danish settlement beautifully and indicates a varying density of place names (and therefore **perhaps** a varying density of Scandinavian settlers). The heartland of the Danish settlement of eastern England lies to the east of the Pennines between the Tees and the Nene, and map **68** indicates the area remaining under the rule of the Ealdorman of Bamburgh (Ordnance Survey 1973).

Scandinavian place names associated with the Norse settlements are also quite extensive in the north-west of England and the far north of Scotland but surprisingly sparse in Ireland (map **69**).

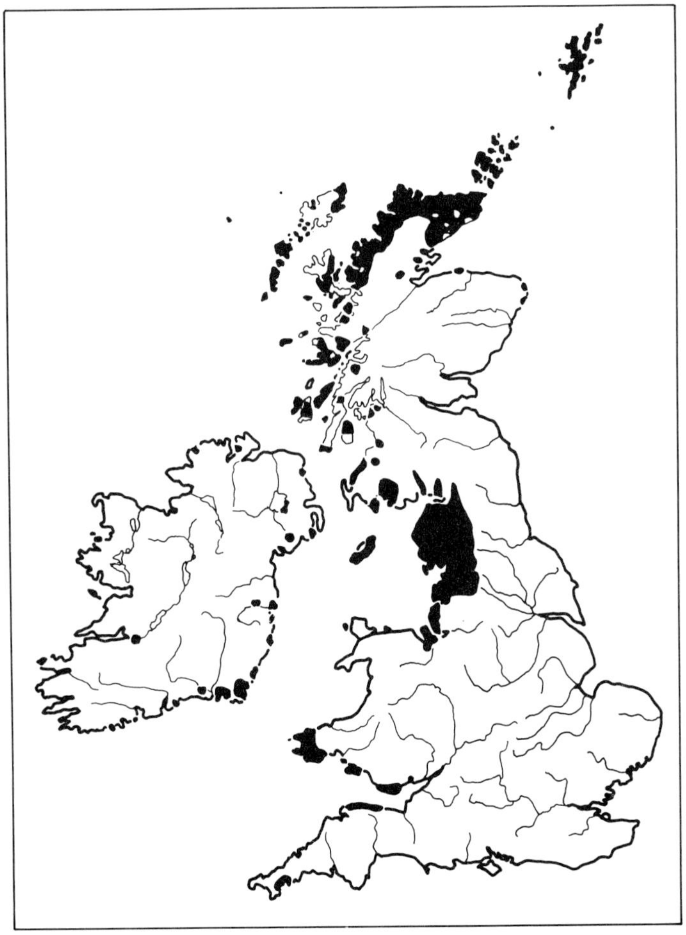

69 Scandinavian place names in the north and west

Mercia 880–906 (70)

The extent and strength of the ealdormanry of Mercia under the overlordship of Alfred and his son Edward the Elder is difficult to judge, but Mercia is the key to an understanding of the Danelaw. A careful mapping of the available evidence does offer a few pointers towards the limits of the surviving Mercian state (map **70**). The places disposed of by charter by the rulers of Mercia (marked on the map as 'places with charter') define a considerable area of influence. In the south and west of the old kingdom of Mercia it is clear that, from at least the early 880s, the areas of the former sub-kingdoms of the Hwicce and of the Magonsætan (indicated by a dotted line, as is the shire of Middlesex) were included together with much land to the north of the lower Thames valley. The northern limits are defined nebulously by the necessity for Cheshire to have formed part of Mercia if any sense is to be made of the north Welsh campaign of 881 and the lands bought in Derbyshire would likewise argue for all of Staffordshire and Cheshire to be included. The distribution of Scandinavian place names makes this likely. The frontier to the east is more problematic, but the map suggests that the 'boundary between Alfred's and Guthrum's kingdoms' had little lasting significance. The question of the extent of the Danelaw is raised by this map, as by **174–177** and **68**. There may be at least six methods of defining this area with little evident correlation between them. Interestingly, from the evidence gathered here it would appear that Gloucester was, for a time, the important centre in Mercia.

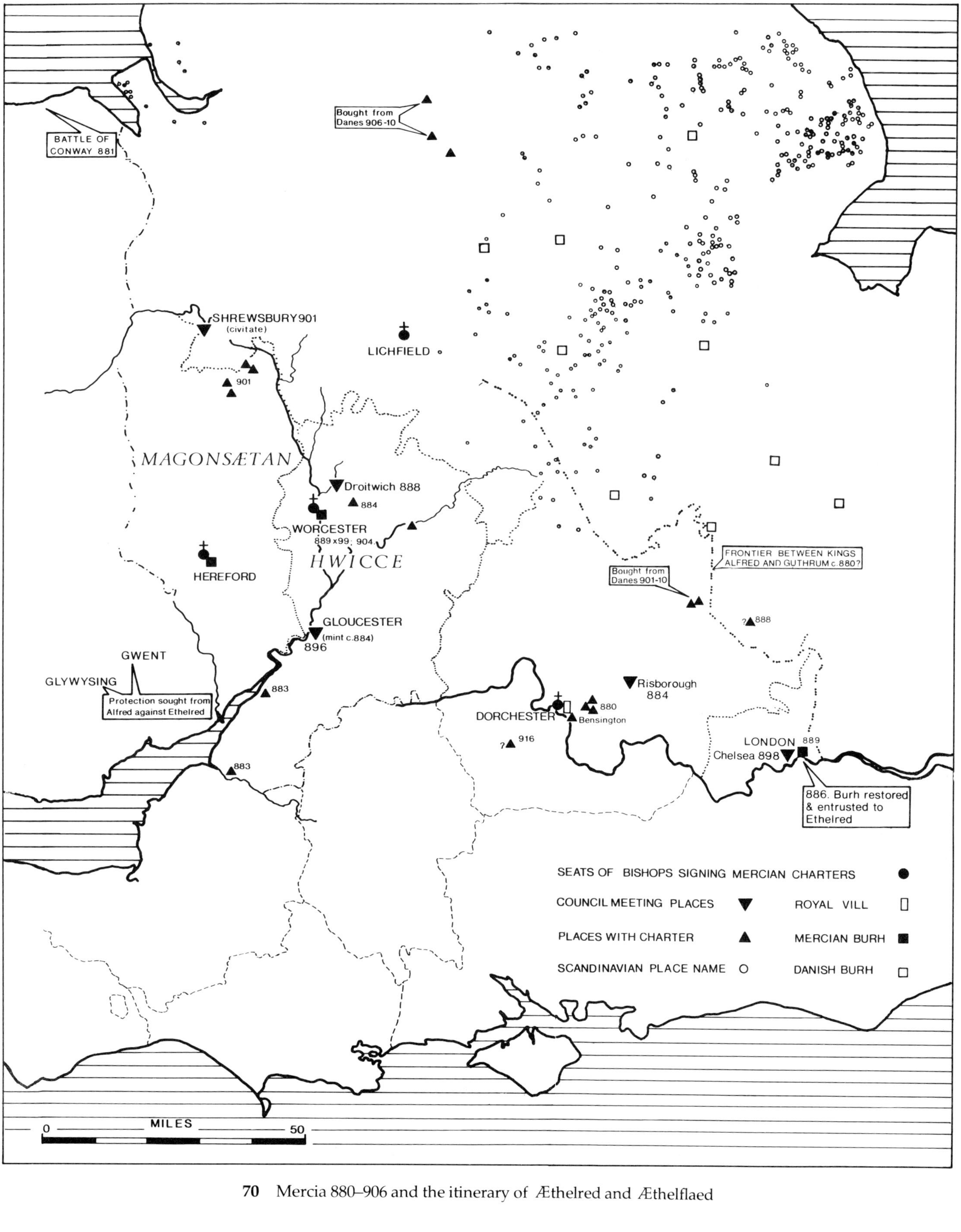

70 Mercia 880–906 and the itinerary of Æthelred and Æthelflaed

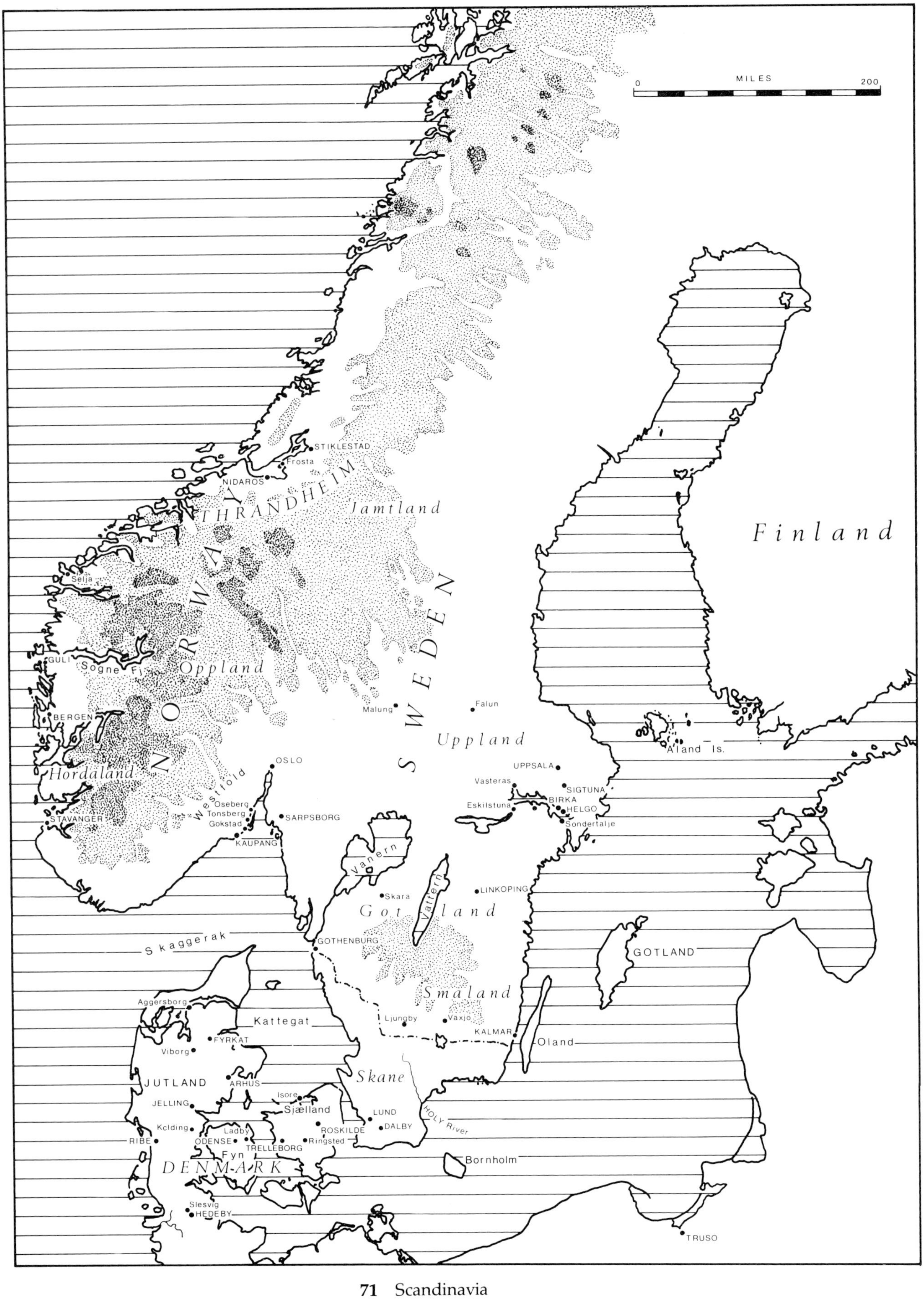

71 Scandinavia

Scandinavia (71–72)

The homelands of the Vikings — Denmark (which included Skane), Sweden and Norway — are very different regions and have differing histories during the period. They are linked by a common language and tradition which gave the Viking the ability to operate with Vikings of another country. Map **71** shows a number of places important for the study of Scandinavian history, without defining them as settlement, fort, town, etc. The relief is indicated and the approximate frontier between Sweden and the Danish province of Skane is shown. The map is intended to assist the reader in general rather than to make any specific point.

It is clear that the areas available near home for Norse and Dane settlement were limited, particularly those areas suitable for farming in Norway where snow often covers the ground for too extensive a period (map **72**). It should be noted that even this limited area is swiftly affected by small climatic variations. In Iceland, similarly, only a limited part of the total area is available for farming. The harsh and restricted environment may explain why peasant farmers were prepared so readily to move out to colonize the Faroes, Shetland, Iceland and beyond.

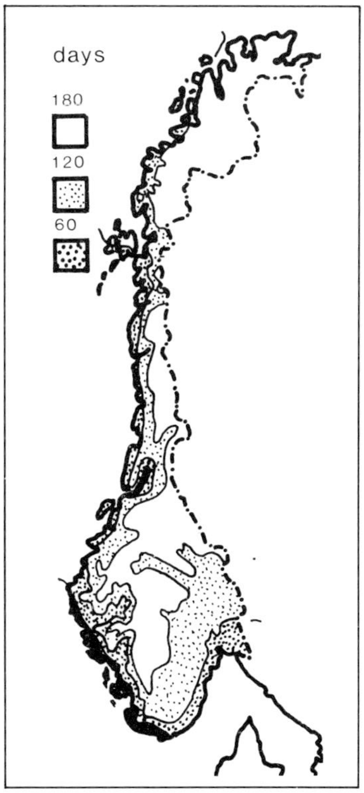

72 Snow cover in Norway

Ireland (73)

It is surprising that the Saga literature of Iceland is part of Europe's cultural and historical heritage whilst the rich and varied sources from Ireland (map **73**) in the same period are largely unknown or, worse, ignored. The English student of the Anglo-Saxon period will know all about the Vinland Sagas or even the **Landnámabók** yet few have read the Chronicles of Ireland which contain much more direct information on England, Wales and Scotland and give a vast amount of information on the Vikings, not least on their raids into England. Irish sources often supply direct causal effects for events in England in the Viking age.

The series of Viking settlements around the coasts of Ireland provided the base for a string of raids on England and also provided the 'other half' of the Viking kingdom of Dublin and York.

ULADH
Ui Neill
Dal Riata
Ulaid
Argialla
Conaille
Breifne
CONNACHTA
Ui Briuin Ai
MIDE
Brega
Ui Maine
LAIGIN
OSRAIGE
Dal Cais
Eoganacht
MUMHA
Deisi
Desmuma
KILMACRENEN
AILECH
DERRY
DUNGIVEN
RAPHOE
COLERAINE
CONNOR
ANTRIM
Bangor
MAGBILE
CRAEB TULCHA
TULACH OC
DROMORE
CLOGHER
ARMAGH
DOWNPATRICK
DRUMCLIFF
KILLALA
RATHMULCAH
Clones
KILMORE
LOUTH
Annagassan
Mayo
GRANARD
Kells
KNOWTH
ROSCOMMON
ARDAGH
TARA
CONG
Tuam
Lough Ree
ATHLONE
LAGORE
CLONARD
UISNECH
CLONCURRY
Clontarf
DUBLIN
(Atha Cliath)
CLONMACNOISE
DURROW
Llamain
Rathangan
NAS
CLONFERT
KILDARE
AILEEN
BIRR
Glen Mama
Glendalough
WICKLOW
TOMGRANEY
AGHABOE
RAITH BILE
MAGNADAIR
KILLALOE
ARKLOW
DINN RIG
ARD LADRANN
GABRAN
FERNS
LIMERICK
(Luimneach)
Cashel
St Mullins
EMLY
WEXFORD
WATERFORD
(Port Lairge)
LISMORE
ARDMORE
CORK
SKELLIG
Lough Foyle
Mourne
Bann
Lough Neagh
Belfast L.
Strangford L.
Lough Erne
Carlingford Lough
Boyne
Lough Corrib
Liffey
Barrow
Nore
Slaney
Loch Derg
Shannon
Suir
Blackwater
Loch Lein
Lea
VIKING (HIBERNO-NORSE) TOWNS
MILES
0
70

73 Ireland

Iceland (74–78)

Iceland drew off many Norse and Viking settlers and so gave Ireland the 'forty years' rest'. Traders and poets passed to and fro and the Sagas record the doings of many of the figures of North European history. The area in which all this happened is constricted both by surface conditions and by weather factors to the coastal strip and to the west of the island (**74**). The **Landnámabók** recounts the taking of the island by Viking settlers and lists all the original settlements. When these settlements are mapped (**75**) one can see immediately the importance of access to the sea and the colonization of all the shores and the valleys of the west.

Without denigrating the achievements of the age, it is likely that access to Iceland (**76** and **77**) and travel generally in the North Atlantic (**78**) area was comparatively easy at the time due to the climatic amelioration.

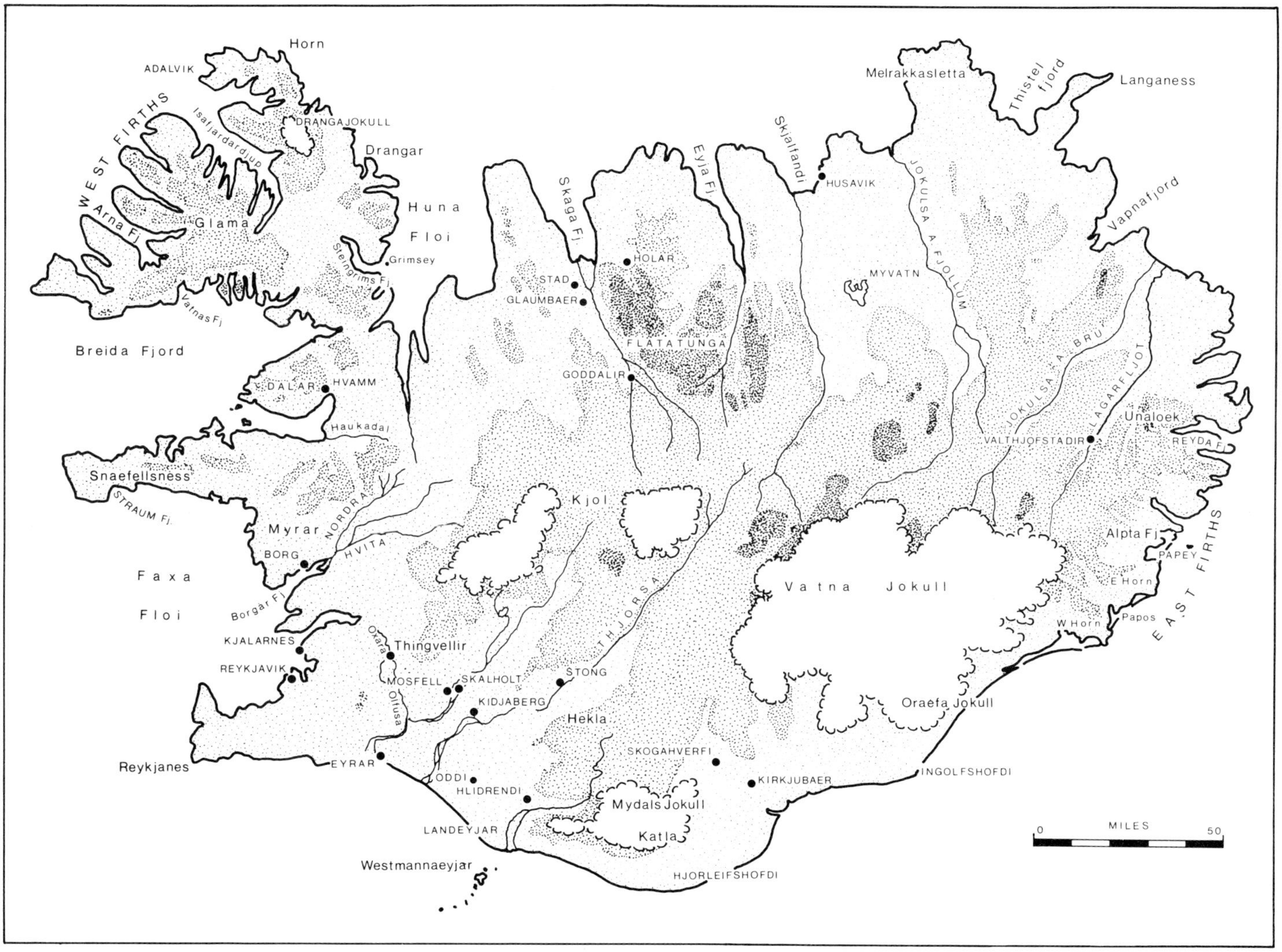

74 Iceland

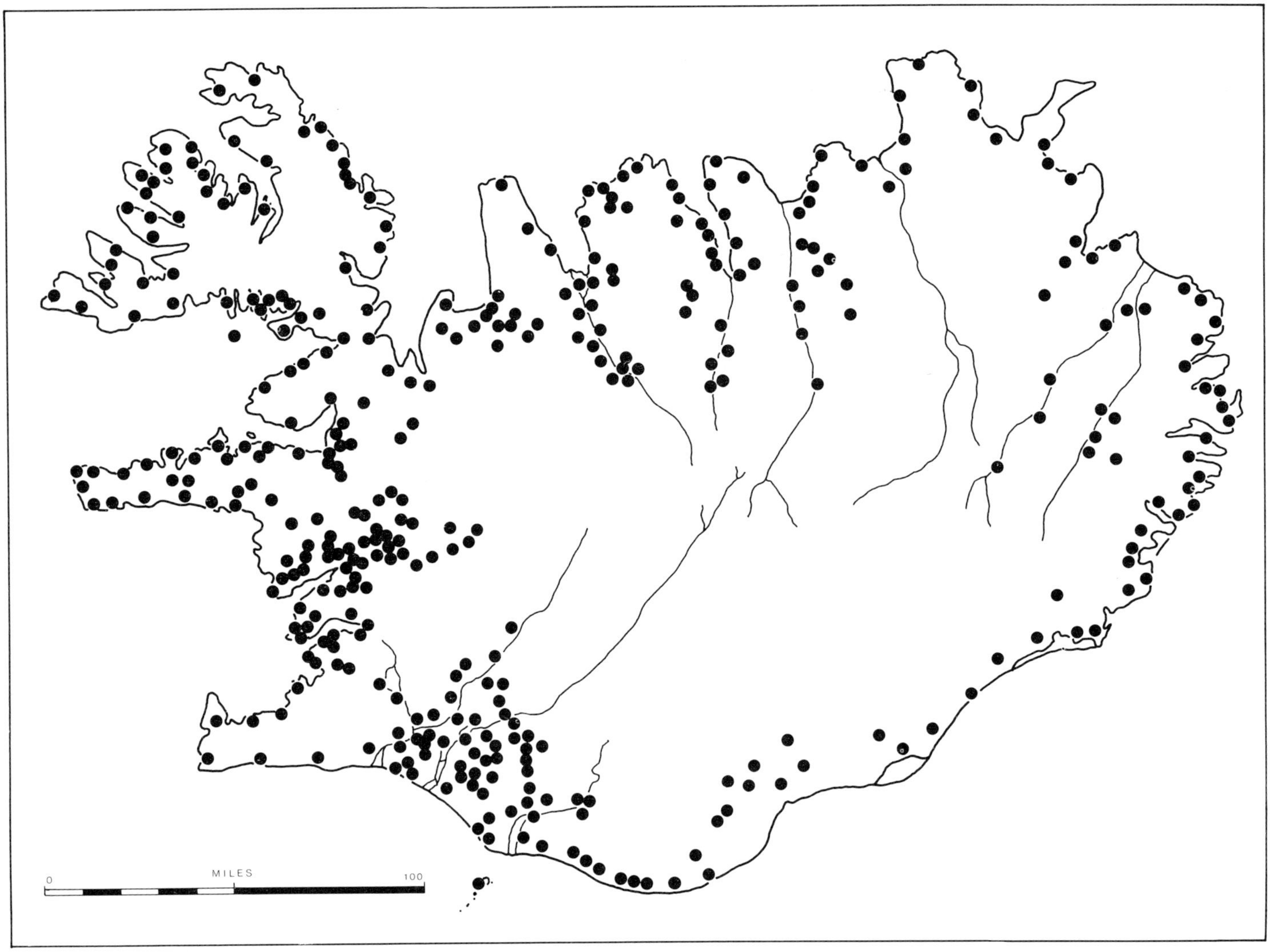

75 Early settlements in Iceland as recorded in **Landnámabók**

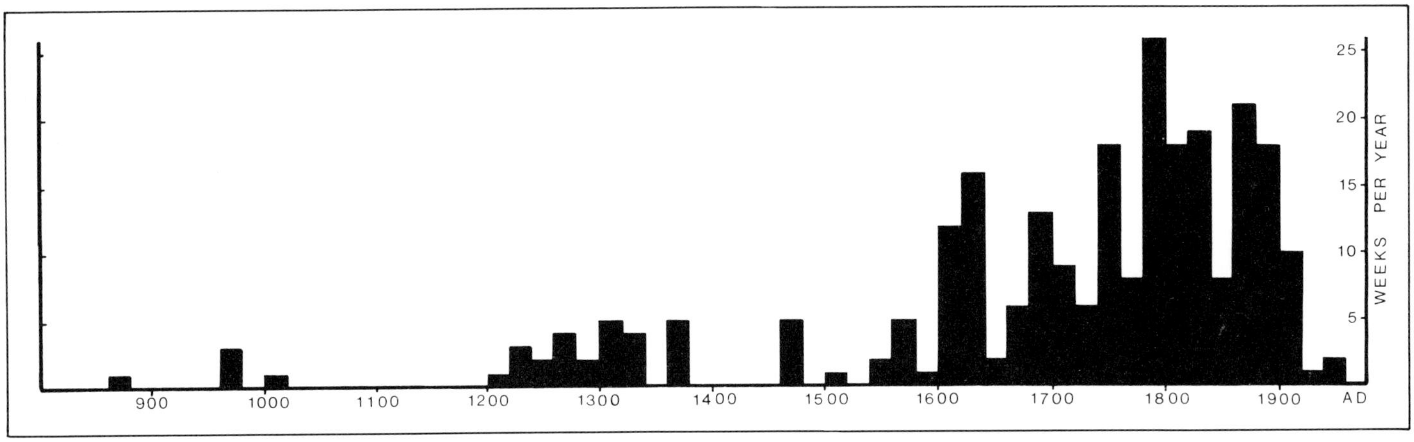

76 Ice-free days on Iceland's coasts 860 to the present (after Koch).
Weeks per year shown as twenty-year averages

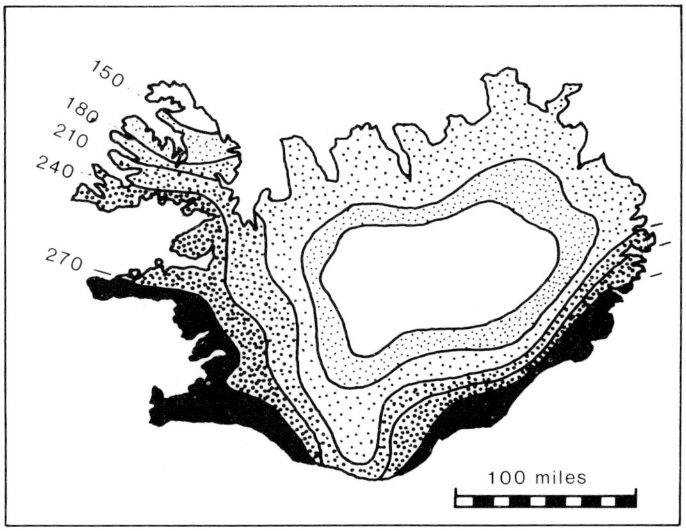

77 Snow cover in Iceland

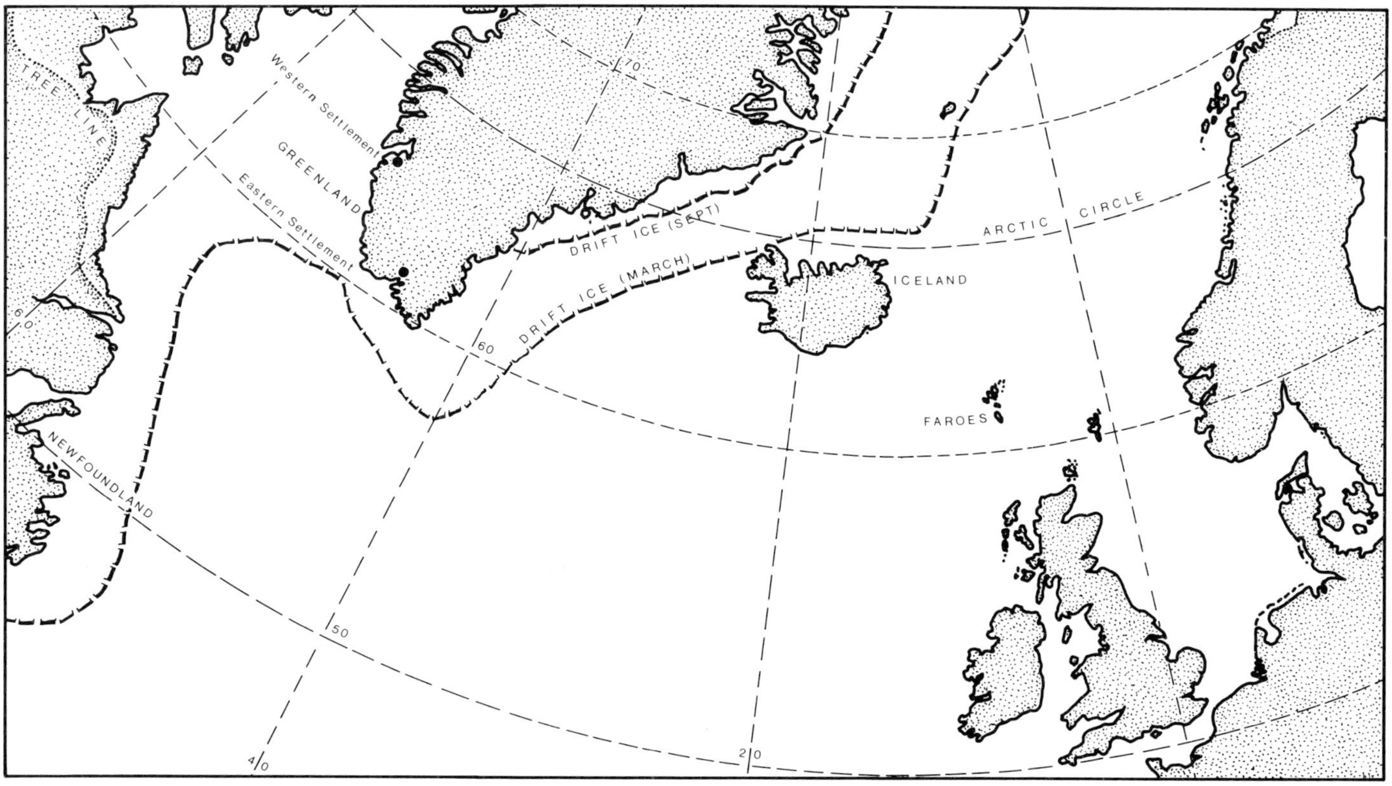

78 The Norse Atlantic

Viking Trade (79–80)

The areas under the control of the Vikings were quite large by the close of the ninth century, the links between them were strong and both the Danish areas and the later Hiberno-Norse successor kingdoms in Northumbria had strong economic and political links with Ireland and the Western Isles. The hoards of coins of the Vikings of East Anglia and of Northumbria mark these areas out (map **79**). Particular emphasis is shown in the Isle of Man and Dublin areas.

The Vikings in the British Isles were part of a much larger economic and trade area using coinage, particularly as bullion. Sawyer has recently discussed in some detail his thesis that the supply of Arabic silver and then its denial had great consequences on the flow of Vikings to the West (Sawyer 1971). It should be noted that much of the silver in areas such as the south Baltic must have reached there as a result of trade out of Scandinavia (map **80**).

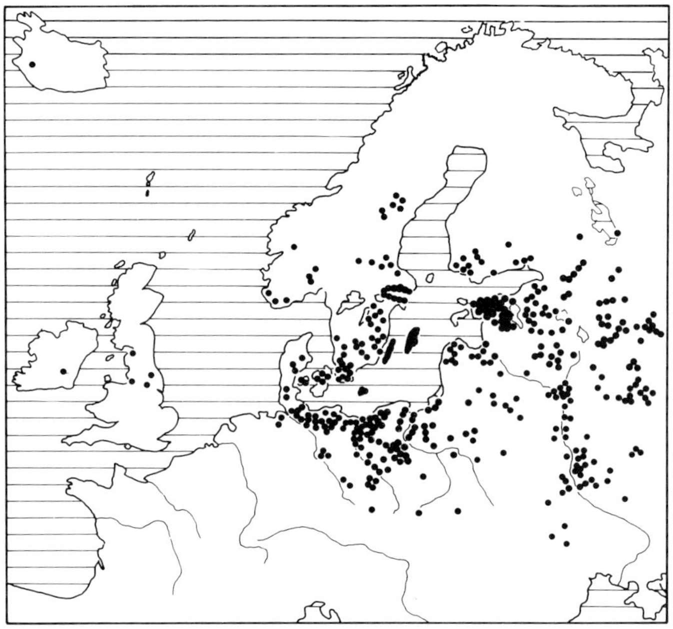

80 Finds of Arabic coins of the Viking Age (after Oxenstierna 1967)

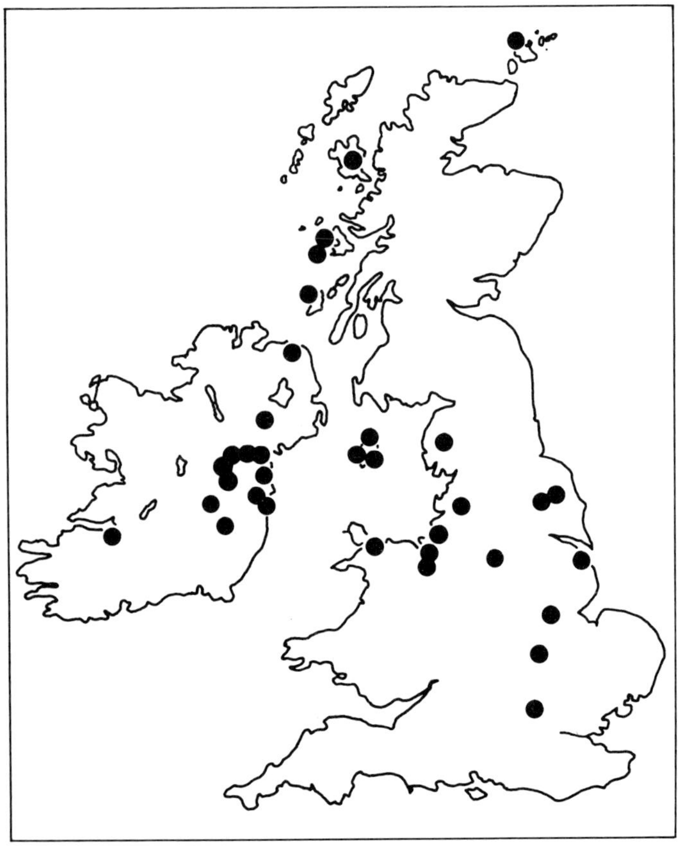

79 Hoards containing coins of the Vikings of East Anglia and Northumbria

The Reconquest 902–921 (81–98)

The campaigns of 892–95 had left a strengthened Wessex facing a series of Danish settlements with no major Danish army roaming the area. This was the setting for the Reconquest. Patrick Wormald (personal communication) remarks that he is rather unhappy with the traditional use of the term 'Reconquest' of the Danelaw. The West Saxons may have attempted to represent their efforts as precisely that. In sober fact, the campaigns represented a West Saxon conquest, and it is far from clear that all Mercians and East Anglians saw their arrival and domination as the happiest answer to their problems. If the word is to stand, and for convenience it must, then we should realize that its use is tendentious.

The disposition of coin hoards for the period c.895–c.965 (map **81**) shows a significant concentration in the eastern part of England, clearly reflecting dangerous times. In the decade 895–905 the initiative passed to Edward the Elder. The raids back and forth did not disguise the fact that the underlying strength of Wessex was increasing (map **83**). The fortified centres, **burhs**, meant that the West Saxons could not suffer a sudden catastrophic collapse such as followed the Danish invasion in 878. Other factors must have affected the Danish areas. The lack of reinforcements, the ageing of the original force and the process of absorption from below, with the swift loss of language and religion, made the Danes more likely to compromise with the West Saxons in order to hold on to their lands.

The areas of the southern armies appear to have given rise to the formation of what were later to be recognized as the shires of the east Midlands. A clue is to be found in the peace of Tiddingford (map **82**), for treaties were often at this period negotiated on the frontiers, as at Dore or Billingsley. Tiddingford does not stand on the so-called frontier of Guthrum (see map **70**). Although the peace was negotiated in 906 the river on which the site stands forms the later shire boundary, which in turn may reflect the army of Bedford's area of control. It is therefore arguable that many of the shires were laid out before 920 in the east Midlands. Tiddingford stands at the point where the Herepath crosses the River Ousel.

These small armies, centred on one **burh**, were too small to face the West Saxons and even the larger units of East Anglia and Essex do not seem to have been either strong enough or sufficiently ready to coordinate their efforts with others to survive.

The pattern of the campaigns was hardly dashing — it was a process of slowly strengthening the West Saxon and Mercian areas with **burhs**, then fortifying the frontier areas with more **burhs**, and finally pushing the **burhs** forward far enough to force the Danes to react. The forced attacks of the Danes on the West Saxon and Mercian defences were always failures, as were their more wide-ranging attacks, and the policy of allowing them to continue to hold their lands after the transfer to sovereignty appears to have made submission preferable to defeat.

The Reconquest was a slow process to begin with. Although the southern Danelaw was gradually eroded, only limited gains were made before 916 (maps **83–90**). The Mercian policy was similar and coordinated with the West Saxons but it was complicated by the fact that considerable efforts had to be made to control the Welsh frontier at the same time. Finally there were the dramatic campaigns of 917 (maps **91–94**) as a result of which the Danelaw submitted in a chain reaction as the surrender of neighbouring armies isolated the surviving armies and exposed their flanks to West Saxon attack.

The final stage of the Reconquest was denied to the West Saxons by two factors, the death of Æthelflaed and the arrival of the Dublin Norse in the Kingdom of York. However, after 917, the pattern of states that had subsisted since 878 disappeared. The Danish states south of the Humber had been amalgamated into the West Saxon Kingdom and the Danish Kingdom of York, along with the lands of the Ealdorman of Bamburgh, became the Hiberno-Norse Kingdom of York linked with Dublin (maps **95–98**).

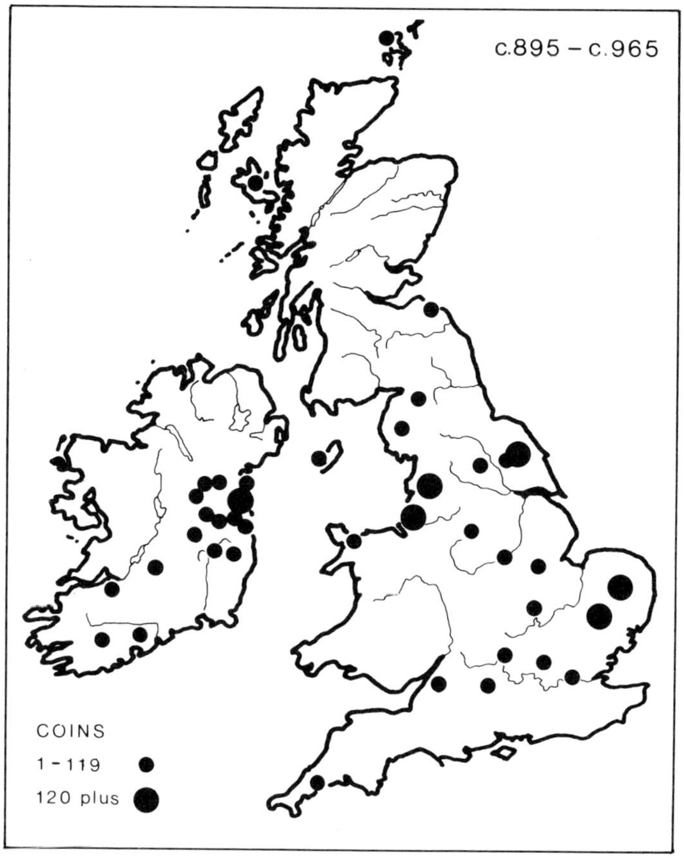

81 Hoards of coins deposited c.895–c.965

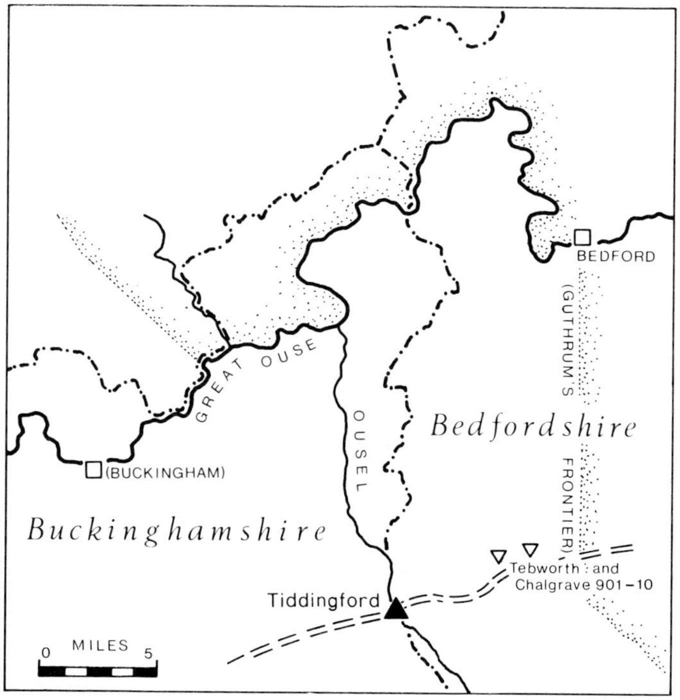

82 The Peace of Tiddingford 906

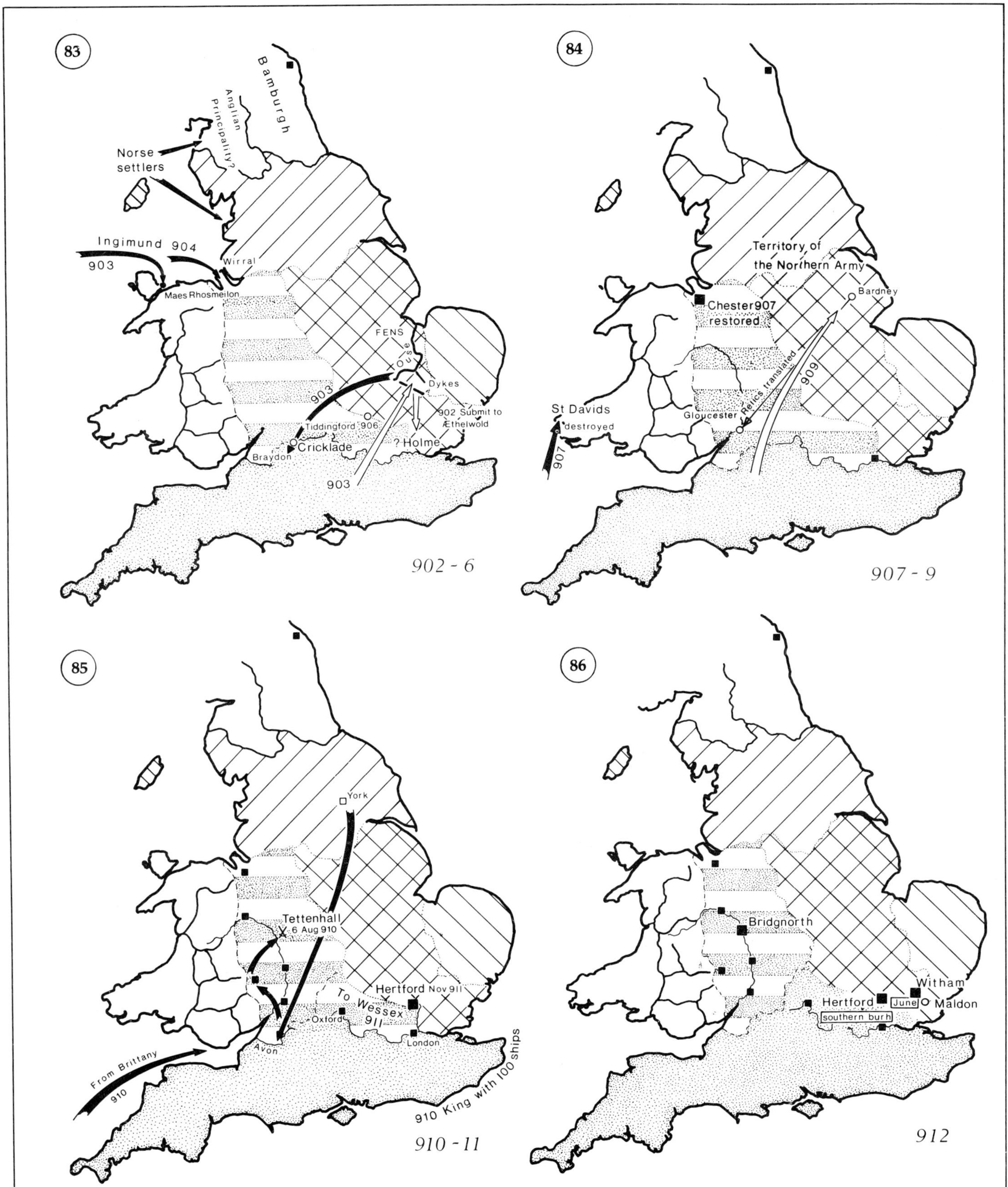

83–86 The Reconquest 902–912. Viking movements shown in black on this and subsequent maps

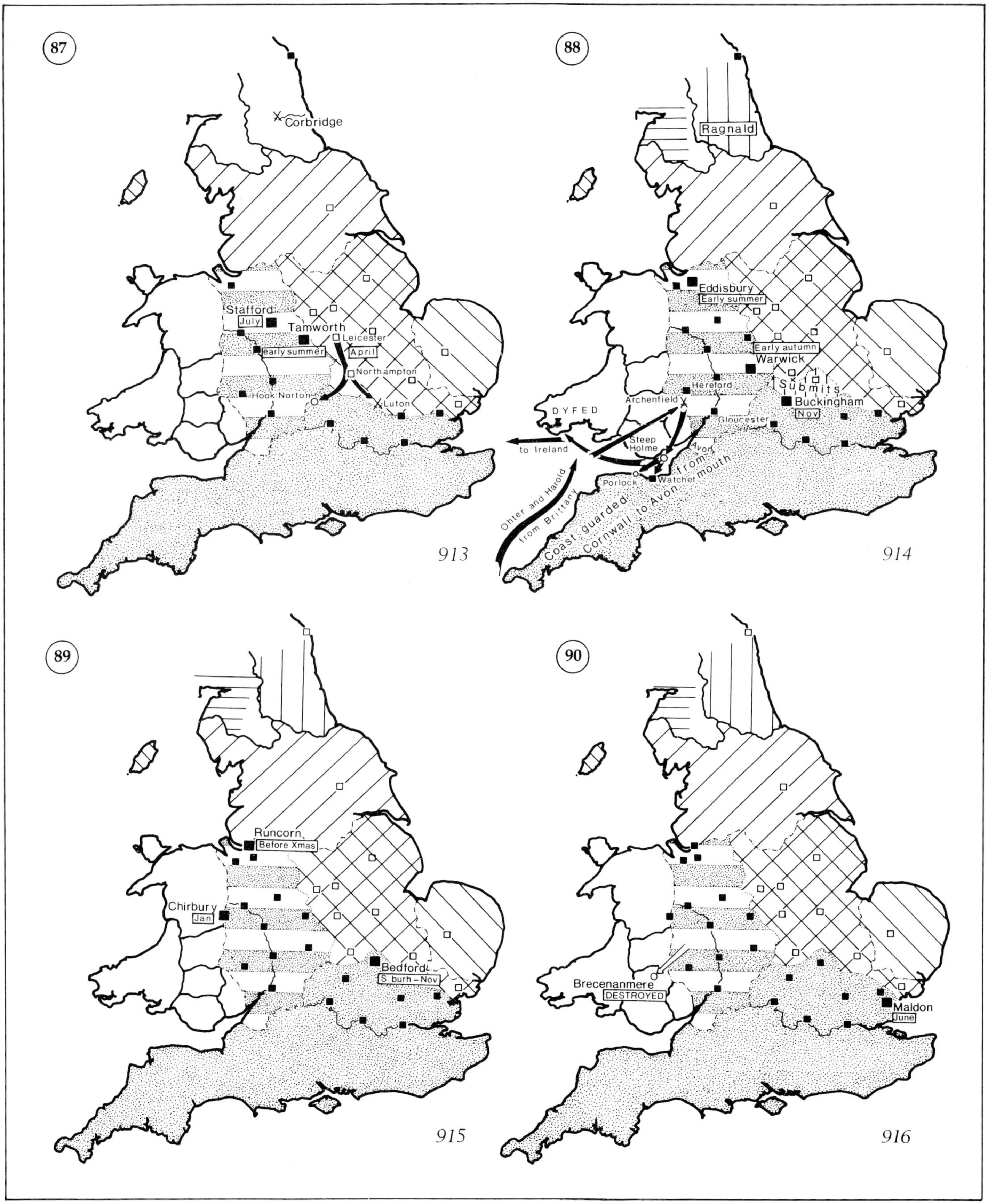

87–90 The Reconquest 913–916

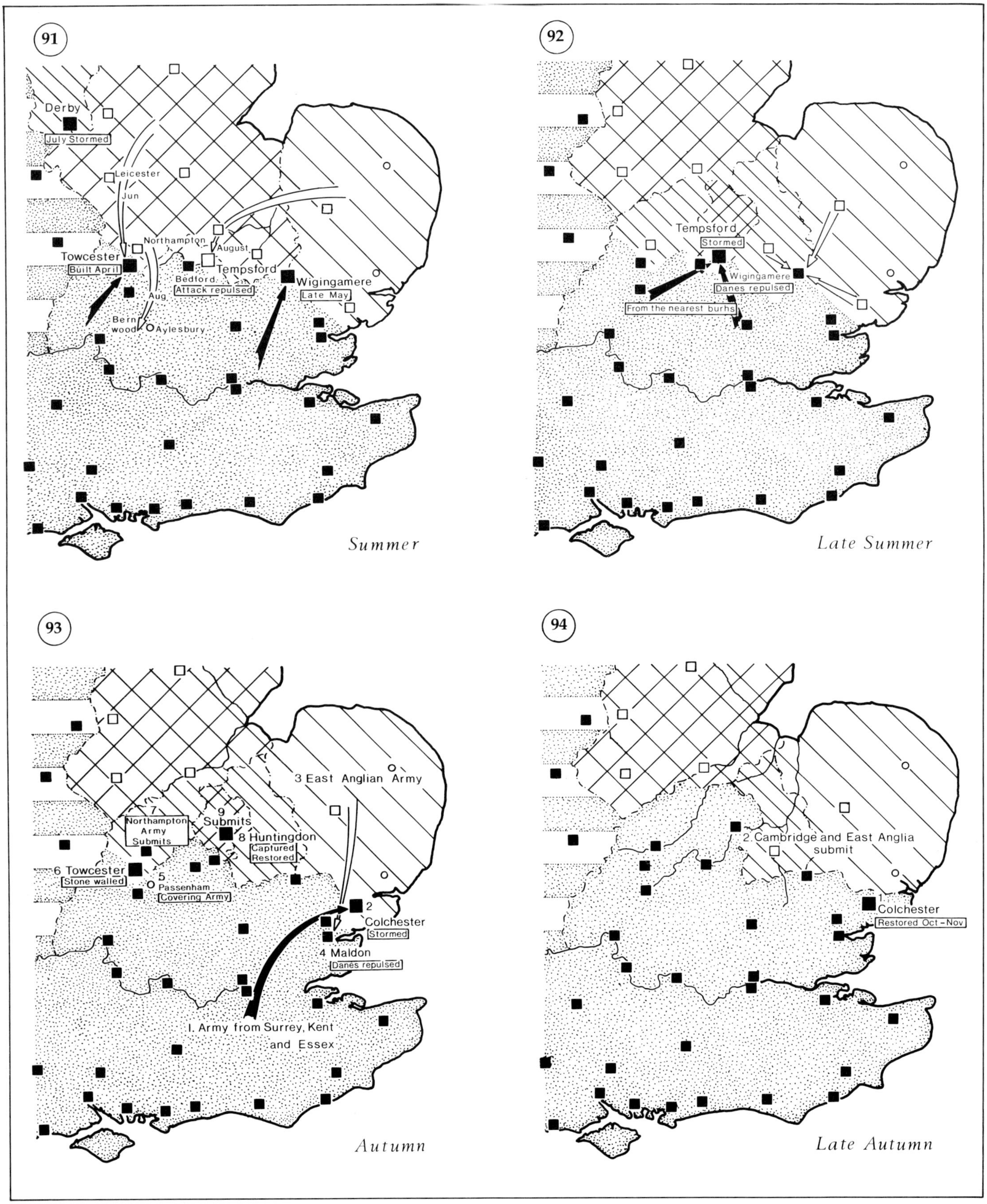

91–94 Campaigns of 917

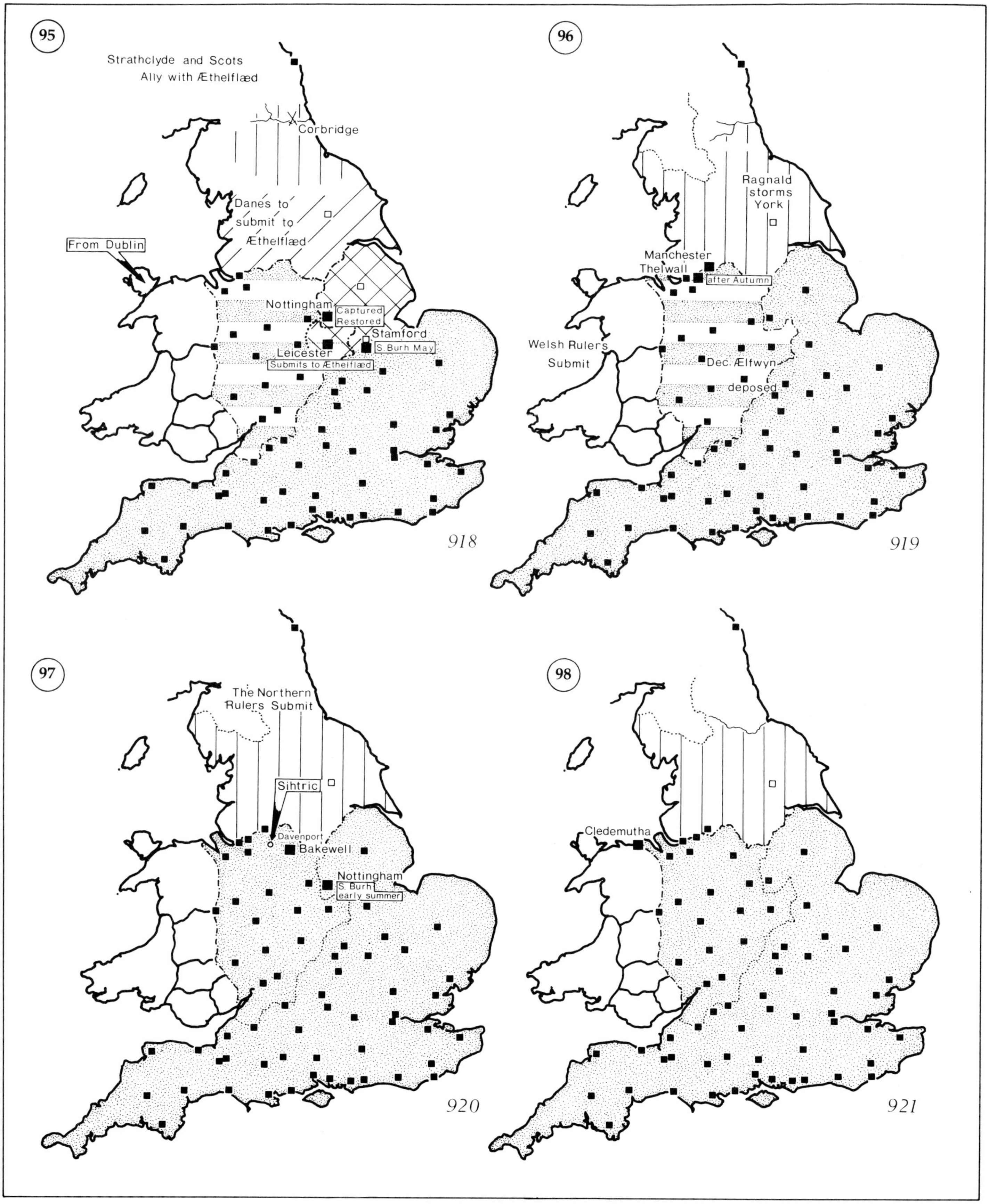

95–98 The Reconquest 918–921

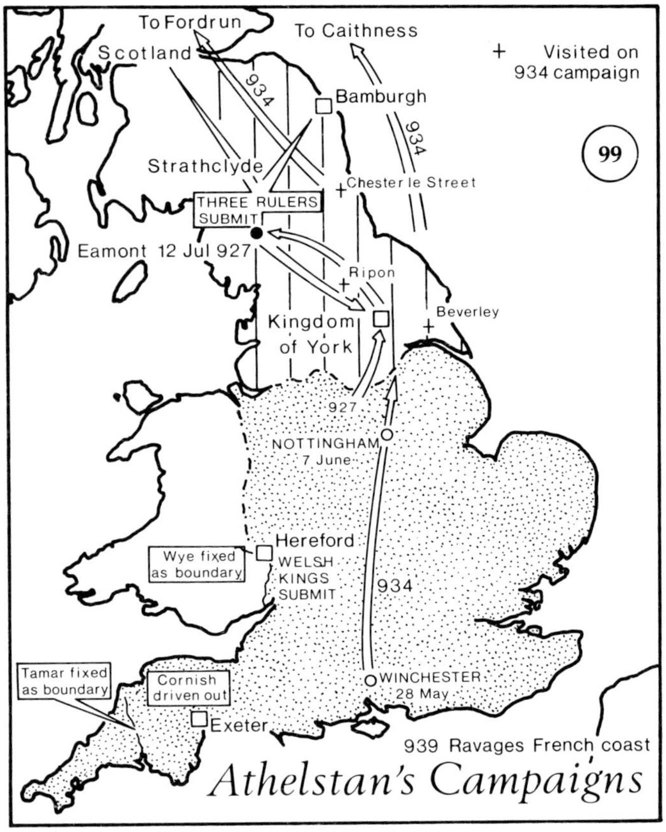

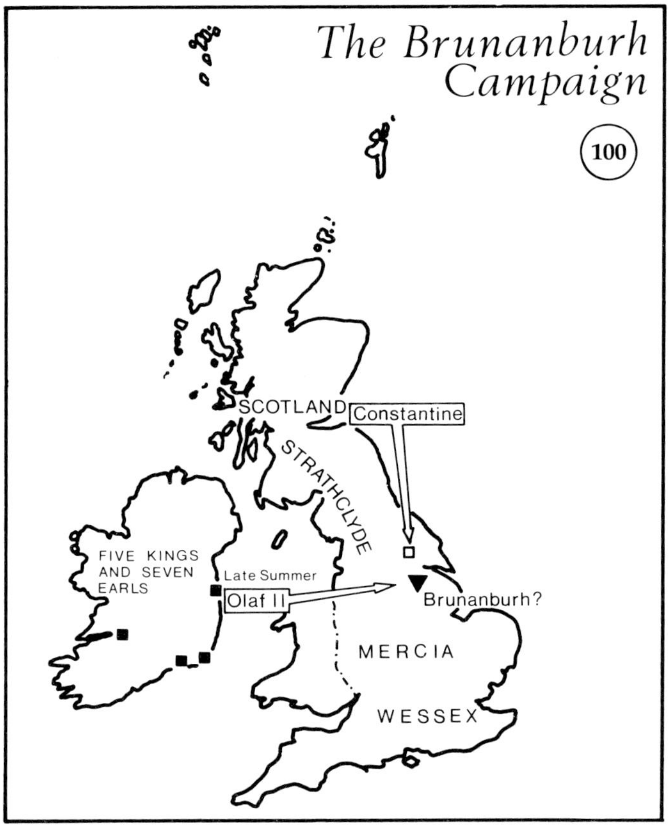

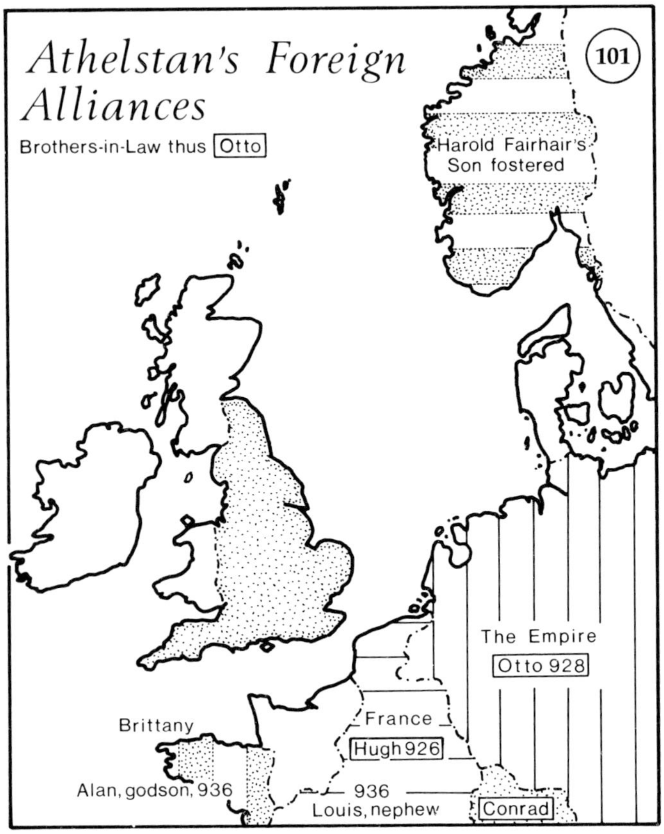

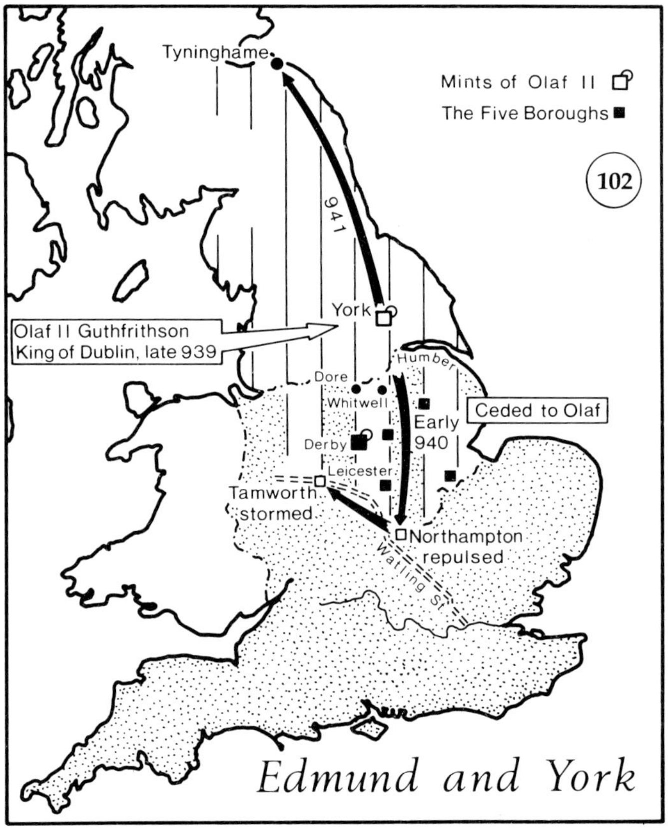

99–102 From Athelstan to Eric Bloodaxe 924–954

From Athelstan to Eric Bloodaxe 924–954 (99–102)

Athelstan began his reign by putting the frontiers of his kingdom in order on all sides and followed this up with an alliance with York (map **99**). The situation appeared to be lost when the great combination of Celtic and Viking powers faced him at Brunanburh but his victory there set a West Saxon king firmly over a Kingdom of England (map **100**). Athelstan went on to become a monarch of European stature, forming alliances both within and beyond the British Isles (map **101**).

The kingdom nearly disintegrated with his death as Olaf Guthfrithson recovered the Danelaw and Northumbria up to Dunbar. The situation was soon remedied, not least because the Danish settlers had had nearly twenty years of West Saxon rule and preferred it to that of the heathen Norse. There was to be a final upsurge of the Norse Kingdom of York with Eric Bloodaxe and Olaf Sihtricson but after Eric's death in 954 the adventure begun in East Anglia in 866 was over (map **102**).

The Submission to Edgar, Chester 973 (103–105)

The events surrounding Edgar's coronation in Bath and the submission at Chester created a scene of medieval splendour which had an impact on the imagination of the time and on that of succeeding generations. His coronation was the consummation of the expansion charted in the preceding maps. Ælfric wrote in his life of Swithun (Skeat 1881):

> *. . . King Edgar*
> *furthered Christianity, and built many monasteries,*
> *and his kingdom still continued in peace,*
> *so that no fleet was heard of,*
> *save that of the people themselves who held this land;*
> *and all the kings of the Cymry and the Scots*
> *that were in this island, came to Edgar*
> *once upon a day, being eight kings,*
> *and they all bowed themselves to Edgar's rule*

The identification of the realms and kings that submitted has been discussed by Stenton (1971, 369–70). Mapping these events and the kingdoms involved sheds an interesting light on the whole affair (map **103**). The best list is provided by Florence of Worcester. Maccus, King of many Islands, expanded his kingdom by occupying Anglesey (in the Welsh Annals he and his brother are 'The Sons of Maccus'). Anglesey was part of Iago's kingdom of Gwynedd and Iago was under the protection of Edgar. After the coronation at Bath Edgar took his fleet (presumably around Wales, for he is recorded as founding St Mary's at Bangor) to Chester. This great fleet must have had a profound effect on Maccus: he and the other sub-kings came to a ceremony of submission. The map makes it clear that the island kingdom was greatly exposed in the face of such a combination, and the cession to Lothian at about this time may well have been linked to securing an alliance against Maccus and the Vikings in the Irish Sea area. We know very little about the state of the Border area at this, or any other early, time; but the distribution of place names (map **104**) makes it clear that the Anglian kingdom of Northumbria had extended far to the north, including the region around present-day Edinburgh, although the Anglian presence in the Solway and Galloway regions is less marked. It may well be that in these areas Anglian names are overlain by later additions.

The hoard evidence (map **105**) supports the general idea of a realm at peace, with only the raids around Chester and a few coastal sites in the latter part of the period showing up.

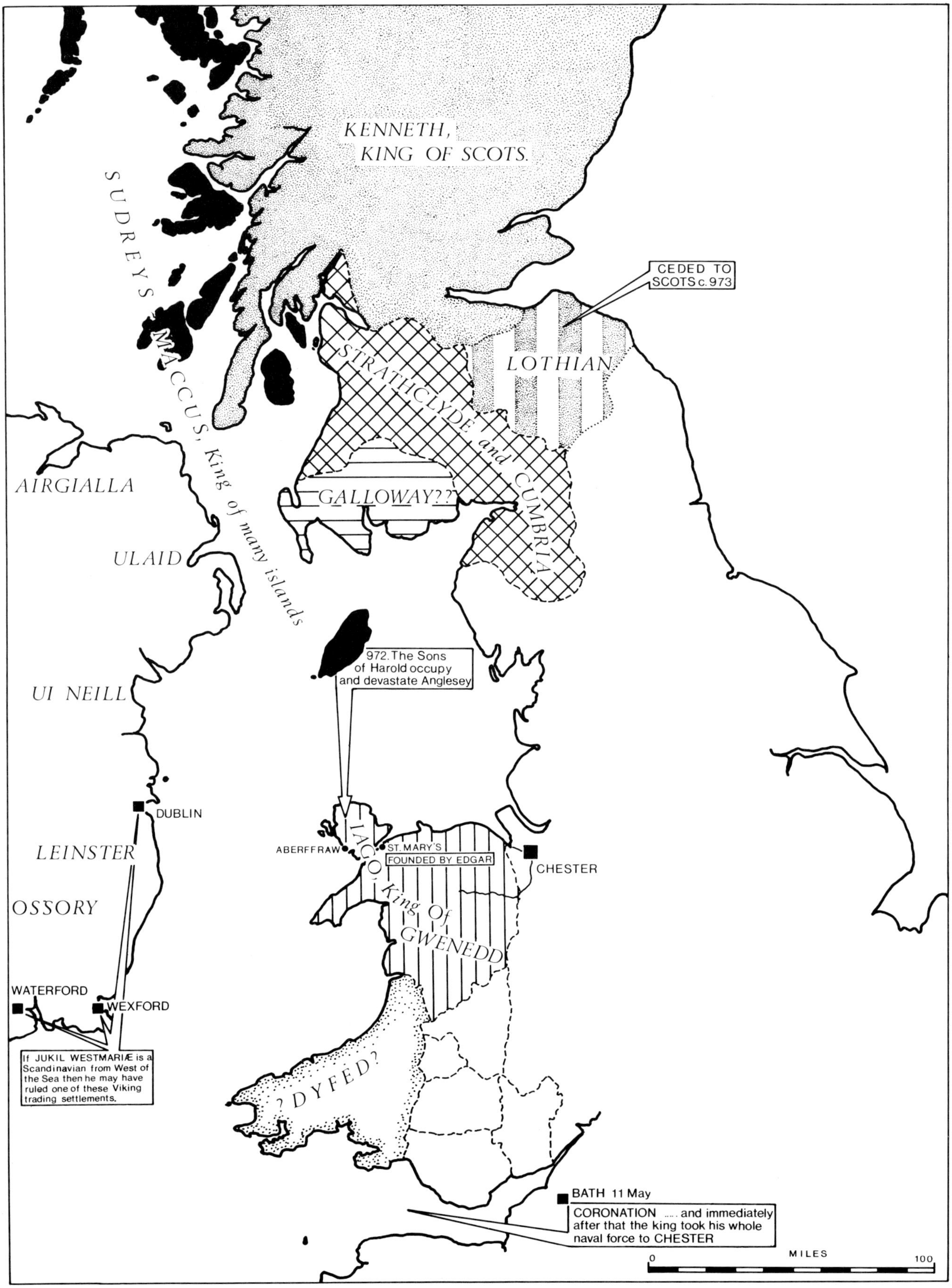

103 The submission to Edgar, Chester 973. Sub-kingdoms stippled

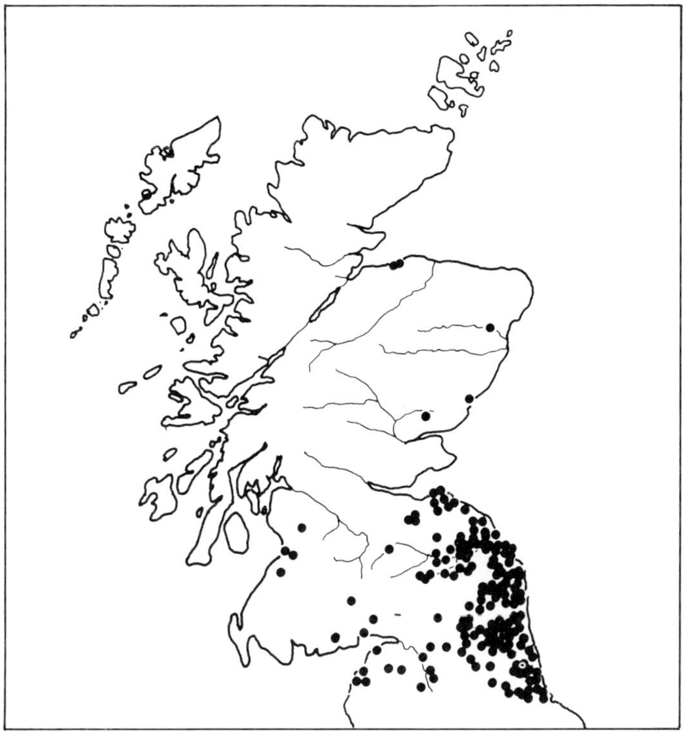

104 Anglian place names in Scotland (McNeill and Nicholson 1975)

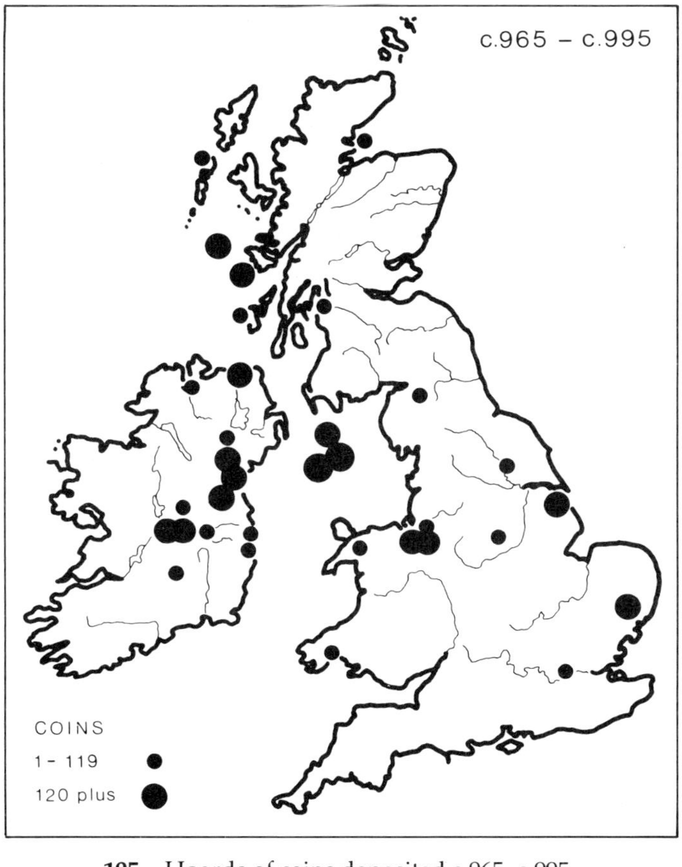

105 Hoards of coins deposited c.965–c.995

The Wars of the Reign of Ethelred the Second (106–129)

The maps that follow are mainly designed to draw together the information carried in the Anglo-Saxon Chronicle and Florence of Worcester and to augment it with the information from the Welsh sources; they may be a useful aid when following the account in the Chronicle or Stenton.

The chronicler's thoroughly gloomy account, heavily biased against Ethelred, is certainly distorted, at least for the early period. The hoard maps (**106**) gives the impression that the Viking raids were on a rather more restricted scale than the Chronicle would indicate. As Dolley has highlighted, the map also shows a contraction of the Viking sphere of influence in Ireland.

The poetic account of the battle of Maldon of 991 (maps **107** and **109**) equally belies the atmosphere of weakness and defeatism conjured by the Chronicle, and it is hard to detect a dying society in the voluminous works of Aelfric.

In maps **108–129** only the places relevant to the years dealt with or to the understanding of those events have been included. It is important to realize that the white areas are not empty and that maps for a particular year should be used together with the maps of mints, towns or churches later in the book.

The renewed Viking attack on England started with sporadic raids around the coast (maps **108–111**), but it is clear that there were two completely different sets of raids: those in the east, which were to prove decisive, and those in the west originating in Ireland with the Hiberno-Norse, which belong to a pattern that Edgar the Peaceable's reign had merely interrupted. These acts of Irish piracy were to continue at odd moments until the Conquest and particularly bedevilled the Welsh and Scots coasts. It is clear from their positioning that the eastern sets of raids were in all probability mounted from the Low Countries (see maps **112–115**) but they were not connected with any general renewal of Viking activity. In fact the scale and direction of these new attacks was very different from those of the Heroic Age. They may have contained an element of Danish imperialism; certainly the Danish kings were soon involved and the war brought out considerable numbers of combatants on both sides. The Danish raids did not take place every year. When the raiders did appear, the English response was very positive, notwithstanding the defeatist tone of the chronicler of this section of the Anglo-Saxon Chronicle, who has tainted our view of the period and certainly omitted or played down successes in the first part of the wars (maps **116–119**). Ethelred made great efforts to reorganize army, fleet and fortifications. In every other branch of Anglo-Saxon life of which we have knowledge the Danish incursions seem to have had little effect until 1006, by which time the English had been resisting steadily for a quarter of a century.

The chronicler's bias against Ethelred led him to decry all the king's moves, which has in turn affected later judgements of history. For example, the campaign against Man and Cumbria in 1000 (map **115**) is often seen as inexplicable or pointless. Yet it was probably part of an English attempt to squeeze the Dublin Vikings who had been thrown out after the defeat at Glen Mama but were still in the Irish Sea region, pehaps in the areas of Norse control known to have existed in Cumbria and Galloway, or in the Isle of Man. The claim (see map **122**) that the shires overrun by 1011 included the whole of south-east England is disproved by the preceding maps and appears to be simple exaggeration.

The second phase of the Viking attack (maps **120–129**) involved some of the most awe-inspiring Viking fighters, including the dreaded Jomsvikings and figures such as Thorkell the Tall, but even then there was no sudden English collapse. They resisted even after seven more years of disasters, which the chronicler would have us believe were unrelieved. It was only the death of Edmund Ironside that finished the campaigns and gave Cnut the kingdom, thirty-six years after the attack on Chester in 980.

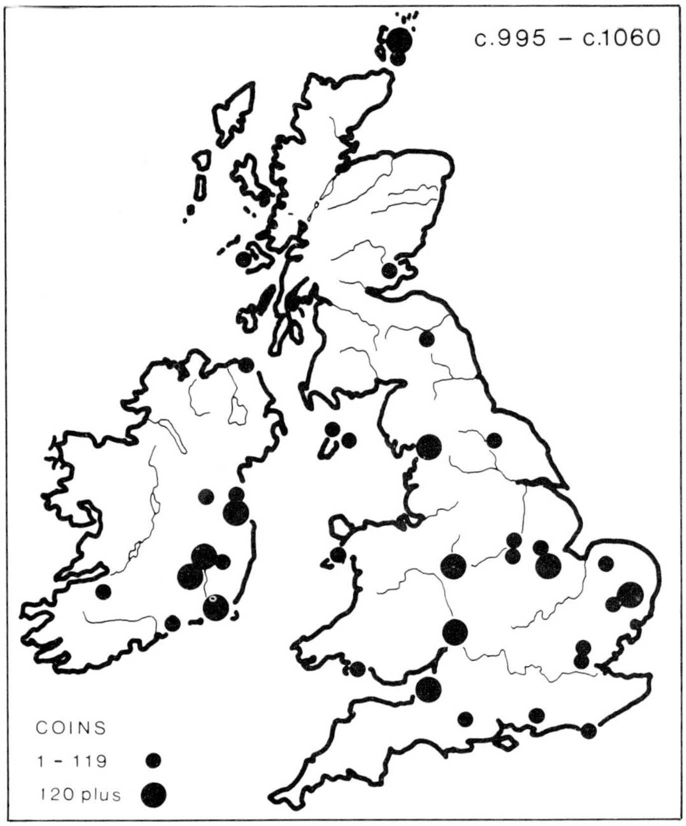

106 Hoards of coins deposited c.995–c.1060

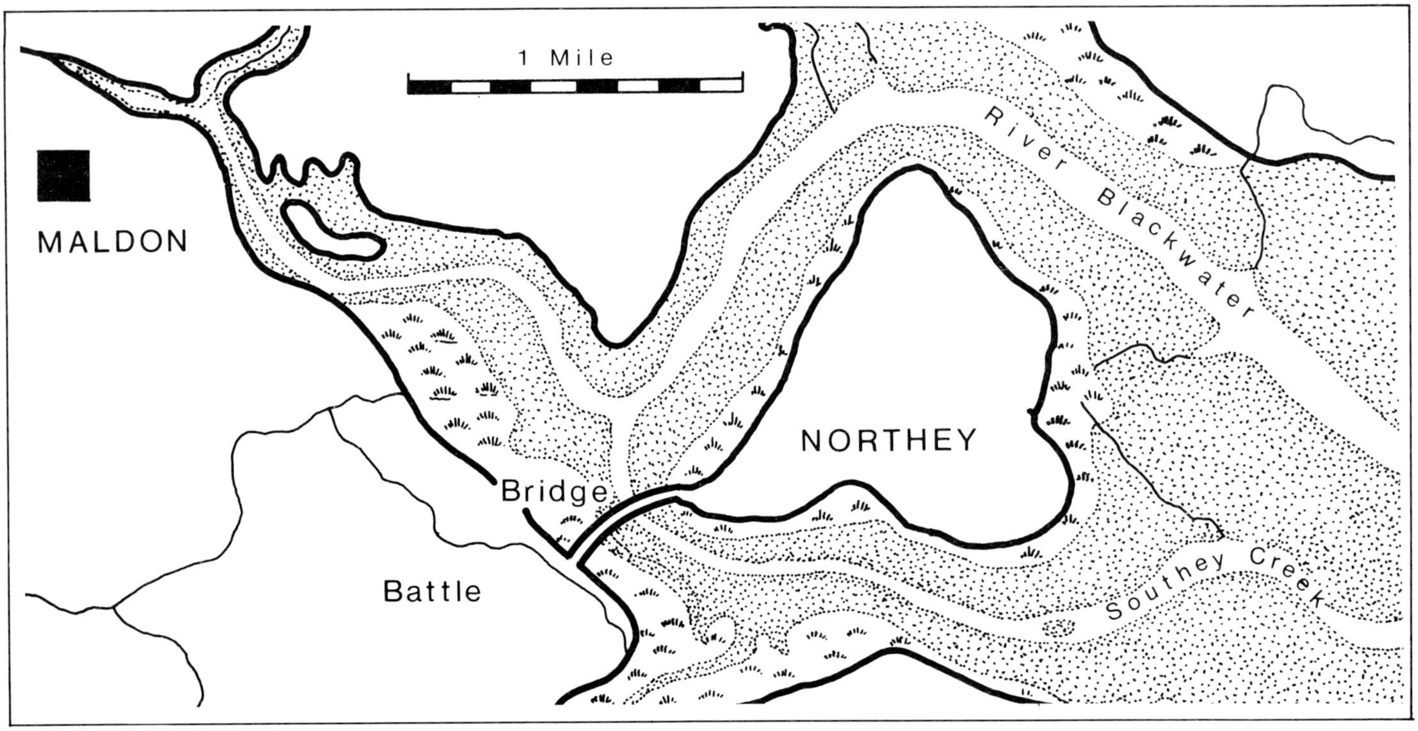

107 The Battle of Maldon 991

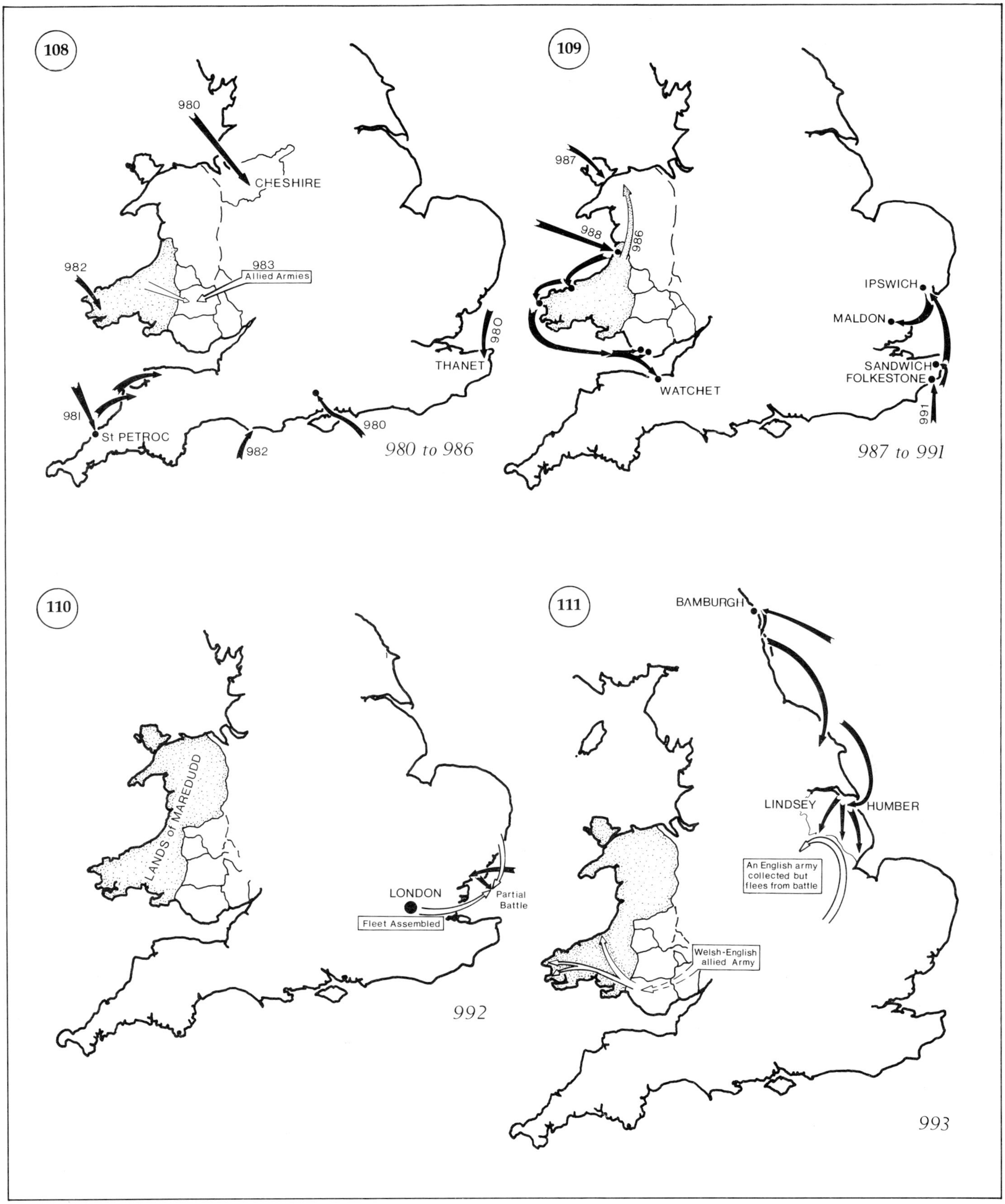

108–111 Ethelred II: the earliest attacks 980–993. Viking movements shown in black on this and subsequent maps

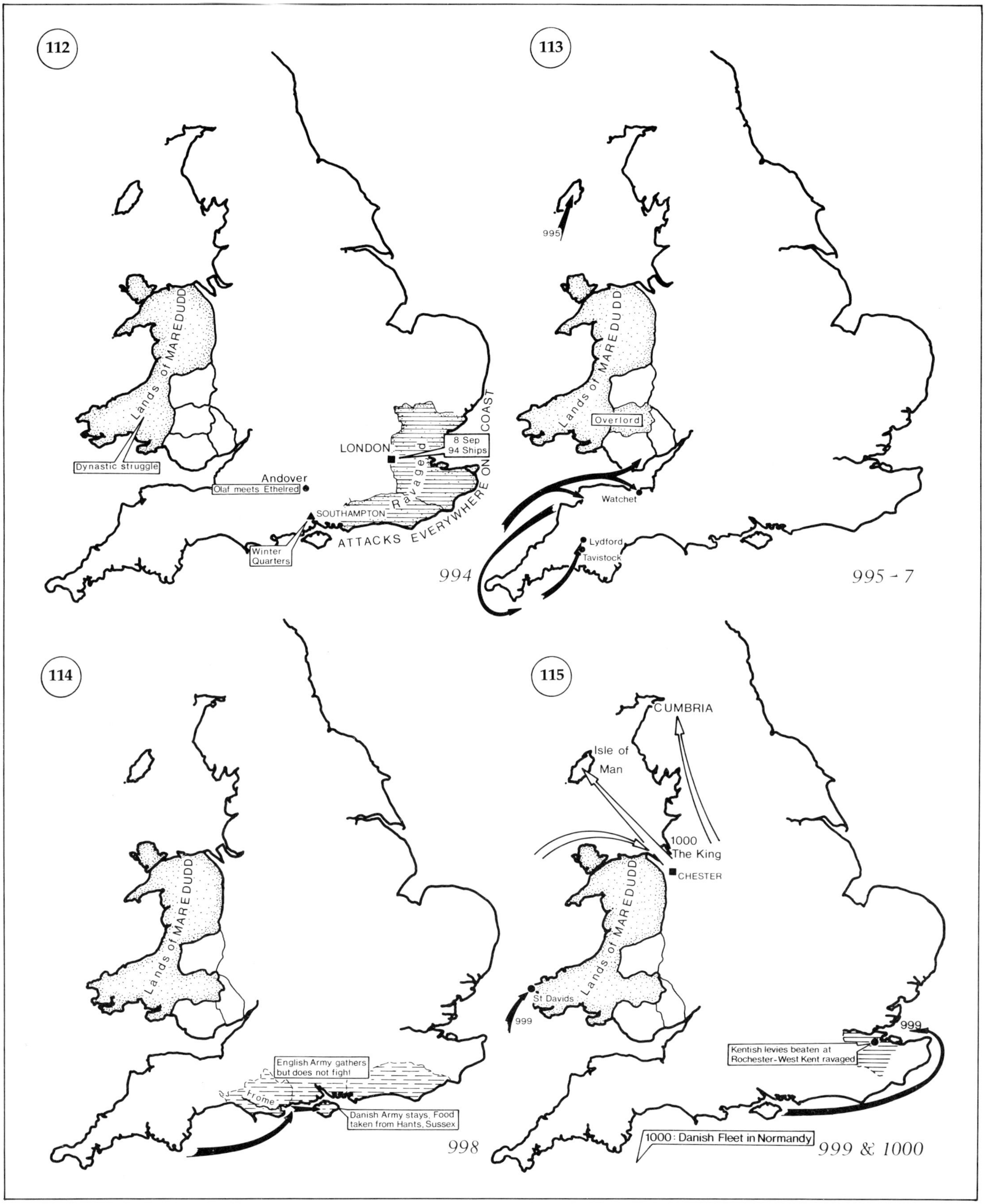

112–115 Raids and campaigns 994–1000

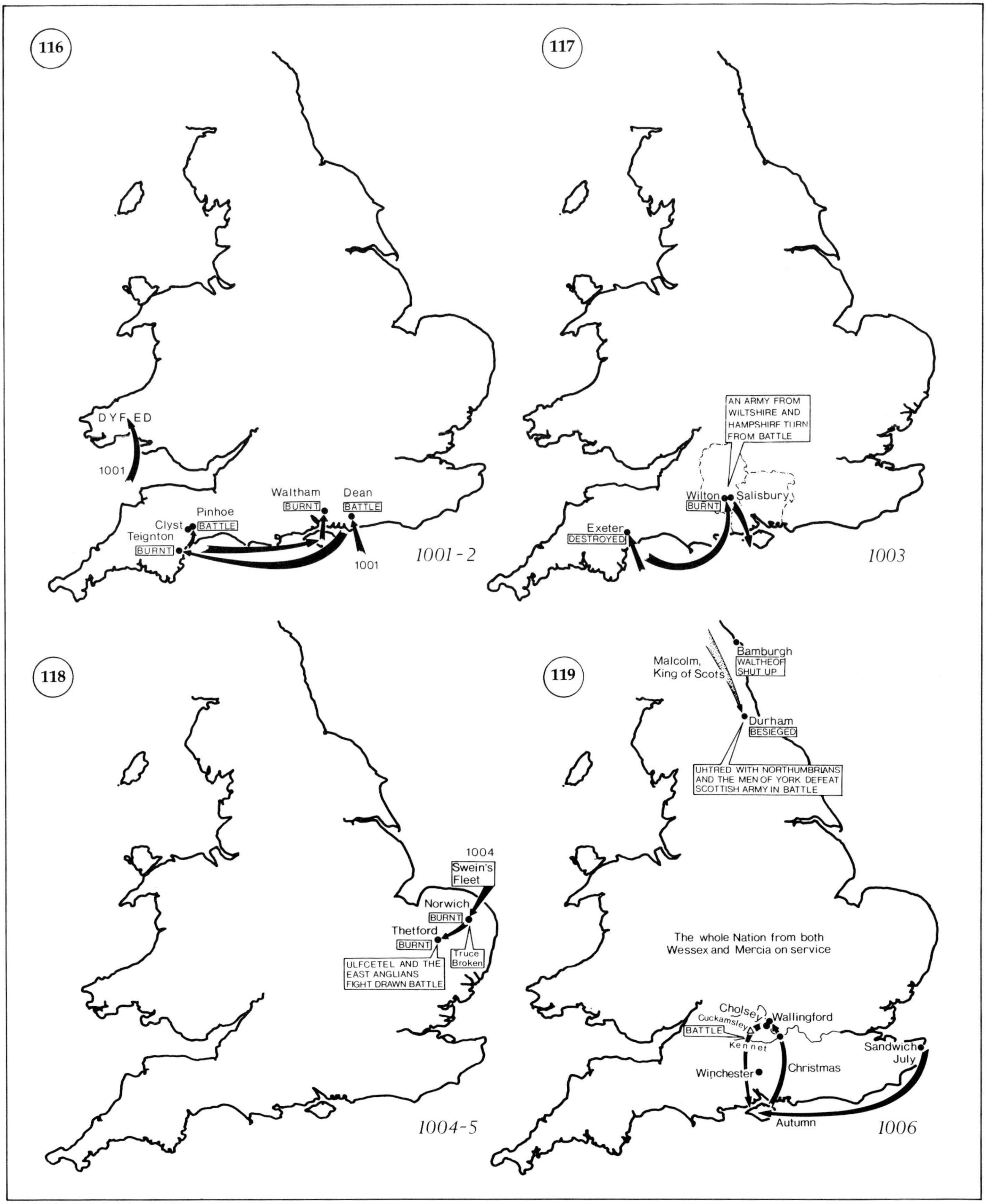

116–119 Raids and campaigns 1001–1006

120

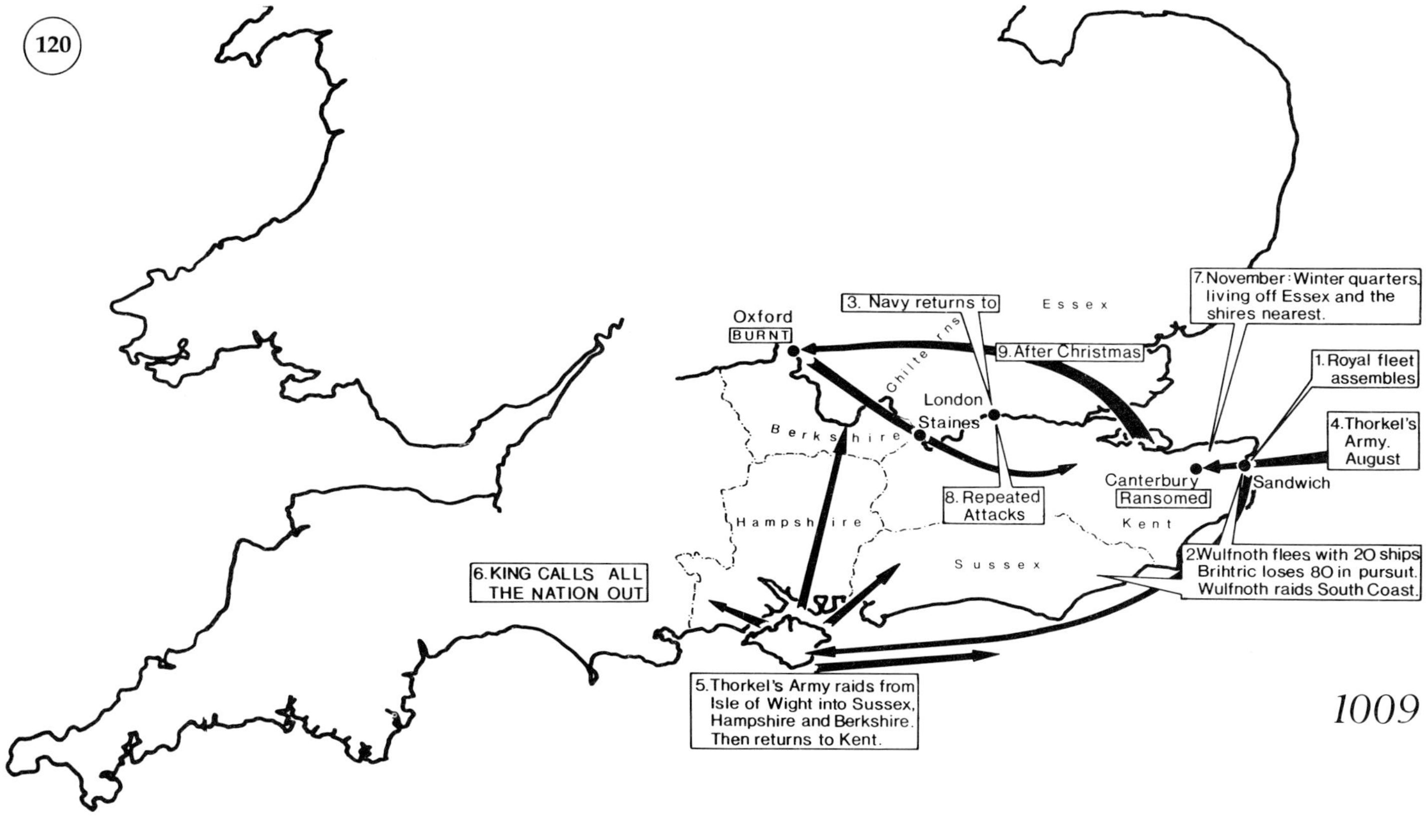

121

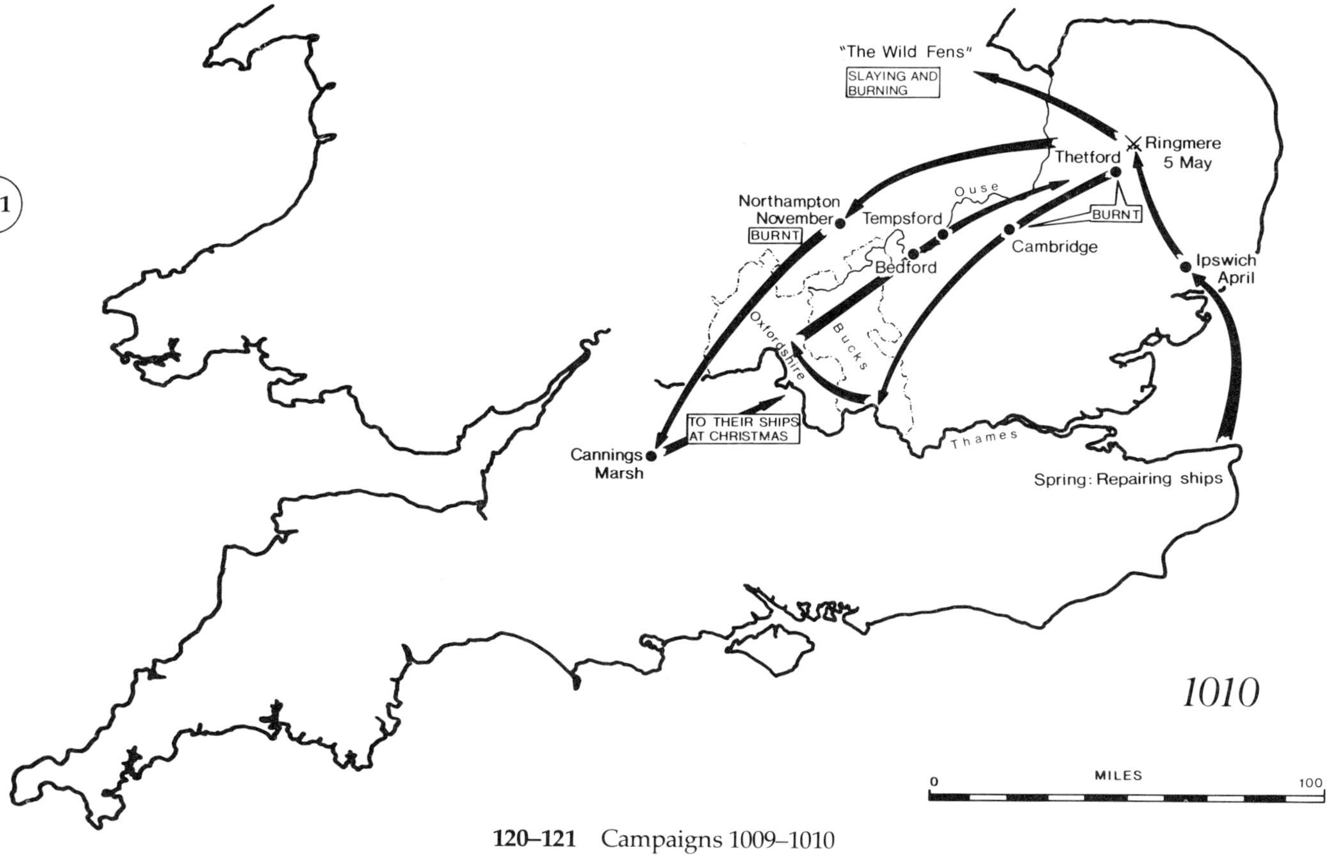

120–121 Campaigns 1009–1010

122

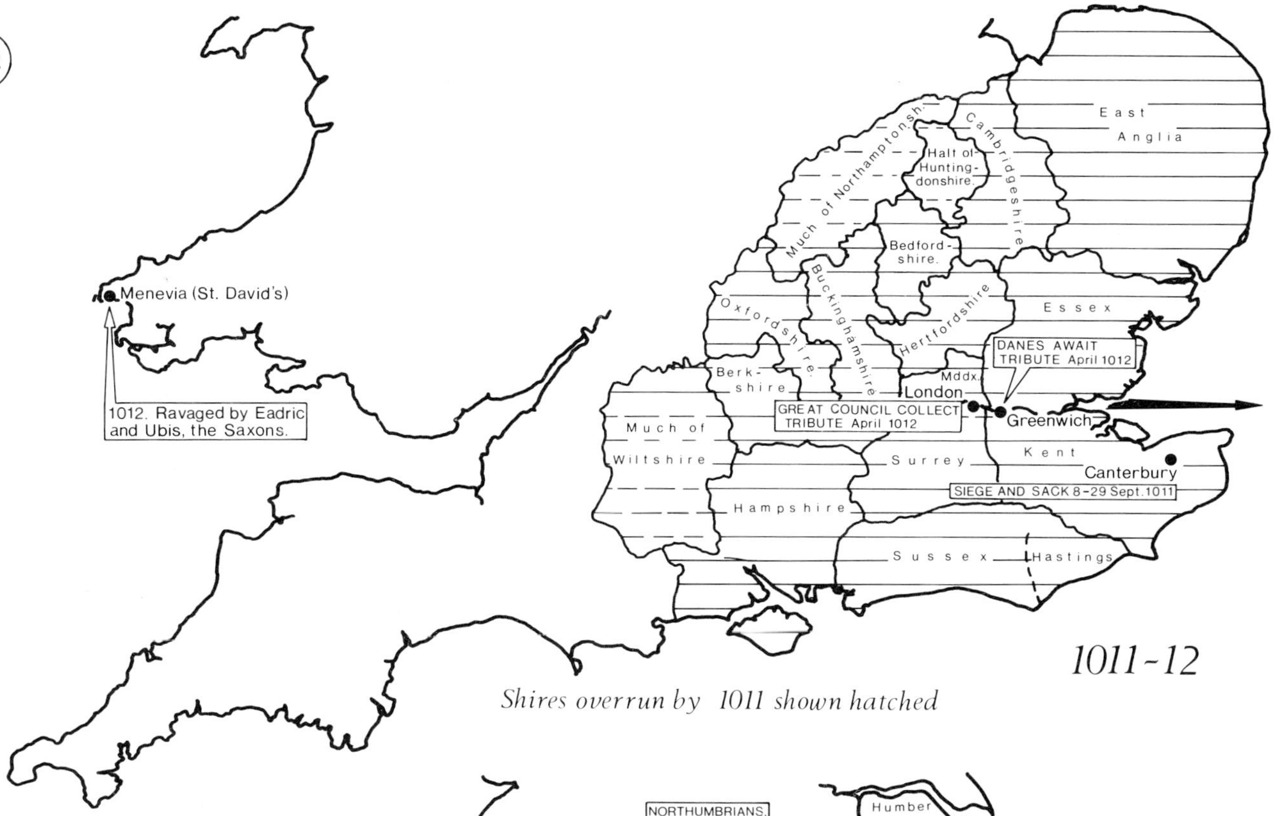

Shires overrun by 1011 shown hatched

123

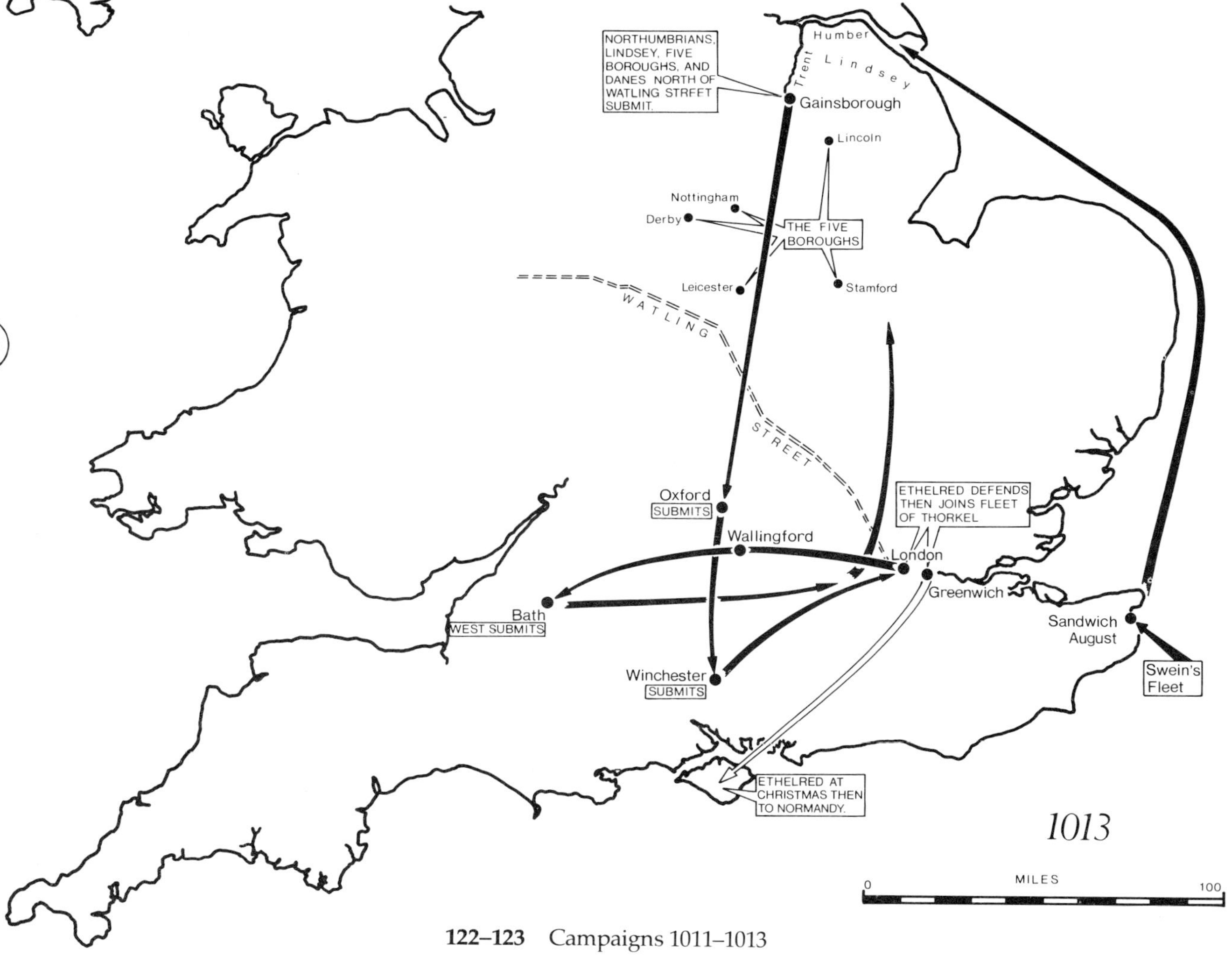

122–123 Campaigns 1011–1013

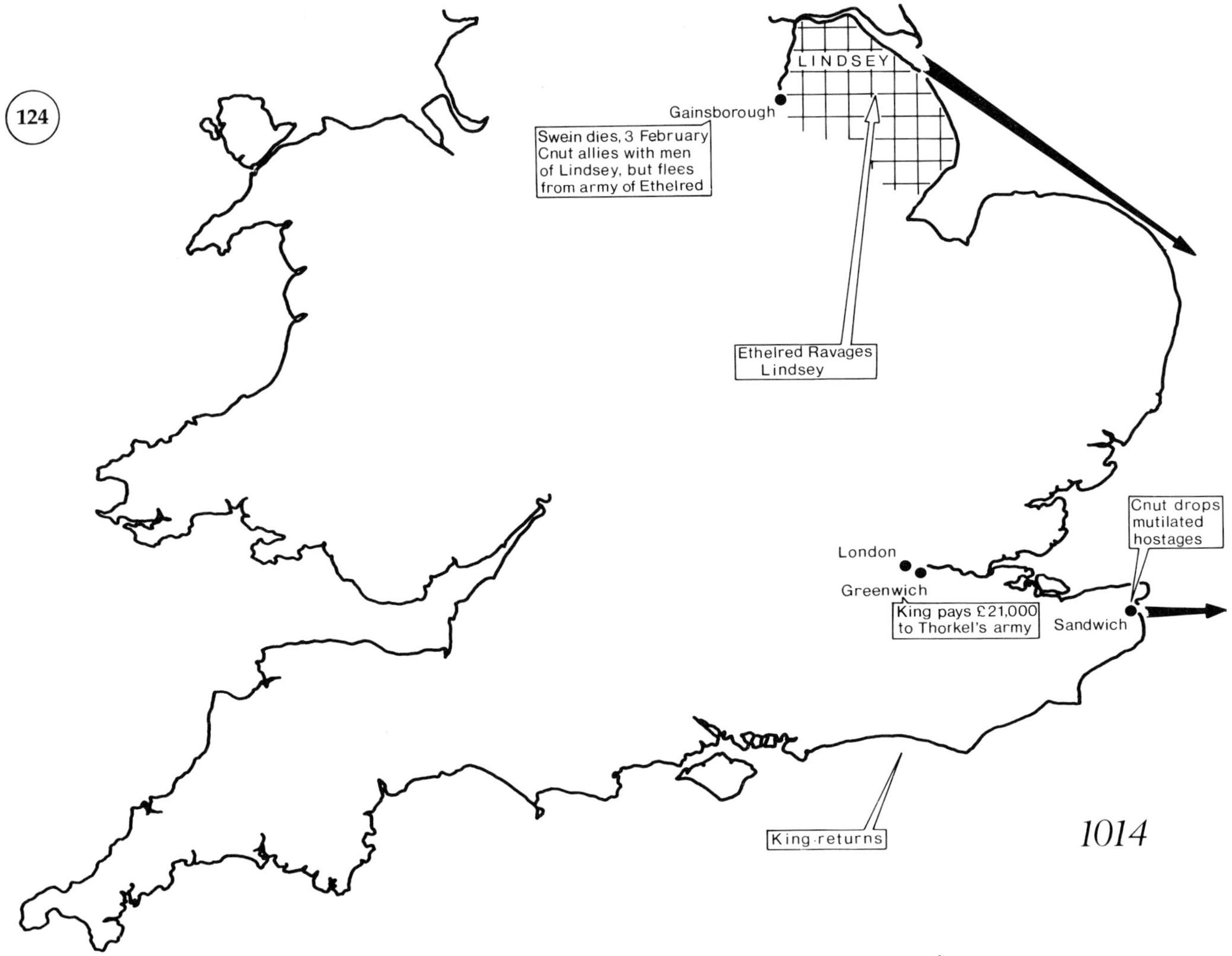

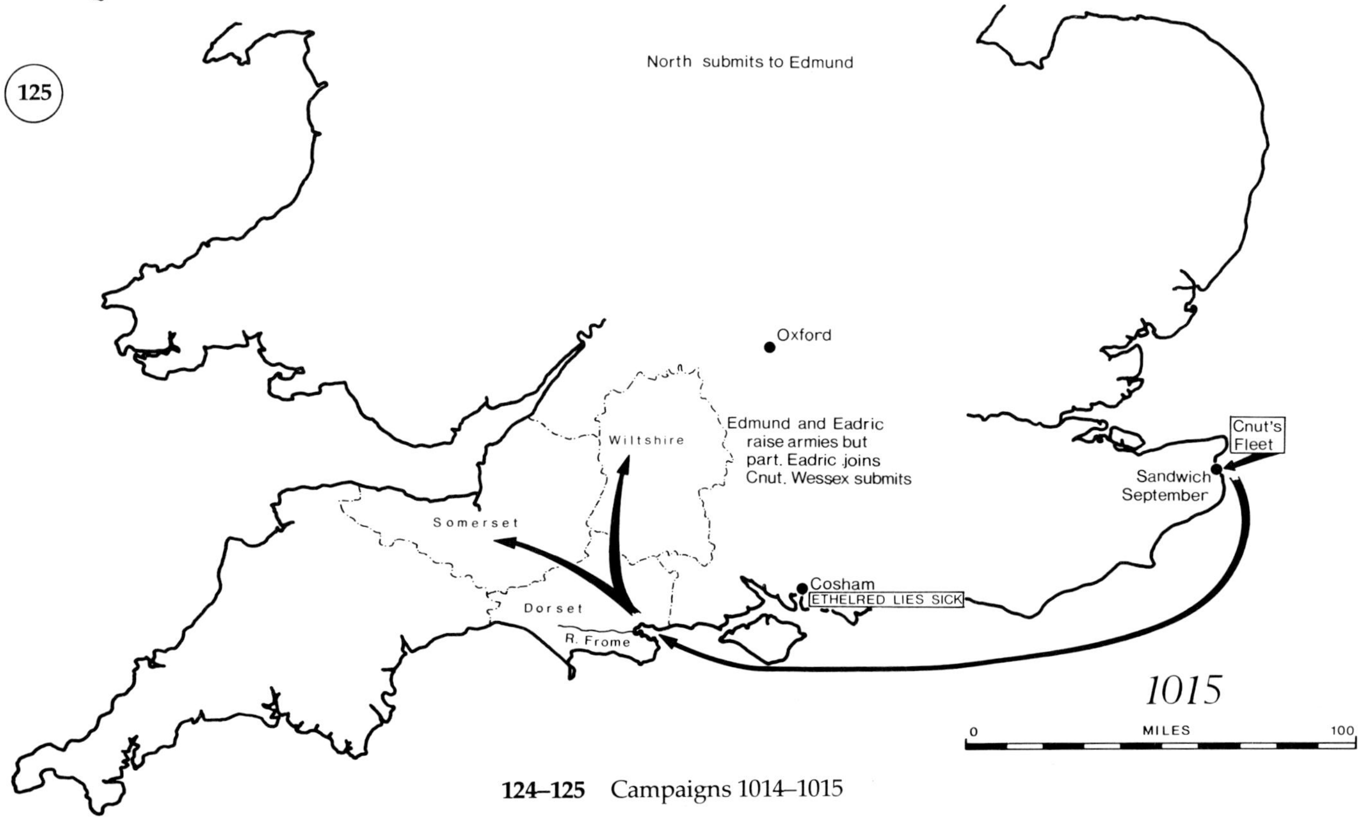

124–125 Campaigns 1014–1015

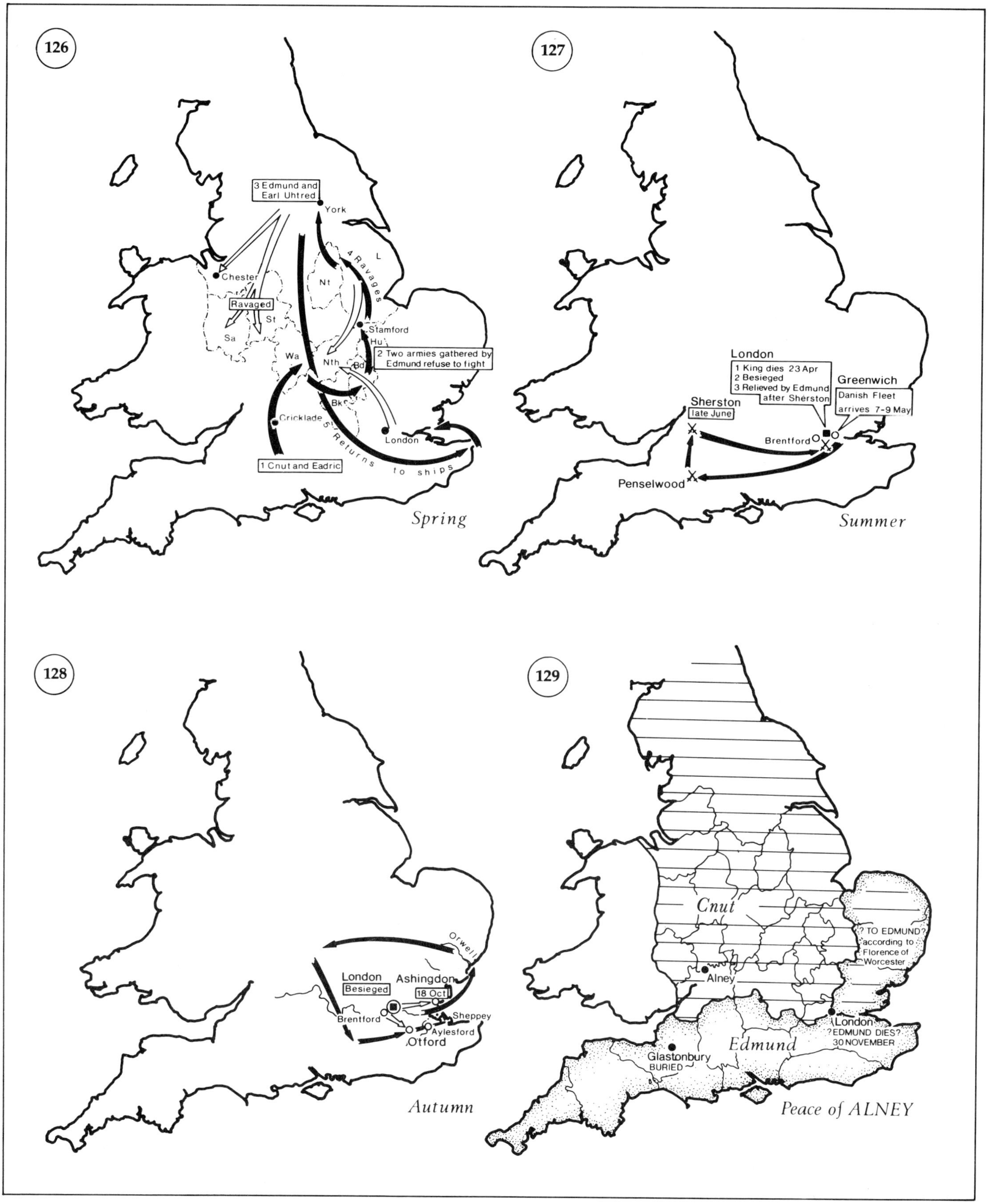

126–129 Campaigns of 1016 and Peace of Alney

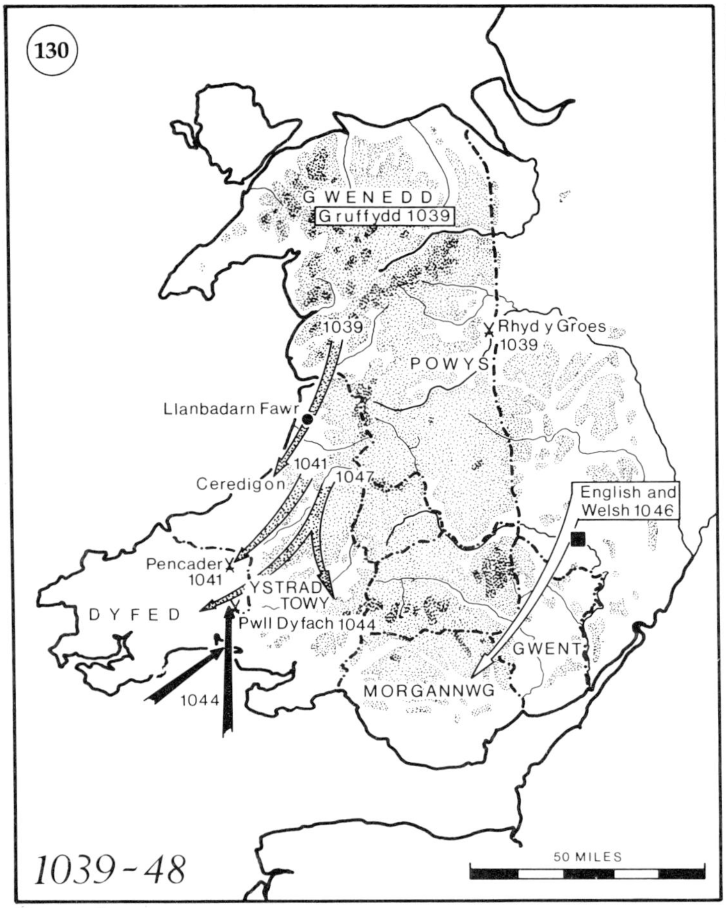
130
GWENEDD
Gruffydd 1039
1039
Rhyd y Groes
1039
POWYS
Llanbadarn Fawr
Ceredigion
1041
1047
English and
Welsh 1046
Pencader
1041
YSTRAD
TOWY
DYFED
Pwll Dyfach 1044
GWENT
1044
MORGANNWG
50 MILES
1039-48

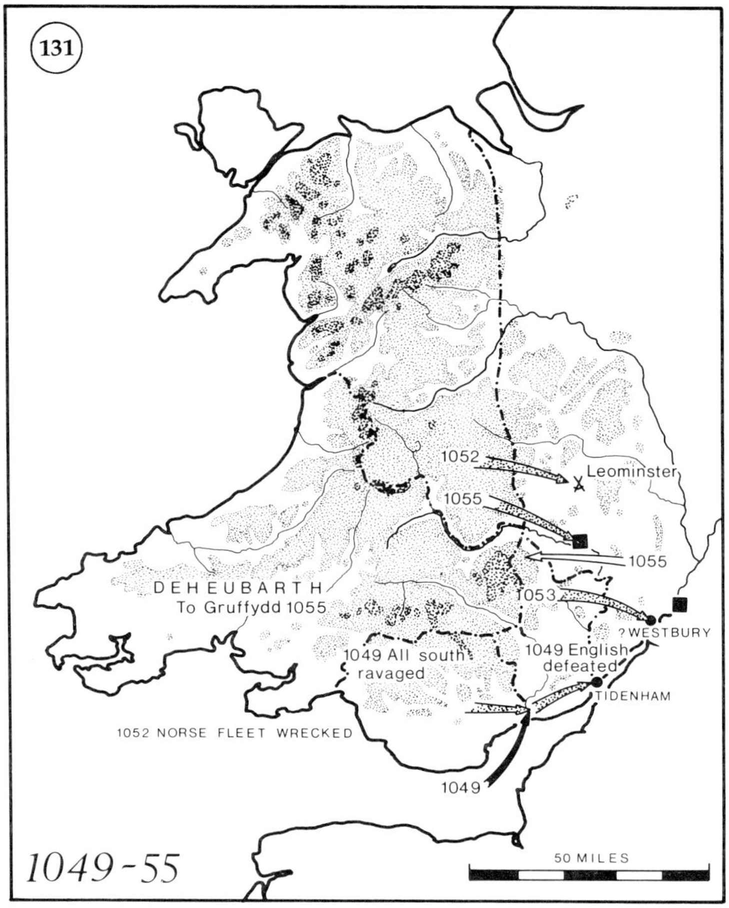
131
1052
Leominster
1055
1055
DEHEUBARTH
To Gruffydd 1055
1053
? WESTBURY
1049 All south
ravaged
1049 English
defeated
TIDENHAM
1052 NORSE FLEET WRECKED
1049
50 MILES
1049-55

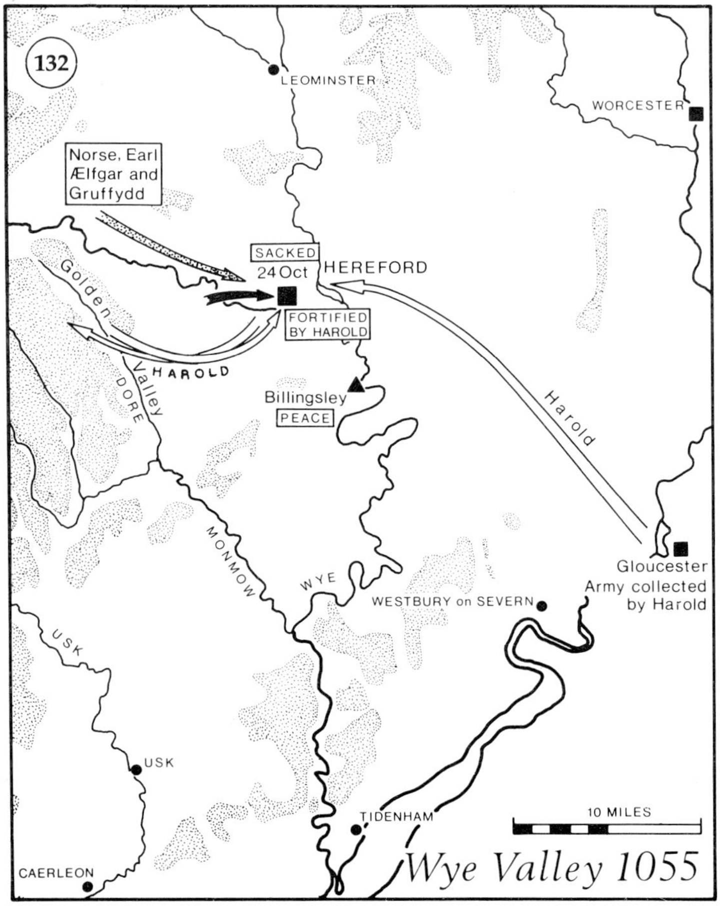
132
LEOMINSTER
WORCESTER
Norse, Earl
Ælfgar and
Gruffydd
SACKED
24 Oct
HEREFORD
FORTIFIED
BY HAROLD
Golden
Valley
DORE
HAROLD
Billingsley
PEACE
Harold
MONMOW
WYE
Gloucester
Army collected
by Harold
WESTBURY on SEVERN
USK
USK
10 MILES
TIDENHAM
CAERLEON
Wye Valley 1055

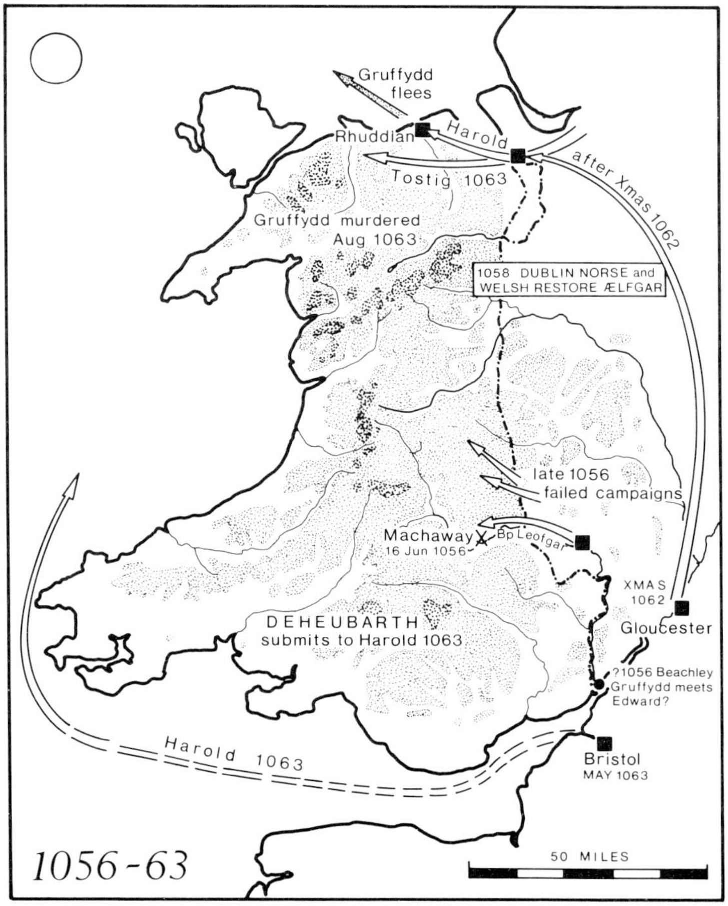
Gruffydd
flees
Rhuddlan
Harold
Tostig 1063
after Xmas 1062
Gruffydd murdered
Aug 1063
1058 DUBLIN NORSE and
WELSH RESTORE ÆLFGAR
late 1056
failed campaigns
Machaway
16 Jun 1056
Bp Leofgar
XMAS
1062
Gloucester
DEHEUBARTH
submits to Harold 1063
?1056 Beachley
Gruffydd meets
Edward?
Harold 1063
Bristol
MAY 1063
50 MILES
1056-63

Wales (130–134)

After the conclusion of the Danish Wars, in the period 1016–66, there were no great campaigns apart from those of Cnut in Scandinavia. But it was a period of significant developments in Anglo–Welsh relations, which have too often been ignored. The rise of Gruffydd ap Llywelyn to become the eventual ruler of all Wales was a long one, his skirmishes with the English were many and he made skilful use of the rivalries of the English houses and of the interventions of the Vikings from Ireland. Gruffydd finally sacked a major English town and escaped retribution, going on to rule all Wales from his palaces and to own a fleet. It took the most powerful man in England, Harold, to bring about his downfall and then only after several unsuccessful forays into Wales (maps **130–133**).

The whole episode commands a considerable amount of attention in the Chronicle, where indeed it is the only Welsh episode to be treated at length. The story illustrates the resources that the Welsh threat could absorb and the attention it could demand and may provide some measure of the troubles Wales posed for the Mercian kingdom in earlier centuries. Maps **181** and **182** show the concentrations of lands held by Harold and the Leofric families on the border, which perhaps reflects the attention that the earls had to pay to the Welsh problem.

Waste estates are noted in many shires in the Domesday Book and are sometimes attributable to historic events. Significantly, there is a concentration of waste places recorded TRE, i.e. in 1066, along the Welsh border (map **134**). Whilst these places may have become waste for a variety of reasons, as in other shires far from the border, the concentration does suggest that the raids recorded for the reign of Edward the Confessor had an effect and may have been the cause of most waste vills. Certainly the four waste vills due to King Caraduach cannot be attributed to any other cause.

130–133 Wales 1039–1063

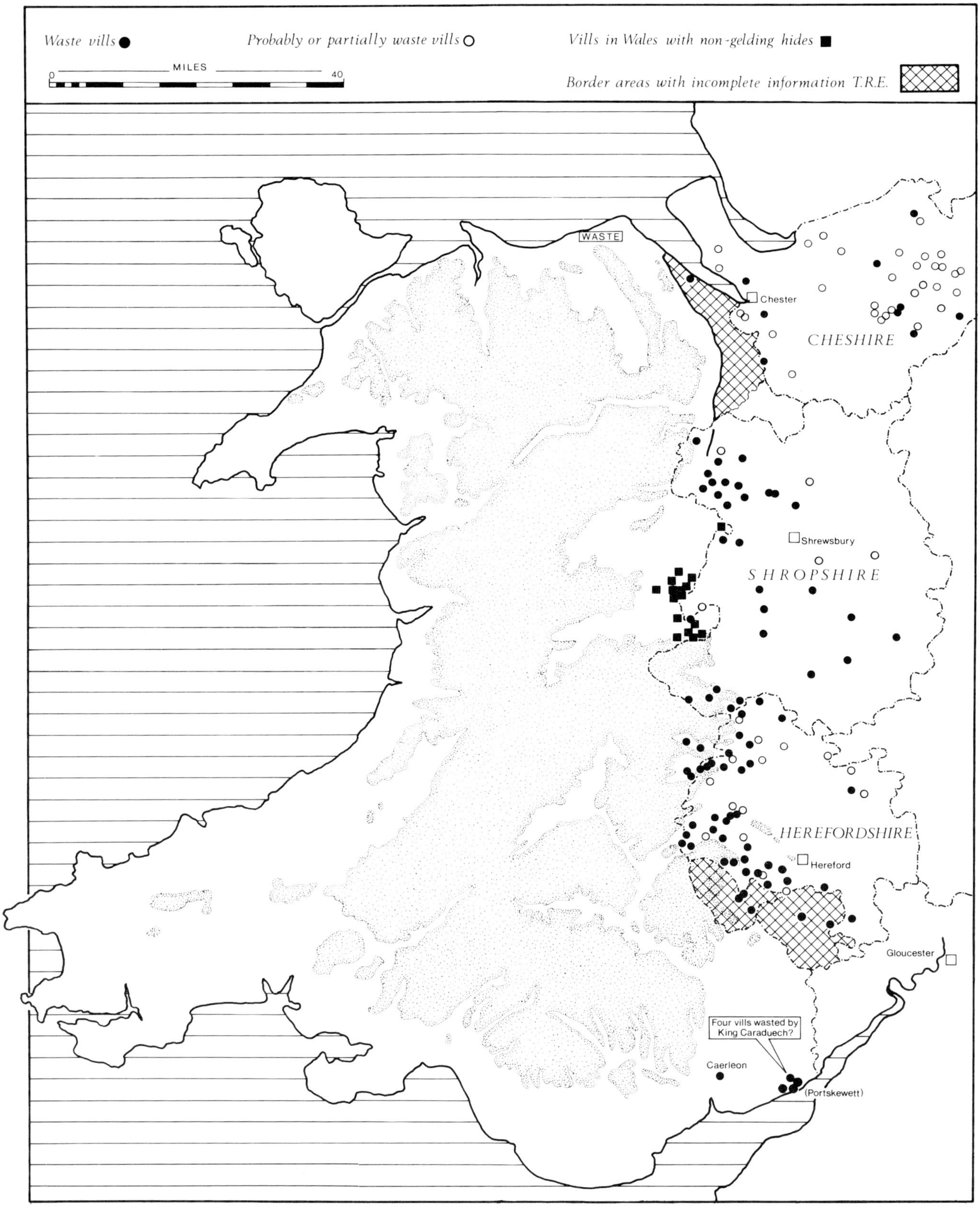

134 Domesday waste in 1066 as an indicator of previous Welsh raids. High ground stippled

Administration

The Administrative Implications of Offa's Dyke (135)

The materials for the reconstruction of the administration of Anglo-Saxon England are extremely sketchy. It is easy therefore to fall into the trap of believing that the administration was rudimentary and to concentrate attention only on the surviving documents, the laws and the charters. However to gain some perspective on the strength of the Anglo-Saxon administrative machinery, it is essential to look at its achievements, for example the frontier system known as Offa's and Wat's Dykes (map **135**). The dykes are longer than the more famous Roman Antonine and Hadrian's Walls added together: they run from sea to sea, cutting off the Welsh peninsula from Mercia. There can be little doubt that the larger dyke was built at the command of Offa; the shorter but stronger dyke must belong to the same period. The dykes are roughly 149 miles long, the probable height of the rampart was some 24 feet above the ditch bottom, and the ditch was some 6 feet deep.

The number of men required to build the dykes and the effort of directing and maintaining them on the border of the Mercian kingdom must have been considerable. The enterprise shows the degree of organization an early medieval society could attain. The whole of England was assessed in tax units which were linked conceptually to the productive capacity of the land. These were hides in most of the country, sulungs in Kent and, later in the Danelaw, carucates. It is probable that the system was to order so many men from a hide-unit, with their tools and food, under the organization of their ealdormen to appear on a given day at a predetermined point on the dyke line. Difficult stretches would already have been marked out with a small bank and ditch; for the rest, a line of marking rods sufficed. This basic system was used by the Carolingians for works such as the great bridge at Pont de l'Arche and was general in northern Europe. As long as there was some idea of the tax possibilities of the realm and its constituent parts then a building project or a tax could be assessed in terms of men or of money and divided first by the total, to arrive at a figure such as one man from every ten hides, or a penny from every hide. The total was divided between shires or **regiones,** the shire reeve or ealdorman would then pass the assessment down to the hundred meeting or its predecessor, and finally the collection would be made and returned back up through the system. Little was needed in the way of book-keeping. That there were some royal memoranda is not in question. Surprisingly, amongst so little in the way of secular documentation, we even have two surviving examples.

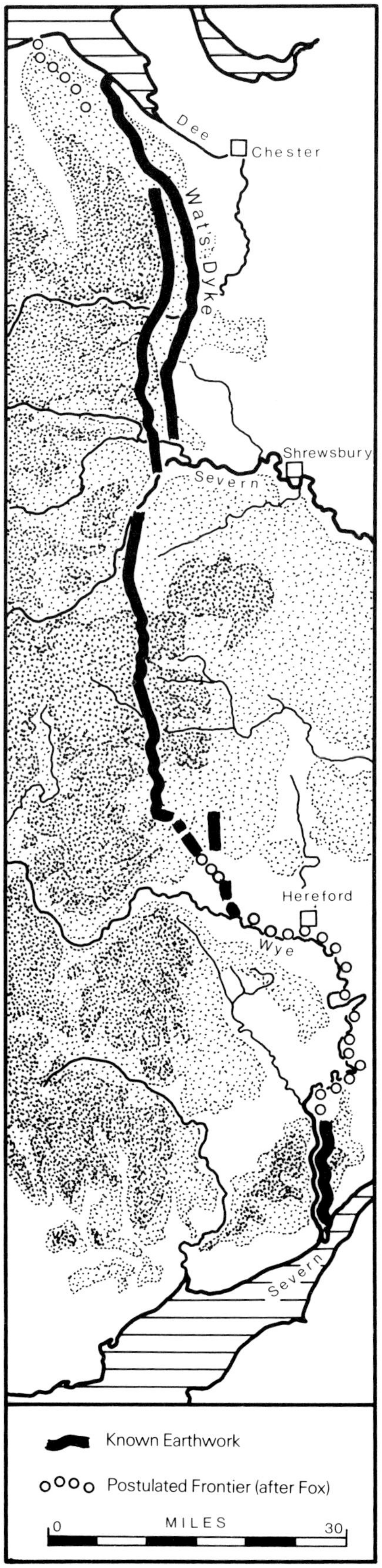

135 Offa's dyke

136 The Tribal Hidage: place names from Harleian MS 3271

The Tribal Hidage (136–138)

One document, known since the days of Maitland as the 'Tribal Hidage', exists in a tenth-century manuscript but there can be no doubt that the exemplar comes from the days of the Mercian Supremacy. Where it should be placed within that period is a subject of debate still awaiting satisfactory elucidation. In the meantime it is safest to reckon it an 'ancient tribute-list of the Mercian kings . . . it should probably be attributed to the reign of Wulfhere, Æthelbald, or Offa. Its great age, to which much of its obscurity is due, shows that it must have been intended to serve some practical purpose' (Stenton 1971, 43, 295–7, 300–1). The names of the various **regiones**, provinces and kingdoms are often obscure and their exact location a matter of dispute (Davies and Vierck 1974; Hart 1971). Map **136** and the diagram and list (**137–138**) offer the information as it stands; further discussion is better left to the authorities cited. Some of the early kingdoms that appear are well known — we can attach other information to them and in some cases even chart their frontiers — whereas others are known only from this list.

137

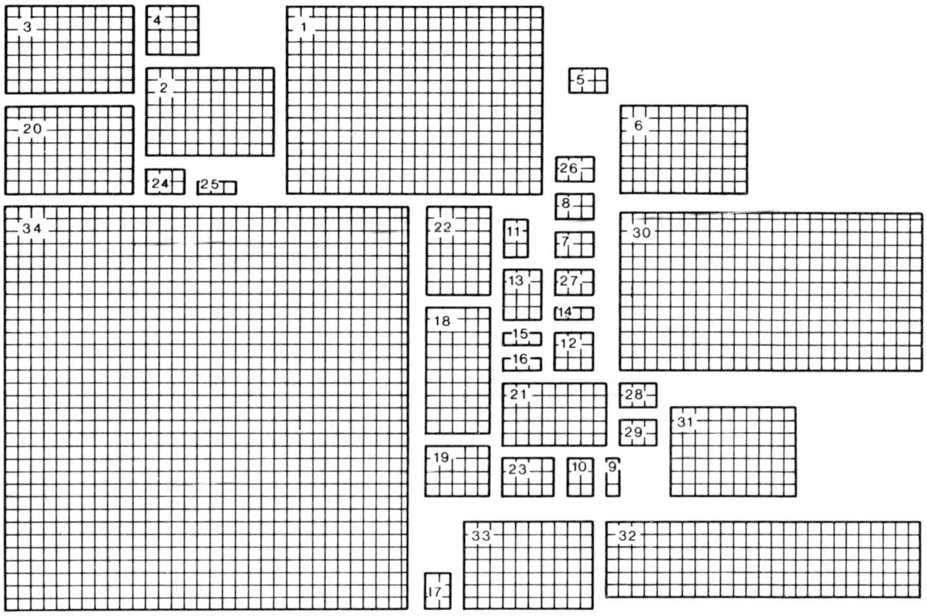

138

		Hundreds of Hides
1	MYRCNA LANDES	300
2	WOCEN SÆTNA	70
3	WESTERNA	70
4	PECSÆTNA	12
5	ELMEDSÆTNA	6
6	LINDES FARONA and Heathfeld land	70
7	SOUTH GYRWA	6
8	NORTH GYRWA	6
9	EAST WIXNA	3
10	WEST WIXNA	6
11	SPALDA	6
12	WIGESTA	9
13	HEREFINNA	12
14	SWEORDORA	3
15	GIFLA	3
16	HICCA	3
17	WIHTGARA	6
18	NOXGAGA	50
19	OHTGAGA	20
	TOTAL	66,100

		Hundreds of Hides
20	HWINCA	70
21	CILTERN SÆTNA	40
22	HENDRICA	35
23	UNECUNG GA	12
24	AROSÆTNA	6
25	FÆRPINGA	3
26	BILMIGA	6
27	WIDERIGGA	6
28	EAST WILLA	6
29	WEST WILLA	6
30	EAST ENGLE	300
31	EAST SEXENA	70
32	CANTWARENA	150
33	SUTH SEXENA	70
34	WEST SEXENA	1000
	TOTAL	247,700

137–138 The Tribal Hidage: comparative assessments and listing

Early Kingdoms (139–143)

At the opening of the period covered by this atlas, England south of the Humber was organized in some degree with reference to the central kingdom of Mercia. By the reign of Æthelbald there was allied kingdoms, subject and tributory kingdoms, provinces and **regiones**. The allied, subject and tributory kingdoms were themselves divided, in the case of Wessex from an early stage, into shires.

One of the these kingdoms was that of Lindsey, one of the few early kingdoms of which the bounds can be accurately drawn (map **139**). These bounds and the early history of the kingdom have been discussed by Stenton (1970, 127–35). The 'island' of Lincoln was cut off on two sides by river valleys and on the other two by the sea and the Humber estuary. Within this isolation the kingdom managed to survive independently into the eighth century, while to the south the rest of present-day Lincolnshire was part of Middle Anglia. The kingdom had to exist under an overlord, which by the middle of the eighth century was Mercia. The kings of Lindsey became permanent tributory kings under Offa and were finally absorbed into the Mercian nobility by 800.

The bounds of the other kingdoms are sometimes embedded to some extent in the dioceses which were originally founded to serve individual kingdoms. It is therefore possible to postulate the extent of the kingdom of the East Saxons by comparing it with the diocese of London (map **140**). There are problems, however, as the northern boundary of Middlesex and the coincident limit of the diocese of London reflect only the edge of the holdings of the Abbey of St Albans. However the map is useful, as the kingdom included the whole of Essex and Middlesex and the eastern fringe of Hertfordshire. The Middlesex and Hertfordshire portions were probably lost between 735 and 755 as a result of pressure from Æthelbald, but it is clear that Middlesex was firmly in the Kingdom before 730, when Bede referred to London as its metropolis, and the Thames would appear to have formed the frontier with Wessex in 704–706, when a meeting was held in Brentford. This would suggest that Wessex had some hold over Surrey at the time. Although no East Saxon king was of national rather than local importance, the kingdom survived in its truncated form into the ninth century when it appears to have been incorporated into Wessex.

Among the longest lasting of the minor kingdoms were the Hwicce and the Magonsætan (map **143**). Although their independence disappeared in the eighth century they remained as territorial units in the eleventh century when their ealdorman still led the group to battle. The grouping had thus survived the Danish wars and the incorporation into Wessex, and even the division of Mercia into shires in the first half of the tenth century. This territorial unity must have been aided by the fact that the Magonsætan were also the people served by the bishopric of Hereford whilst the Hwicce were served by the bishopric of Worcester. As the map shows, the later division of the area into shires cut across these early kingdoms.

That the use of the diocesan boundaries is an acceptable approach towards the reconstruction of the early boundaries is shown by the distribution of charters issued by the kings of the Hwicce. In map **141** the charters of the kings of Hwicce are plotted in relation to the later diocesan boundary of the bishopric of Worcester and the two clearly correlate. At one time, as the map shows, there was also jurisdiction over Bath, a fact born out by the intineraries of the Mercian kings; a certain fluidity in the boundaries is only to be expected.

This fluidity was operating upon the Hwicce and the Magonsætan at the end of the ninth century, when it would appear that there was some extension of Saxon control into the areas of the Welsh kingdoms. The Welsh kings finally abrogated authority over the area known as Archenfield sometime after 900 — when the series of Welsh charters dealing with the area ceases (Davies 1978, 26). When the authority of the old divisions broke down as a result of the Danish wars the dioceses of Hereford and Worcester seem to have taken responsibility for areas which originally belonged to the Wrocensetnan and the Tomsætan (map **142**). These two peoples are named after the Wrekin and the Tame (in the same way that one must assume the Magonsætan were named after the old Roman site at Kenchester, Magnis).

The few charter references which allow us to guess at the extent of these areas put some part within the dioceses representing the Hwicce and the Magonsætan. This same evidence points to the Tomsætan as a large unit. The evidence of map **142** must act as a caution against drawing frontiers too uncritically using apparently early materials (Ford 1976, 281).

There is a series of articles discussing these kingdoms (Finberg 1961, 167–81, 217–24; Smith 1965; M. Wilson 1968). They had ceased to function at all independently by 750 although the names of their kings were still recorded into the last years of the eighth century when, like many other small divisions, they were absorbed into Mercia.

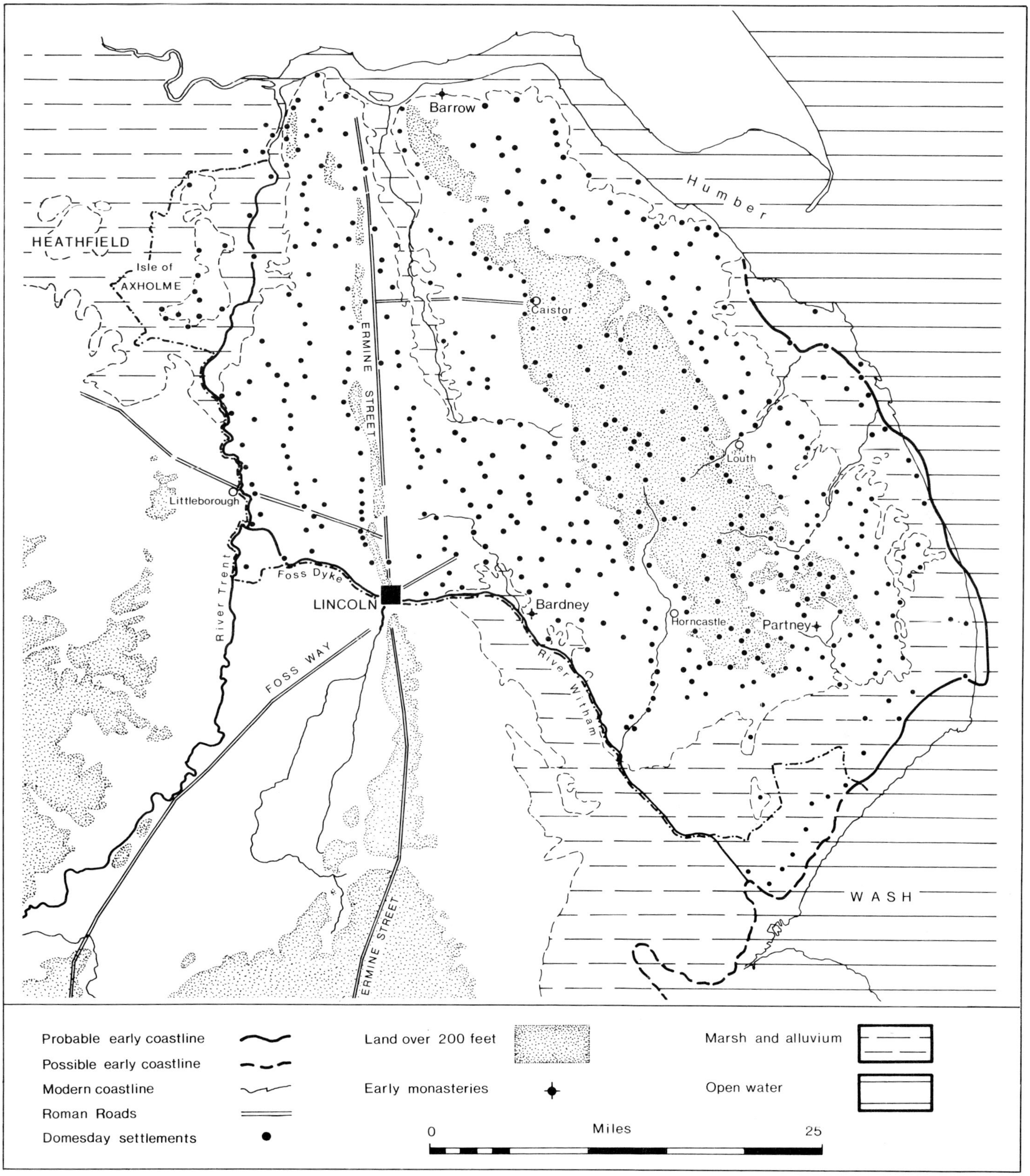

139 Early Lindsey

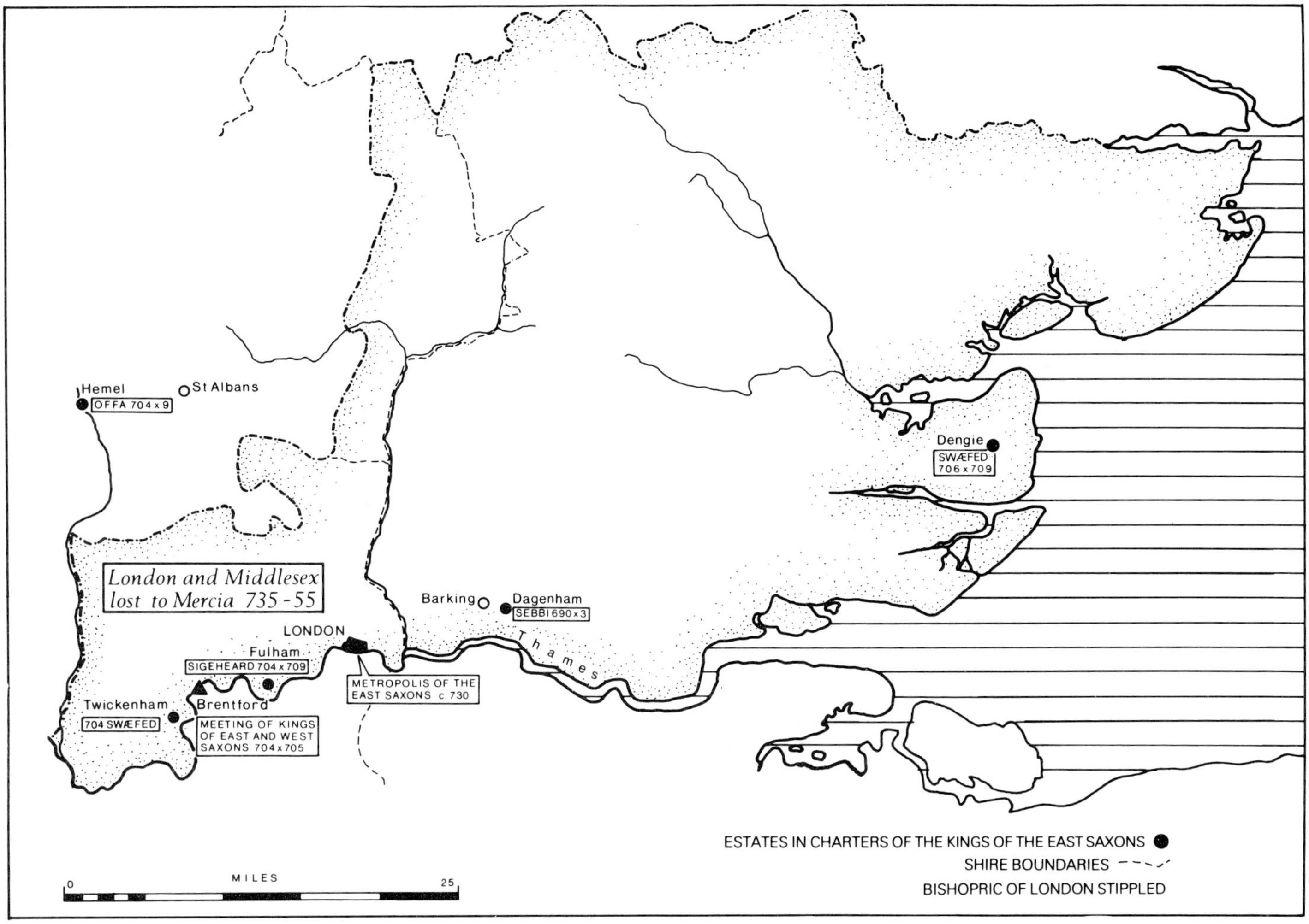

140 The Kingdom of the East Saxons

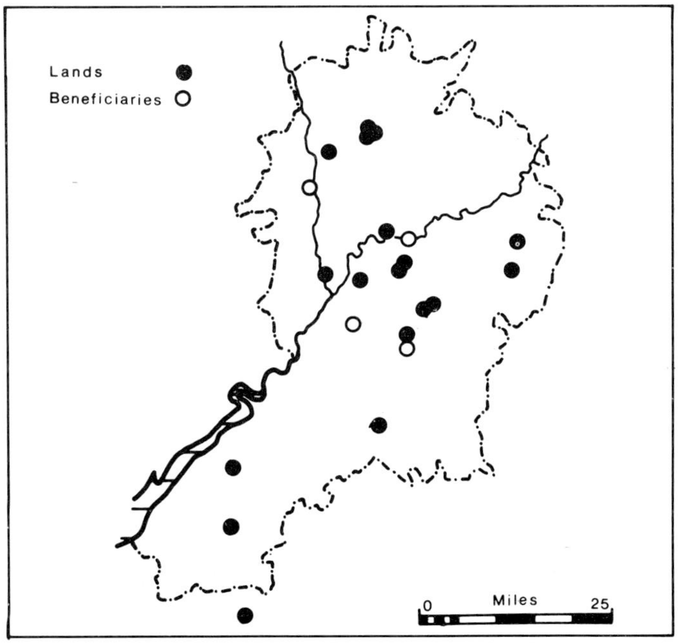

141 Charters of the kings of Hwicce

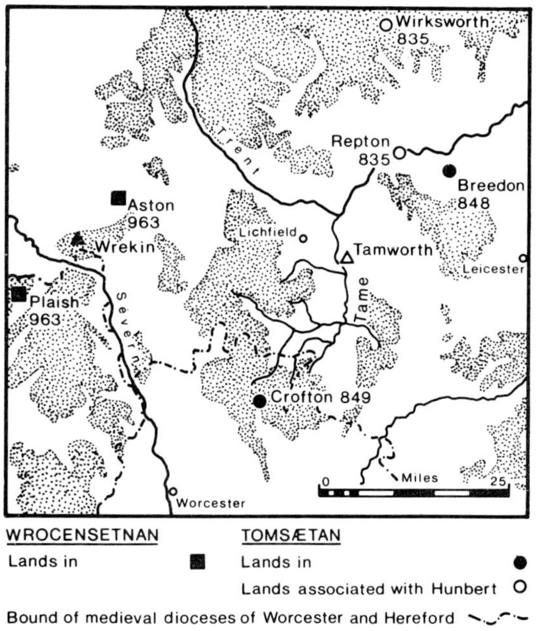

142 The Tomsætan and Wrocensetnan

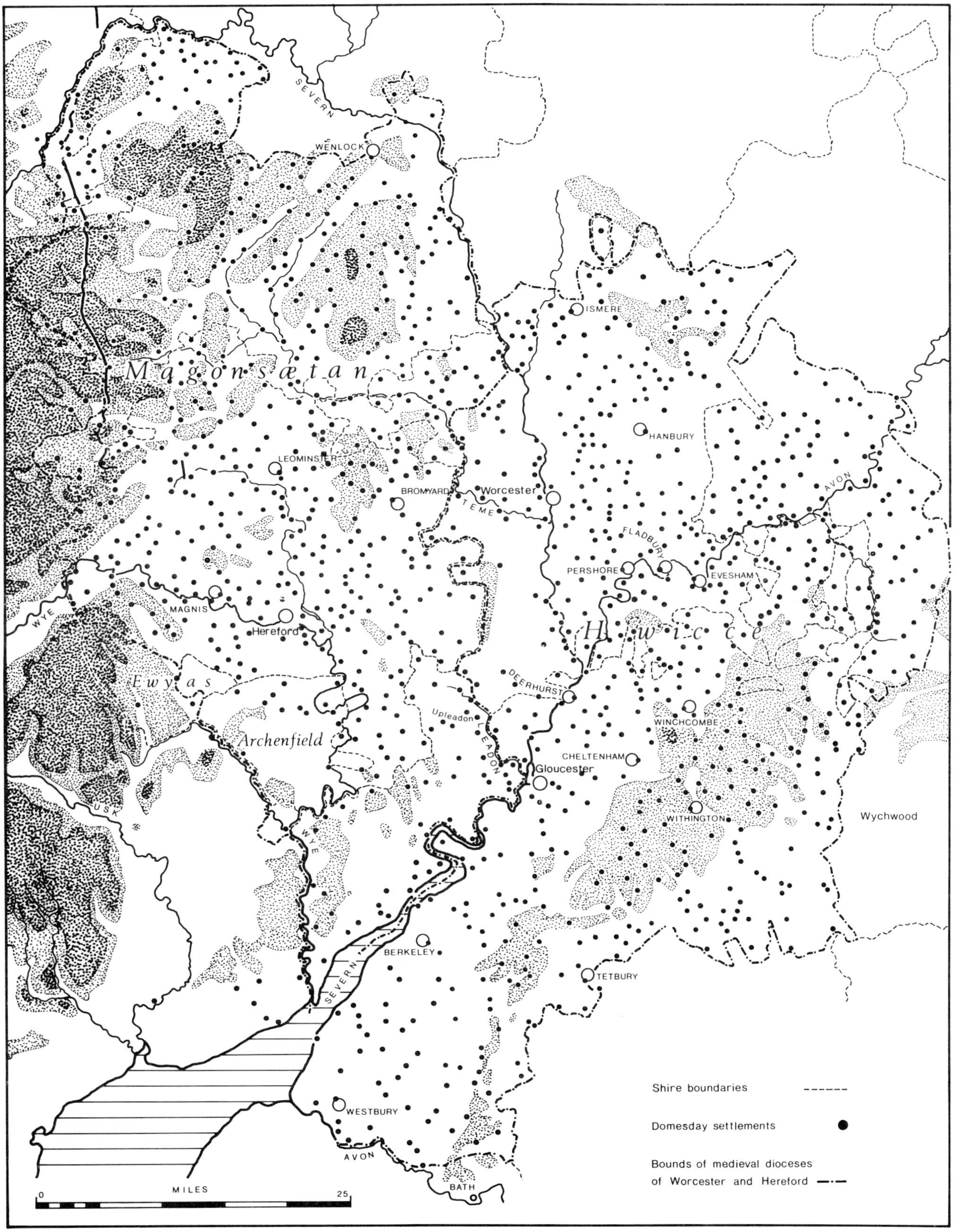

143 The Kingdoms of the Magonsætan and Hwicce

The Itineraries of the Early Kings (144–148)

Itineraries of rulers of the early medieval period in Europe have often been drawn and found useful by scholars. Examples are the itineraries of Charlemagne (map **144**) and Henry the Fowler. Such material becomes increasingly common after the Conquest. It is a little less certain that the effort will produce any clear results for the more fragmentary movements of the Anglo-Saxon kings. However the maps have been compiled, and although they are not exhaustive, they show some interesting patterns which may have important implications and inferences. All the itineraries show civil rather than military movements.

The itinerary of the Mercian kings (map **145**) reveals little that is new, as it is substantially the same as the map of 'the Mercian Kingdom' in Stenton (1971, 201), although the version here does bring out the importance of Tamworth rather more strongly. The itinerary of West Saxon kings (map **146**) has several interesting features: first, the Berkshire area is bereft of meetings, which, taken with the Mercian map, opens up the question of exactly where the frontier between the two kingdoms was up to 850, as does the fact that Bath was a place that Mercian kings visited. The West Saxon kings showed an early preference for the four shires of Hampshire, Wiltshire, Dorset and Somerset, a preference which continued into the late tenth century when all England was theirs to choose from.

Alfred the Great showed an interest in all parts of his kingdom which is reflected both in his itinerary (map **147**) and in his will (map **148**). The evidence suggests that the king held east Cornwall in his own hands, perhaps as a relatively deserted band between him and whatever remained of the Cornish state to the west of Bodmin Moor.

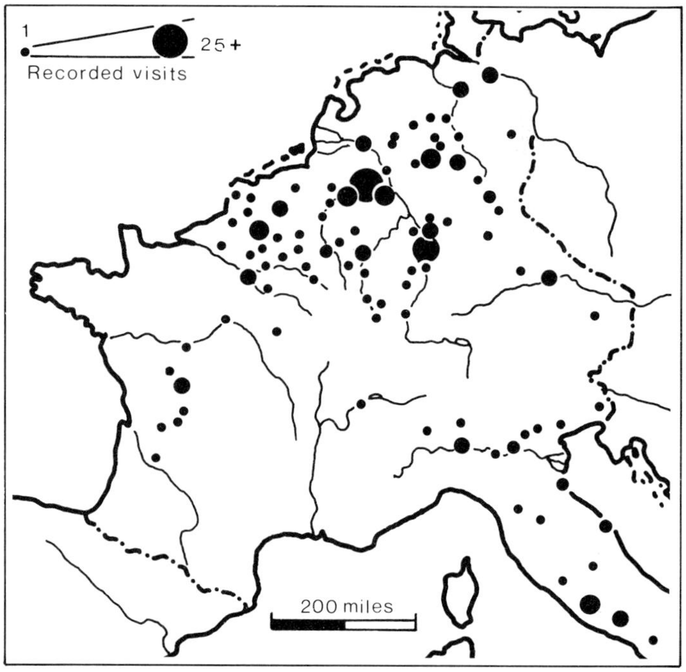

144 The itinerary of Charlemagne

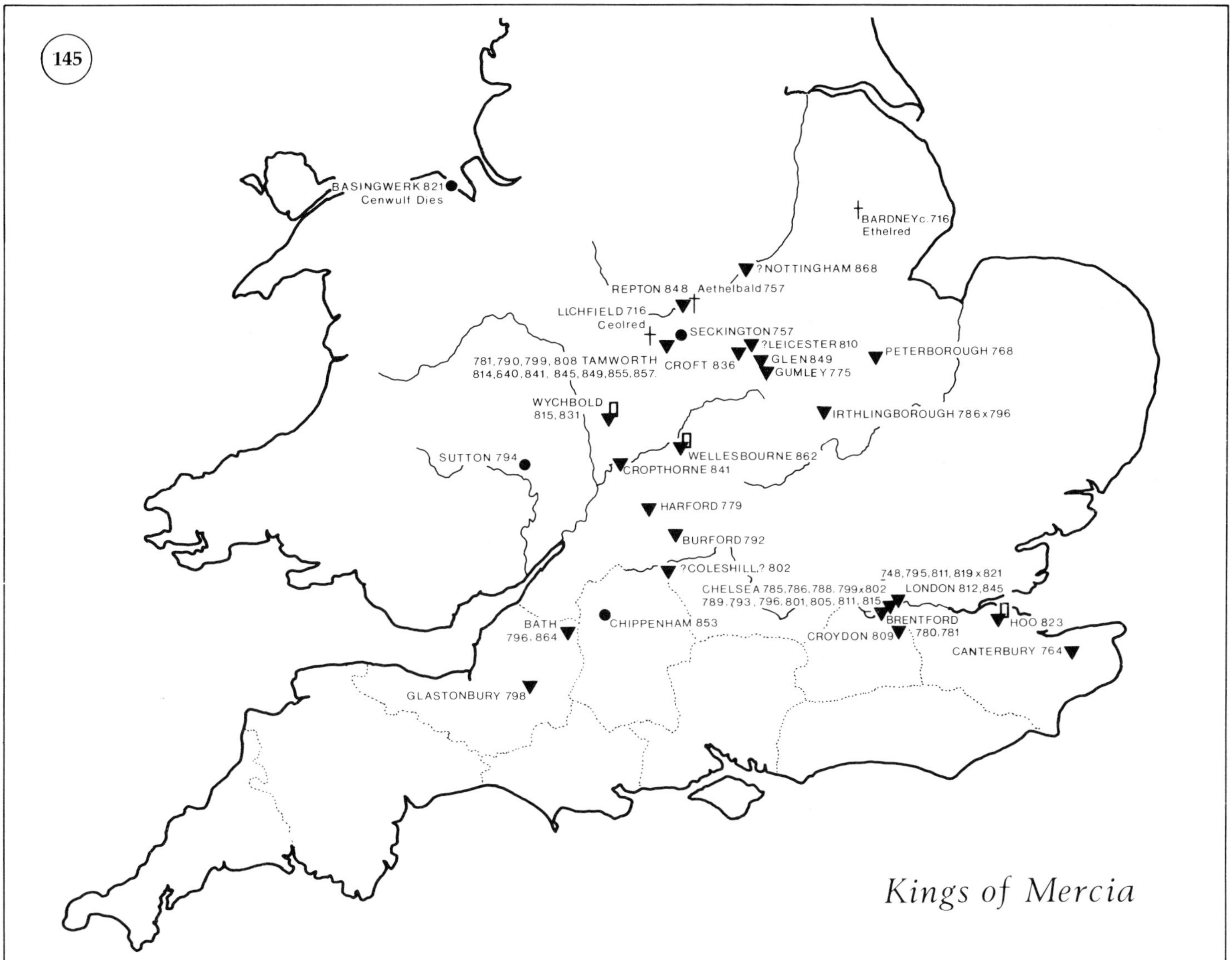

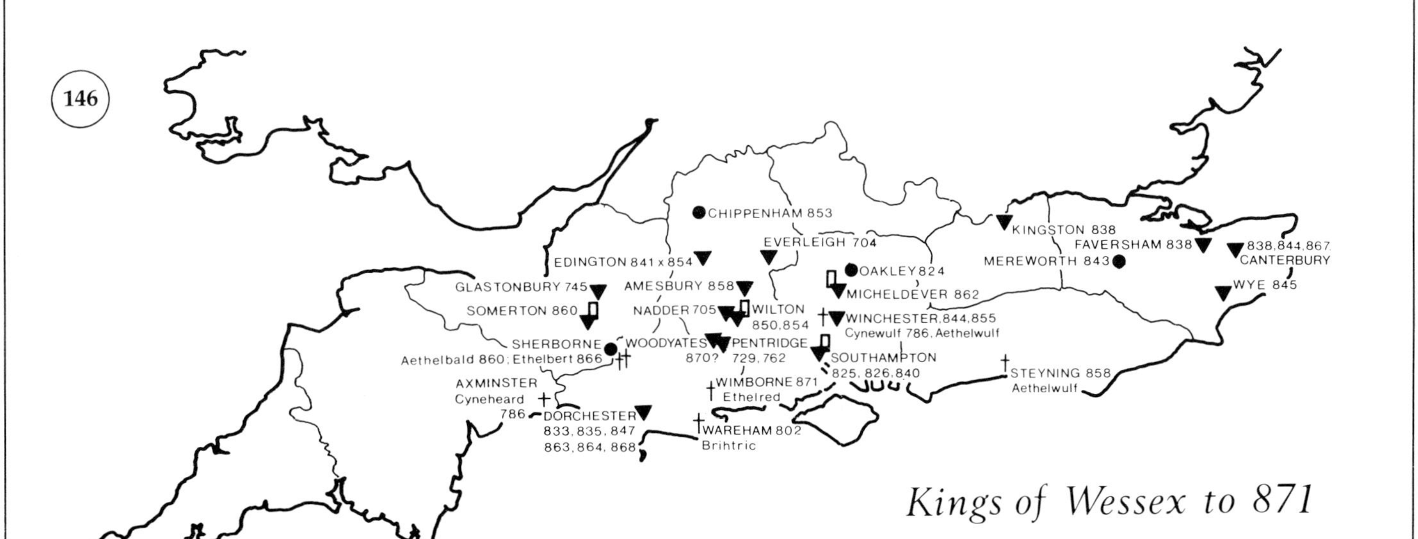

145–146 Itineraries of the Kings of Mercia and of Wessex to 871

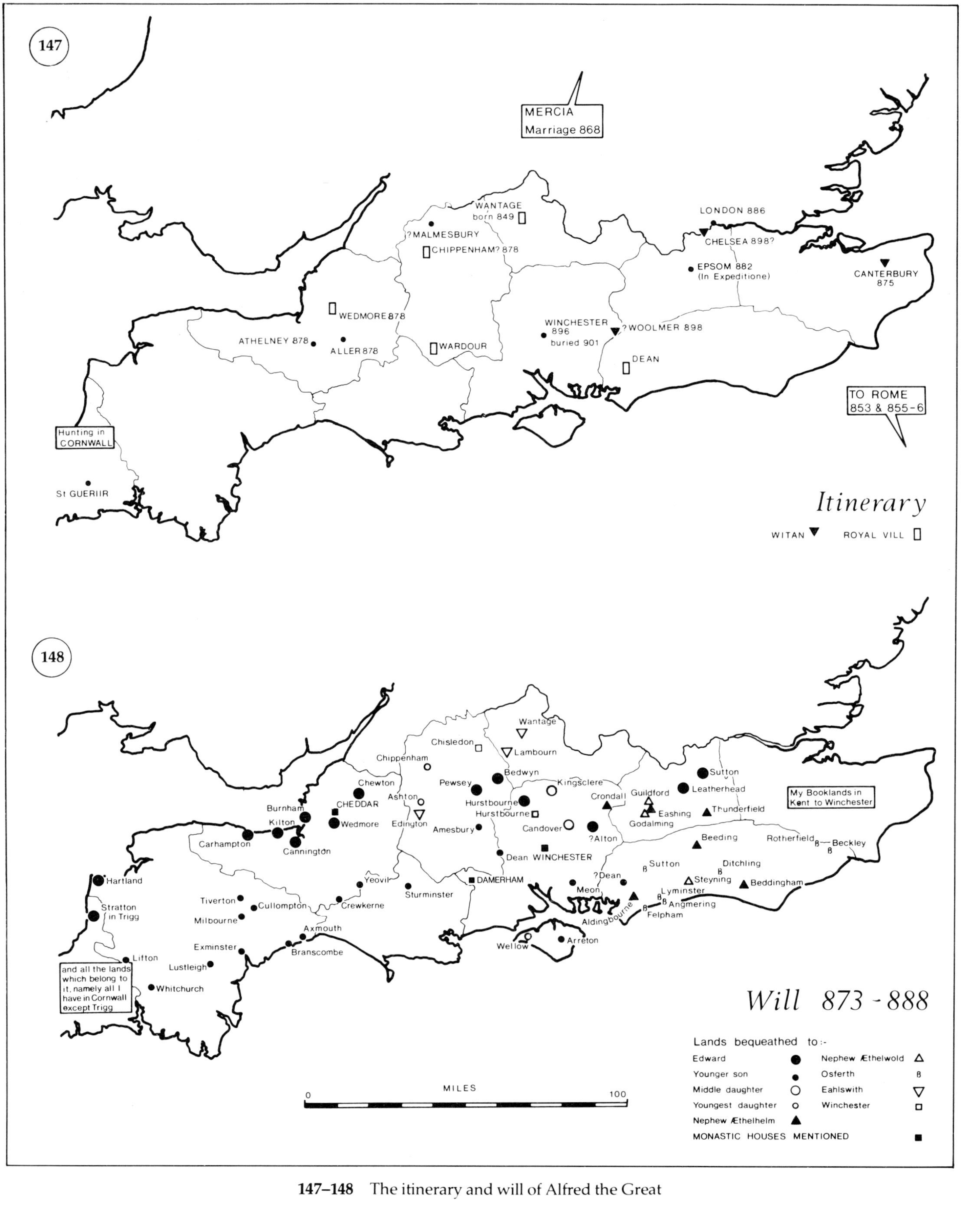

147–148 The itinerary and will of Alfred the Great

The Burghal Hidage (149–153)

The survival of this royal memorandum is of great importance in the study of the development of towns and fortifications under Alfred the Great and his children. It consists of a list of West Saxon **burhs**, fortified places, set out in order around southern England, omitting Kent, London and most of Mercia (**150–153**). The places are each assigned a number of hides and a concluding paragraph allows one to deduce the length of defended wall (**149**), so that we can be certain what places were defended at a given time, 919 (for a discussion of the date and other important points see Brooks 1964). This conversion from the tax assessment in hides to length of wall is obviously of great import if it is possible to confirm the exact extent of a defended area at a fixed moment of time (Hill 1969), and the figures given in the text can be checked against the actual lengths, giving a surprising degree of accuracy. In fact the whole document is a piece of early mathematics which can be seen to work, from the complex conversion table to the totals at the end of the second version of the text. If the correlation apparently demonstrated in **149** is correct we have much to learn of the early history of Exeter and Chichester which show such a deviation from the norm.

Thus the one document allows us to examine the early topography of a town, know that it was walled at a given time, at the king's command and that there was an area of a known size dependent in some way on it.

The Burghal Hidage stands alone in importance and it is doubtful even now if we have realized its full significance in relation to the development of royal government as well as in the more urban field. (Loyn 1971, 117)

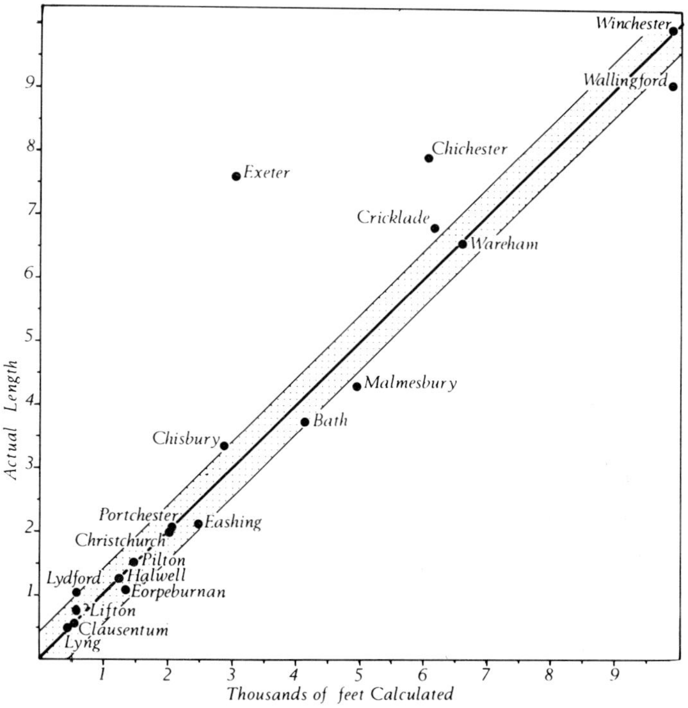

The Itineraries of the Kings of England from Edward the Elder to Cnut (154–163)

In the whole of the tenth century, when the King of the West Saxons was, with interruptions, King of all England, it is remarkable how rarely he is to be seen travelling outside of the south of England, and more particularly the four heartland shires of Wessex. This may have some general relevance apart from a very sensible preference for the better part of England. It explains how the remark that Ethelred II was 'eating his foodrents' in Shropshire in 1006 was meant to be ironic, for no other king is known to have been in that shire in the preceding century. More generally, however, it is clear that it must tell us something of the nature of royal administration. Only Athelstan (map **155**) appears to have spent any considerable portion of his time in Mercia and it follows that the whole realm had to be administered from the centre of Wessex where the king decided to be. It should be noted that it was not from the towns, Winchester or Dorchester, that the king mainly ran his affairs but from estates in the countryside, Cheddar, **sede regali**, Frome or Amesbury. If Edgar the Peaceable (map **160**) wished to administer his kingdom from Cheddar he would need a skilled household, dependable subordinates in the outlying regions and good communications. There is little here of the king travelling restlessly, grazing the pastures of his estates and eating up his foodrents. This is a sophisticated system and not run from 'a box under the bed'.

There is a change apparent with the stress of the Danish Wars, and about AD 1000 a drift in the centre of affairs towards the Thames Valley is noticeable with some indication of the special links that Ethelred had with London (map **162**). But for Ethelred and Cnut (maps **162–163**) there seems little attempt to travel the heartlands of the Midlands. One thing which puzzles me, and for which I have yet to find an explanation, is the insistance on the part of successive kings that they be consecrated at Kingston upon Thames, a place which is neither in Wessex nor the heart of Mercia.

149 The Burghal Hidage: correlation of wall lengths. The stippled area represents the 'rounding up' of 50 hides

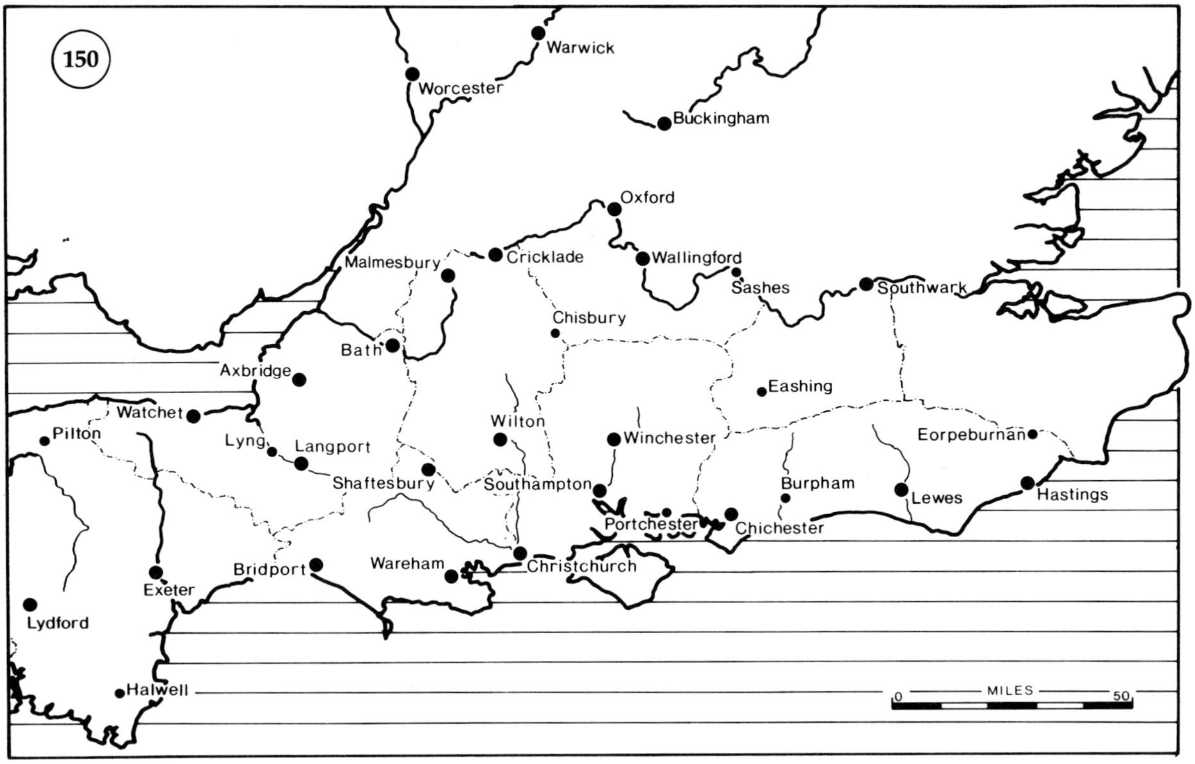

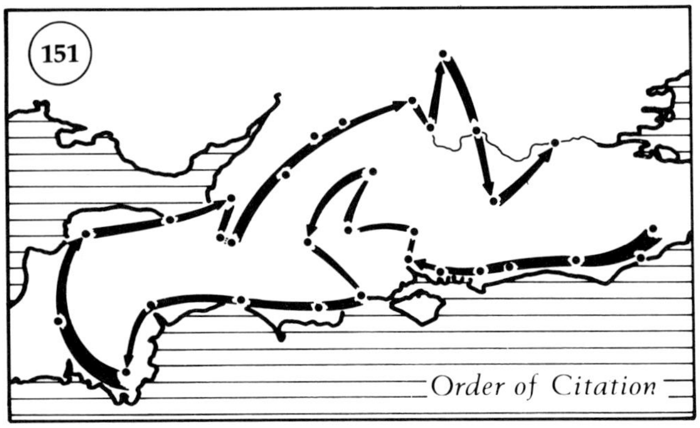

152

	ASSESSMENT (HIDES)	EQUIVALENT (FEET)
1 EORPEBURNAN	324	1336
2 HASTINGS	500	2062
3 LEWES	1300	5362
4 BURPHAM	720	2972
5 CHICHESTER	1500	6187
6 PORTCHESTER	500	2062
7 SOUTHAMPTON	150	619
8 WINCHESTER	2400	9900
9 WILTON	1400	5775
10 CHISBURY	700	2887
11 SHAFTESBURY	700	2887
12 CHRISTCHURCH	470	1939
13 WAREHAM	1600	6600
14 BRIDPORT	760	3135
15 EXETER	734	3028
16 HALWELL	300	1237
17 LYDFORD	140	577
18 PILTON	360	1485
19 WATCHET	513	2116
20 AXBRIDGE	400	1650
21 LYNG	100	412
22 LANGPORT	600	2475
23 BATH	1000	4125
24 MALMESBURY	1200	4950
25 CRICKLADE	1500	6187
26 OXFORD	1400	5775
27 WALLINGFORD	2400	9900
28 BUCKINGHAM	1600	6600
29 SASHES	1000	4125
20 EASHING	600	2475
31 SOUTHWARK	1800	7425
TOTAL FOR WESSEX	27.070	
32 WORCESTER	1200	4950
33 WARWICK	2400	9900

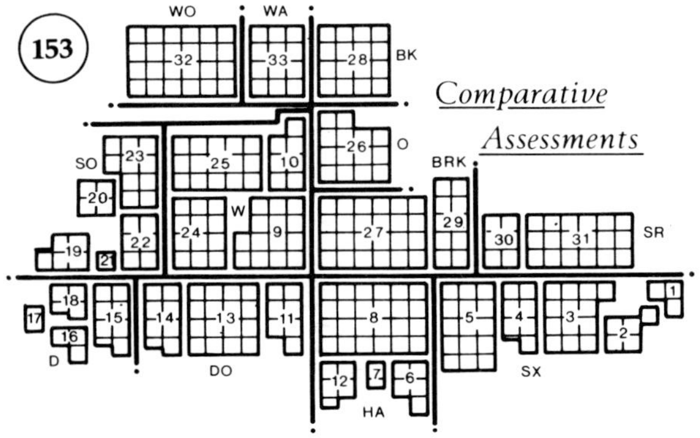

150–153 The Burghal Hidage

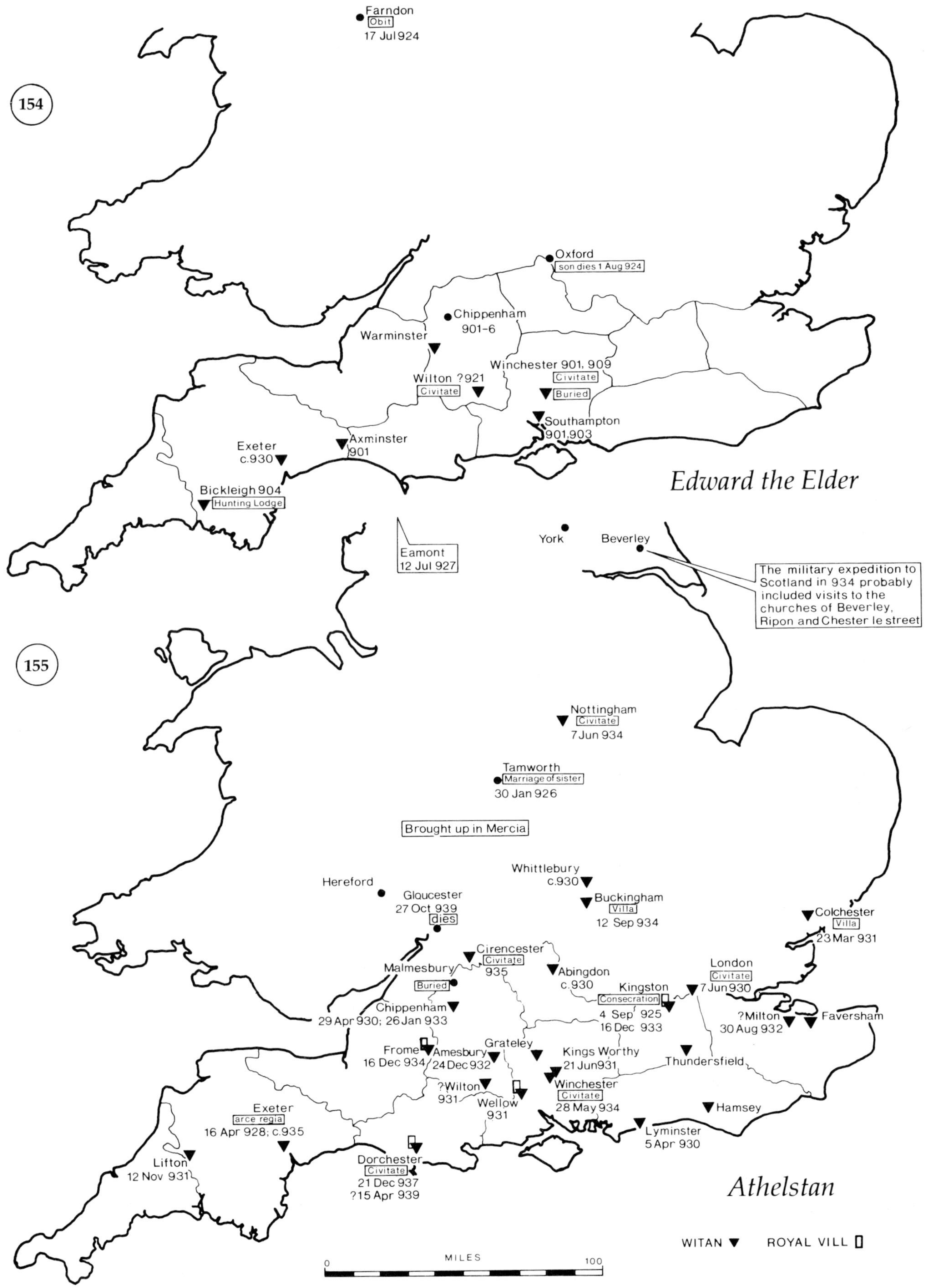

154–155 Itineraries of Edward the Elder and Athelstan

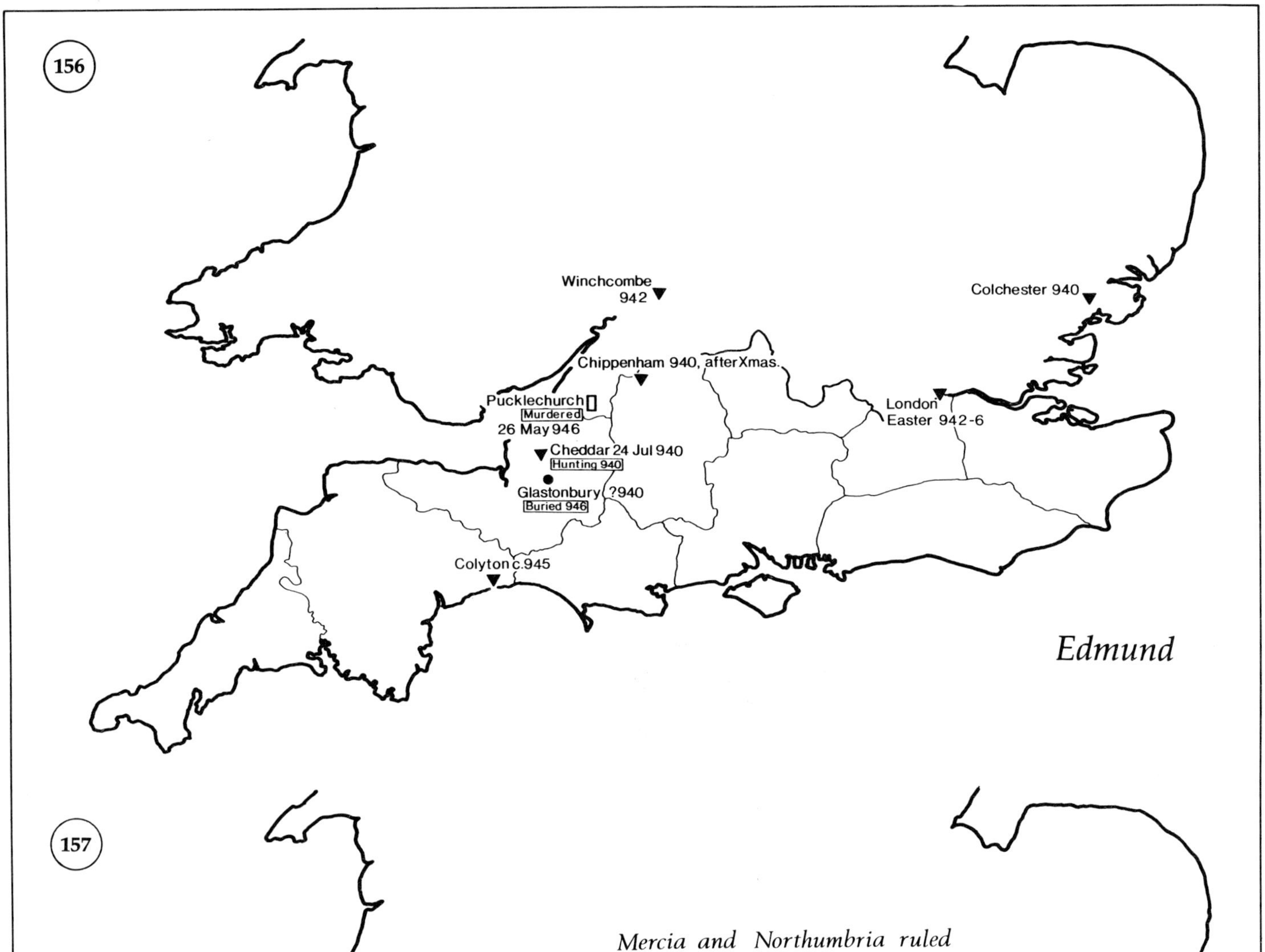

156–157 Itineraries of Edmund and Eadwig

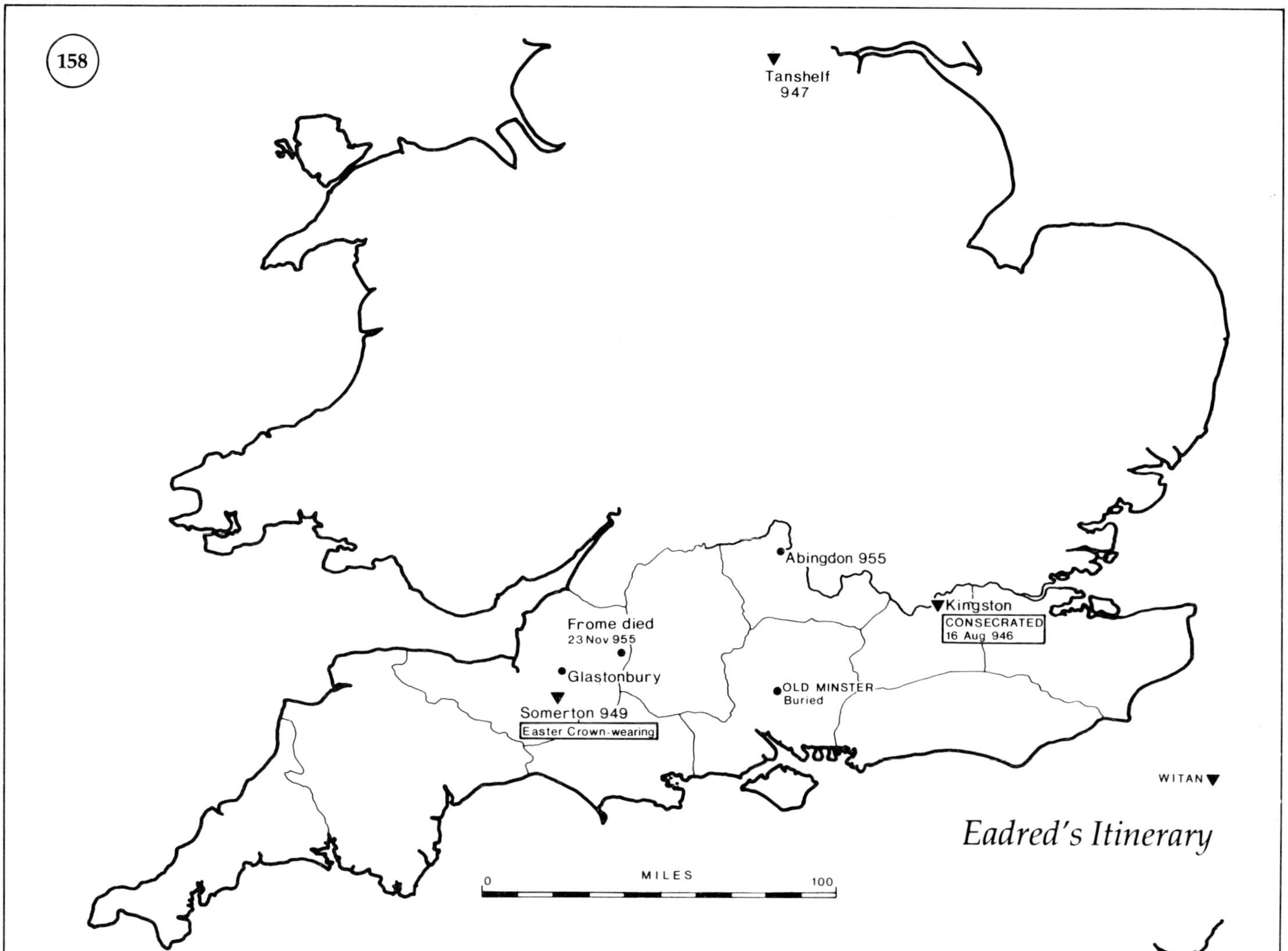

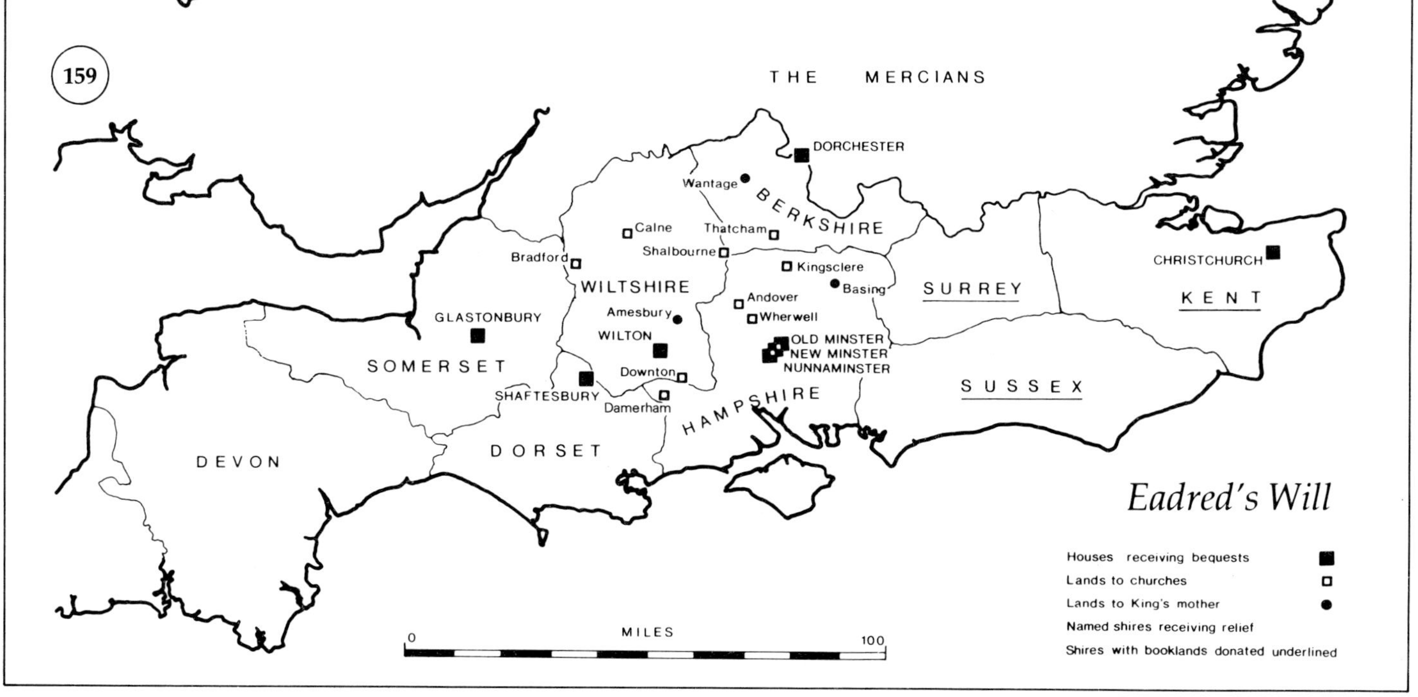

158–159 Itinerary and will of Eadred

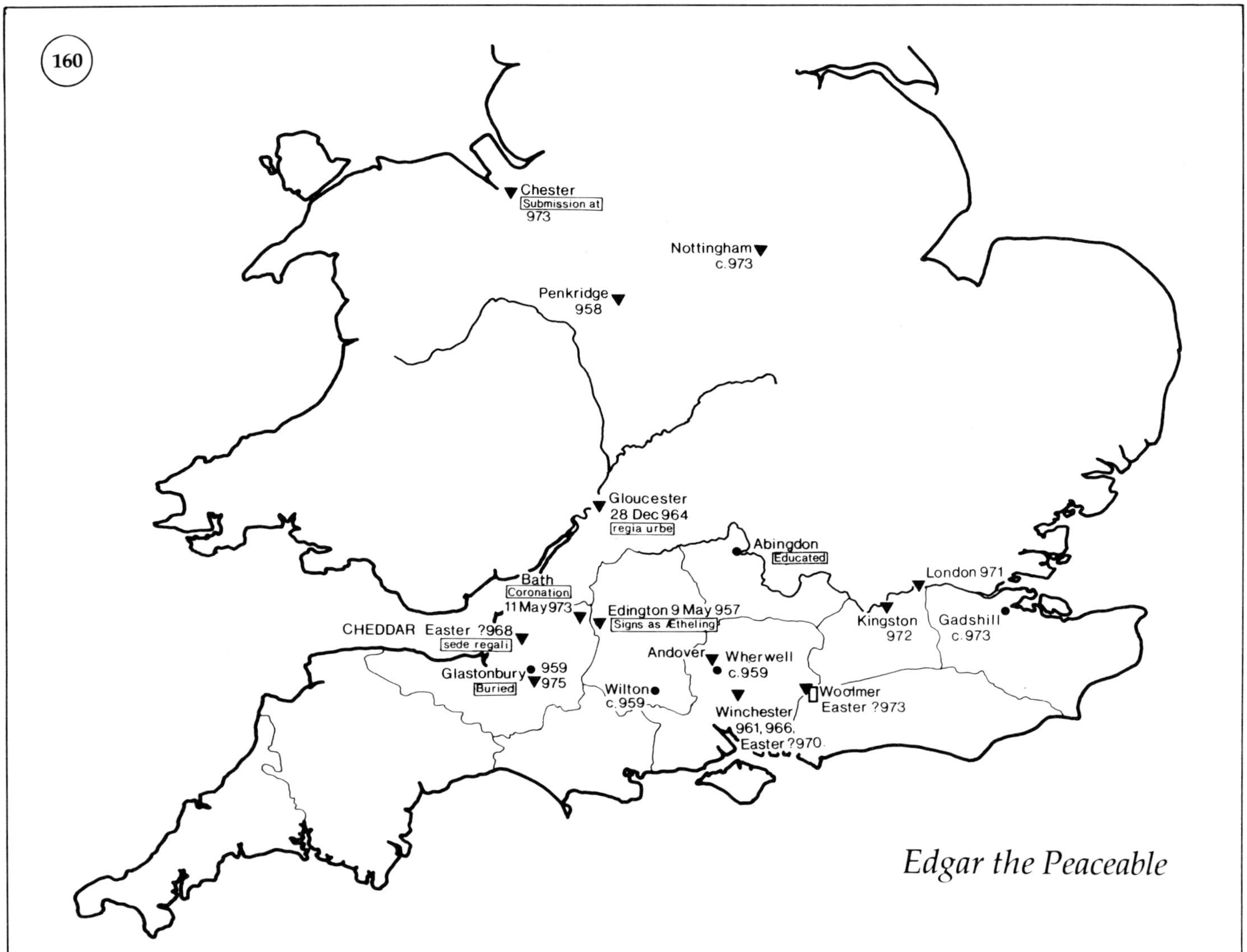

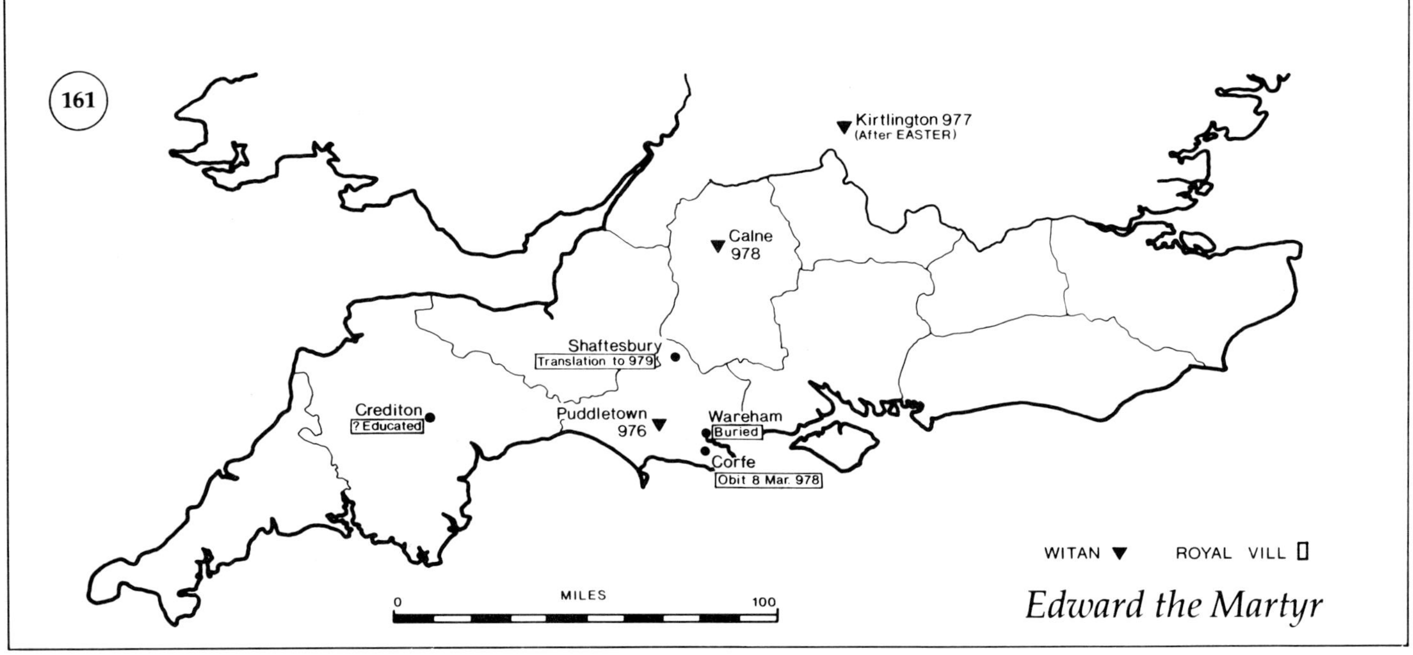

160–161 Itineraries of Edgar the Peaceable and Edward the Martyr

162

163

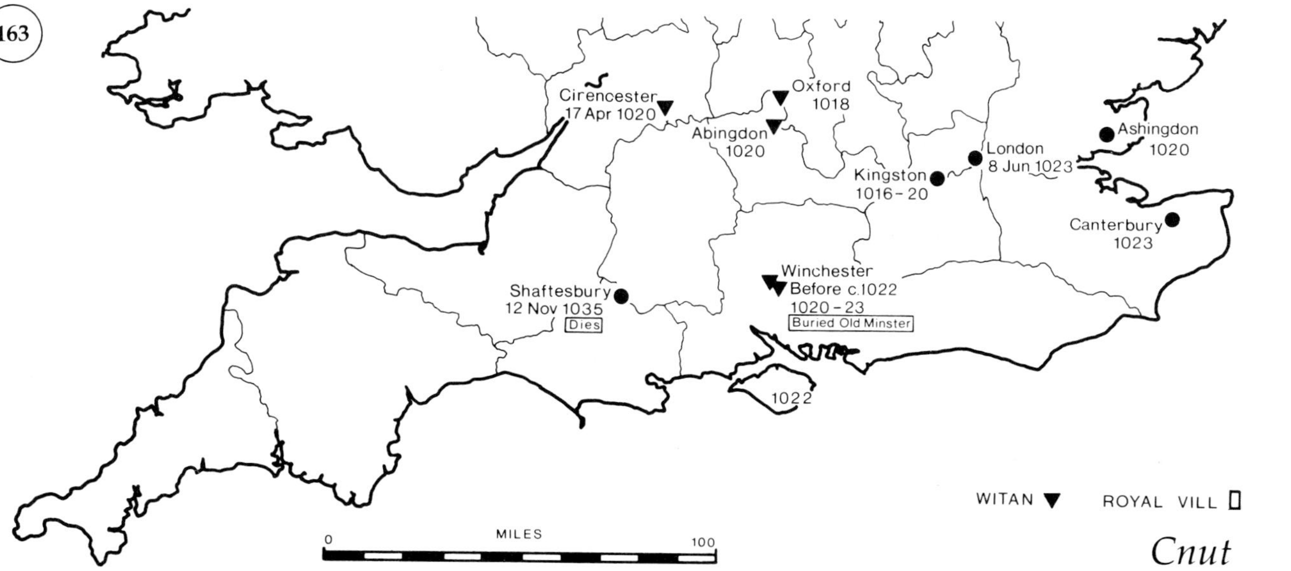

162–163 Itineraries of Ethelred and Cnut

The Fleet (164–166)

1008 *In this year the king ordered that ships should be built unremittingly over all England, namely a warship from 310 hides, and a helmet and corselet from eight hides. (Anglo-Saxon Chronicle)*

The importance of the fleet in late Anglo-Saxon England is often overlooked, but it was active from the days of the kings of Wessex, through the reigns of Alfred the Great and Athelstan to its high point during the reign of Edgar the Peaceable, where it could be seen as an instrument of policy as well as a fighting machine. The fleet was part of a defensive scheme that included the army, which could be called upon in several stages, the **burhs** in which the population sheltered, the **herepaths**, along which the armies moved, and the beacon system which warned the various parts of the system and the fleet.

The evidence for the beacon system has yet to be fully worked out but it appears to be a direct ancestor of the Armada system, the Hampshire portion of which is shown in map **164** with the beacons for which Anglo-Saxon evidence could be inferred named in heavy type. Where these documents (Robertson 1939, no. 72) fit with the evidence for a coastwatch (for example Sawyer, charter no. 1383) is difficult to determine. The first document is a list of those estates belonging to the church of St Paul's in London which sent men to ship; the second is constructed from a letter where another bishopric, that of Sherborne, is complaining that whereas he should have 300 hides to provide a ship, he has lost 33 of those hides.

The administration that lay behind the fleet pre-dates the order of 1008 noted in the Chronicle entry above (Whitelock 1955) as the St Paul's document (map **165**) shows. The involvement of the bishops would appear to be an administrative convenience, but all landowners were liable. The stipulation that a ship should come from 300 hides with a crew of helmeted and armoured men would lead to a figure of some 90 ships and 3,380 armed sailors from Wessex alone (map **166**), and there would be other fleets from the other parts of the kingdom. The threat they were facing could hardly have been a small one.

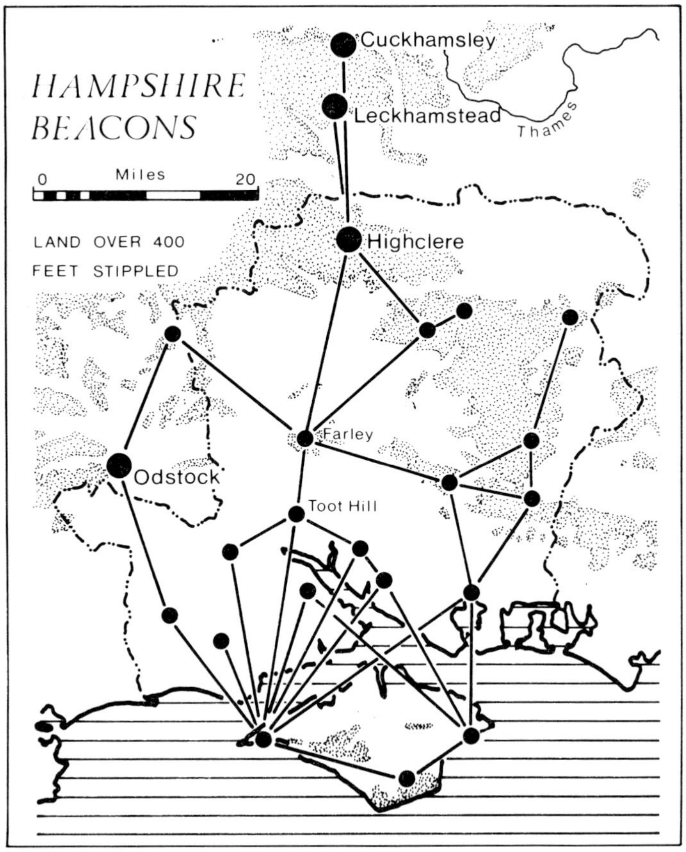

164 Hampshire beacons

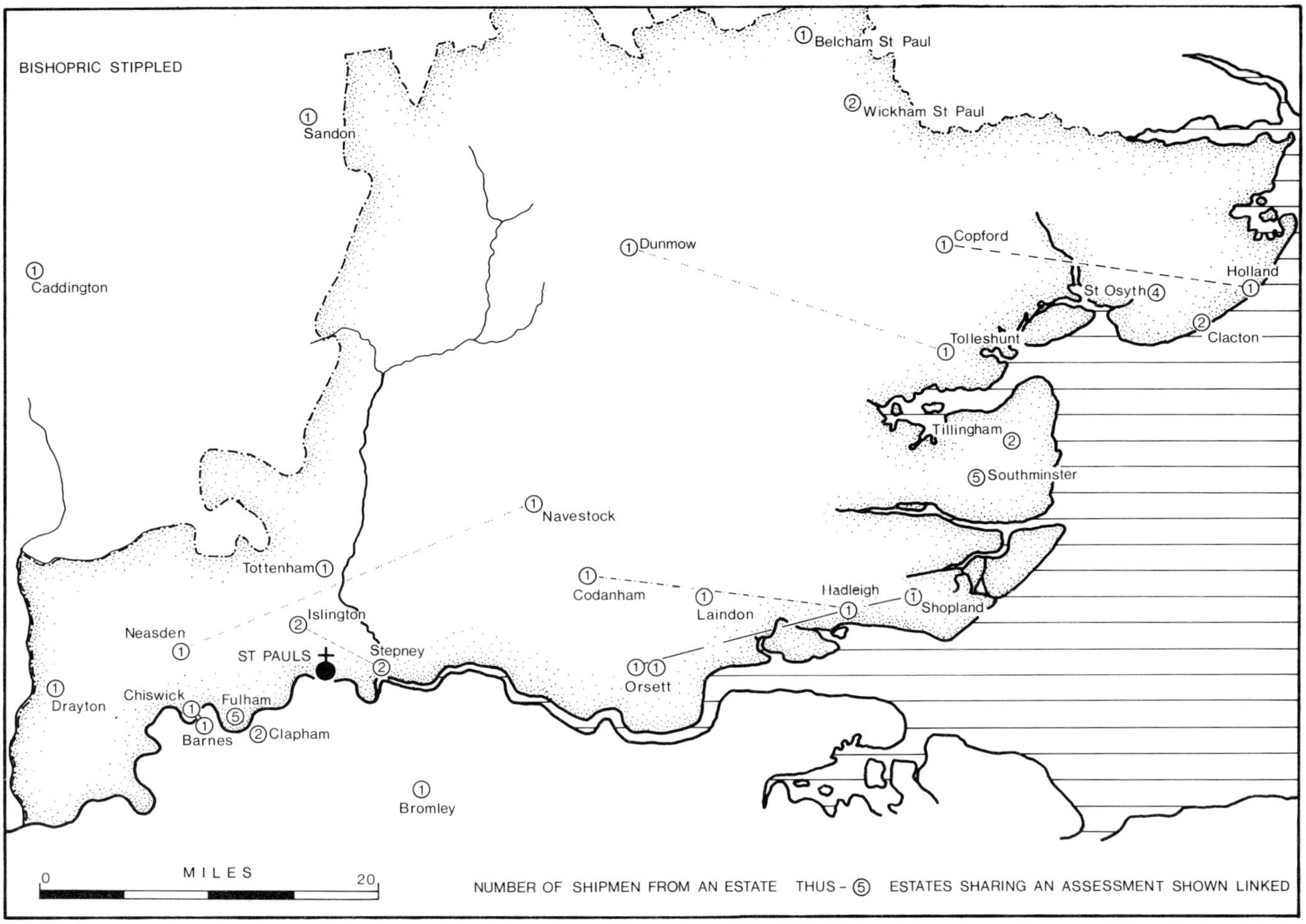

165 Manning a ship from St Paul's Estates 995 × 998

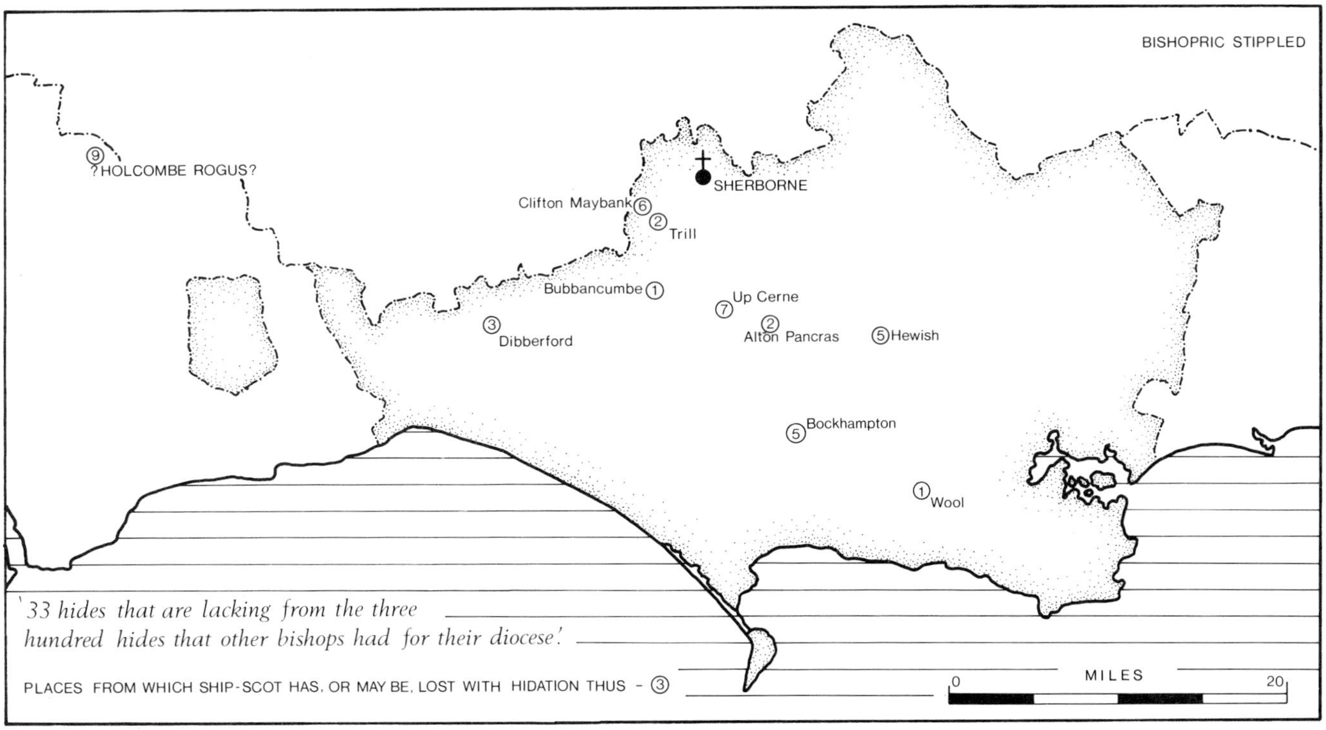

166 Ship-scot for the Bishop of Sherborne 1001 × 1012

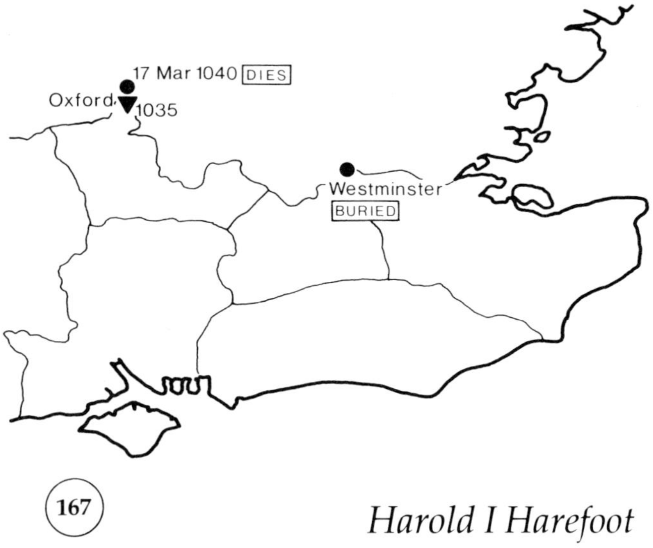

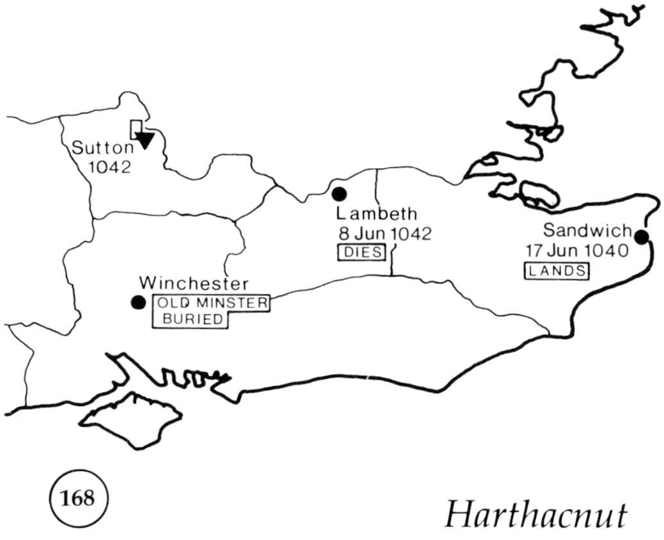

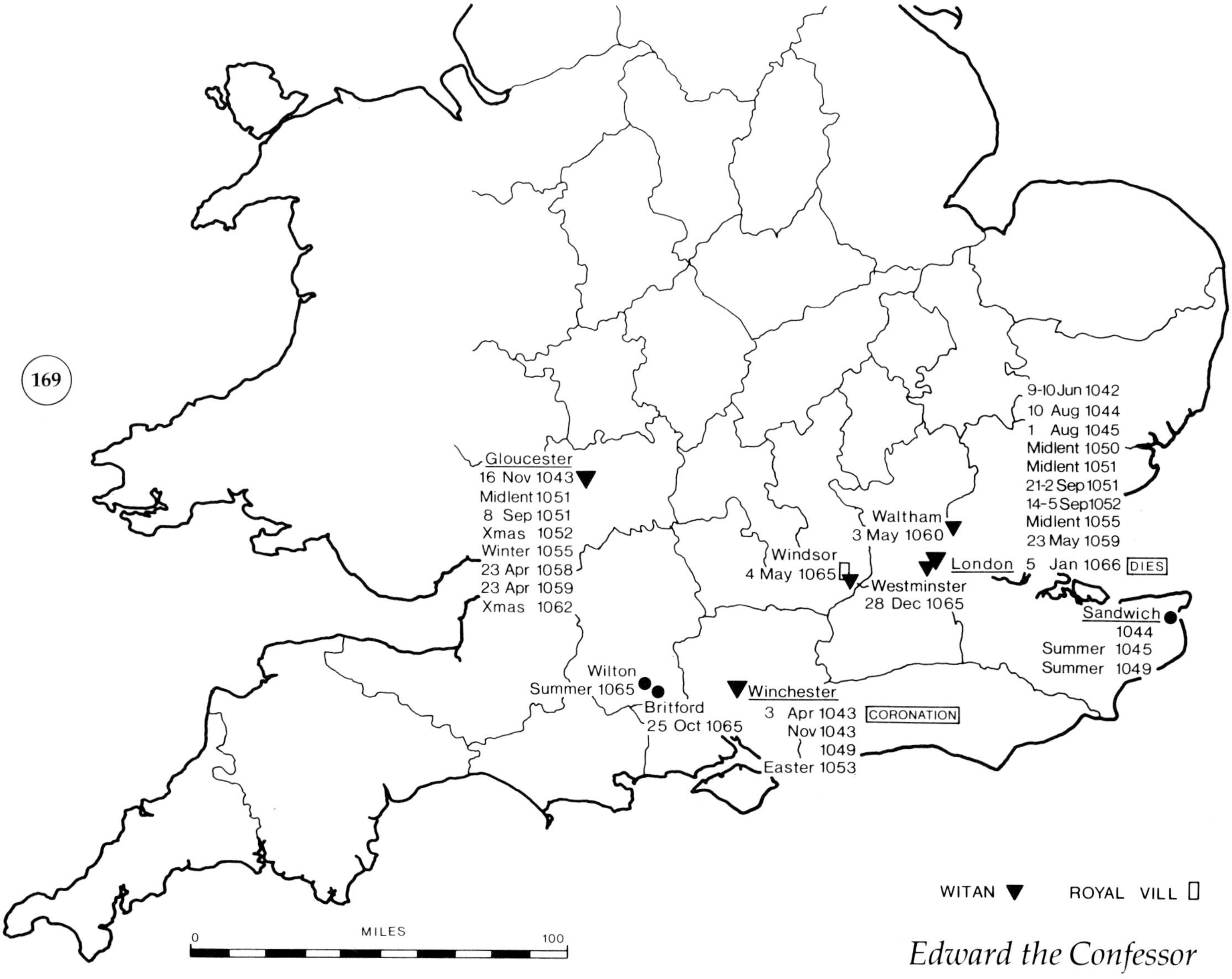

167–169 Itineraries of Harold I Harefoot, Harthacnut and Edward the Confessor

Itineraries of Harold I Harefoot, Harthacnut and Edward the Confessor (167–170)

The small amount of evidence for the reigns of Harold I Harefoot (map **167**) and Harthacnut (map **168**) is hardly enough to sustain the argument that their movements were similar to those of Ethelred and Cnut, with an axis along the Thames Valley.

It is clear that when Cnut died there was a division of the kingdom between Harthacnut's followers and those of Harold. The Chronicle records 'Earl Leofric and almost all the thegns north of the Thames chose Harold to the regency of all England'. There is further information in Florence of Worcester: 'the kingdom of England was divided by lot, and the north part fell to Harold, and the south to Harthacnut.' This situation, which lasted from late in 1035 until 1037, is reflected by the pattern of mints striking in the name of the absent Harthacnut (map **170**).

The itinerary of Edward the Confessor (map **169**) differs from the itineraries of his predecessors in that the king had three urban centres, London, Gloucester, and on a rather smaller scale, Winchester. Perhaps the years spent abroad coupled with the Danish interregnum broke with the traditions of the past and the hunting lands of Somerset had no childhood memories for Edward (he was born at Islip) or perhaps his father had already broken with the past. It is notable that he was crowned at Winchester and not at the traditional site at Kingston.

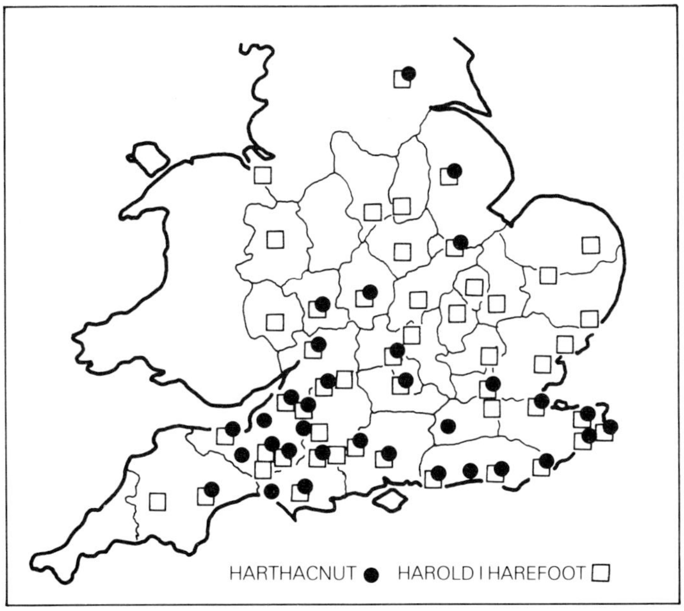

170 Mints for the 1035–1040 issue

171

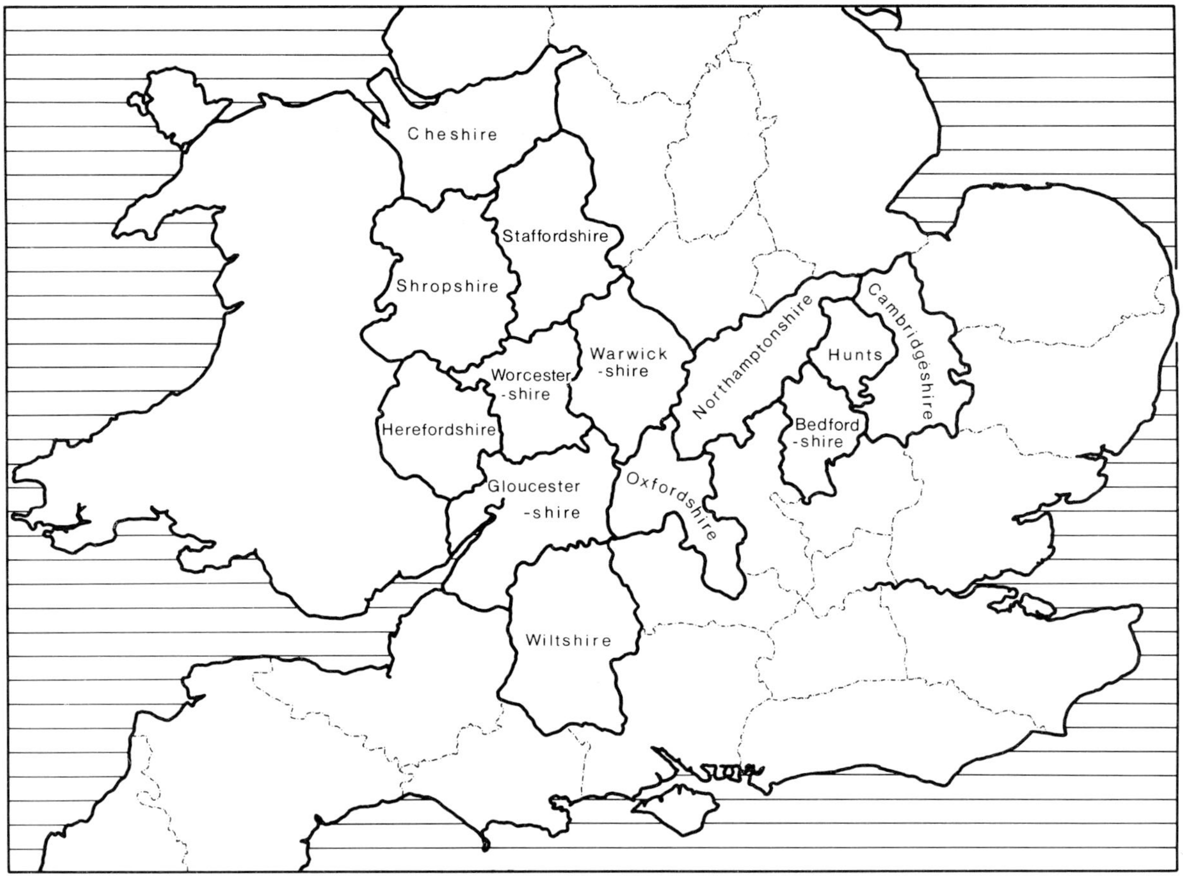

172

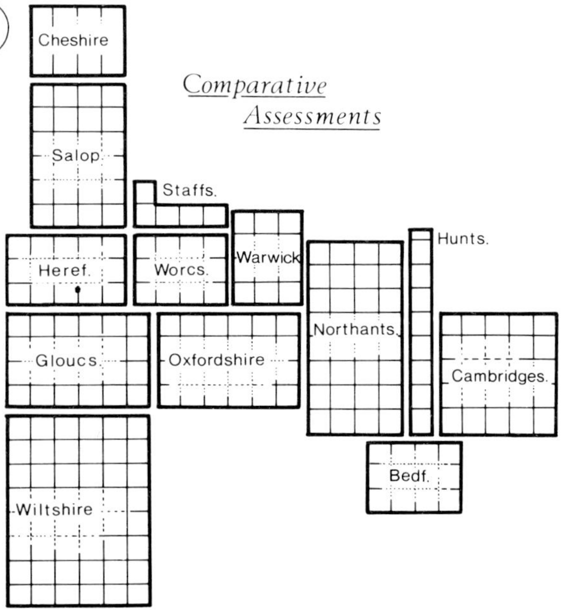

173

COUNTY	COUNTY HIDAGE	Domesday Hundreds	Domesday Hides
WILTSHIRE	4800	40	4050
BEDFORDSHIRE	1200	12	1193
CAMBRIDGESHIRE	2500	17	1315
HUNTINGDONSHIRE	850	8	747
NORTHAMPTONSHIRE	3200	32	1356
GLOUCESTERSHIRE	2400	39	2388
WORCESTERSHIRE	1200	12	1189
HEREFORDSHIRE	1500	16	1324
WARWICKSHIRE	1200	10	1388
OXFORDSHIRE	2400	22	2412
SHROPSHIRE	2400	15	1245
CHESHIRE	1200	12	512
STAFFORDSHIRE	500	5	505

171–173 The County Hidage

The County Hidage (171–173)

Recent work by David Austin has cast doubt on whether the document known as the 'County Hidage' is pre-Conquest, or even if it contains any pre-Conquest material. Whatever it is, the document is interesting, as it deals with an area of Midland England and assigns hidages which are considerably at odds with the Domesday assessments (**171–173**). On balance it may represent a tradition of early assessments and has therefore been included. As the document has often been quoted it is useful to have the information set out. The figures follow Austin whose appraisal appears sound. For another view see Sawyer (1978, 228–9).

Law and Land (174–178)

In late documents we are told that England was divided into three laws, the West Saxon, the Mercian and the Danelaw (map **174**). From this comes the expression for the area of Danish and Scandinavian settlement and influence, the 'Danelaw'. The versions of the 'Law' divisions attached to the county hidage represent the largest extent of the Danelaw in any of the versions known to us, as even London, Middlesex and Buckinghamshire are included.

The Domesday Book contains other indicators of Danish influence. The smallest area of the Danelaw is represented by those shires (map **175**) which were divided into the wapentake rather than the hundred. The area where the tax unit was the carucate and not the hide (map **176**) is rather larger, including Norfolk and Suffolk, whilst the area where land units were counted not in fives, as in the south, but in the Scandinavian twelves is an amalgam of both areas (map **177**). Division into these groups is not always clear cut, as in Essex, where there are a few groups of five-hide units.

These permanent alterations in the legal traditions of the land do not fit comfortably with other definitions of the territory of the Danelaw, such as the treaty line between Alfred and Guthrum (map **70**) or the distribution of place names (**68**) or graves (**67**).

In the first half of the tenth century the old divisions of Mercia were abolished by the West Saxons, who then proceeded to shire the area in their hands. This would seem to have been part of the organization of the defences, for each shire was designed to contribute to, and be protected by, the **burh** within it. Thus the shires of the West Midlands received the names of their **burhs**: Gloucestershire, Warwickshire and so on. One of these shires was set up around Winchcombe but the shire was annexed to Gloucestershire during the ealdormanry of Eadric Streona 'who tore up shires as if they were paper'. That this is not the whole story is clear from map **178**, which shows that the work of Eadric Streona in the early years of the eleventh century involved the inclusion of large areas of lands belonging to the church of Worcester into that shire thus giving the whole area the patchwork effect that survived into this century. The map itself is based on Cotton Tiberius A xiii, Hemming's Cartulary, which contains the earliest surviving charter collection (as opposed to individual charters). Although the cartulary is biased against Eadric, it is an essential source for the period and area.

The reconstruction of the shire of Winchcombeshire has been attempted (Finberg 1961, 228–35) but it is likely that this shire ran to the north of the boundary of Gloucestershire and reached the Severn.

174–177 Law and land

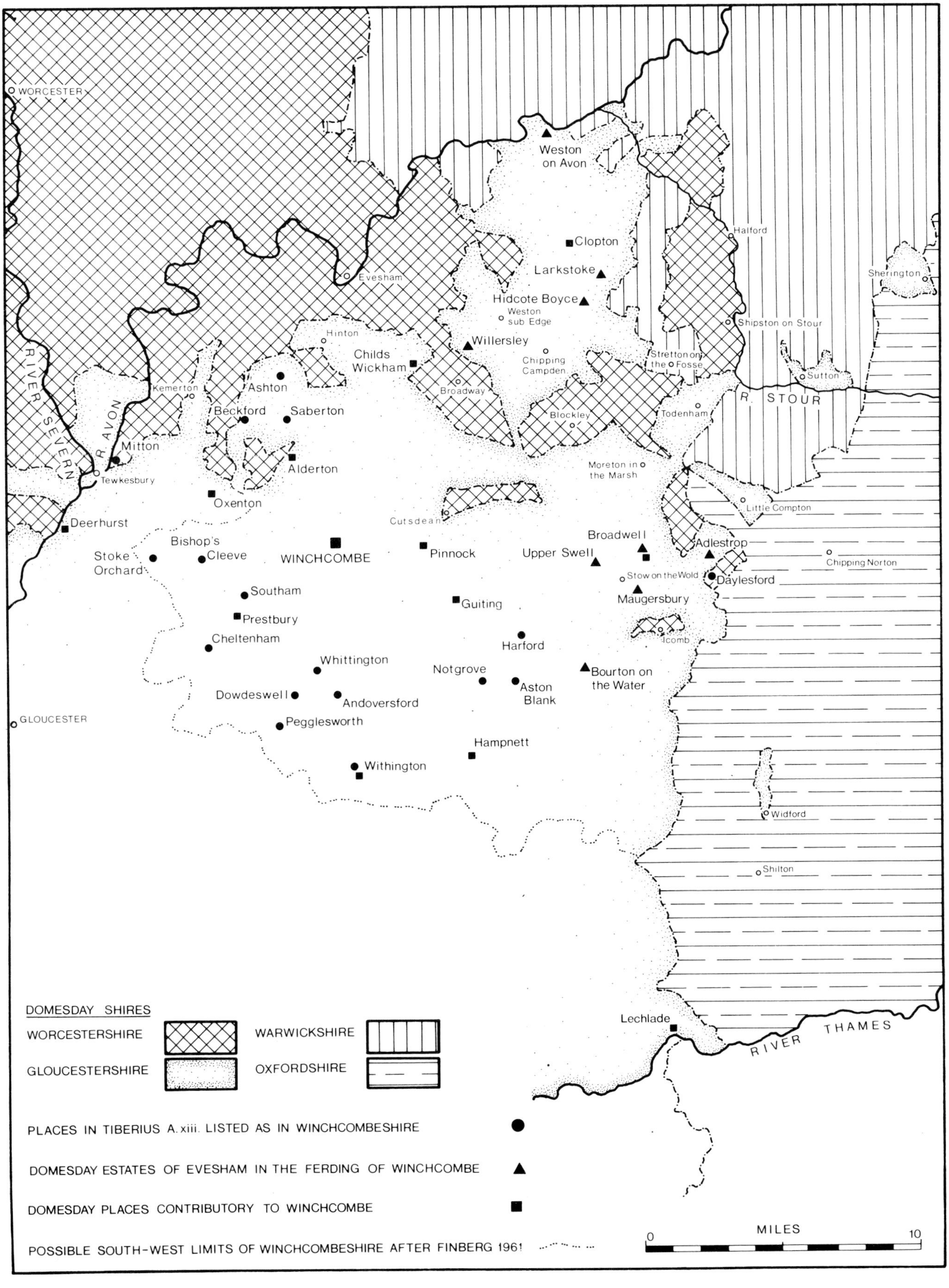

178 North-east Gloucestershire showing changes in shire boundaries

Landholding in 1066 (179–187)

The Domesday Survey used juries of local men to reconstruct the ownerships of a particular district in January of 1066, as this was the time of legal probity before the usurper Harold and the disturbances which followed. We therefore have an accurate statement of the holdings of the late Anglo-Saxon monarchy, the earls, the church and the thegns. Although it is at the end of the period, it allows us to examine the eleventh century and also to see patterns extending back at least to the monastic revival and, in the case of the king's holdings, back to the West Saxon state.

The major secular landholders in 1066, TRE, the time of King Edward, were the king himself (**179**), the Queen (**180**), the widespread Godwin family (**181**) (of which Queen Edith was a member), and the family of Leofric (**182**). When these holdings are calculated in value, as in **183**, then it will be seen that the holdings of the king, in demesne lands, are almost equalled by the holdings of the Godwin family. The holdings of Harold II, Godwinson, must have been enormous as they brought together both sets of lands. It is a moot point, however, whether the kings of the first half of the tenth century had fewer lands than Edward the Confessor; it is quite possible that the holdings of Athelstan, incorporating the royal holdings of Wessex, Mercia and Northumbria, were considerably larger than Edward's. It was the mid-tenth century 'reforms' that may have dissipated the royal domain.

In 1066 Harold held the largest individual holding and it may have been larger, as it is not known who actually held those lands entered in Domesday as belonging to Earl Godwin (who had died in 1053). These lands were mainly in Sussex and were possibly administered by Harold along with his own. The Leofric family holding compares badly with the Godwin family total.

The earldoms were mapped by Freeman (1870) and Barlow (1970, 358–9) as a useful aid to the understanding of the late Saxon office of earl (maps **184** and **185**). The mapping is based on the addressing of the royal writs and it can be appreciated that this information is far from complete, especially when one is attempting to follow changes in a short period (see map **32**). From the reign of Cnut the holdings of the family of Godwin are paramount in the south, with the family of Leofric in control in the midlands. The earldom of Northumbria followed its own line of descent for most of the period. It would be possible to map all the earls' holdings in Domesday but the two, lands of Earl Harold, map **181**, and the lands of the Leofric family, map **182**, appear to be the most informative. When the two are compared, the clearer division of responsibility for the important Welsh border region can be seen.

The values of the holdings shown in **183** should be seen in relation to the strength of the Church. On **249** the total income of Church holdings is something in excess of £9,550, larger than the king's holdings and the holdings of the house of Godwin combined. These figures do not include the amounts for the lands of the bishops, houses of secular canons or parish churches.

There are other ways of showing the vast holdings of the Church at the close of the reign of Edward the Confessor, and it is arguable that the proportion had not changed greatly in the eleventh century. One way is to arrange the holdings into a 'pie' diagram (**186**) for two typical shires, and it can be seen that the Church forms the largest block of holdings.

A second way is to take two other shires and equate Domesday holdings with ecclesiastical parishes of the early nineteenth century, marking the owner of the holding. The resultant cartoon (map **187**) may not be correct in detail but it is extremely informative in general. In these shires there were perhaps unusually large holdings of the church of Winchester around Taunton, the monastery of Glastonbury's extensive holdings in east Somerset, the Bath Abbey estates, the lands of the church of Malmesbury, the bishop of Ramsbury's holdings north of Bedwyn and the nunnery of Wilton's holdings in south Wiltshire. Against this it should be remembered that this was the home area of the tenth-century kings, although the estates in south Wiltshire had passed to the church since Alfred's day, and one must assume a similar diminution of the royal demesne around Cheddar and Axbridge. The map does show the attempts of the kings to increase their revenue from the royal estates by the founding, mainly in the eleventh century, of the small market centres, **ports**, on their lands.

Maps **179–182** show distributions of demesne lands only, and in some cases the size of the holdings has been calculated from the ploughlands. Carucates have been treated, together with sulungs, in the same way as hides. The attempt has been to create the visual image, and a close similarity would have been achieved using values; however, it is felt that the value of the lands in the south-west is still underrated.

The lands of the king do show a concentration in the south and west, with northern Mercia not well represented. The large estates in Wiltshire, Somerset and Dorset show up well, but the king has a series of estates in the Thames valley. The value of royal rights in the towns and from various other dues are not shown.

The queen's dower lands in Somerset are shown and there are some unexplained holdings in Hereford and Worcester; the dower lands in the Thames valley date back at least to the birth of Edward the Confessor but the western holdings are probably more ancient. Winchester was held to be the queen's morning gift.

The succession of earldoms held by Harold are well represented on the map showing his lands and it is complemented by the lands of the Leofric family which covers those shires not covered by Harold, although the Leofric estates are also to be found around London, presumably to give them a base when called south on royal business.

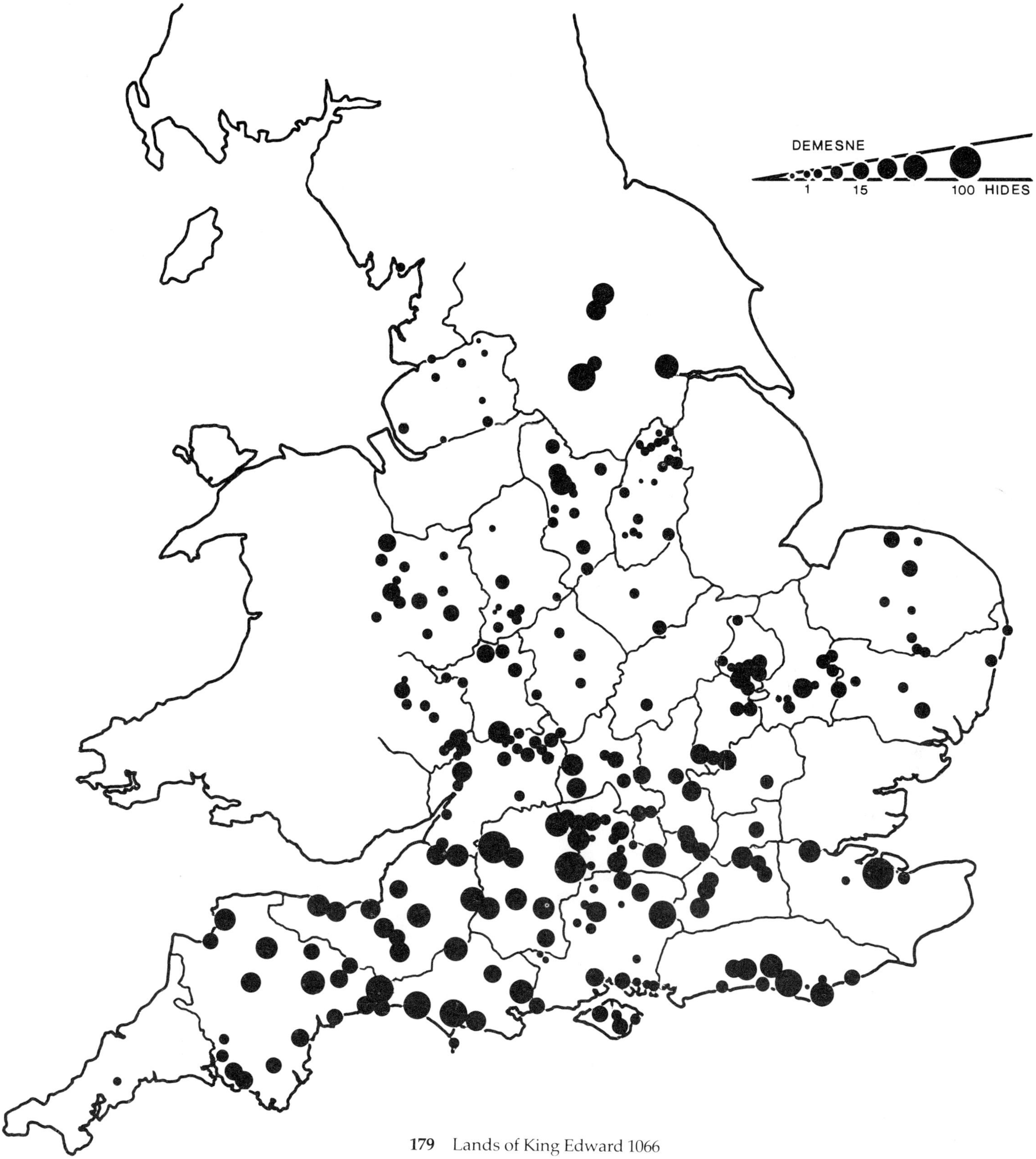

179 Lands of King Edward 1066

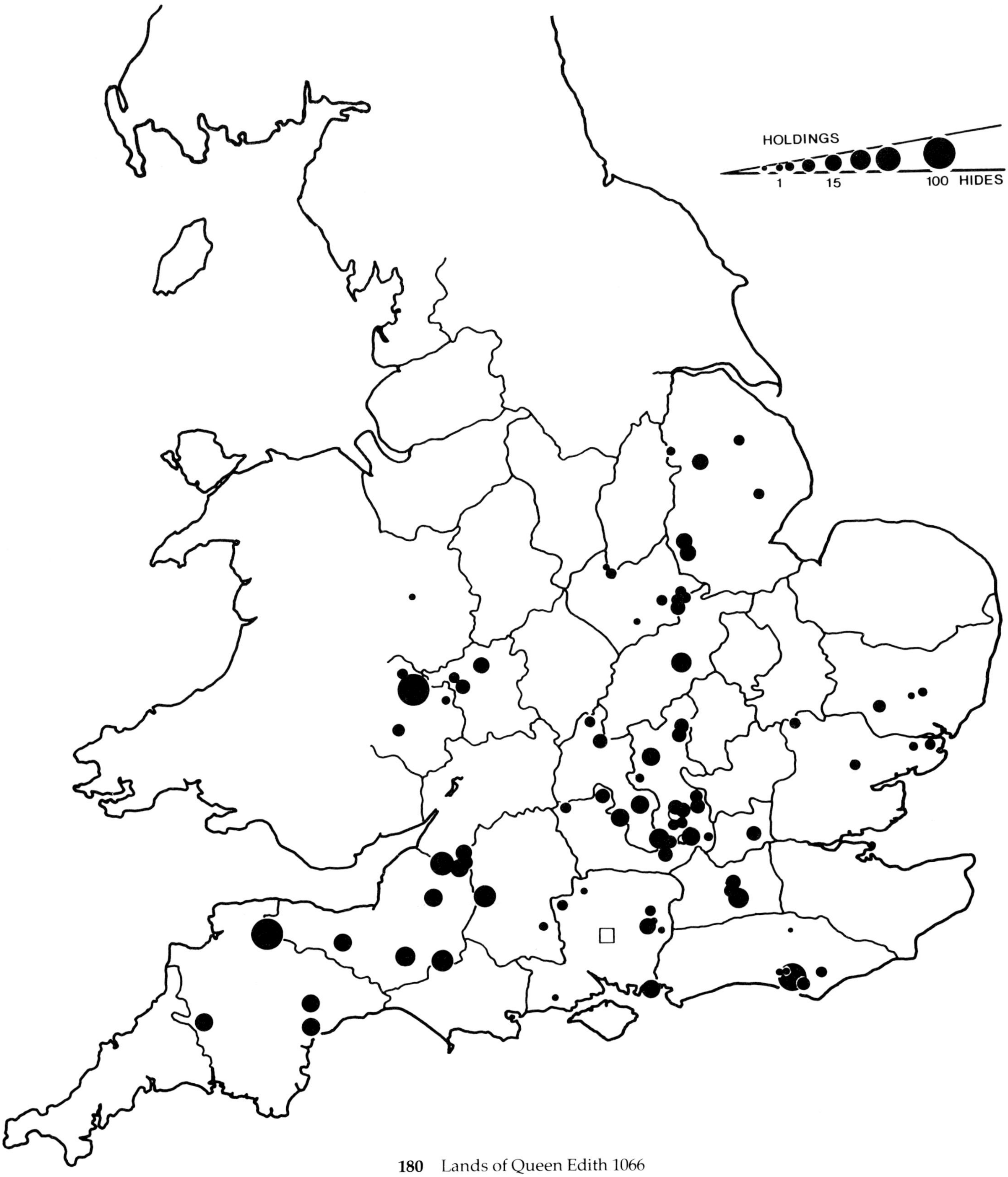

180 Lands of Queen Edith 1066

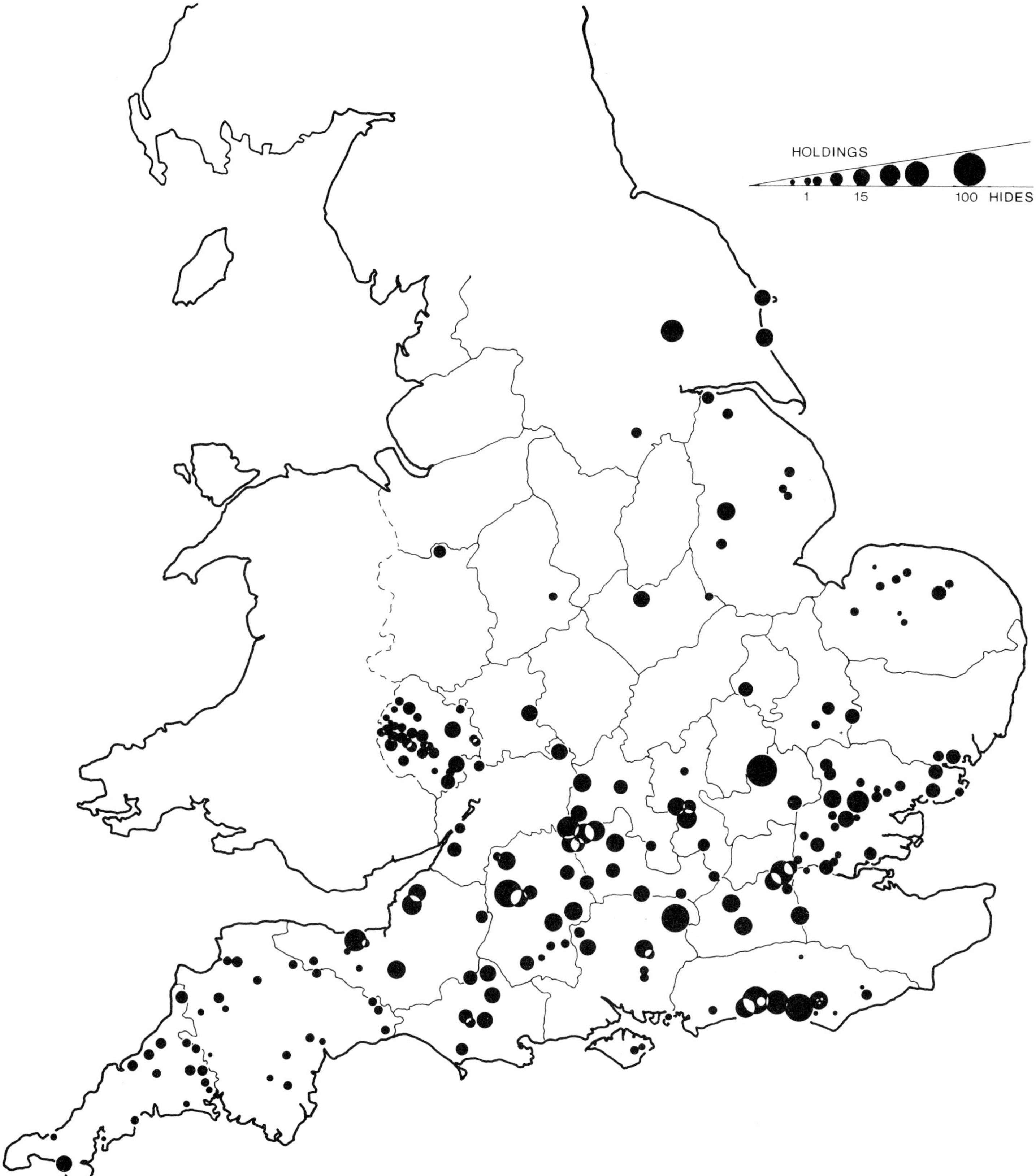

181 Lands of Earl Harold 1066

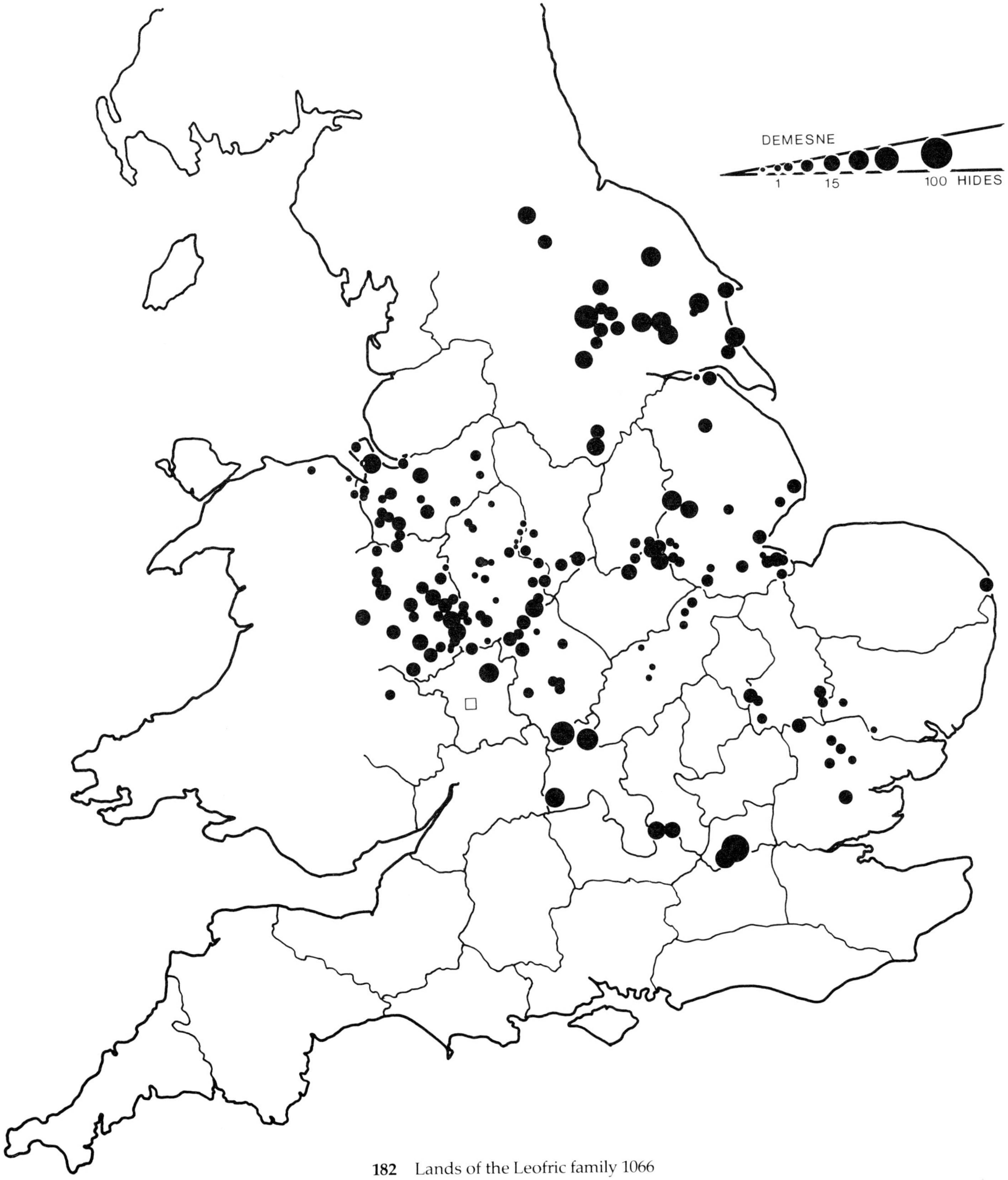

182 Lands of the Leofric family 1066

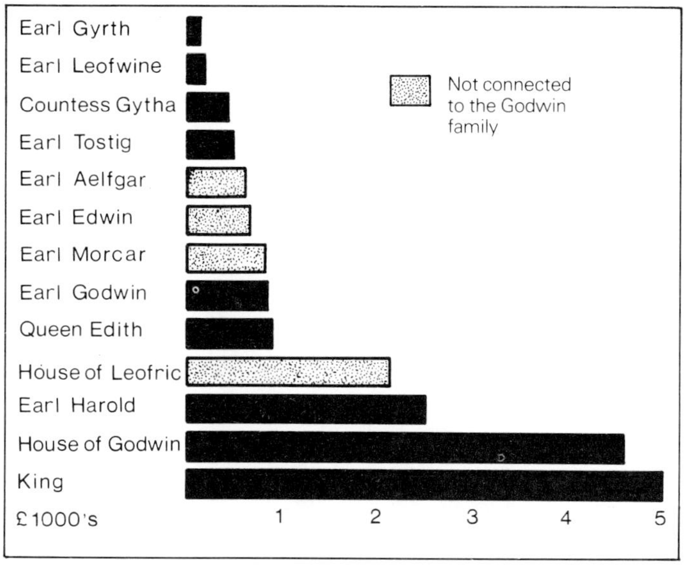

183 Value of lands held by the king and leading families in 1066

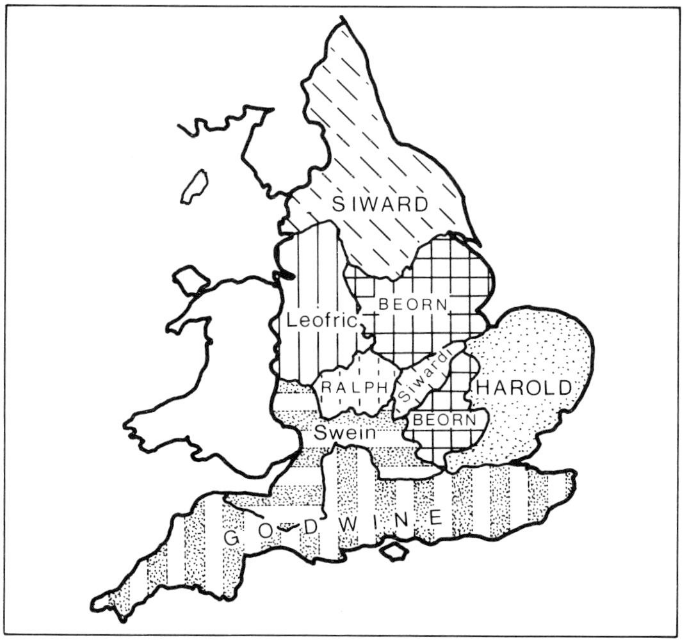

184 Earldoms in 1045 (after Freeman 1869–75)

185 Earldoms in 1065 (after Freeman 1869–75)

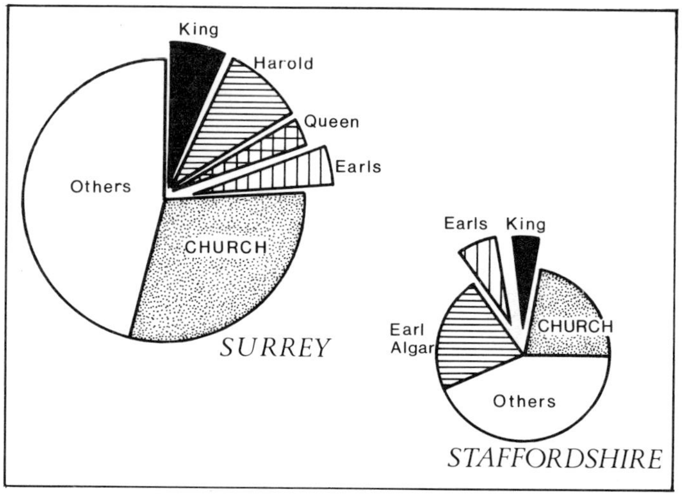

186 The proportional holdings of demesne lands in the shires of Staffordshire and Surrey in 1066

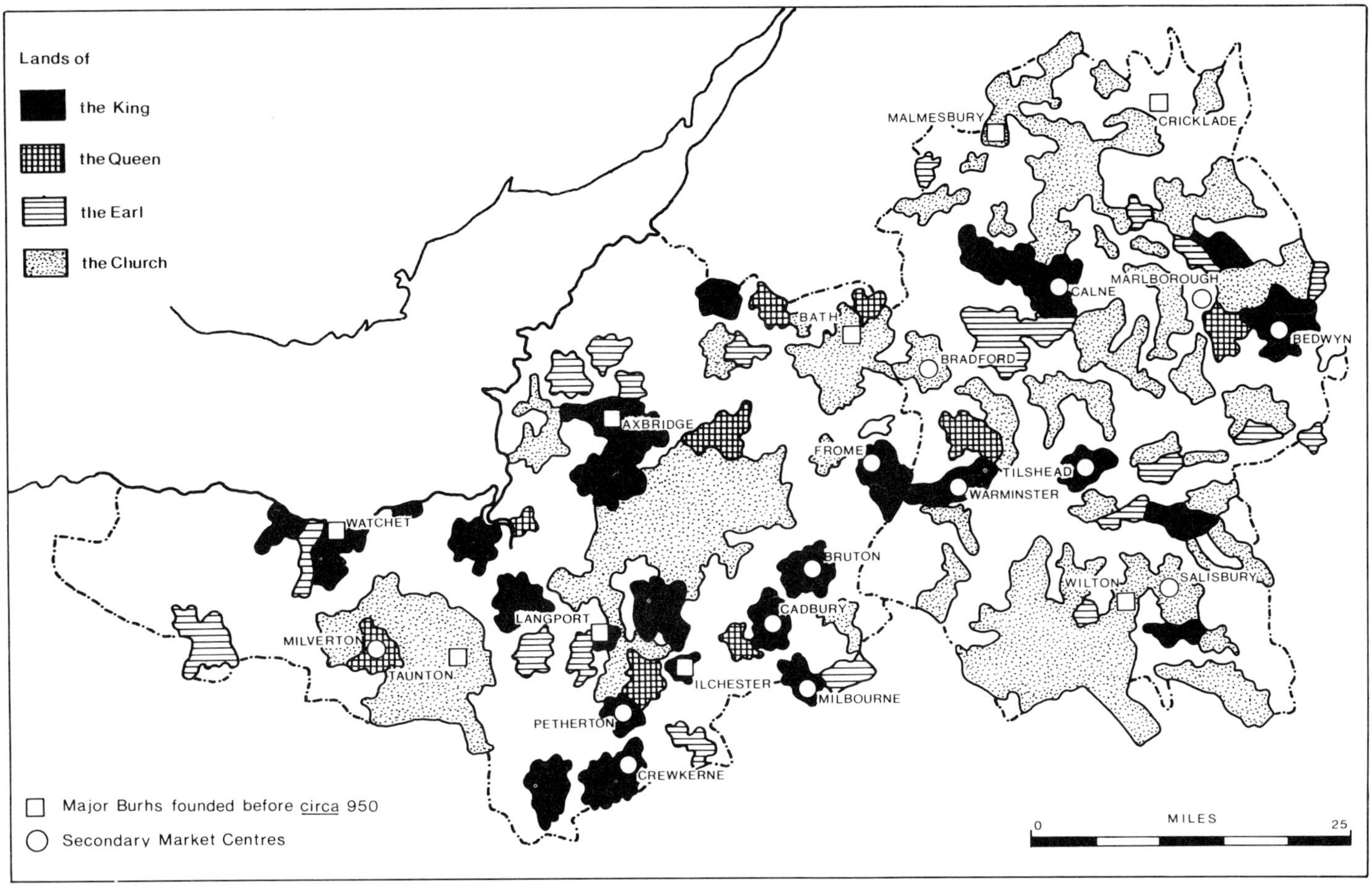

187 Landowners and markets in Somerset and Wiltshire in 1066

The Economy

Research into the early medieval period has progressed beyond the point where it is possible to believe in the extremely simple economy once postulated for the period. It was once, wrongly, supposed that most estates, vills, villages or settlements were self-sufficient. Everything needed on the estate was produced on the estate, trade was limited to a tiny amount of luxury goods for the nobility and the king, the surplus of any estate was eaten up by the king, noble or bishop travelling with his retinue 'eating up his rents'. The village sat in the middle of its fields; beyond, the meadow; beyond that the waste and finally the great wild wood. In fact, the charter bounds show that many estates had their fields abutting and one of the commonest features on the boundaries was the road, way or path with its bridge or ford — all indicating frequent movement from place to place. Common sense shows that many commodities were unavailable on the 'average' estate — few of them would have been naturally endowed with supplies of iron, salt, lead, hone and building stone, wine, fish, flax, antler and the hundred and one requirements of the late Saxon economy. Many of these commodities are the product of specialist communities — charcoal, metals, salt and fish spring readily to mind. The following maps highlight those parts of the economy that can be charted but it should always be remembered that from the time of Offa onwards estates had to find an increasing part of their taxes, dues and renders in coin: the only way to obtain this was by the export of goods or services.

Before embarking on discussion of the economic life of Anglo-Saxon England the limitations of the evidence should be clearly recognized, as these are inherent in distribution maps in particular and should be borne in mind when using this section. The problems of one of the most important classes of evidence (pottery and ceramics) are such that it has been decided not to attempt to cover an extremely difficult and rapidly expanding subject. The situation has recently been summarized (Hurst 1976) and sounds the warning that in the last two decades the earlier distributions and received truths have been torn up and discarded. The warning note sounded in Hurst's paper applies to much else in the study of the economy but it should be remembered that pottery was being made and traded from many centres in middle and late Saxon England. There was also a thriving import trade from many centres from the Rhineland to Aquitaine. All this has developed so rapidly that maps drawn in 1958 have now to be discarded.

Minerals, Salt and Lime (188–192)

There is a unique charter reference to an iron mine in Kent as early as 689 (see map **188**). The rest of the evidence is scattered but with the collation of archaeological and Domesday evidence TRE the pattern emerges of widespread ironworking. It would be fatuous to add a map of iron artefacts as this would simply show excavated settlements where the soil conditions are suitable for the preservation of iron. The spread of ironworking must have been extensive due to the widespread sources of iron; the blooms of iron would then be traded to those areas lacking their own sources.

The same range of evidence that is available for iron can be used for salt even though archaeological evidence is lacking (map **189**). The importance of salt in the early economy is obvious and it is not surprising that it is widely represented in the charter evidence. Three areas can be recognized for supply and distribution: the important Droitwich brine springs serving most of Midland England through a series of pre-Conquest saltways, a pattern confirmed by the Domesday evidence; the east and south served by coastal saltpans (it should be noted that there are none in the Bristol Channel, presumably due to the turbid and silty waters); and the perhaps later Saltwichs of Cheshire serving the north.

It becomes clear from contrasting the availability of limestone and chalk with the known pre-Conquest mortared stone buildings (map **190**) that some lime would have to be moved considerable distances to the mainly religious building sites.

The evidence for lead-working comes both from archaeology, in that it is a common find on archaeological sites of the period, and from charter mentions, either of a mine in the bounds at Stoke Bishop or of lead renders as at Wirksworth (map **191**). It was known abroad and was used in England for roofs and, more importantly, for the construction of brine vats in the salt-making process, an example of the interlocking of two specialist communities. It is usually thought that silver was obtained by the cupellation process from lead but it should be noted we have no evidence for it in England, nor do we have evidence of the working of lead in the Mendips or the far north.

There are claims, though I do not know their basis, for the working of the Shropshire copper deposits and there is the inferential evidence that the Trewhiddle hoard was found in a tinstream for the working of that metal (map **192**). However, apart from the fact that the metals are found in use as objects or slag, we have no evidence for the sources of these metals in England at the time

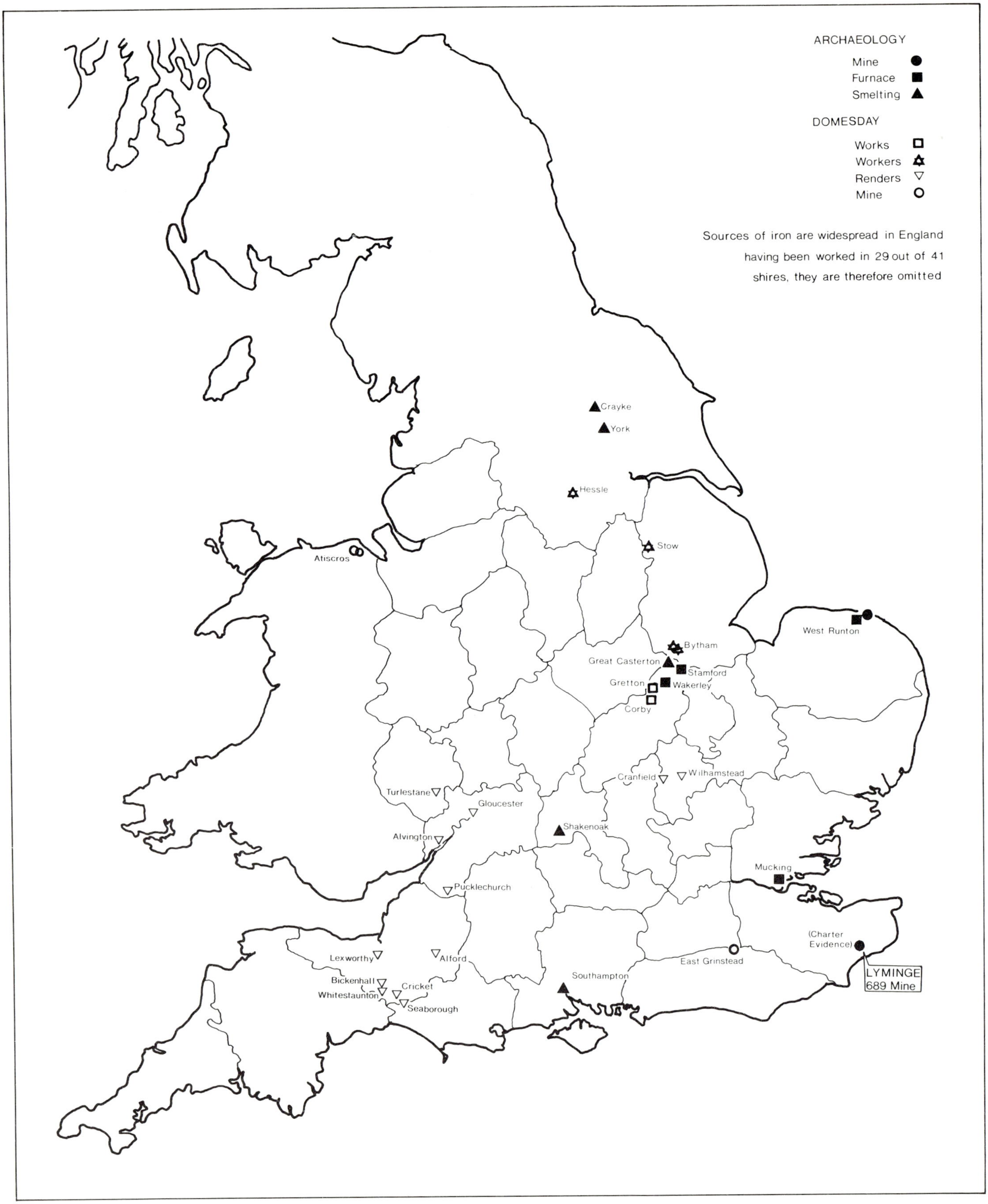
ARCHAEOLOGY
Mine
Furnace
Smelting
DOMESDAY
Works
Workers
Renders
Mine
Sources of iron are widespread in England having been worked in 29 out of 41 shires, they are therefore omitted
Crayke
York
Hessle
Stow
Atiscros
West Runton
Bytham
Great Casterton
Stamford
Gretton
Wakerley
Corby
Cranfield
Wilhamstead
Turlestane
Gloucester
Alvington
Shakenoak
Mucking
Pucklechurch
(Charter Evidence)
LYMINGE
689 Mine
Lexworthy
Alford
East Grinstead
Southampton
Bickenhall
Cricket
Whitestaunton
Seaborough

188 Iron

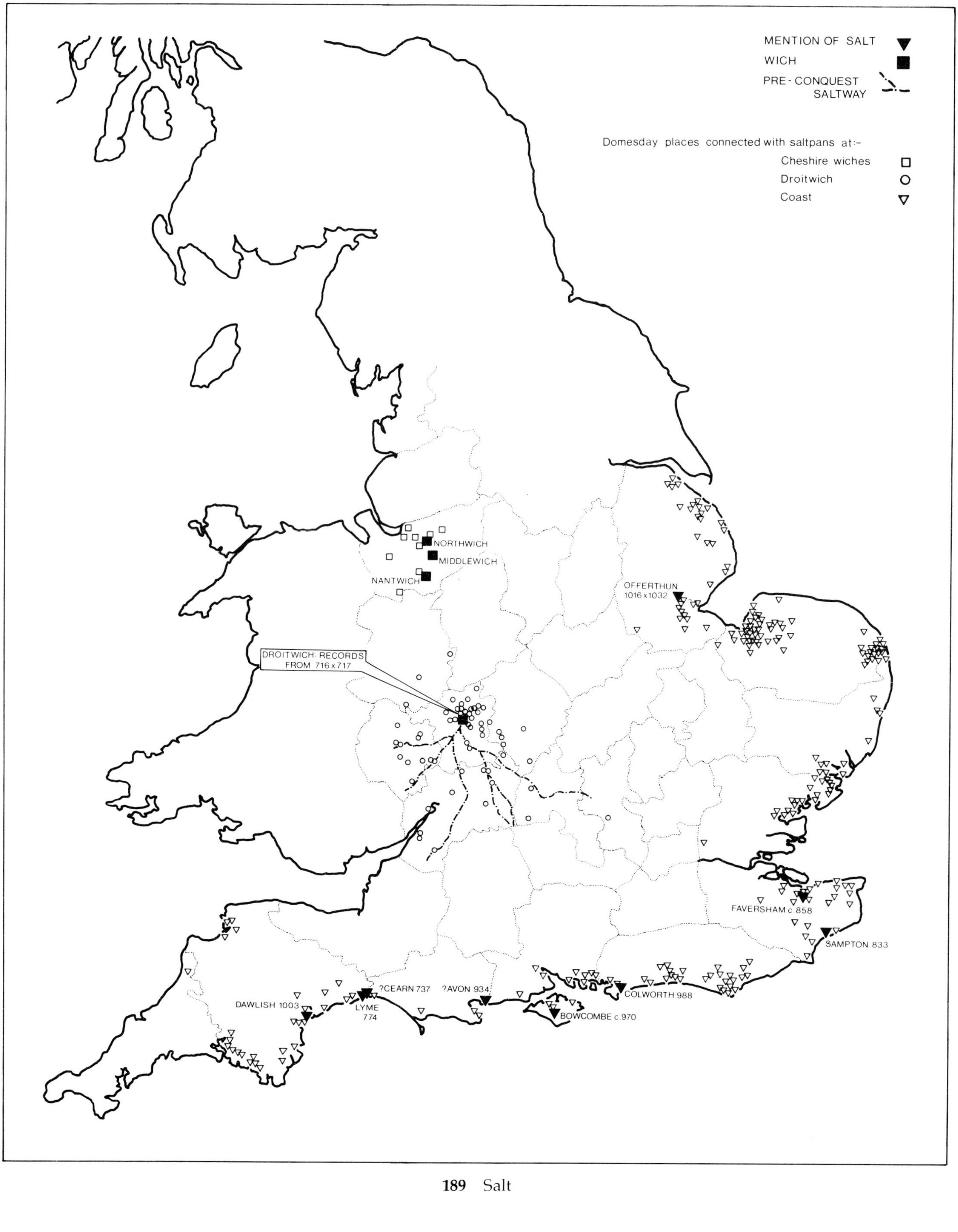

MENTION OF SALT
WICH
PRE-CONQUEST SALTWAY
Domesday places connected with saltpans at:-
Cheshire wiches
Droitwich
Coast
NORTHWICH
MIDDLEWICH
NANTWICH
OFFERTHUN 1016 x 1032
DROITWICH: RECORDS FROM 716 x 717
FAVERSHAM c. 858
SAMPTON 833
?CEARN 737
?AVON 934
DAWLISH 1003
LYME 774
COLWORTH 988
BOWCOMBE c. 970

189 Salt

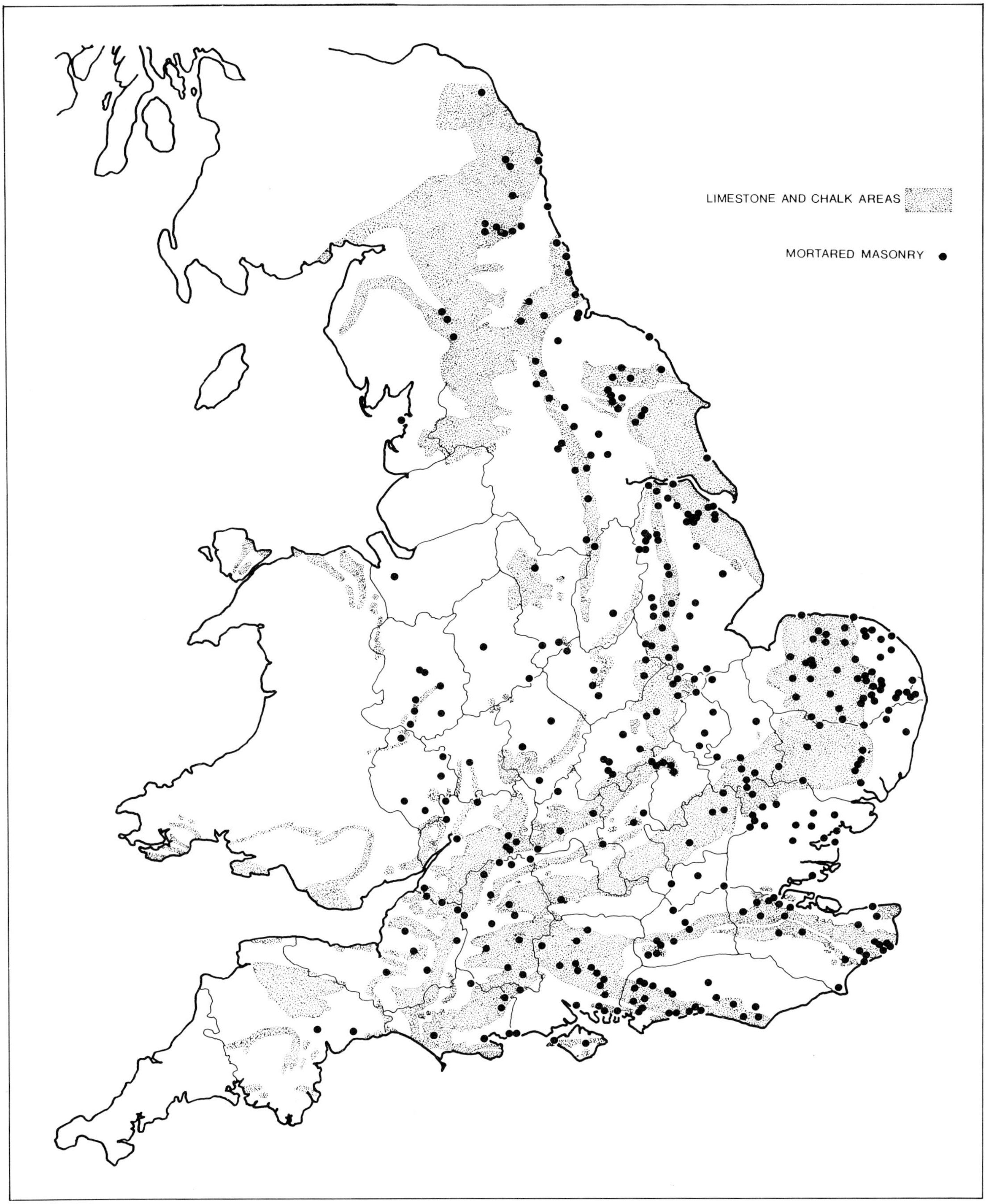

190 Lime

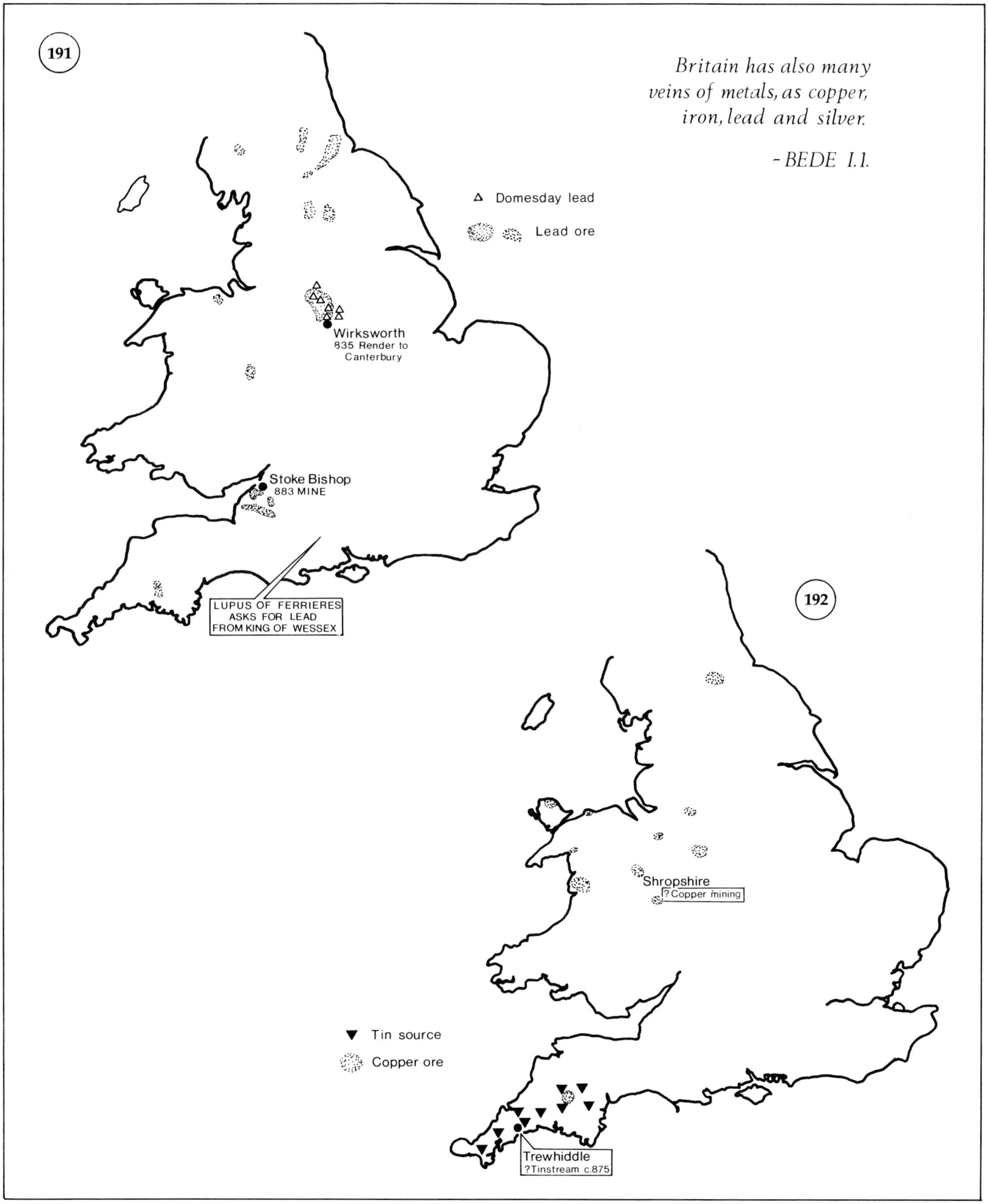

191–192 Lead and other metals

Agriculture (193–196)

This atlas unfortunately includes very little information on the subject of agriculture: 'it is one of the real scandals of Anglo-Saxon archaeology that we still know less about the context and practices of the Anglo-Saxon "village" than we do about the Iron Age farm and the Roman Villa' (Graham-Campbell 1977, 520). The medieval distribution of the open-field system is well known and many inferences have been drawn from it by earlier historians of the Anglo-Saxon period (map **193**). It may be that the system is early and is linked with the entry phase of Saxon settlement. When this problem is finally faced we shall expect the answer to throw light on the parallel problems of the open-field systems in France (map **194**). They appear to have some correlation in this area with the distribution of Germanic place names, indicating settlement as opposed to areas of hegemony in the Frankish entrance phase (map **195**).

Of the agricultural maps that can be drawn only the one of vineyards has been included as all the rest contain so little information as to be practically useless. The vineyard map (**196**) is of interest even if in fact it shows more information on climatic amelioration than on general agricultural practice.

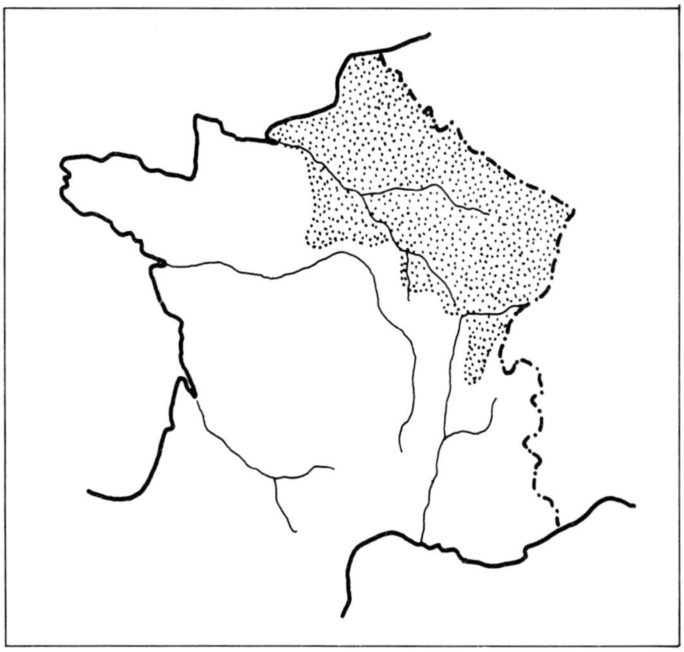

194 Open fields in France

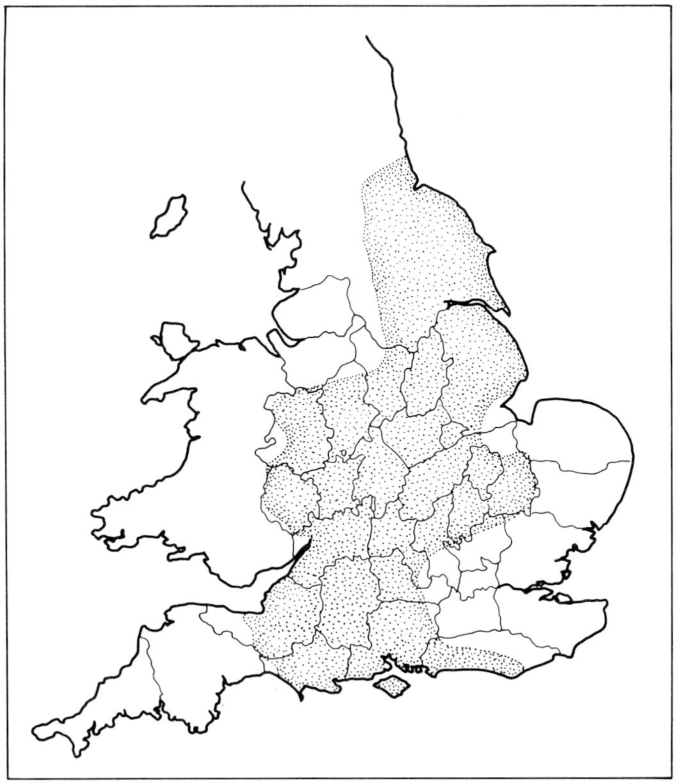

193 Medieval open fields in England

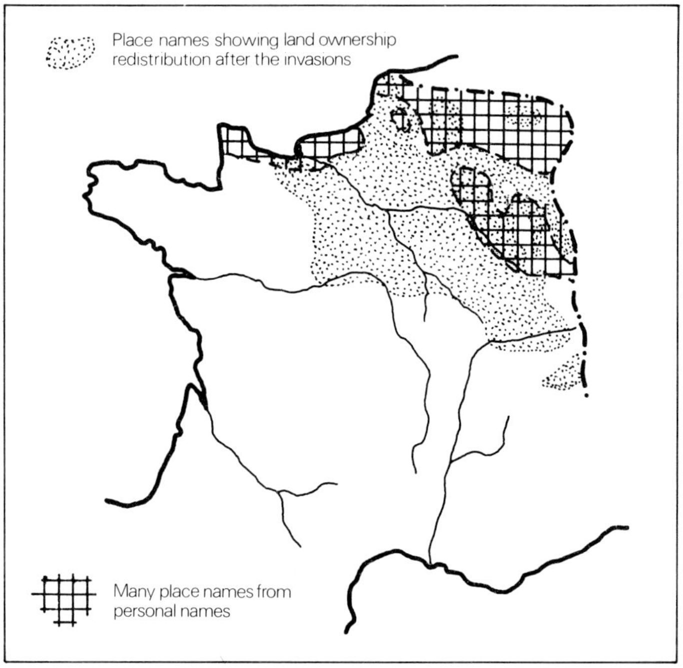

195 Germanic place names in France

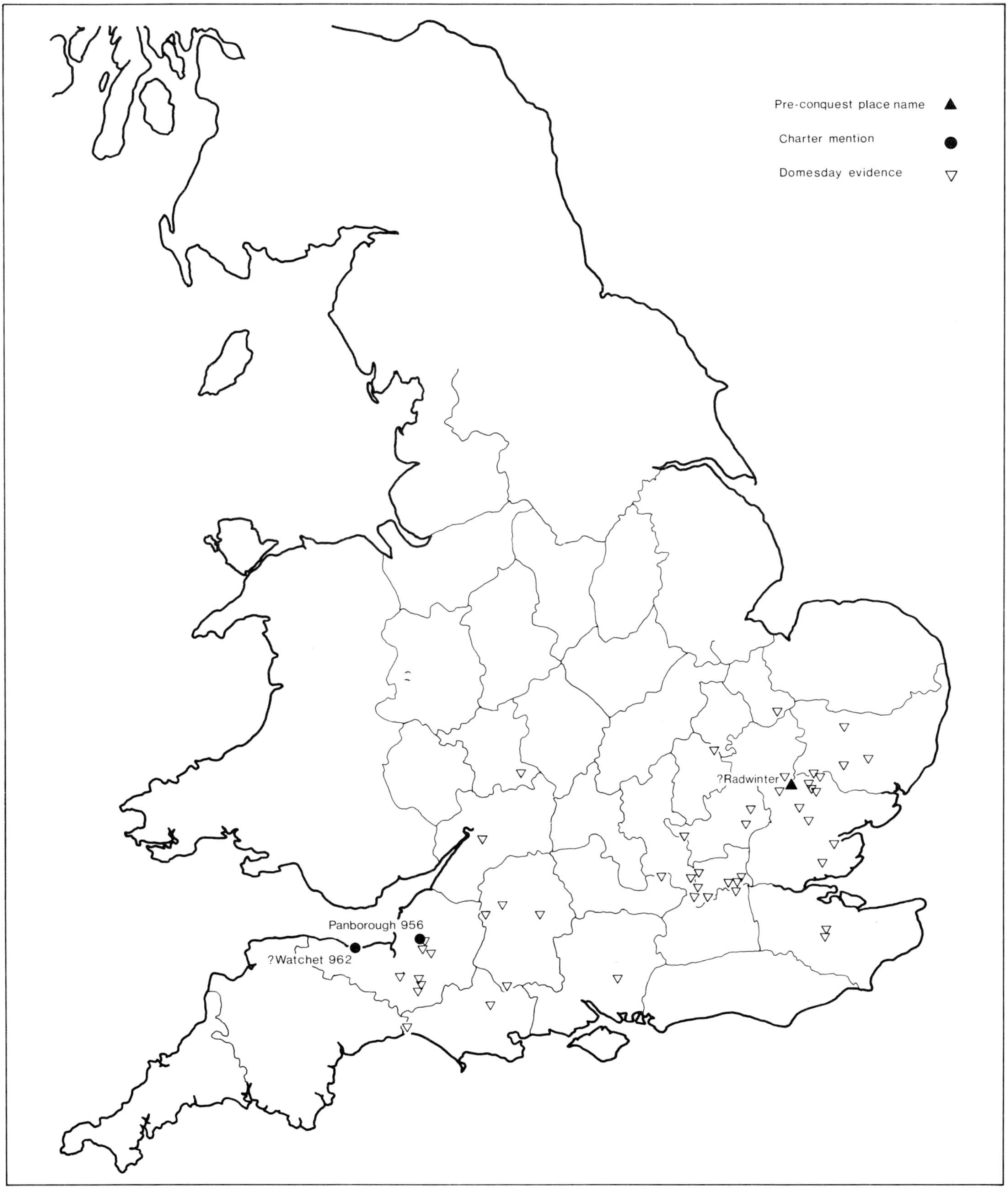

196 Vineyards

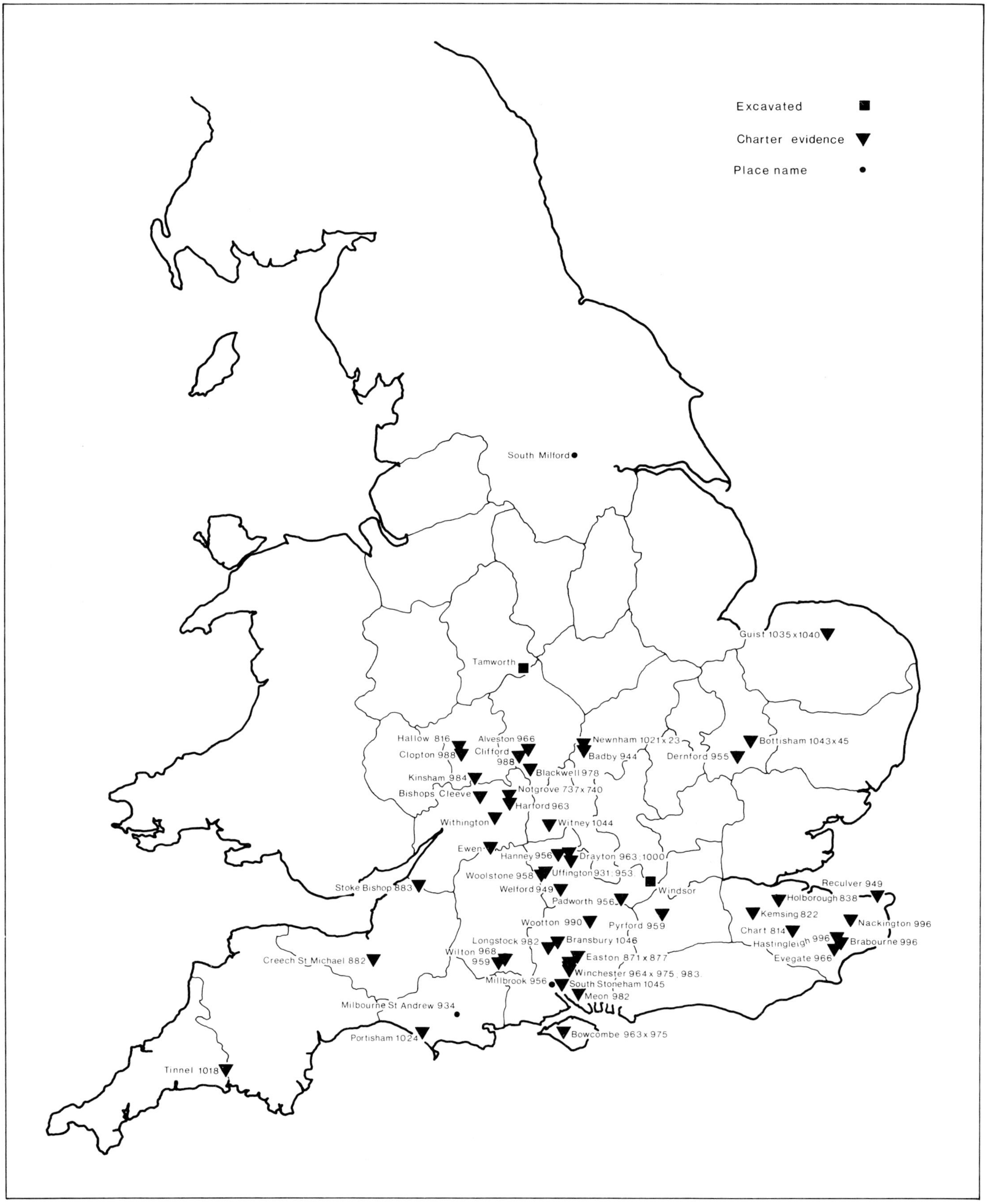
Excavated
Charter evidence
Place name
South Milford
Guist 1035 x 1040
Tamworth
Hallow 816
Alveston 966
Newnham 1021 x 23
Bottisham 1043 x 45
Clopton 988
Clifford
988
Badby 944
Dernford 955
Blackwell 978
Kinsham 984
Notgrove 737 x 740
Bishops Cleeve
Harford 963
Withington
Witney 1044
Ewen
Hanney 956
Drayton 963; 1000
Woolstone 958
Uffington 931; 953
Stoke Bishop 883
Welford 949
Windsor
Reculver 949
Holborough 838
Padworth 956
Kemsing 822
Wootton 990
Pyrford 959
Nackington 996
Chart 814
Longstock 982
Bransbury 1046
Hastingleigh 996
Brabourne 996
Wilton 968
959
Easton 871 x 877
Evegate 966
Creech St Michael 882
Winchester 964 x 975; 983
Millbrook 956
South Stoneham 1045
Meon 982
Milbourne St Andrew 934
Portisham 1024
Bowcombe 963 x 975
Tinnel 1018

197 Mills

Mills (197)

With the excavation of the Tamworth mill (Rahtz 1978) there has been more interest shown in this form of Anglo-Saxon technology. They are a common feature in charters from the ninth century and show that the vast numbers to be seen in the Domesday Survey were not a new feature. As it is not possible here to discuss all of the early place names, only three pre-Conquest examples are shown on map **197**.

A few mills had considerable engineering works attached to them to bring water from some distance, and all represent a mixture of skills and technologies, involving carpentry, millstones, metals and siting.

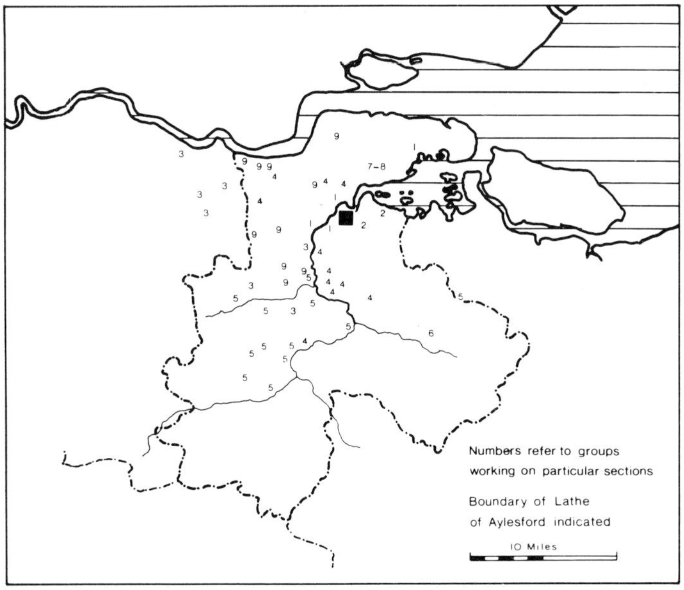

198 Estates owing work on Rochester Bridge ?973 × 988

Roads (198–199)

In a rare lapse, Stenton decided that the highway was unknown in Anglo-Saxon England. He was wrong. Long-distance thoroughfares were in use throughout the late Saxon period; some can be identified because they carry the name of their far-distant destination, as with the London Way; some use the same name throughout their length, as with the Foss; some are directly referred to, as with the road from Nottingham to York (map **199**).

That a system of 'king's highways' protected by royal prerogative existed in our period we should not doubt. Athelstan's journey with all his court from Winchester to Nottingham in eight days, the moving of Saint Aethelwold's body sixty miles in two days from where he died to his burial in Winchester (an example of the unexpected insights to be gained from such unlikely sources as the Life of Saint Aethelwold or the History of the Translation of Saint Aelfheah), Harold's dash from Yorkshire to Hastings, or the movement of lead from Wirksworth to Canterbury could hardly have been undertaken by people creeping apologetically along the margins of irate peasants' fields, or blundering through trackless woods. The insistence of the charters on bridgework points also to the royal interest in communications. Although these bridges had a defensive role in some cases, it is not possible that works of this complexity, widely scattered over the face of Anglo-Saxon England, connected two muddy lanes and were only part of a system of farm tracks. The bridges form part of a system of thoroughfares, for although the reference to the Royal Roads is strictly post-Conquest it refers to a period before 1066, and one at least of the roads (Watling Street) was called a 'royal street' in 940.

An example of the widespread responsibility for bridges throughout the countryside is provided by Rochester (map **198**) where a surviving document lists the obligations of various estates for work on the bridge, detailing the actual part of the structure concerned.

The bridges at London and Rochester were two of the great engineering feats of the age; there were similar bridges at Pont de l'Arche and at Paris and a greater and more famous example at Mainz. Einhard's **Life of Charlemagne**, chap 17, records:

The bridge over the Rhine at Mainz, which is five hundred feet long, this being the width of the river at that point. The bridge was burned down just one year before Charlemagne's death. He planned to rebuild it in stone instead of wood.

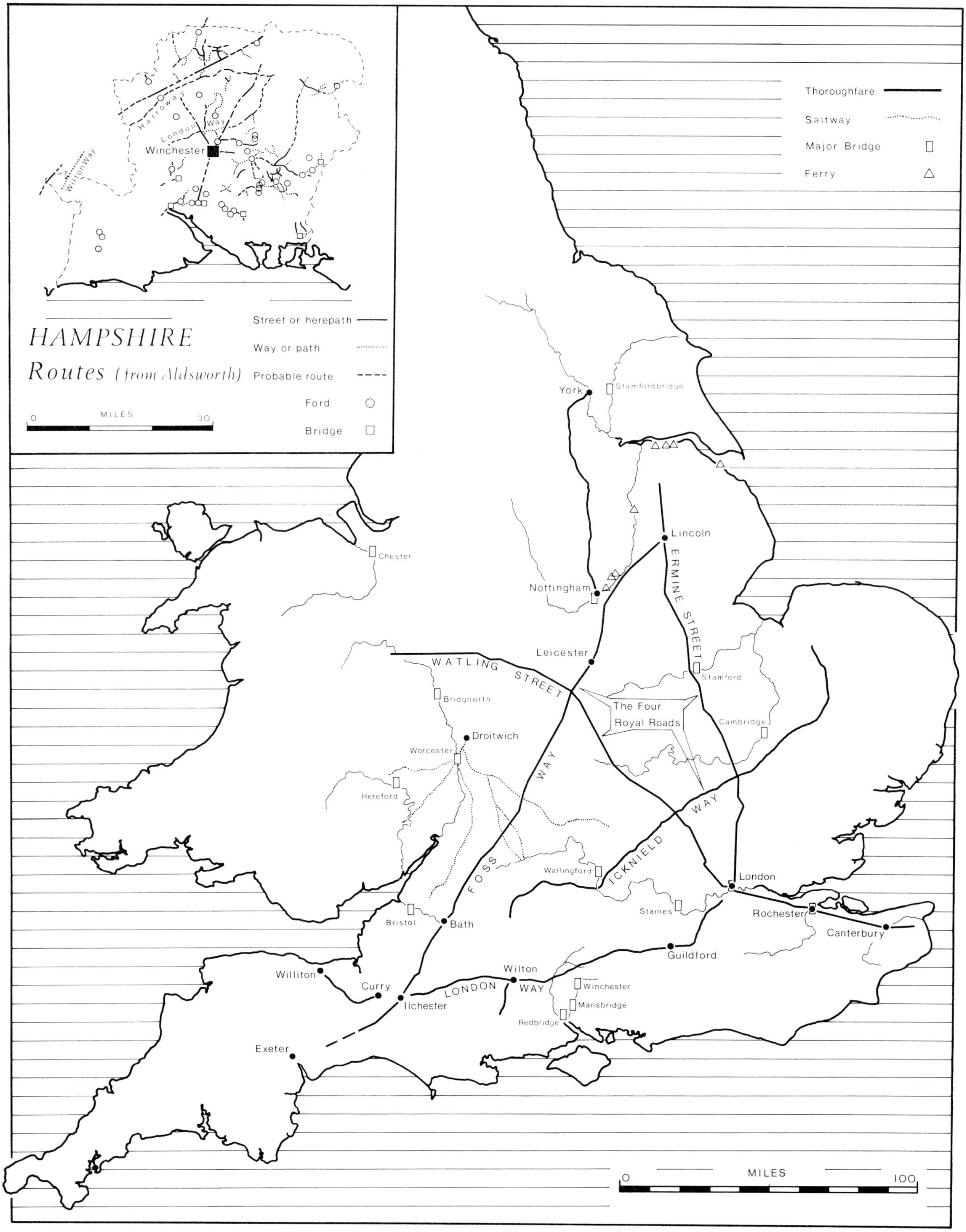

199 Major roads in Anglo-Saxon times with an inset of Hampshire routes (from Aldsworth)

Building Stone (200–202)

In a pioneering piece of research Professor Jope has identified the building stones in churches and memorials across southern Britain (map **200**). From this he has shown that the material came from four great quarry areas and was transported across considerable distances (Jope 1964). Half-ton quoins were moved over sixty miles, a fact which points to communications, organization and planning of a high degree. It should be realized from map **190** that there are other stone buildings using stone gathered from a variety of sources, but the idea that all Saxon stone structures, religious or secular, were cobbled together from old Roman buildings must be discarded.

The patterns of trade are affected by the political patterns of the time, and the early identifiable mica schist honestones from the Eidsborg in southern Norway travelled widely in the Danelaw and even farther afield (map **201**). It would appear that some may have travelled directly across either as ballast or as a part cargo, whilst some may have been traded via Rokleiv and Dorestadt. Whichever way they came they supplied a necessity, for every Saxon peasant carried with him a knife and, hanging on a string around his neck, his hone to sharpen it (Ellis 1969).

In the lava flows of the Eifel mountains there are quarries dating from all periods, from prehistoric to modern. The quality and ease of working of the stone from Mayen (usually known as Niedermendig after one of the villages in the area) has ensured its wide and continuous use (map **202**). The enclosed bubbles of air in the stone mean that as the millstones or querns made from the lava wear down the surfaces remain abrasive, while the bubbles also make the querns light. Querns from this material are to be found in Carolingian forts in Saxony and widely in the north-west of Europe in the period 700–850. They were carried as blanks to Dorestad and over to Hamwih (Saxon Southampton), and the worked querns are then found in such settings as the Tamworth watermill. These are probably the stones referred to in the correspondence between Offa and Charlemagne (Whitelock 1955, 781). They are an indicator of trade in basic commodities at an early period and have a strikingly similar distribution to the sceatta coinage.

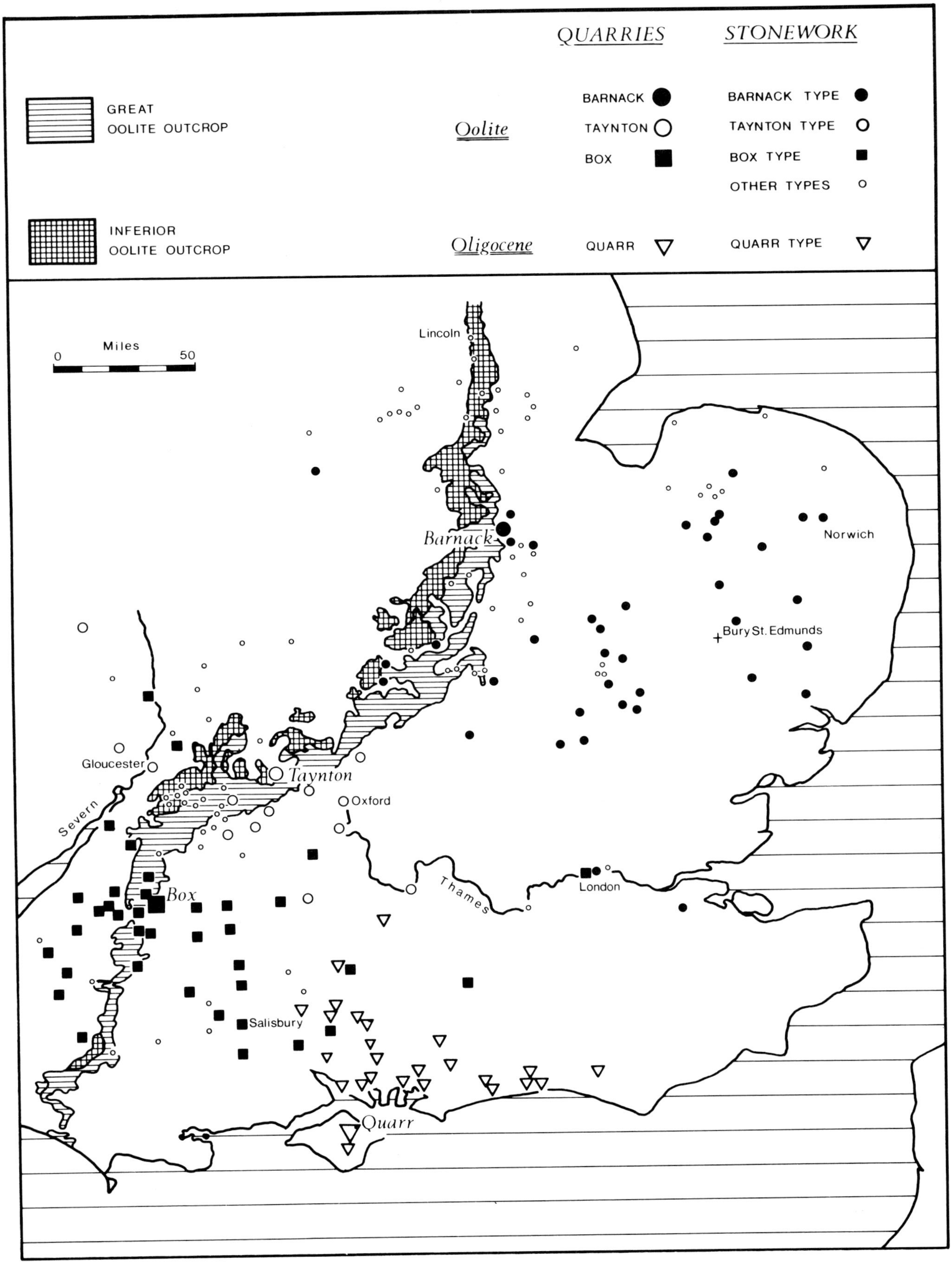

200 Fine building stone eighth to eleventh centuries (after Jope (unpublished))

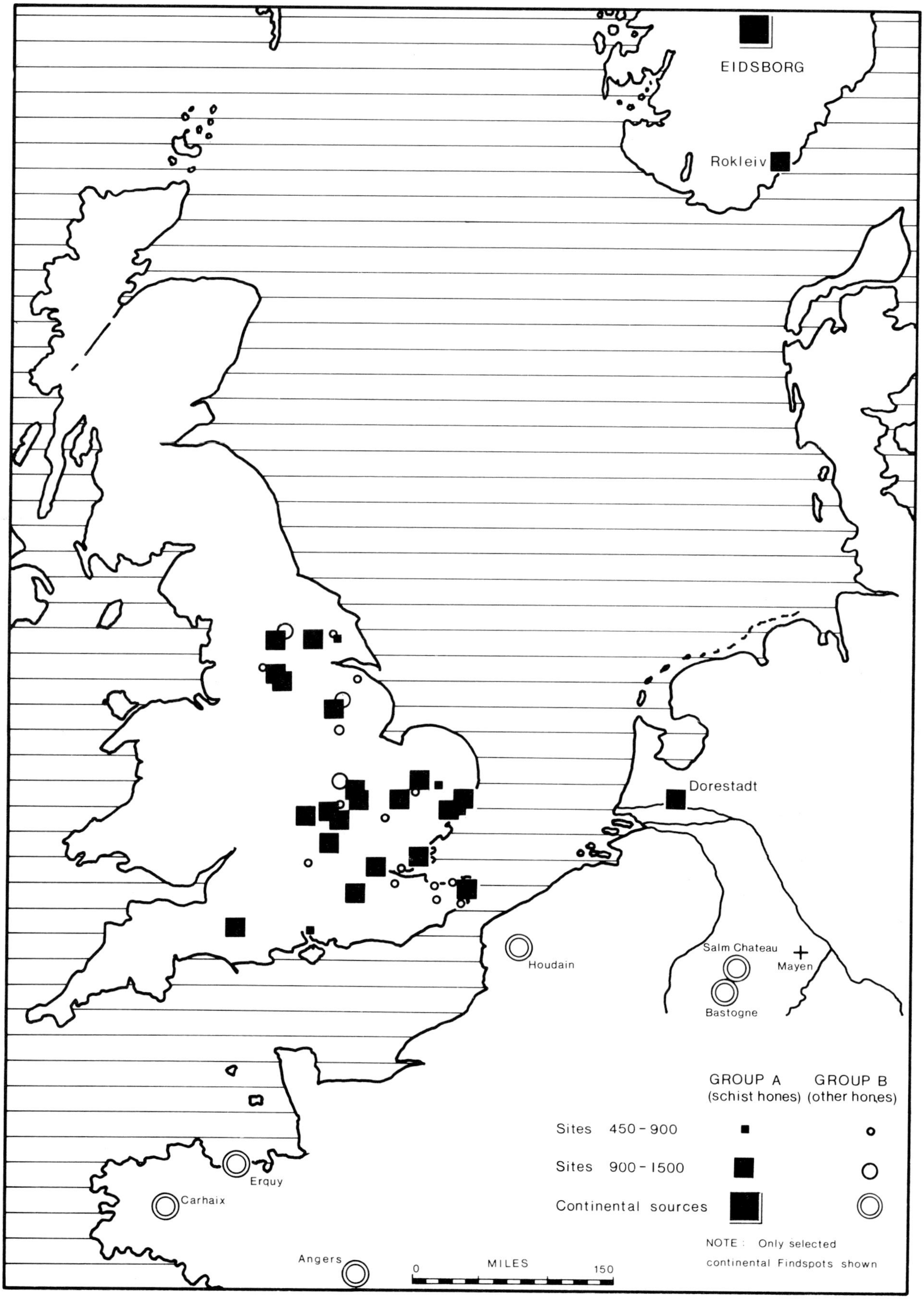

201 Honestones

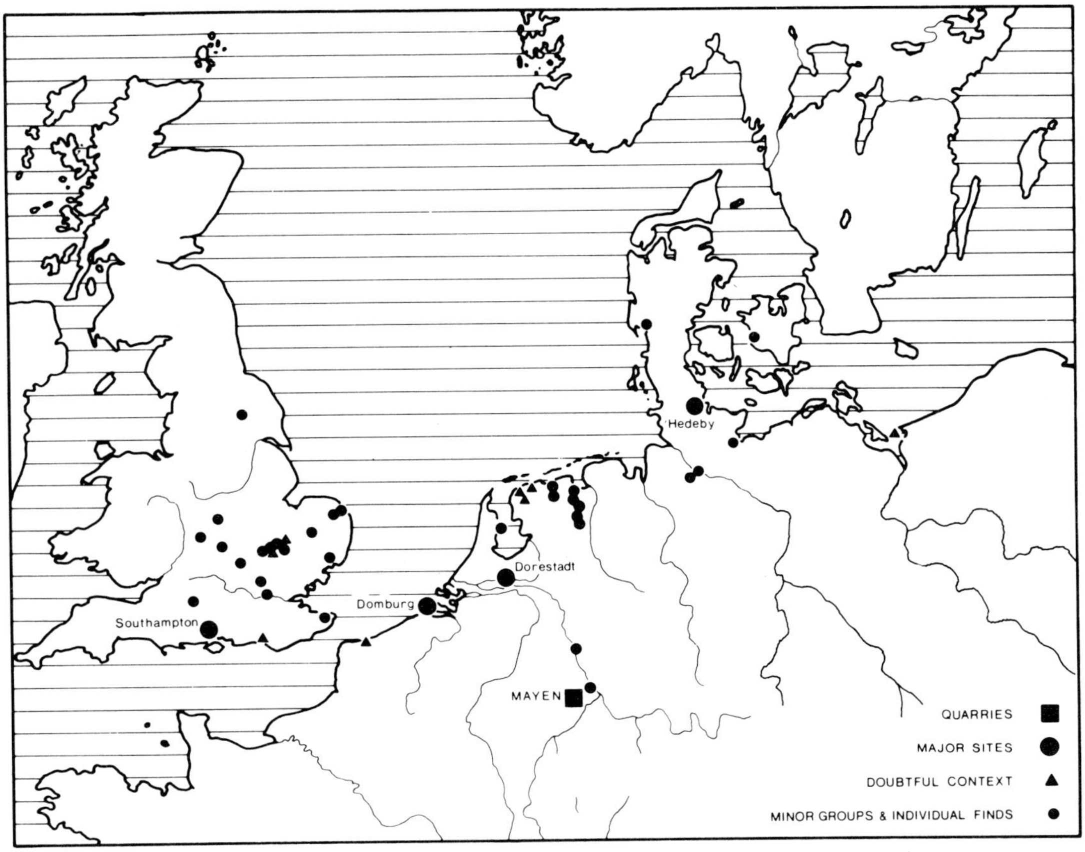

202 Niedermendig lava (after Parkhouse (unpublished))

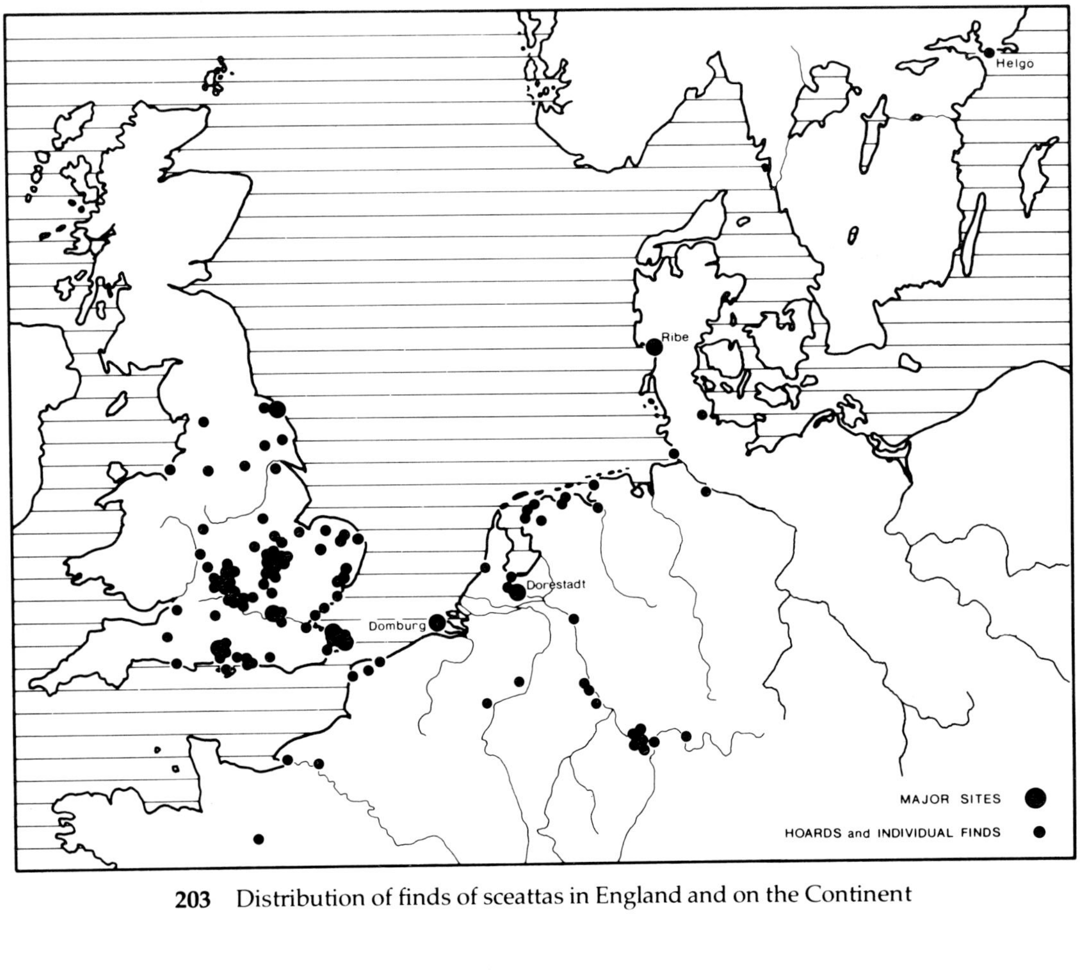

203 Distribution of finds of sceattas in England and on the Continent

Coins (203–207)

The small flan deniers of silver known by the antiquarian name of **sceattas** come in a wealth of designs mostly without any inscription. They date from around the 690s, when they replaced the **thrymsa**, until they were in turn replaced by the coinage of Offa and the Kentish kings, although there is a hiatus of uncertain length between the two coinages (map **203**). They were struck at a number of centres, in the same way as the contemporary Merovingian coinage (map **204**) and with little central control. The sceattas (regrettably, Dolley's suggestion that they should be known as proto-pennies has not been taken up) were struck at London, Canterbury, Rochester, York and Southampton and have the distinction of being found widely across northern Europe, particularly in large hoards in Frisia. One point which is often missed is that with the multiplicity of issues in Merovingian Gaul the anepigraphic issues of sceattas would be acceptable anywhere in Gaul. In fact the evidence of the hoards in France together with the distribution in the Rhineland shows that it would be helpful to regard the sceattas as the northern fringe of Merovingian coinage, mixing with it where the two coinages overlapped.

The distribution of the sceatta finds in England is very specific, and rather inexplicable (map **205**). The concentration around the east Kent coast is what one would expect when one takes into account the lively trade with Domburg, Dorestadt and the Rhineland, but there is a wider distribution along an axis from north Wiltshire to Norfolk, southern Mercia. There are also sceattas in southern Northumbria and on the south coast, but the southern Mercian concentration is striking. It may, as with the Niedermendig lava, reflect a trade for England to the Rhineland of Mercian woollen goods carried, in the main, by Frisian traders from London, Kent and Southampton.

The particular finds from a large number of Roman sites and from some Iron Age hillforts raise questions about the role of these sites as central places in the eighth century.

Following the reorganization of the Frankish coinage by Pippin III, 'Pepin le Bref', in 755 and the marking of that reorganization by a new coin, the denarius on a wider flan, the Saxons issued a new coinage. The penny was of similar type to the denarius and was first struck by the kings of Kent in small quantities. Offa followed c.780 with a penny series which is outstanding in both quality and design. It is noticeable that the distribution of finds of the coins of Offa follows that of the sceattas (map **206**). In the north the Northumbrians went their own way continuing the sceatta series with an increasingly debased coinage which soon became the base metal, fiduciary, issue the **stycas** which was out of step with the rest of European coinage and survived until the Danish invasions (map **207**).

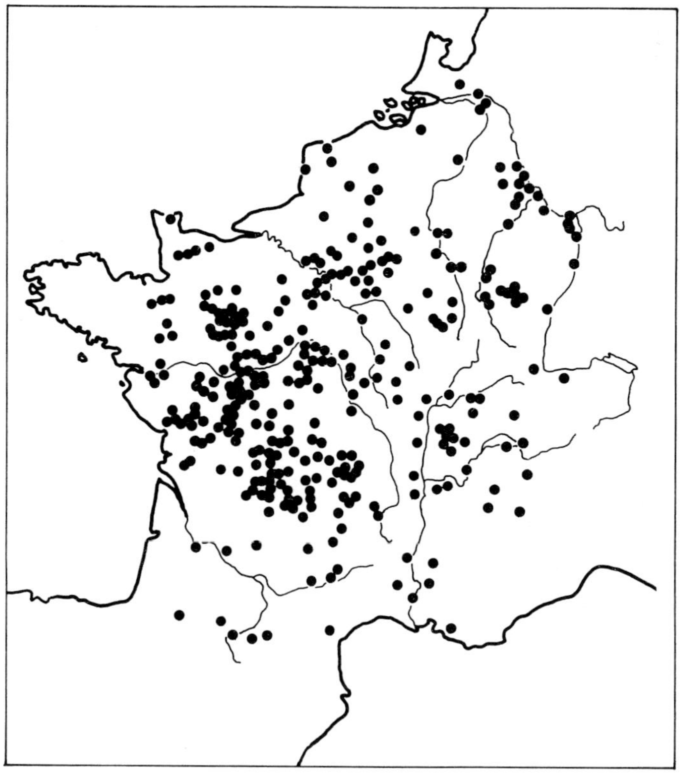

204 Merovingian mints

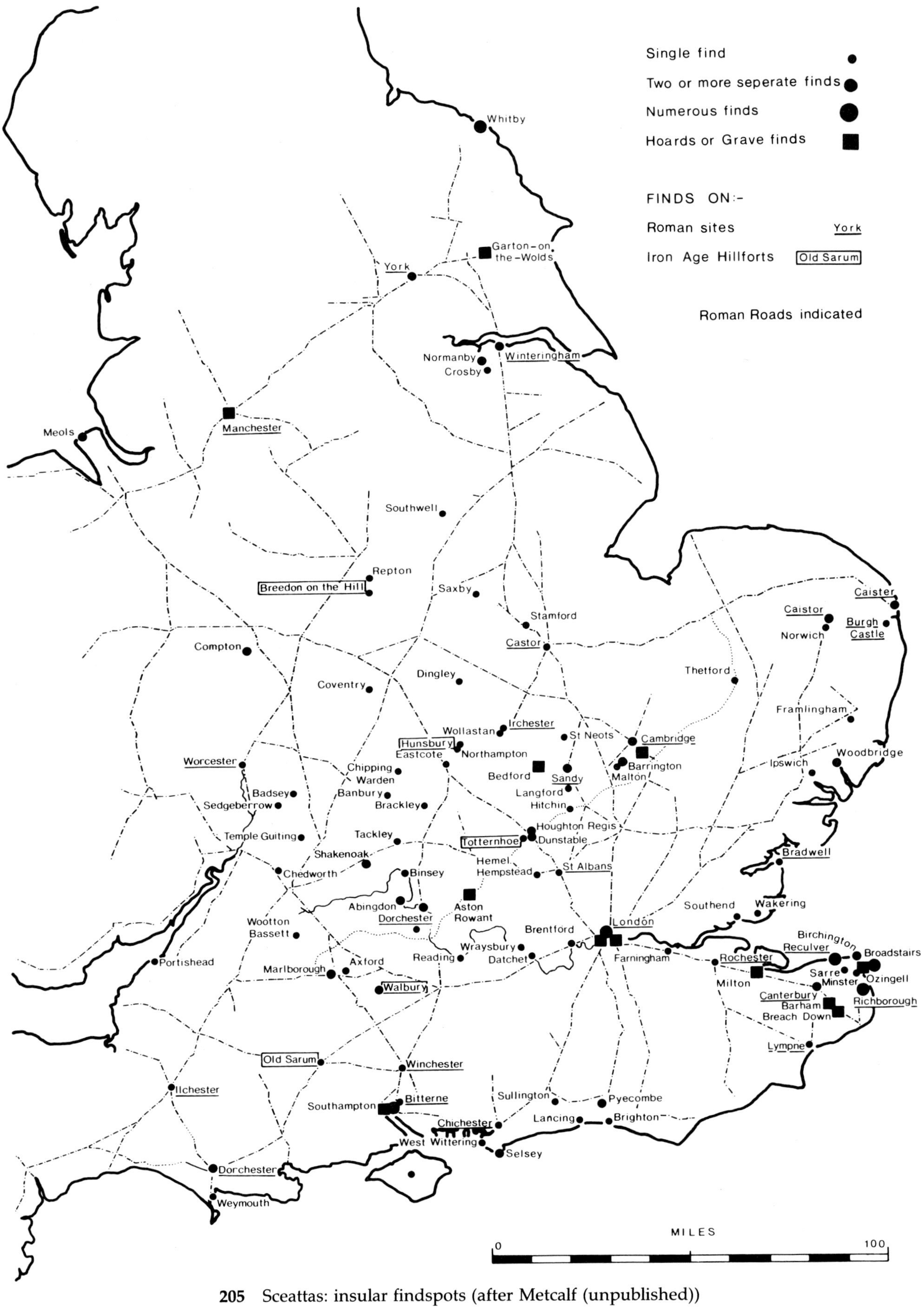

205 Sceattas: insular findspots (after Metcalf (unpublished))

206 Offa's coinage: findspots

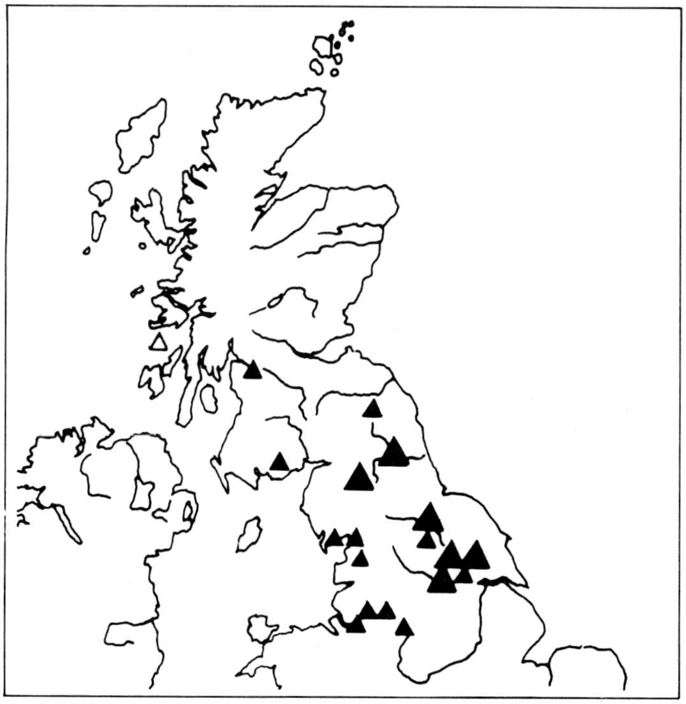

207 Stycas: distribution of hoards

The Mints of Carolingian Europe (208–211)

The rise of the towns of Anglo-Saxon England, their multiplication and their association with the expansion of minting, is also intimately linked with trade and town patterns in Northern France. It is useful as a control for our thinking about the English situation to consider the places with which the Saxons were trading on the other side of the Channel.

The number of mints in France and their concentrations are not matched in England until a century after the distribution in France charted on these maps (**208–211**). In the reign of Charles the Bald, a time of intense Viking attack and of civil war, there seems to have been a considerable expansion of minting, and (one may speculate) also of urban activity (map **210**). It is of interest to note that the full citation of the place names on the coinage of Charles the Bald includes a designation of the status of the minting place and these can be used to show a typology of towns that was in use in the ninth century. This typology should have some validity when compared with those constructed by more recent scholars. It should be noted that, in common with Gildas and Bede (map **43**), the Franks were aware of the Roman origins of their towns and these towns have the title **civitates**, the **de novo** sites are carefully named with what appears to be some technical sophistication (map **211**). Unfortunately, although there is some Frankish influence on the Anglo-Saxon coinage, it is rare for English coins to carry these descriptions; some do appear on the coins, particularly those of Athelstan; London, Winchester, Bath, Canterbury, Chester, Chichester, Exeter, Gloucester, Leicester and Rochester are all **civitates**, a style which does not have here the specialised meaning of 'cathedral city' but means 'walled place of Roman origin'. Four mints are designated **urbs**: 'Darent'. Lewes, Southampton and Oxford; all are walled but none are Roman. This distinction in the use of the terms is obviously a real one as can be seen from Asser '**de civitatibus et urbibus renovandis et aliis, ubi nunquam ante fuerant, construendis'** (what of the cities and towns he restored, and others, which he built where none had been before?).

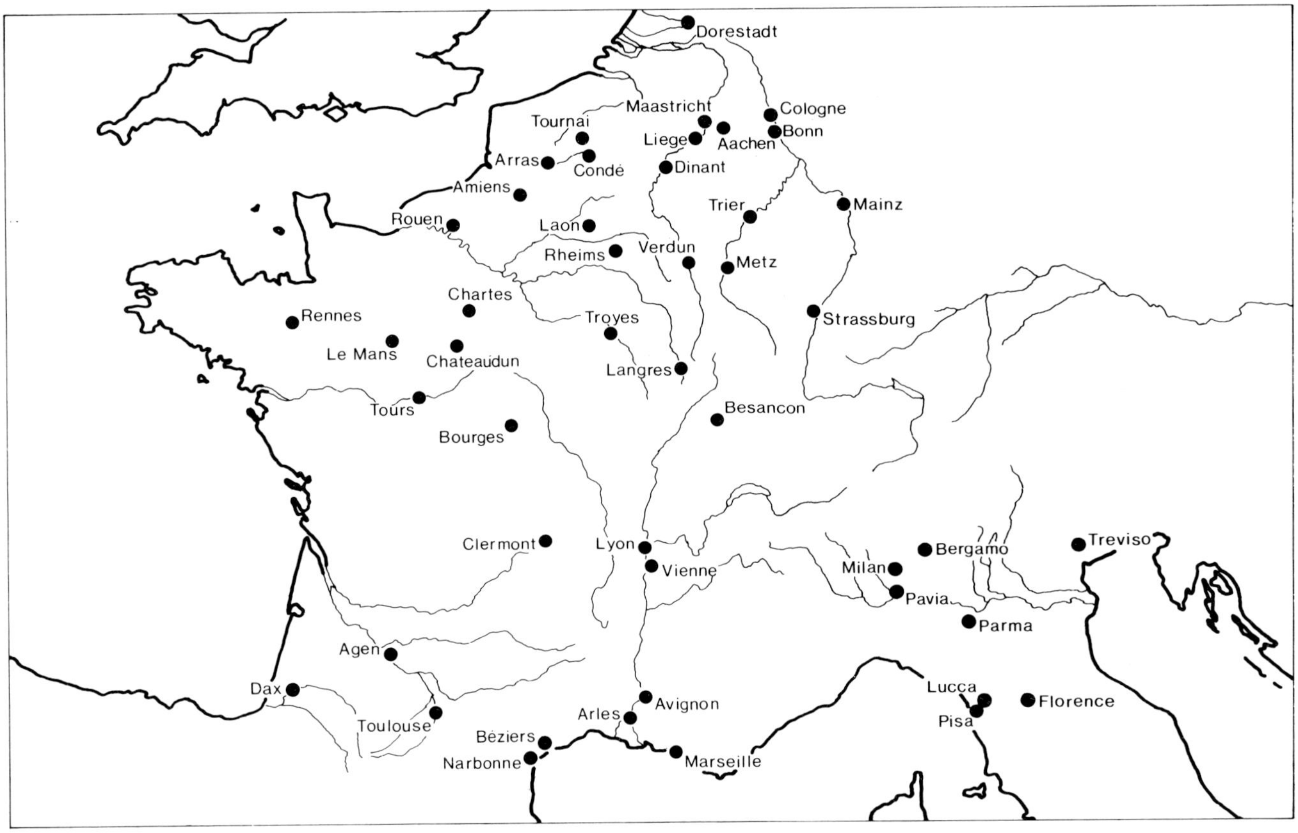

208 Mints of Charlemagne 768–814

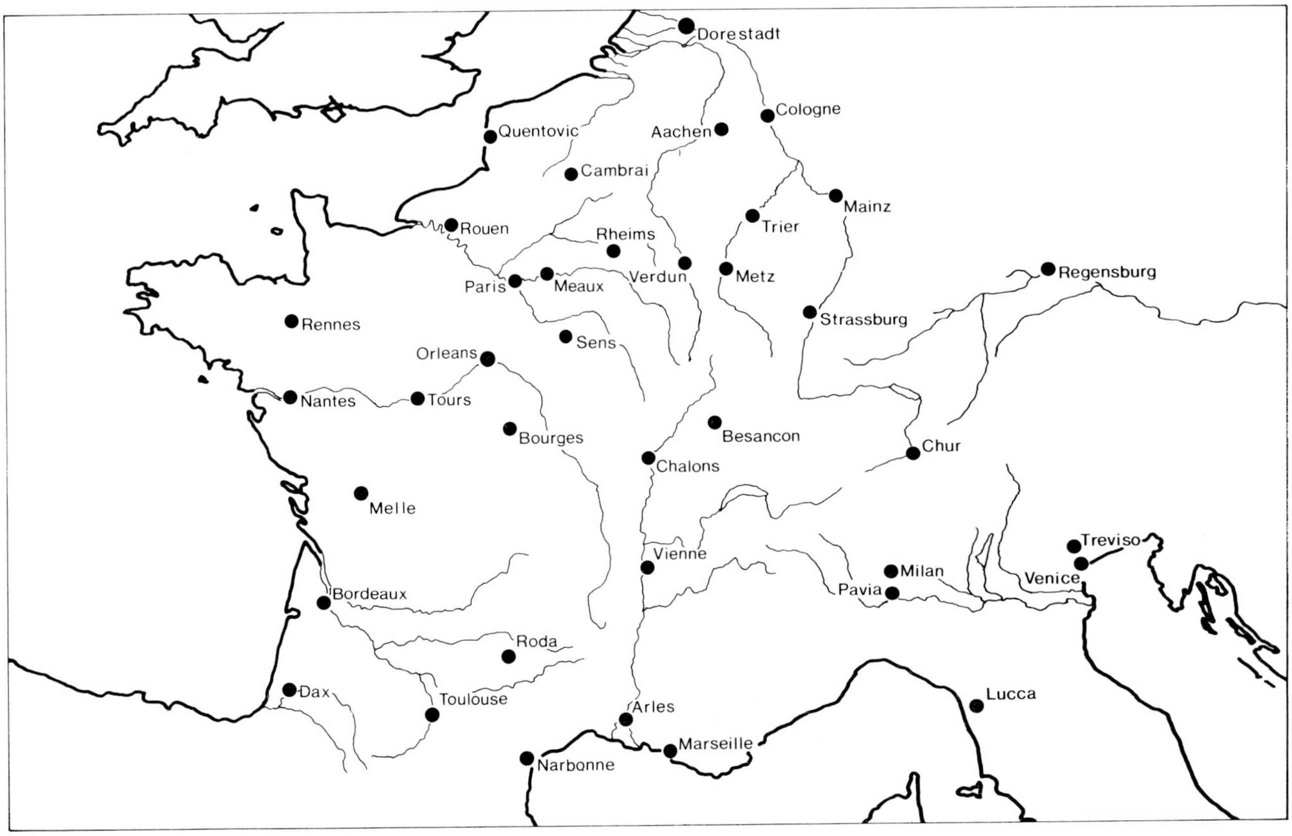

209 Mints of Louis the Pious 814–840

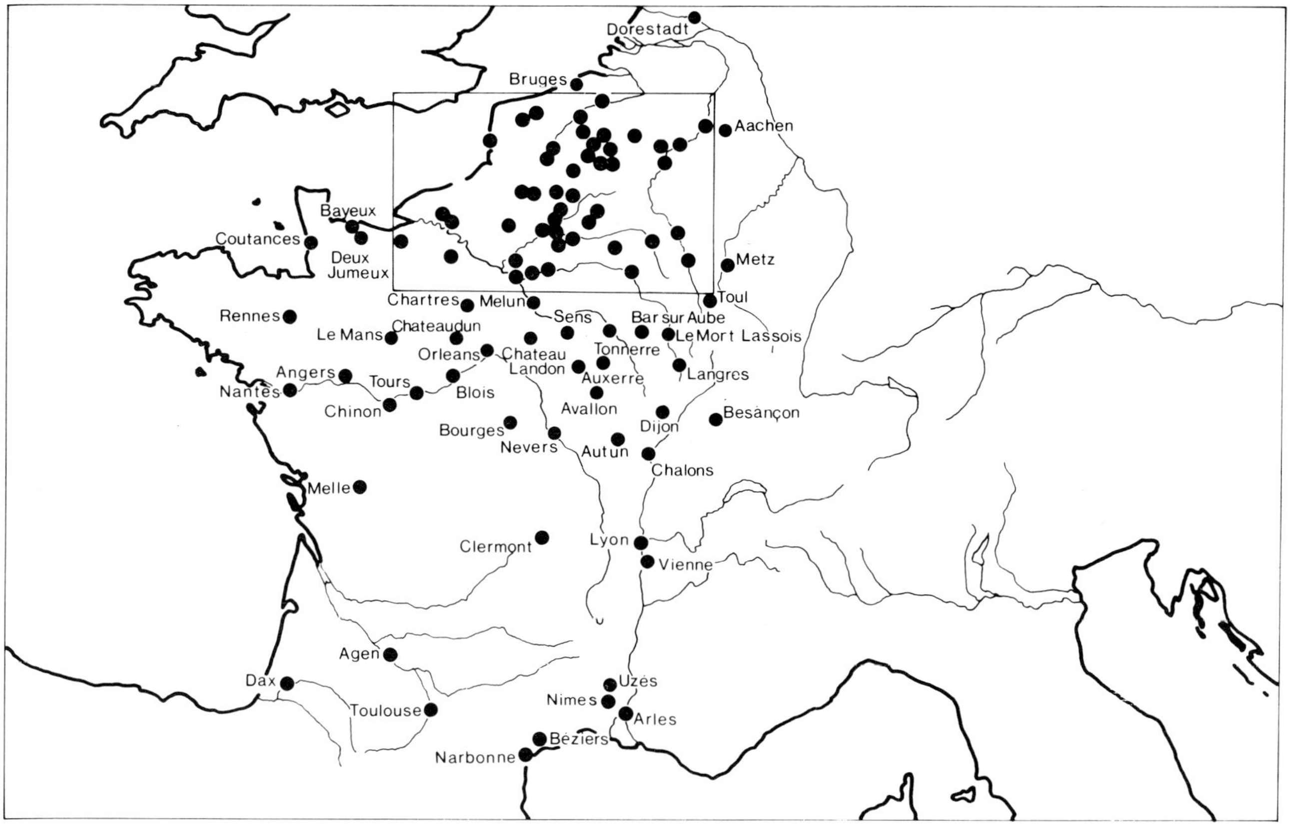

210 Mints of Charles the Bald 840–875

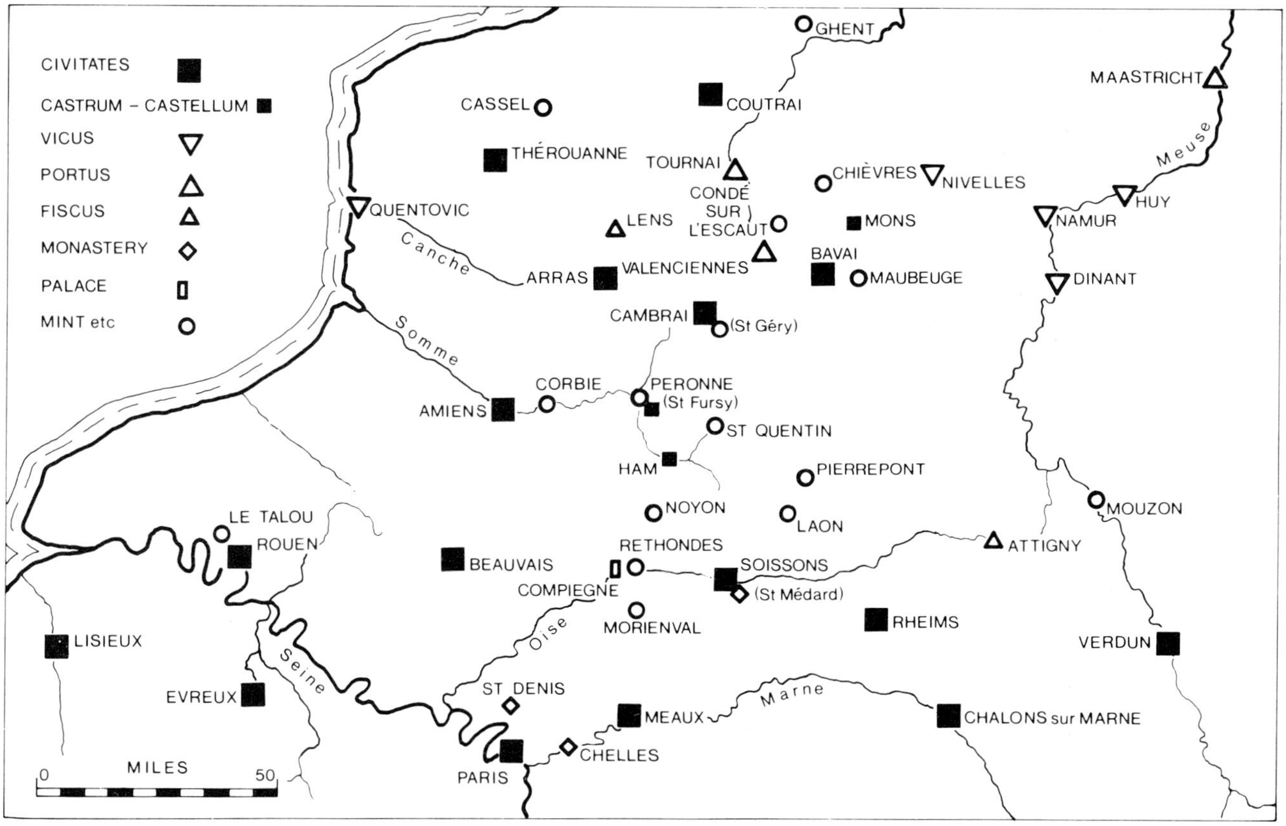

211 Northern area in the time of Charles the Bald

Mints in England (212–225)

The velocity of circulation of coinage in Anglo-Saxon England was remarkable (Metcalf 1978, 168), indicating a very brisk interchange of money, constant travel around the country and a national currency. It should not be thought that at this period the multiplicity of mints indicates purely localized coinages or localized areas of circulation. An example of this movement is the composition of the Pemberton's Parlour hoard from Chester (map **212**). This hoard was deposited c.979–80, which means that the earliest coins were no more than six years old. Yet the mints represented cover most of England, particularly the east Midlands. The farthest coin comes from Totnes in Devon.

The increase in mints during the period is charted by maps **213–221** (North 1963). On the later maps (**218–221**) only the new mints are named. Note that the visual effect of the maps can be deceptive as a small and intermittent mint can be seen alongside a major centre such as Lincoln. The exact location of these mints can be studied on the detailed town sheets (maps **226–234**). The maps are a little misleading in that many of the coins did not carry the name of the mint until the reform under Edgar in 973. Thus the mints of Edward the Elder (map **214**) reflect nothing except that two places are identified on the coins as mints. The later maps (**218–221**) reflect a pattern of surprising concentrations in the South and South-west whilst in the Midlands and the North one mint to a shire would seem to be general. The later reigns have the addition of minor mints reflecting the foundation of small, secondary, market centres.

A simple charting of the Anglo-Saxon mints does not enable us to make sensible judgements about these mints. It is possible to rank the mints and the method used here has been to count the number of known moneyers (**222–223**). This has been preferred to equating the number of surviving coins or recognized dies with the output of the mint, both for the sake of simplicity and to eliminate some of the factors of chance survival, it being felt that a moneyer's coin is more likely to survive than a coin from a particular die. This obviated some of the pioblems arising from the overrepresentation in the survivals of the mints of eastern England. The percentages have been worked out for each reign after 973 and then the average taken from the total reigns, thus making the whole calculation as insensitive as possible (for another, and probably superior approach see Metcalf 1978).

The chart (**223**) makes some interesting points but the map (**222**) gives a visual impression of the mints in their setting. It is clear that there is a ranking which would seem to reflect the role of the various mints: thus there are the great national mints at London, Lincoln and York; what would appear to be provincial centres at Exeter, Winchester, Stamford and Chester; shire centres such as Shrewsbury and Oxford; down to the minor mints and secondary market centres at such sites as Steyning and Frome. The map does issue a useful **caveat** against treating these places as being too much alike.

The greatest achievement of Anglo-Saxon studies since the war has been the clarity and order that has been brought to the study of the coinage, in particular by Professor Michael Dolley. Coins now rank as one of the major sources of insights into the administrative and organizational abilities of the Anglo-Saxon state. It is difficult for many scholars to break out of their particular field or for the general student to acquire the expertise of a specialism, and in fairness it is often true that certain areas of research do not assist the general student, for the rim forms of pots may not seem too relevant to the layman nor will the glories of diplomatic or scriptoria reveal themselves easily to all. But the numismatist has a great deal to offer in practically all fields and the evidence of the coin is so central to the mainstream of research into pre-Conquest England that the effort should be made. Suffice to say here that the management of the coinage and through it the general direction of the economy was so advanced in the last century of the Anglo-Saxon state that we must wonder at the sophistication of the directing personnel. The coinage was changed every six (later three) years, the old issue being demonetized, thus allowing a wealth tax to be taken; the weights could then be adjusted, either up or down, with effects on the rate of exchange and thus on exports and imports; mints were set up and standards controlled all over the kingdom. These and many other aspects of the coinage command attention.

The charts in **224** and **225** show which mints were striking coins at a particular time. Since they are based on obsolescent evidence (North 1963), they are but an interim statement to give some idea of the issues struck at each mint and the first appearance of that mint. It should be noted that when a mint struck for someone other than the named king (i.e. as a Viking mint) it is not included on these charts.

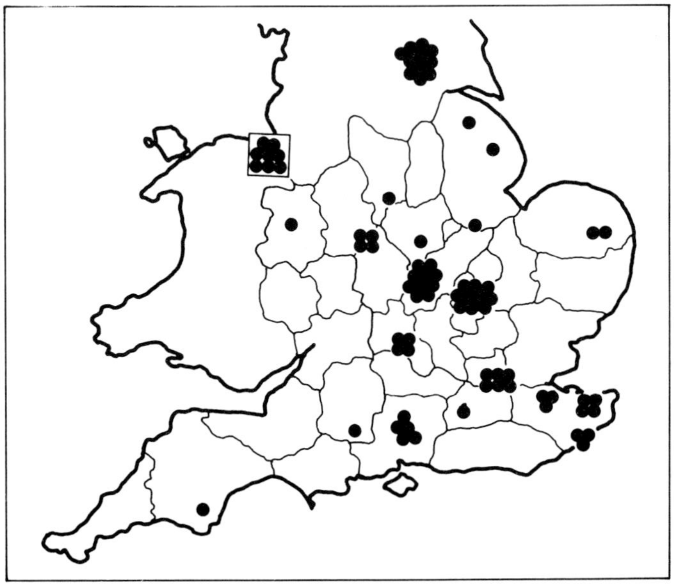

212 Mints of origin of coins in the Pemberton's Parlour hoard, Chester

213

214

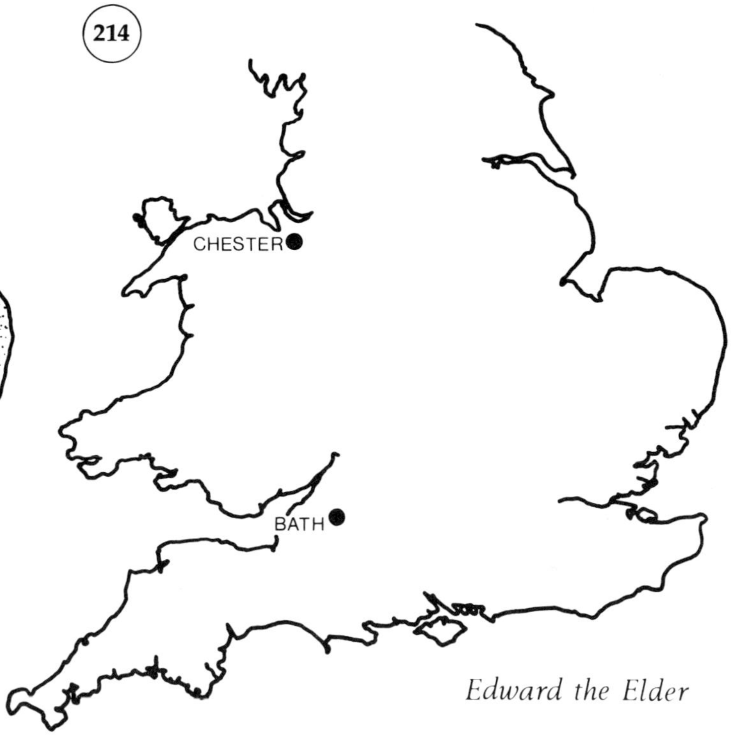

215

216

213–216 Mints 871–959. The large dot shows new mints; the smaller dot existing mints

217 Mints 957–1016

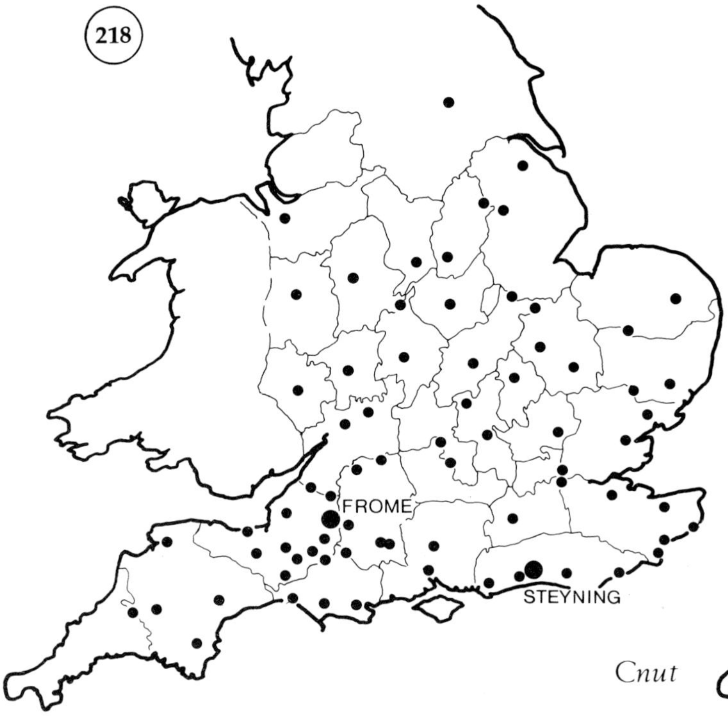

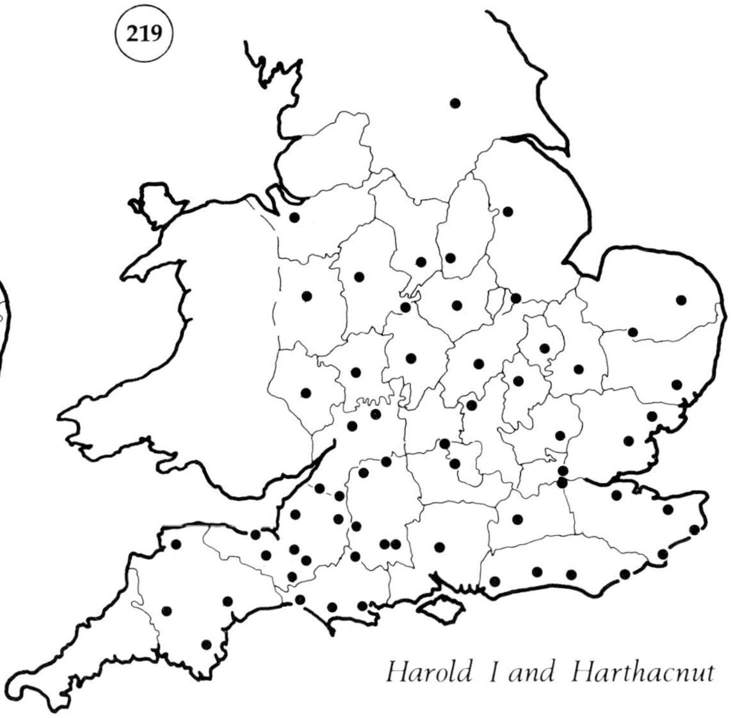

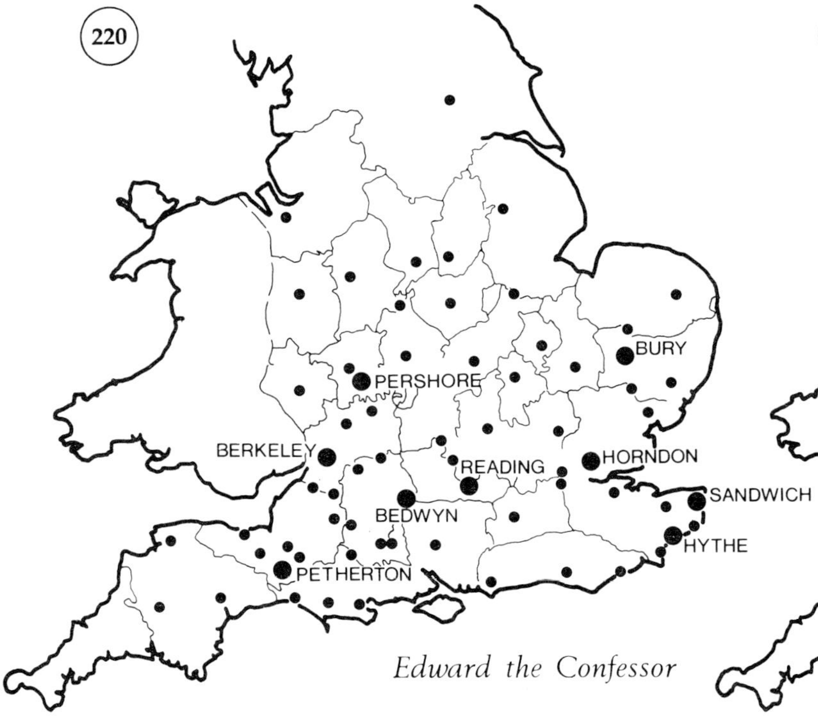

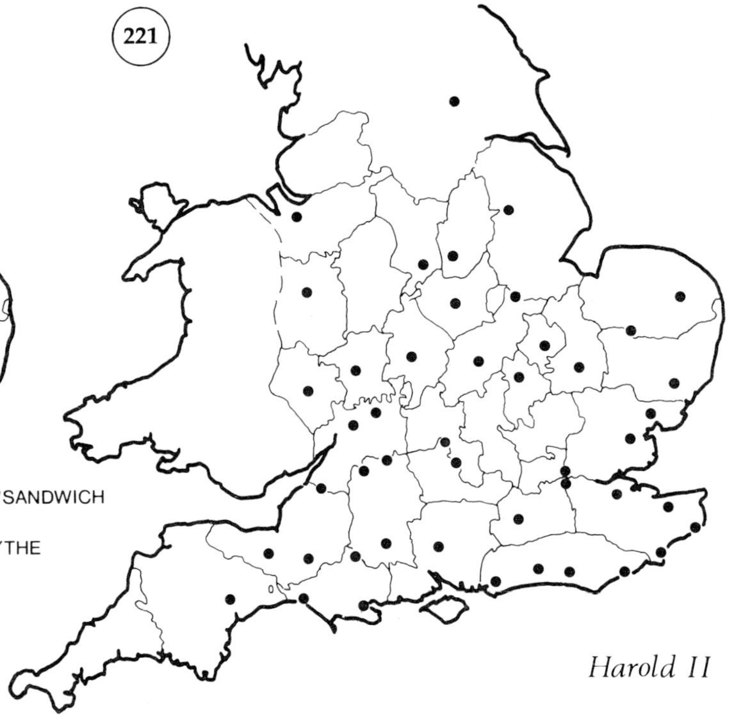

218–221 Mints 1016–1066. The large dot shows new mints; the smaller dot existing mints

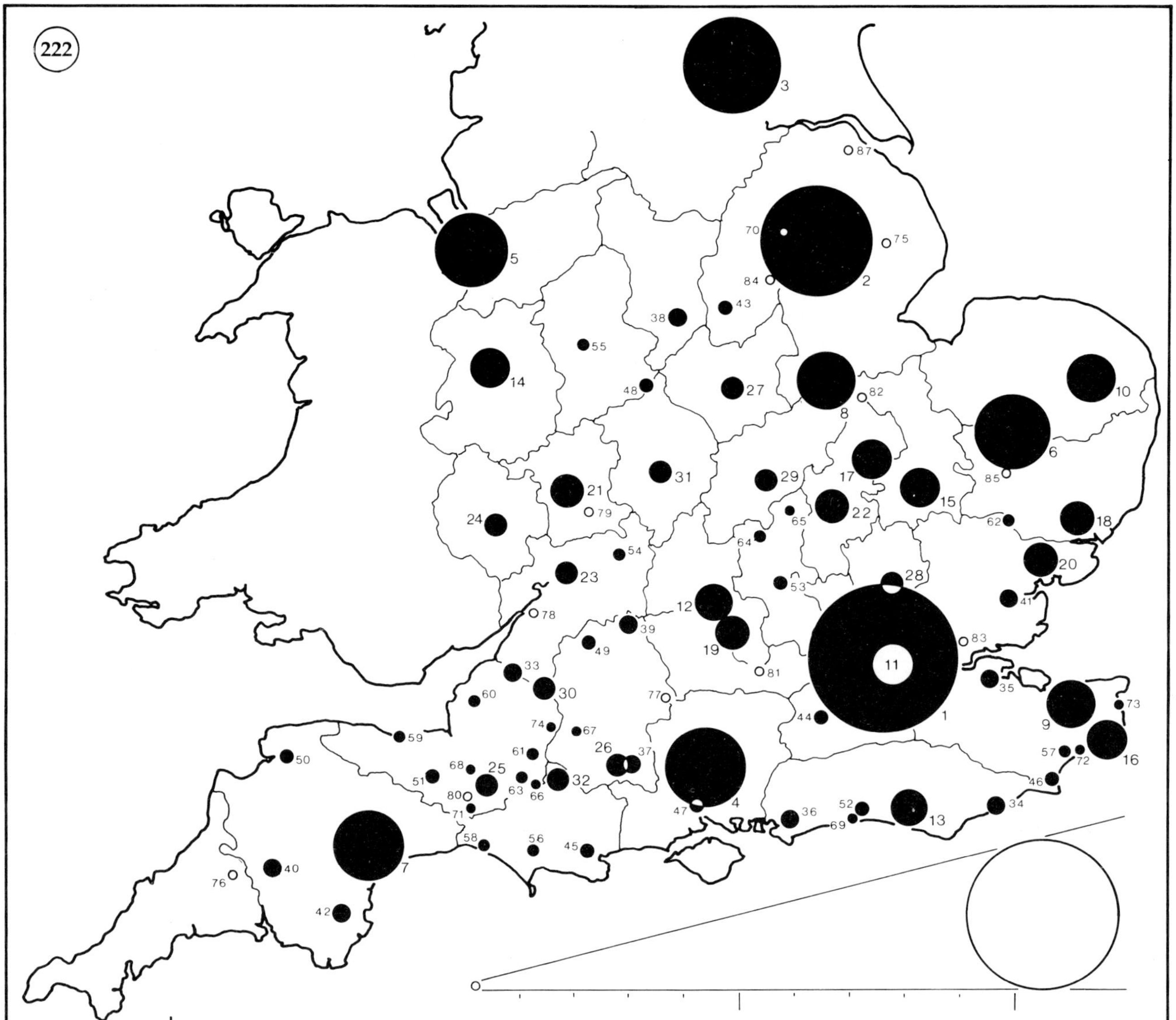

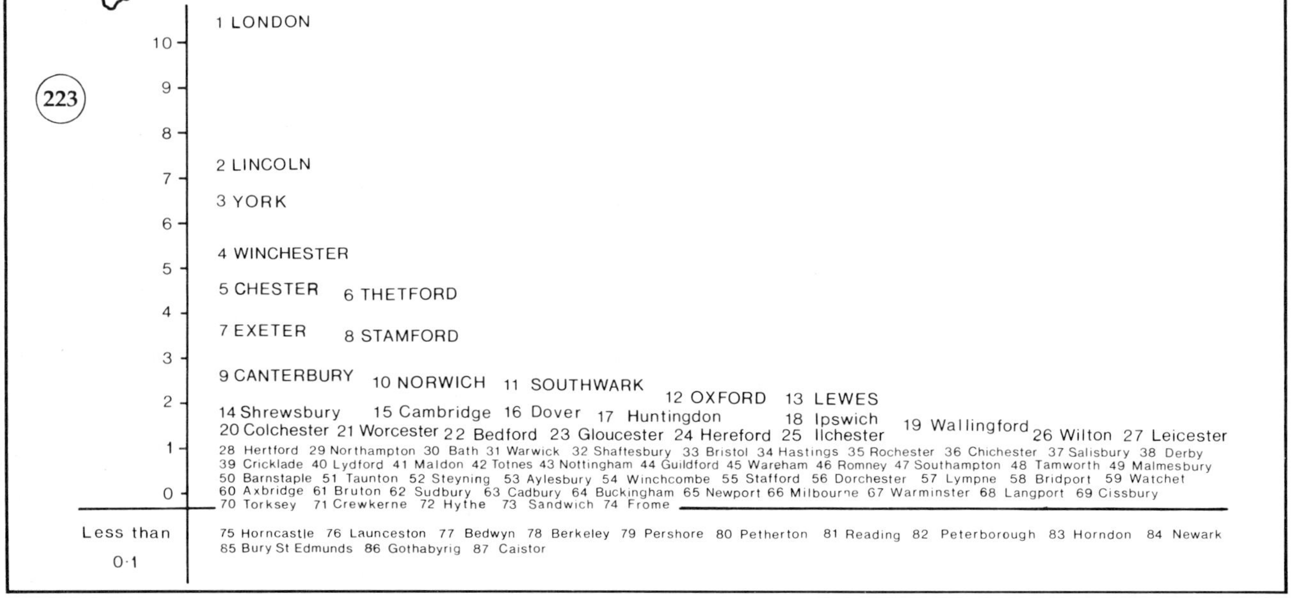

222–223 The ranking of mints expressed as a percentage of total known moneyers

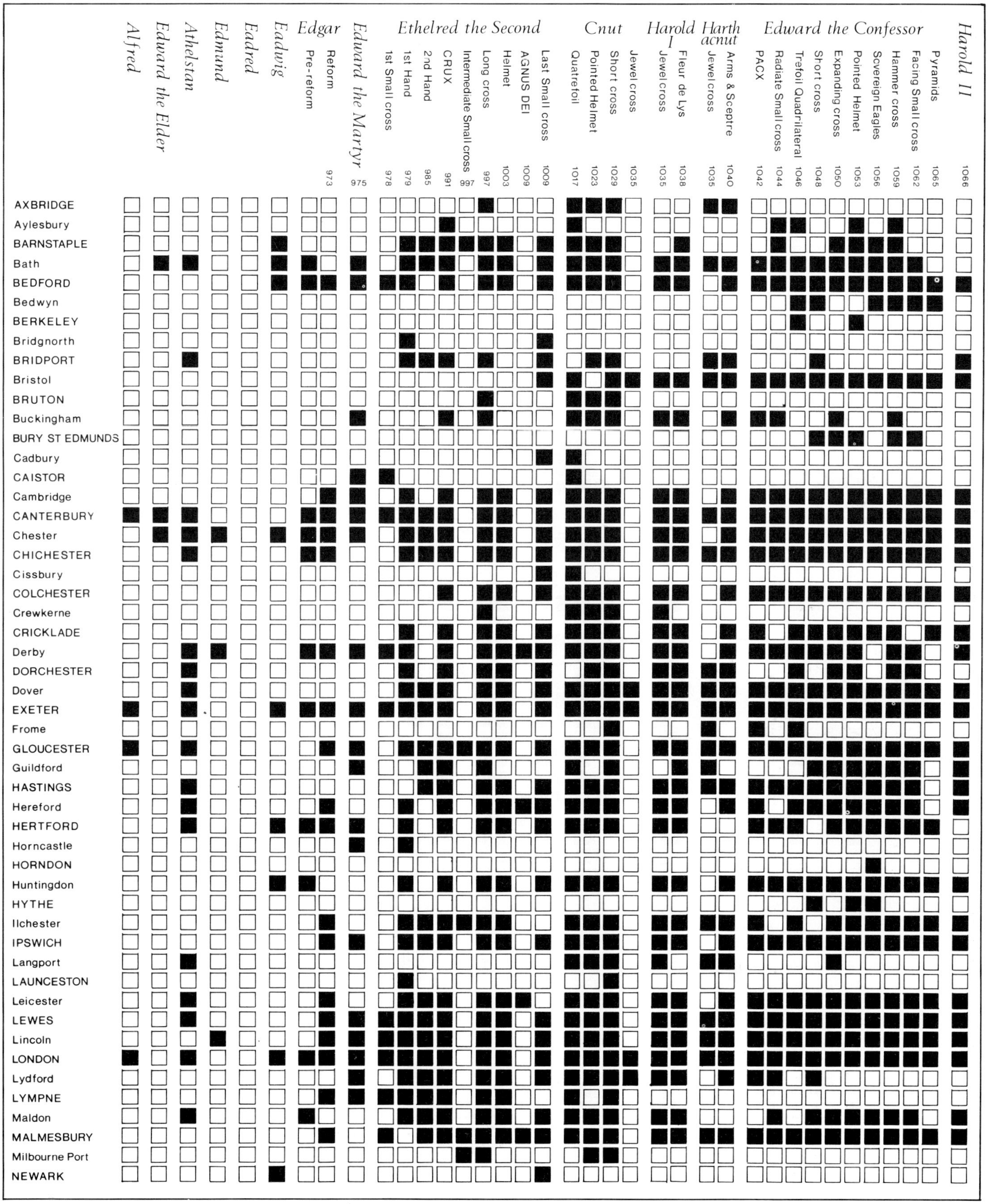

224 Mints striking 871–1066: part I

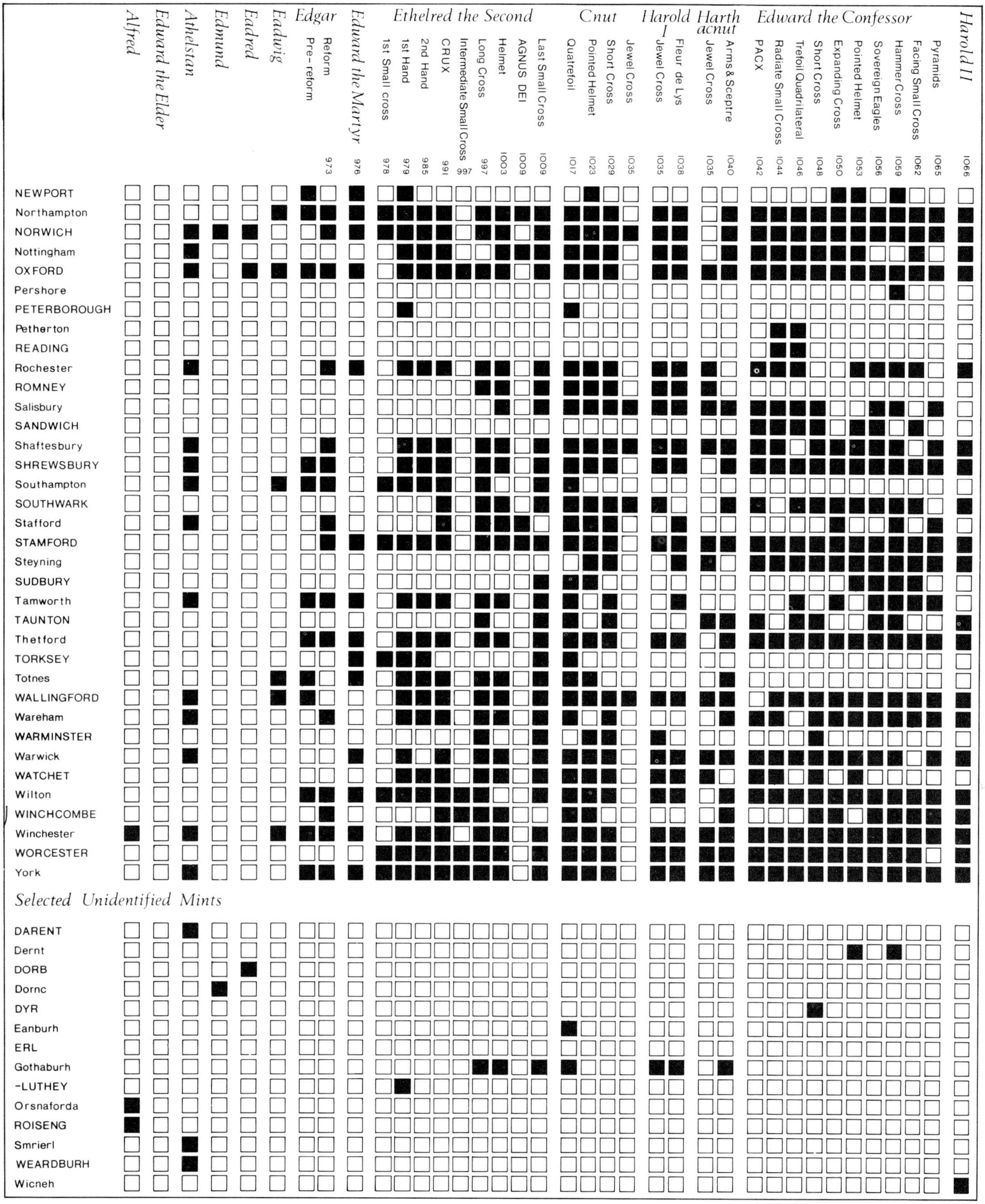

225 Mints striking 871–1066: part II

Towns and their Distribution (226–234)

A great deal of effort has been put into the study of the Anglo-Saxon town in the past two decades and the subject has been revolutionized by the work of urban archaeologists such as Martin Biddle (recent work is conveniently reviewed in Biddle 1976). This atlas is not the place in which to publish detailed and comparative town plans. The area-by-area maps (**226–234**) show only the distribution of all places which have claims to be considered a town, a fort, a mint or a market in the period 700–1066.

The series attempts to show all the forts and towns of which we have evidence. A division is made between fort and town, and between the late market centres and the earlier foundations which have a larger defensive role. Mints are underlined but the function of market cannot really be shown satisfactorily due to the haphazard nature of the evidence.

The town evidence is set against a background map showing evidence thought to be relevant. For example, roads are included but are only Roman roads known to have been used in medieval times; doubtful cases are shown broken; shires are shown with their boundaries as chain dotted lines (taking Domesday shires as the base); and relief is indicated. The maps have also been used as an index series in that sites shown on general maps can be located more accurately on these sheets — places indicated by small white circles have no urban significance.

It would be wrong not to remind the reader that the complexities of the early medieval town, indeed its sophistication, have been established in the past few decades. The king founded forts or walled towns (both termed **burhs**) which were also made into mints or markets (**ports**) by the royal prerogative if he so wished. The towns had their own law, officers, administration, they were often planned and the regular street patterns consisted of streets regularly maintained. In at least one case, Winchester, a water system served all the lower town. The pattern of towns built up slowly from a number of places with some of the attributes of a town in 700, through the few additions that we know about during the eighth century, to a great range of foundations in the period 870–930, followed by the foundation of a set of secondary centres in the years before 1066.

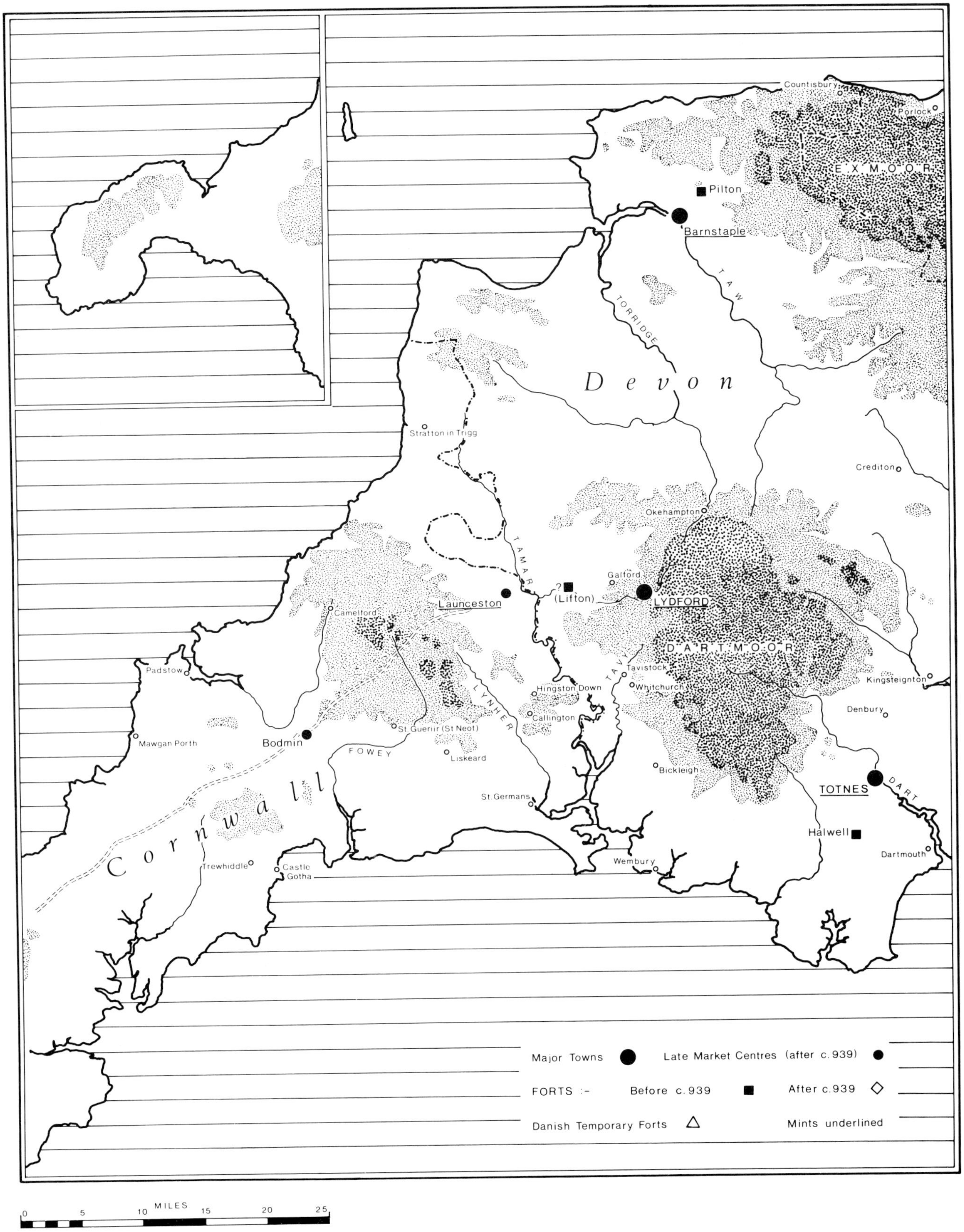

226 Towns in the south-west

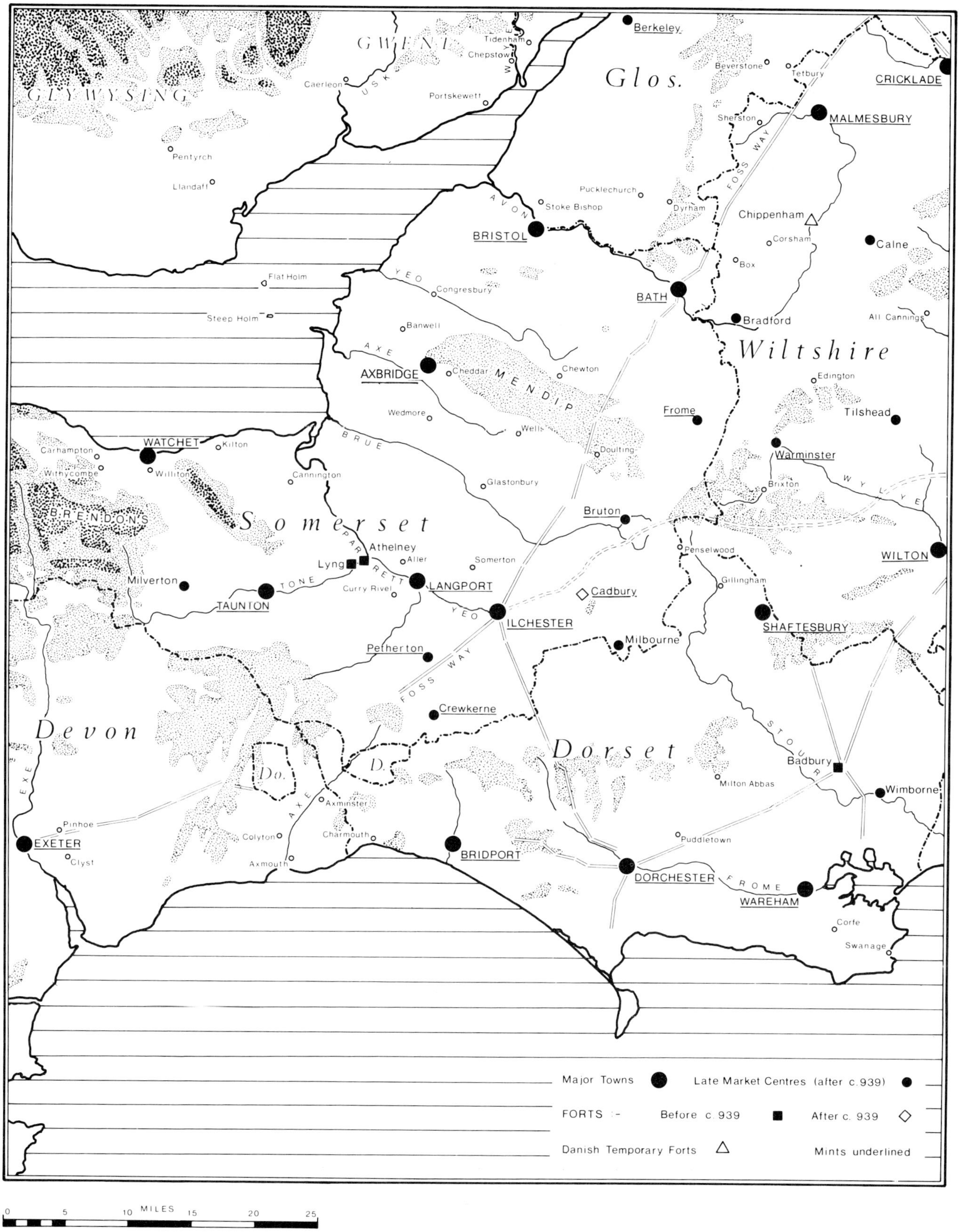

227 Towns in Somerset and Dorset

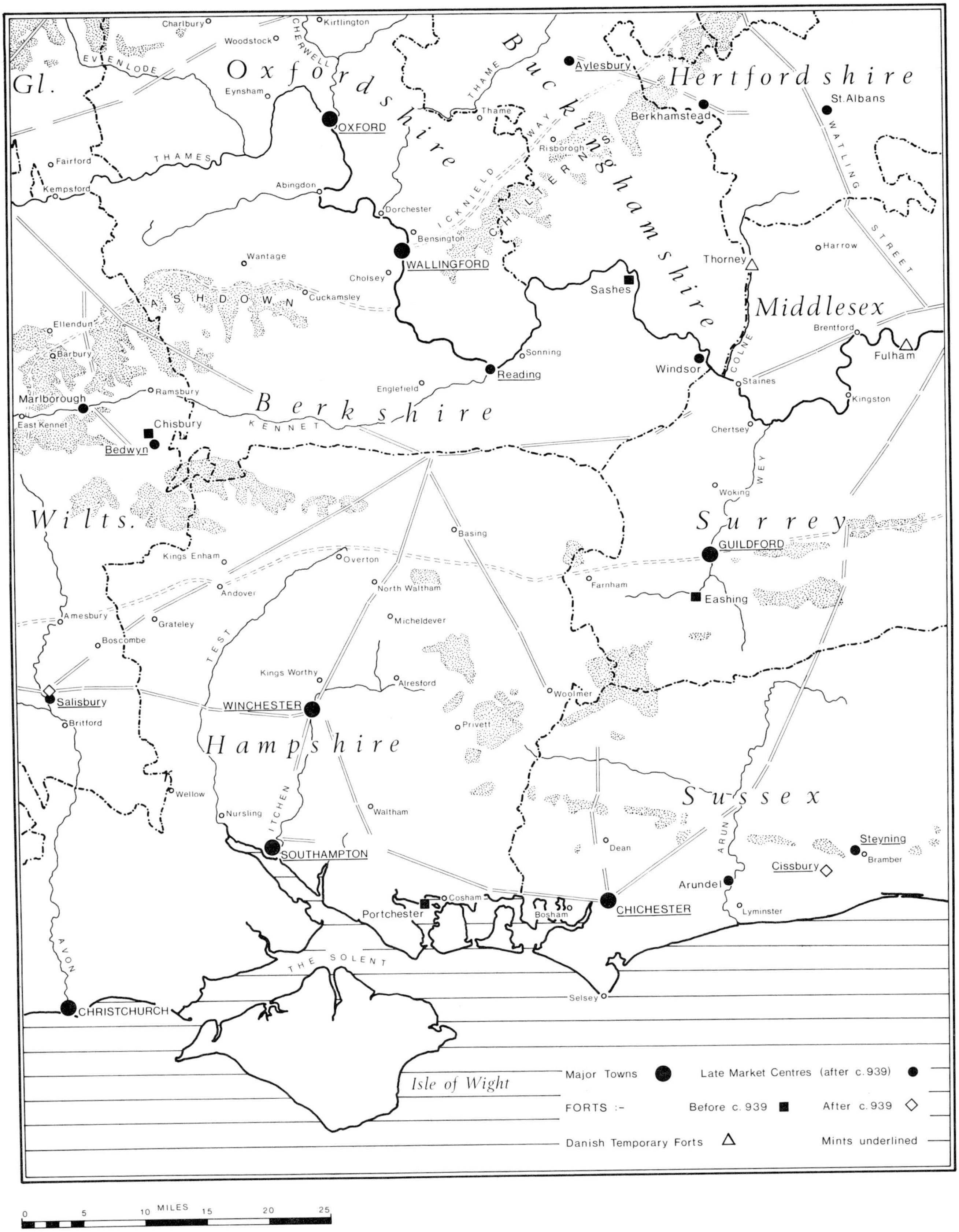

228 Towns in the south

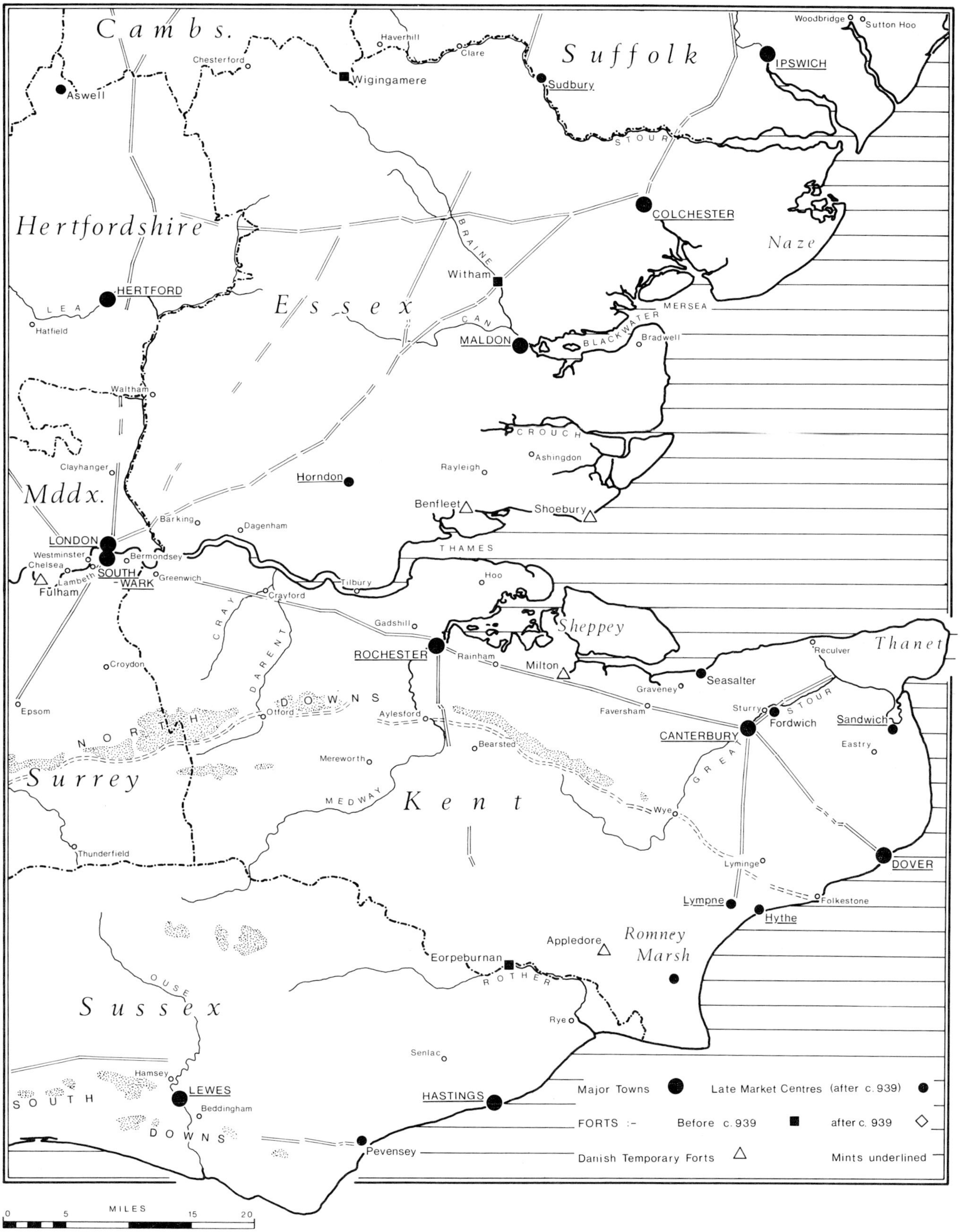

229 Towns in the south-east

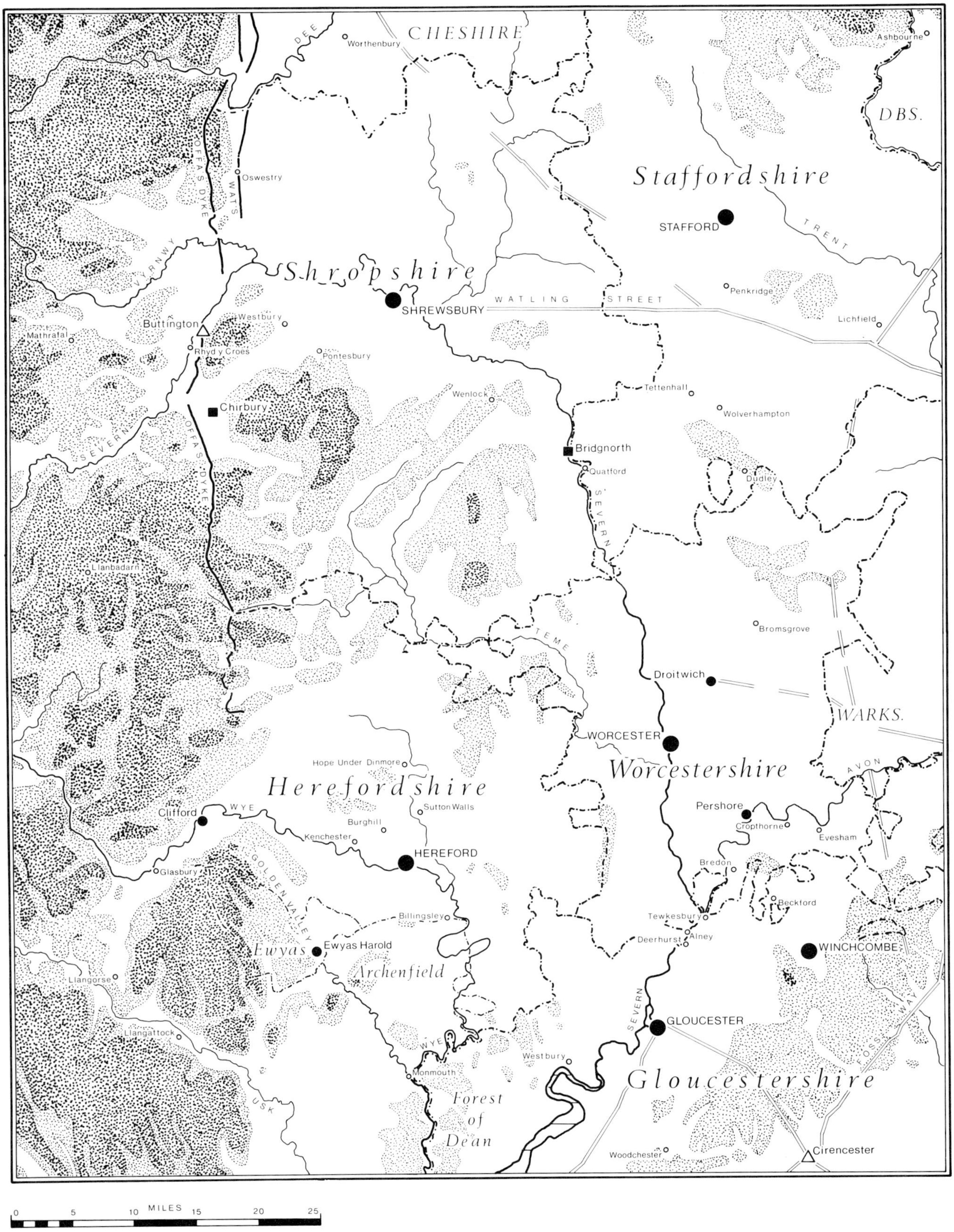

230 Towns in the west Midlands

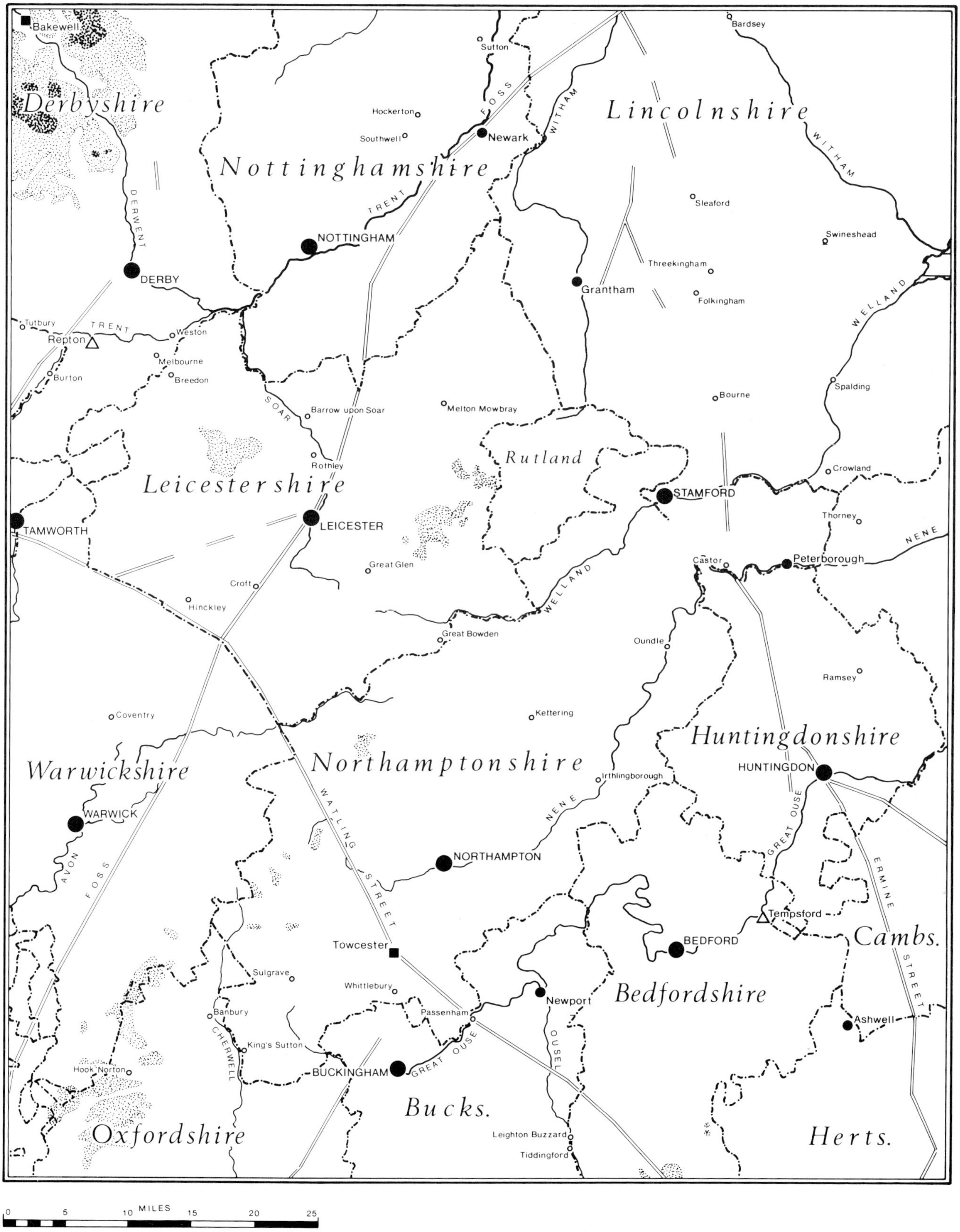

231 Towns in the east Midlands

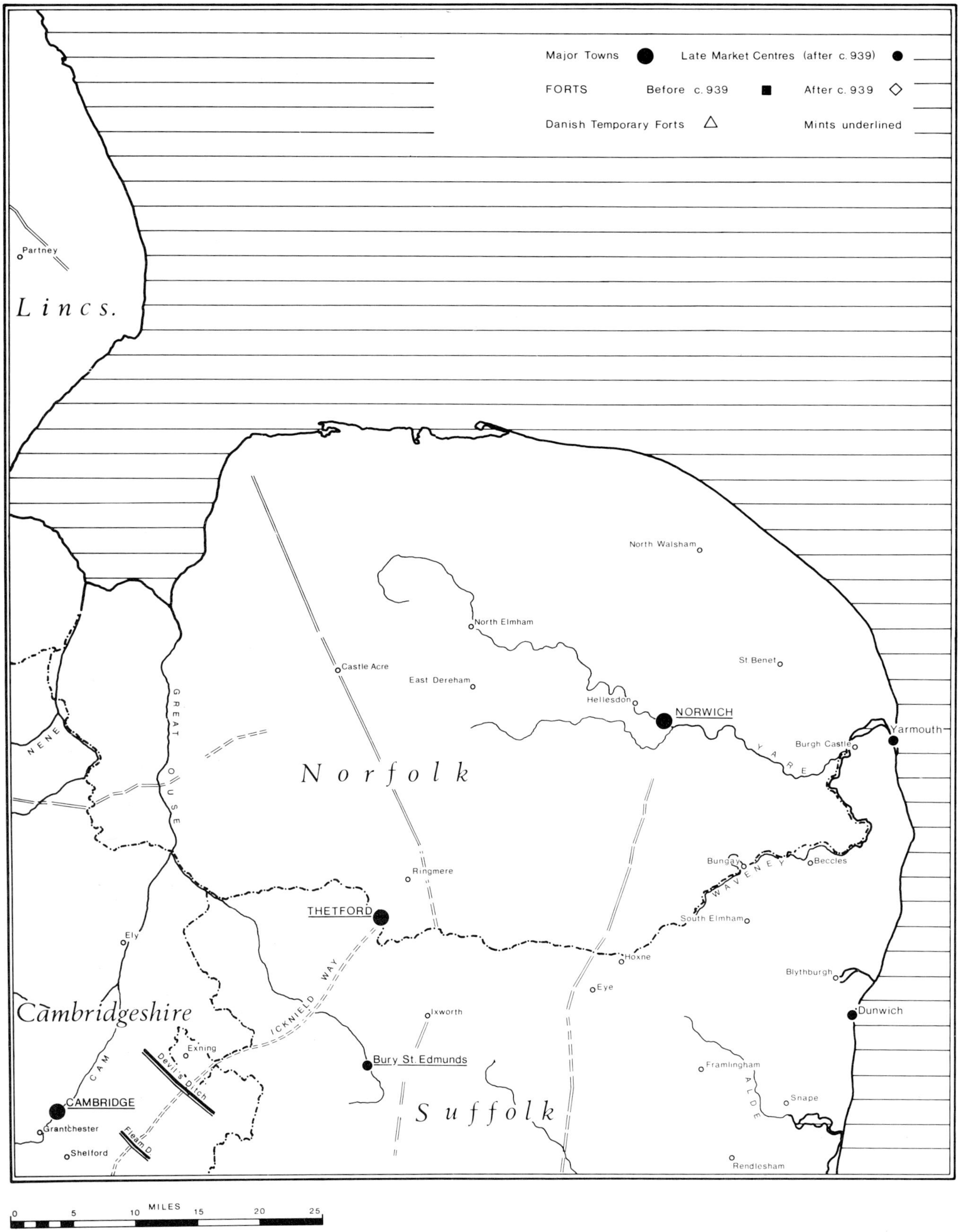

232 Towns in East Anglia

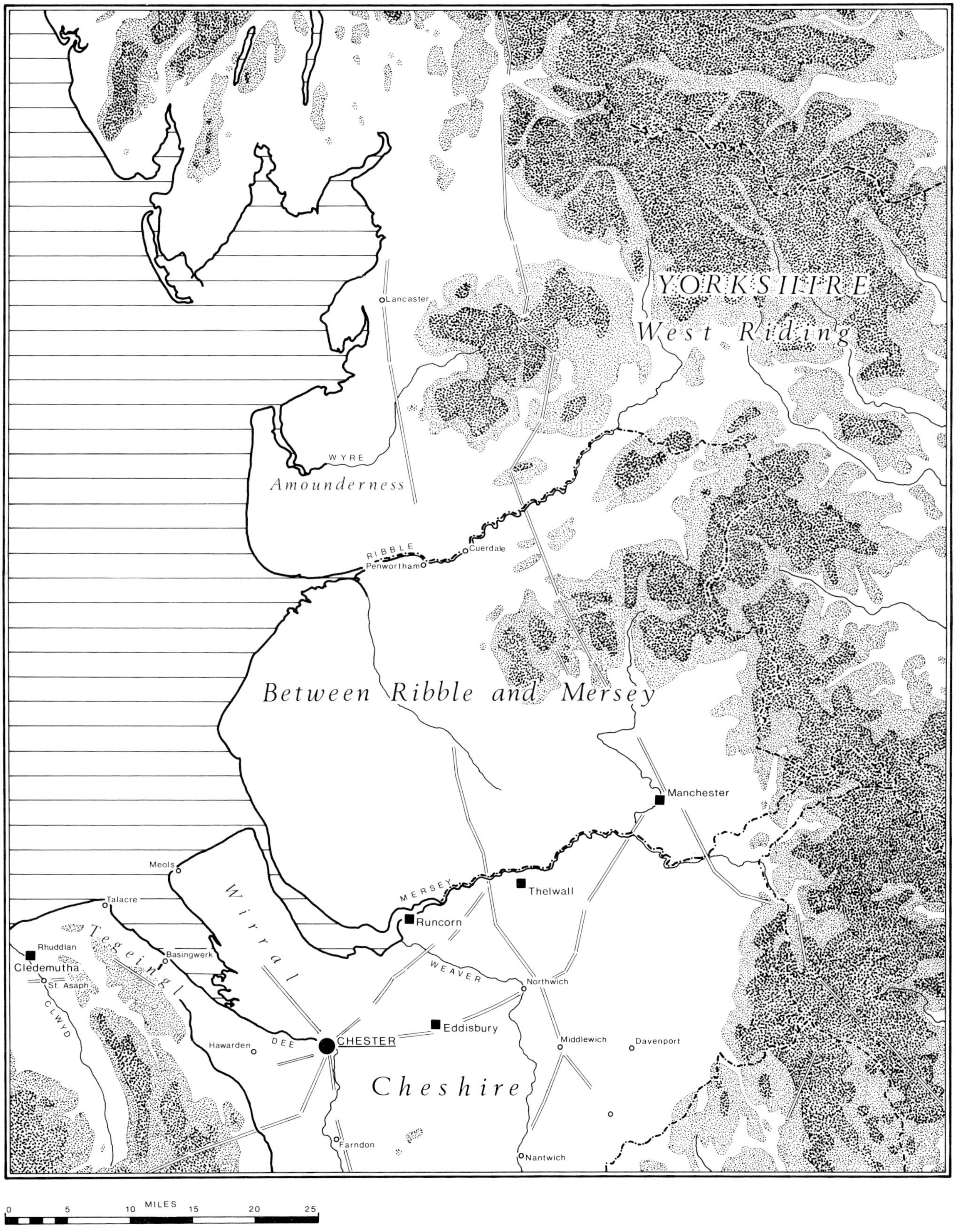

233 Towns in the north-west

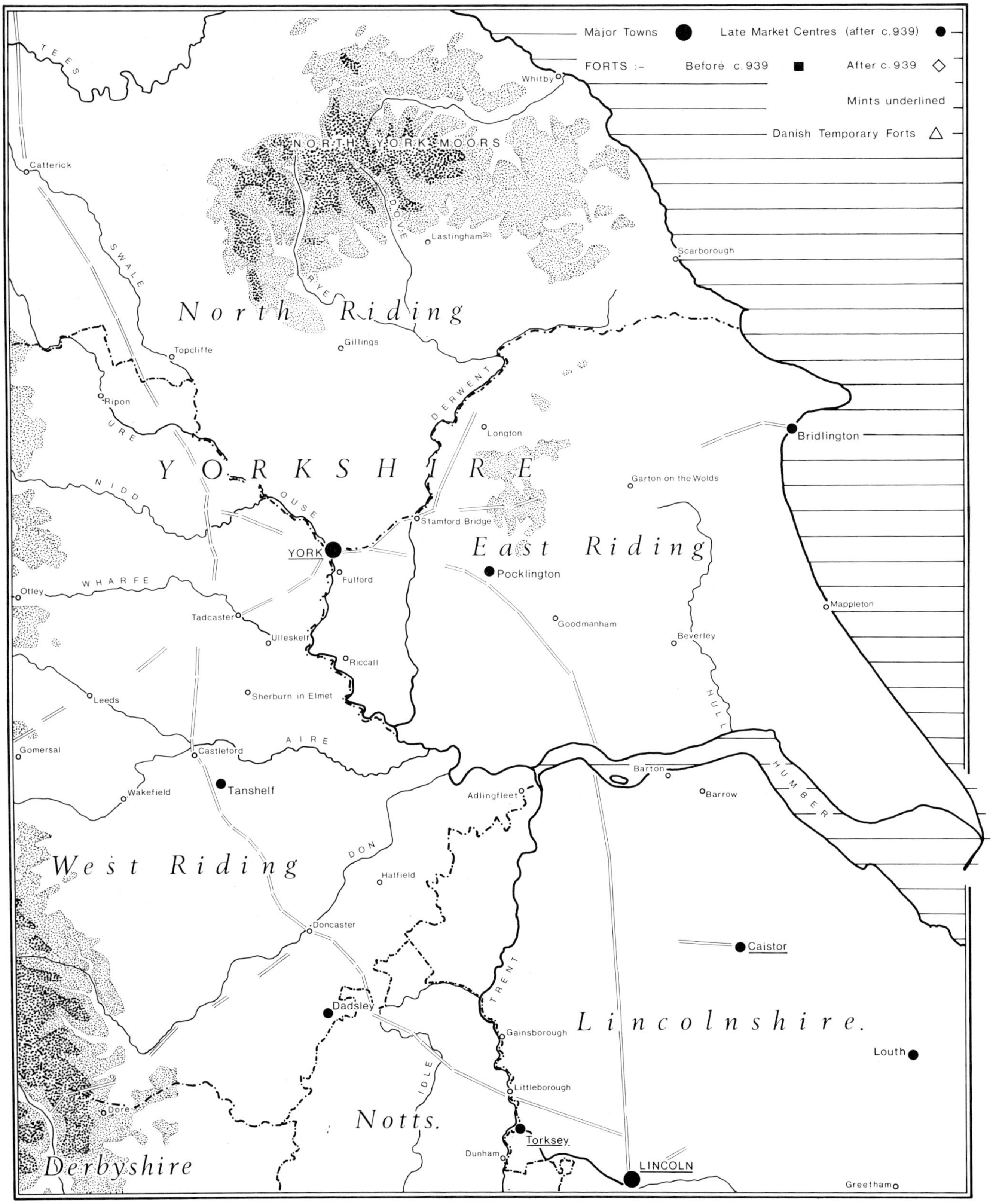

234 Towns in the north Midlands and Yorkshire

The Size of Towns and Forts (235–236)

In the central period (870–930), when the bulk of the **burhs** were founded, it should be clearly understood that the King founded forts or he founded towns — towns did not grow out of forts nor did they appear spontaneously. As this is an important fact I should explain briefly how we can be sure, and as the map series makes the distinction between fort and town that distinction should be justified. The walled area of a **burh** represents the plans and aspirations of its founder. It may fail, in which case the internal area will not be taken up by houses, streets, churches and markets. It may succeed beyond the founder's expectations, in which case it will form suburbs. In the known area of these **burh** foundations we have fossilized the policy of the Anglo-Saxon kings. If these areas are plotted (**235**) against date and we then mark in black those foundations that went on to become towns, we can see a clear pattern. The index of success used is whether the **burh** went on to achieve borough status in the Domesday Survey. If the diagram is simplified the pattern can be further emphasized (**236**).

It can now be seen that before the reign of Athelstan sites founded with less than 16 acres did not become towns, while those with over 21 acres were towns by 1066. The correlation is too great to avoid the conclusion that towns and forts were being founded as such. Some sites — Canterbury, York and London, for example — were towns before 850 but they are few in number, and we must realize that one of the grounds for choice of a site would be pre-existing settlements on that site, whether agricultural, religious or administrative. After the reign of Athelstan the pattern changes and we can see the emergence of centres where the defensive role was unimportant. Map **187** showed a series of secondary market centres burgeoning on royal holdings as the king attempted to increase revenue from his estates (see also Sawyer 1978, 61–2, and 73–4).

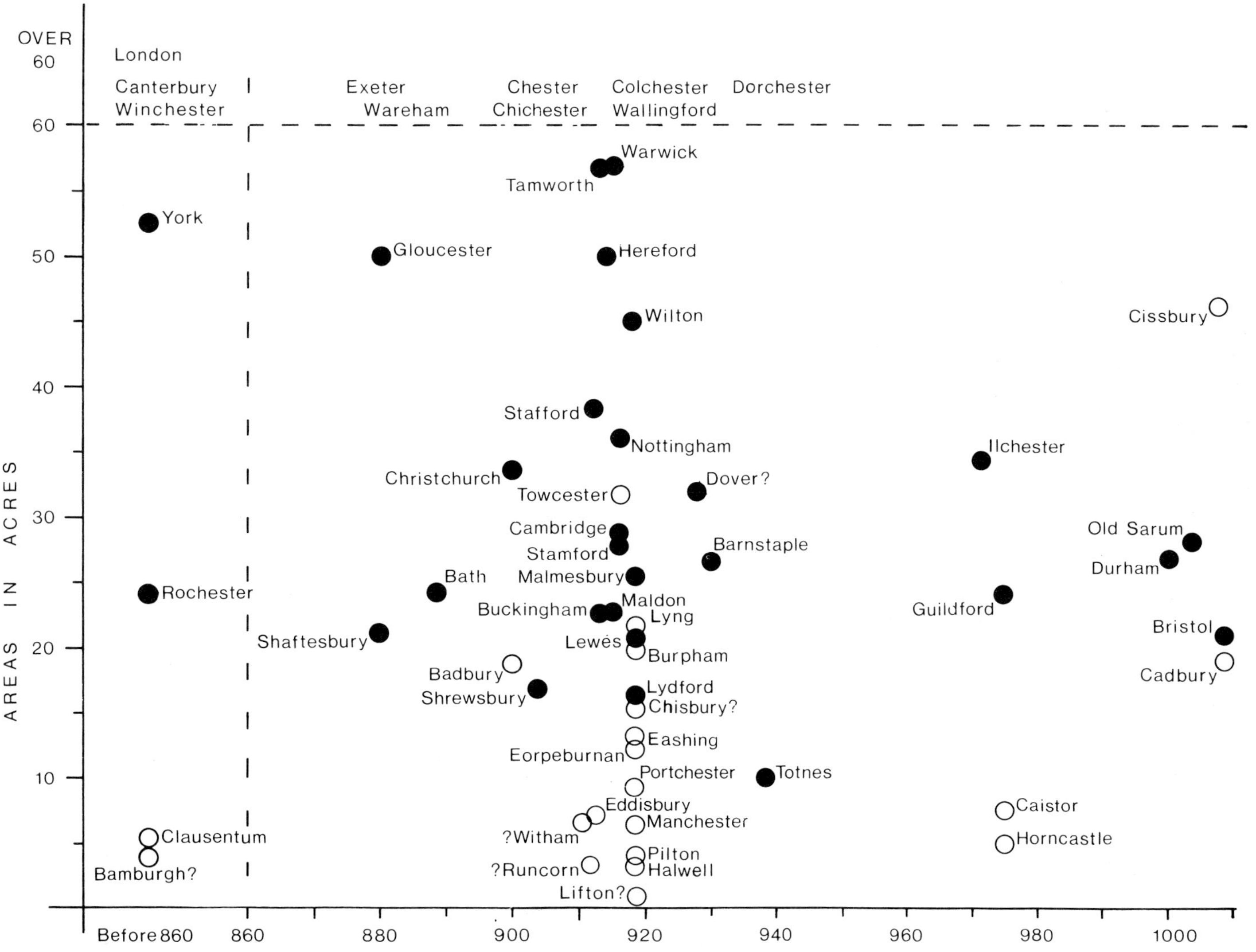

235 Areas of burhs. Those sites with an area of more than 60 acres are shown, correctly for date, across the top of the diagram

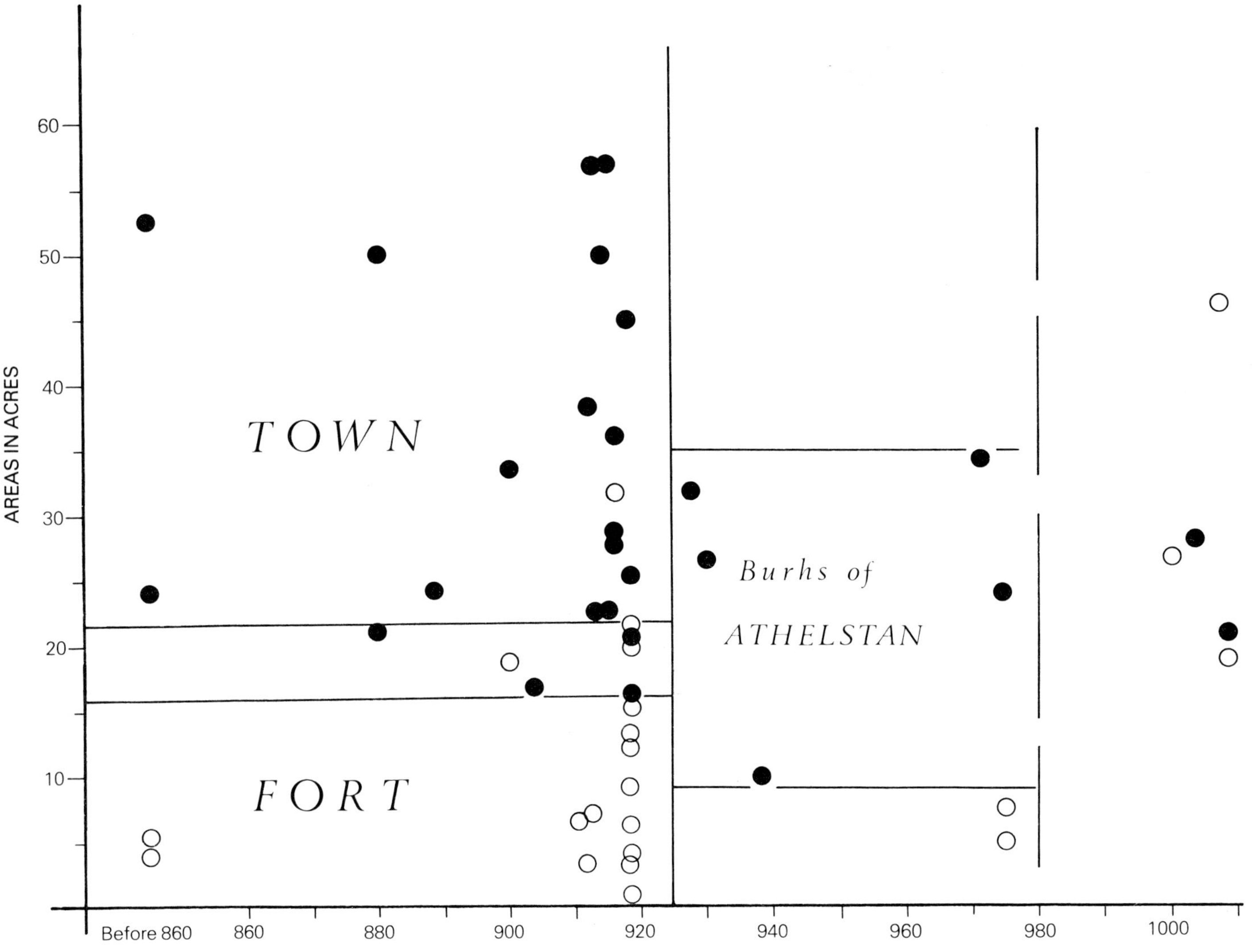

236 Areas of burhs: an abstraction

The Church

Introduction (237)

The Church was a great institution in Anglo-Saxon England with immense influence and a growing power. By the time this atlas takes note of it, paganism was for all major purposes dead, although it regained influence in the Danelaw for a while on a very minor scale.

The major advance of the period, and one not charted here, was the expansion of the parochial system, so that by 1066 most of England was organized into parishes. The other great concerns were the heroic efforts of the Anglo-Saxons to convert to the true faith the lands of their Continental ancestors and the monastic revival of the tenth century.

Before launching into the church history of the period 700–1066, or that part which is easily illustrated by maps, it may be as well to spare one background glance. The background and setting of the Roman mission of Augustine was such that it influenced the Anglo-Saxon Church, with its unique devotion to Rome and the Pope, throughout our period. A glance at map **237** will show two things: the vast numbers of bishoprics in the Mediterranean area (it should be noted that 'Archbishoprics' are an anachronism for the period: these were really 'Metropolitan Bishoprics'), all set by decree of the church fathers in cities not in villages; and the fact that Western Christendom would soon become a thin band across Europe once the Moors broke into Spain. All the churches of Spain and Africa would come into the hands of the Arabs and only North Italy, France and the British Isles were left to Rome. The Church in England was therefore an important part of the Catholic world. The borders of Christendom in the West were to rest in the early eighth century on the Rhine and the Pyrenees, the missions to Germany found it strategically necessary to broaden this narrow corridor between paganism and Islam.

The decree of the Church that no bishop should set up his seat in a village meant that Roman sites in England, perhaps long deserted, received a new lease of life with the arrival of Augustine's mission, and we must therefore treat with caution the choice of places on dogmatic grounds as evidence for continuing urban life in these centres.

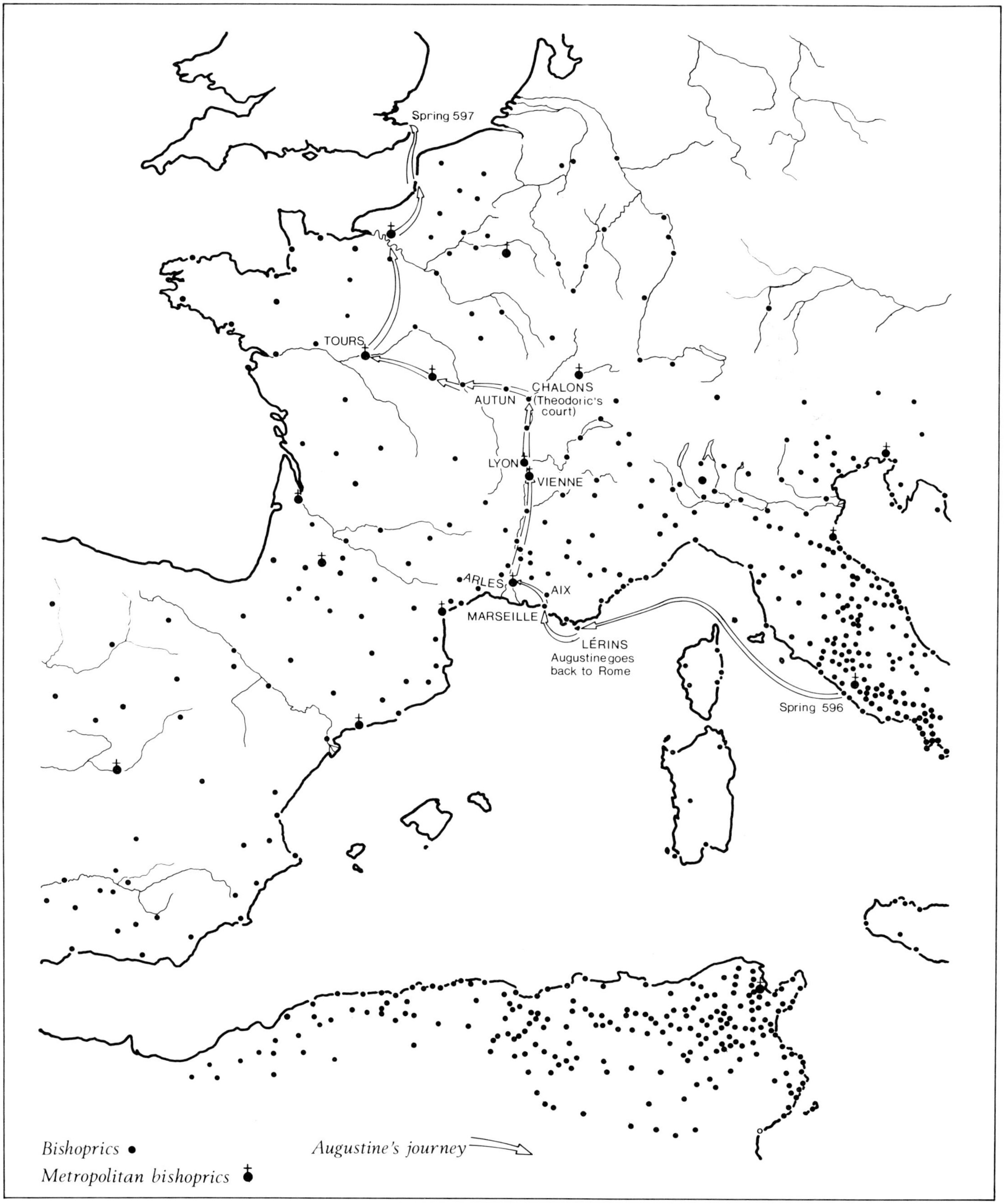

237 Western Christendom c.597

Dioceses (238–241)

The plan of Gregory to consecrate two metropolitans, one at London and one at York, each with twelve bishops under them, was never realized. It is doubtful whether the plan was made on the basis of accurate reports of the state of Britain at the time, or on some tome of late Roman geography in the Vatican library — whichever it was, neither was of much use. The twelfth suffragan of Canterbury was consecrated at Leicester in 737. York never obtained that number, nor did the southern metropolitan remove to London. There was provision for bishoprics for each of the various peoples and kingdoms, the Middle Angles, the West Saxons, the East Saxons and so on. In fact some sees were known by the folk name and not the seat: the Bishop of the Hwicce, was only later called the Bishop of Worcester.

The Mercian bishopric was split in 737 into Lichfield and Leicester, the West Saxon bishopric split into 'east and west of Selwood' (the sees of Winchester and Sherborne), and Selsey was founded to minister to the South Saxon Kingdom (map **238**). The situation then stayed constant, apart from one controversy over a new Archbishop for Mercia under Offa, until the Danish invasions.

The Danish invasions led apparently to a complete disruption of the North Midlands, East Anglian and Northumbrian church organization (map **239**). York continued in some form for most of the period, Lindsey, Hexham, Elmham and Dunwich disappeared completely, Leicester and Lindisfarne moved the site of the bishop's seat (map **240**). The body of St Cuthbert, the principal relic of Lindisfarne, was taken by the monks on their wanderings. The Lindisfarne community settled for many years at Chester-le-Street and finally moved to Durham. All this may be an oversimplification but the cessation of evidence for the area at this time must be significant.

After the Reconquest only Elmham was refounded, the Midlands and the north having to be content with the loss of two dioceses. York was left so impoverished that it was often linked to the wealthy bishopric of Worcester in an attempt to improve its finances.

In the area south of the Thames the West Saxon kings reorganized the bishoprics to give most shires a bishop of their own. The reorganization was completed by Athelstan founding a Cornish bishopric. There were problems, however, in finding a sufficient endowment and some amalgamations took place in the eleventh century (map **241**).

The boundaries of the sees are very conjectural before 900. The bounds of the dioceses of Worcester and Hereford appear to have expanded somewhat to the north in the period of the Danish invasions. The state of Northern and Eastern England in the late ninth century is badly documented. More detailed maps of the dioceses of Hereford, Worcester and East Saxons are to be found on maps **143** and **140**. The medieval boundaries of the dioceses are used on maps **250–258**.

Some of the changes affecting the dioceses can be followed more readily on the charts in **259–260**.

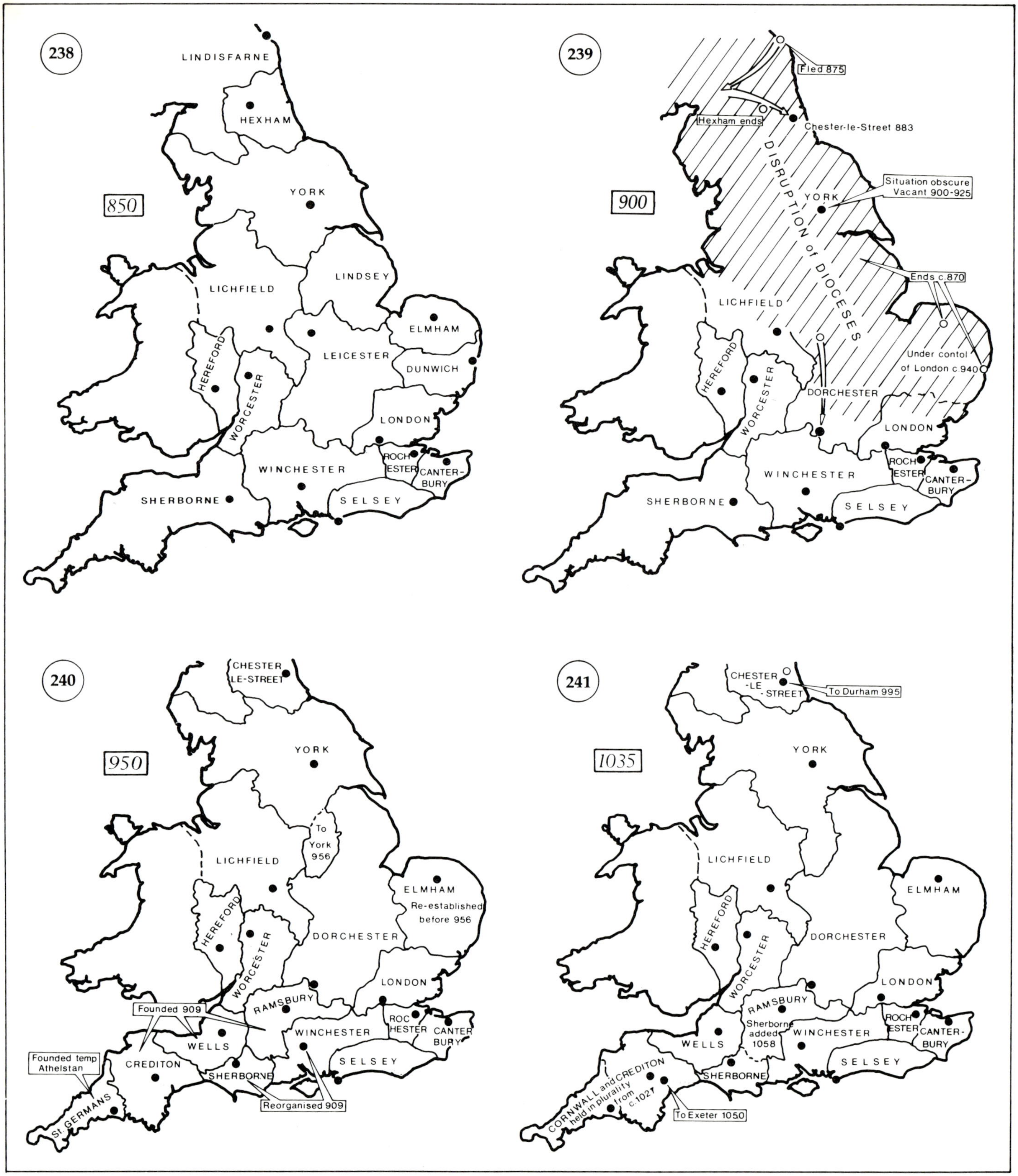

238–241 Dioceses 850–1035

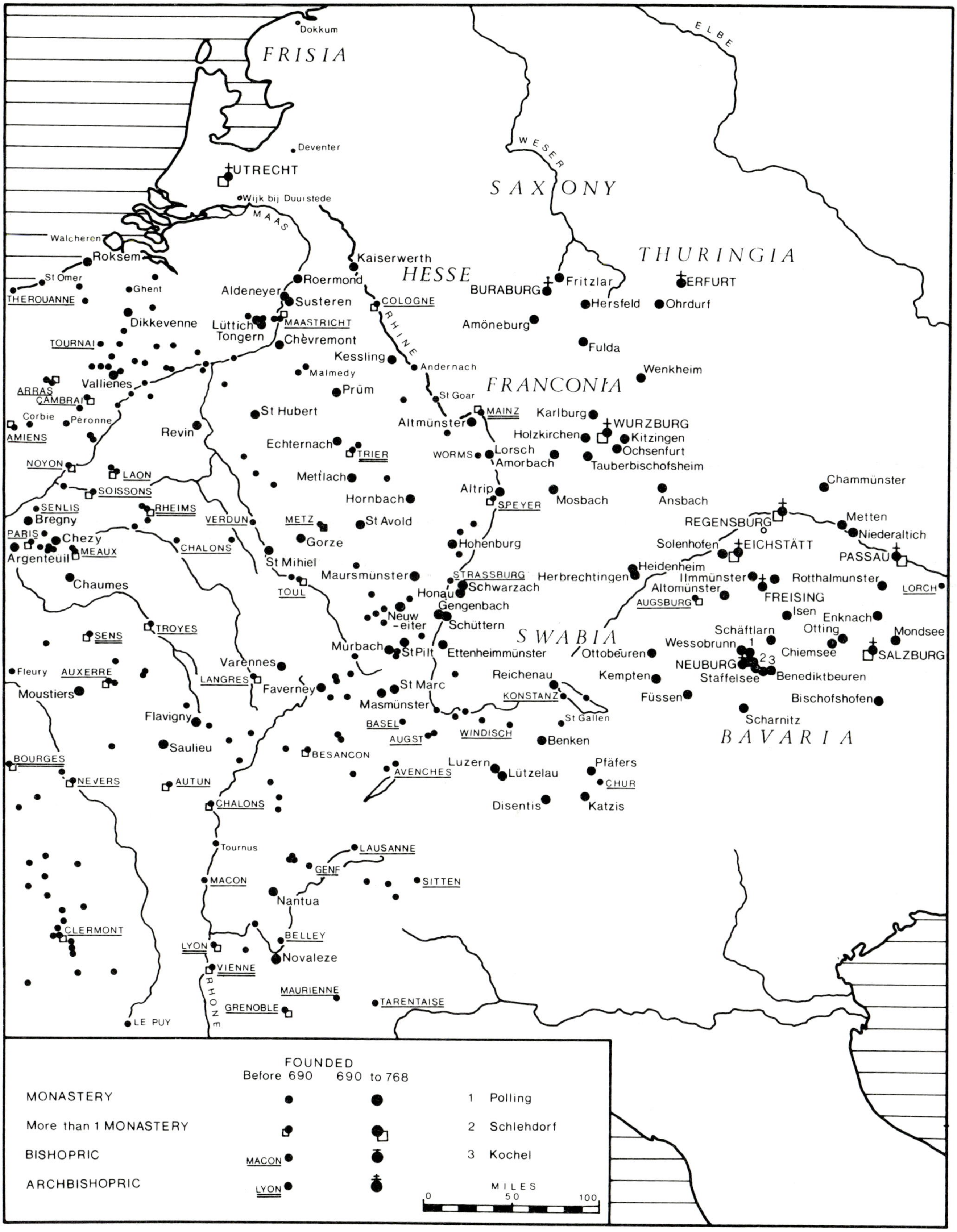

242 The Church in East Francia

Missionary Efforts (242)

The English Church's efforts to convert the heathen Germanic homelands started before the conversion of England was completed in Sussex. In 677 Wilfrid made some attempts to evangelize Frisia on his way to Rome. There was a succession of missionaries, Wihtberht, Willibrord, Boniface and Willehad, and their efforts are well documented in Stenton or more fully in Levison (1946). Map **242** is an attempt to place these successes in their Continental setting and to show that from the stagnation of the Merovingian Gallic Church to the completion of the mission the frontiers of Christendom had been pushed firmly forward from the line on which they rested for all of the seventh century to a new line by 768. By then the Church was firmly established in Bavaria and middle Germany. An impressive string of new bishoprics and monasteries supported this conversion and the stage was set for Charlemagne's attempts to move the missions still further. It should be noted that not all of the new foundations shown are either Anglo-Saxon influenced or Irish influenced.

Anglo-Saxons took part later in the conversion of the north, their most important contribution being in the early eleventh century in providing clergy for Norway.

The Monastic Revival (243–249)

The major ecclesiastic event of the tenth century was the reformation of monastic life (map **243**). History tends to be concentrated where the documentary evidence is thickest and the wealth of material on the saints of the reformation and their churches has meant that the subject is well covered. The standard works all have good accounts and Loyn (1962, 244) has charted the revival, with its houses and derivations; the matter is discussed in great and scholarly detail in Knowles (1963).

The Revival was necessary because of the decay of monastic life in the ninth century and not, as all the monastic chronicles reiterate, because of the Danish invasions. Many houses survived the period as secular colleges, establishments of canons which were very popular in the ninth and tenth century, and described in the charters as 'monasteries'. They were despised by the intolerant chroniclers of the reformed houses and have been little regarded since.

The Revival was only part of a much wider Revival of reformed monasticism in Western Europe in which Glastonbury can be seen as part of a chain from Cluny and Brogne to Ratisbon (map **244**). It is, of course, a great simplification, considering the interrelations within countries: for example, Fleury's influence was marked at Abingdon. The impact of the new monasteries and their ability to attract large benefactions in land should not be underestimated. The Revival had wide economic and political consequences.

A list exists (in several versions) of the relics of various saints and the places in which they rest in England. The date for the text as it now exists is c.1032; but it is clear from the layout and content of the surviving text that it is a conflation of an earlier, Mercian, text with a later, West Saxon, one. Map **245** shows all of the places mentioned, although some of the saints of Thorney and Winchester have had to be omitted through lack of space. The sites mentioned are those which were considered worthy of pilgrimage and as such they show a different aspect of popular religion, for Aelfric's **Lives of the Saints** shows that lengthy journeys were made around England in search of healing or blessing at the various sites, again an indication of the mobility of society. There are also some topographical observations within the text (Liebermann 1889; Rollason 1978).

All the monasteries of the Anglo-Saxon period known to me are shown on maps **250–258** below. The distributions change over the years and the houses are not contemporaneous. Map **246** gives the distribution of Benedictine monasteries and nunneries c.1060 (Godfrey 1962) and map **247** that of the Colleges of Secular Canons. It can be seen that the two tend to complement each other, although it would seem many colleges of secular canons still need to be added, e.g. St Frideswide's, Oxford. The secular canons are found mainly in the north-west Midlands and the North whilst the reformed houses are south of a line from Humber to Severn. This may also have some relevance to the attitudes taken against the Reform by various local magnates; certainly there seem to be provincial loyalties to various types of establishments.

The early Benedictine houses have been extensively studied (Knowles 1963) and it is instructive to examine the relative wealth of the monasteries. They are valued in Domesday and the results can be seen on map **248** and the chart in **249**. There were some very large landholders amongst them and the total approaches the value of the holdings of the king himself. Some of the holdings are of ancient foundation, resting on early benefactions of the kings and local magnates, for example, Glastonbury, Winchester and Canterbury; some belong to the great foundations of the Reform, and the efforts to raise funds for the benefices can be realized by the extent of the lands held in 1066; and some were only just coming into the first rank of landholders, for example, the seventh rank of Westminster must rely heavily on the benefactions of Edward the Confessor. These houses did not always receive 'fresh' benefactions and as a result of a change of policy of the royal house a monastery could be suddenly impoverished. Pershore, for example, must have been dramatically affected when its lands were appropriated elsewhere. The picture presented is only true of the mid-eleventh century although there are elements of an earlier picture.

The leading nunneries were Wilton and Shaftesbury, both rich from their royal associations in the tenth century. A confusing factor is the extent of the holdings of the bishops, and a similar map could have been drawn for these. Worcester was the richest but in many cases the ownership of lands was intermixed, as at Winchester, between the bishop and the monastic community living cheek by jowl with him.

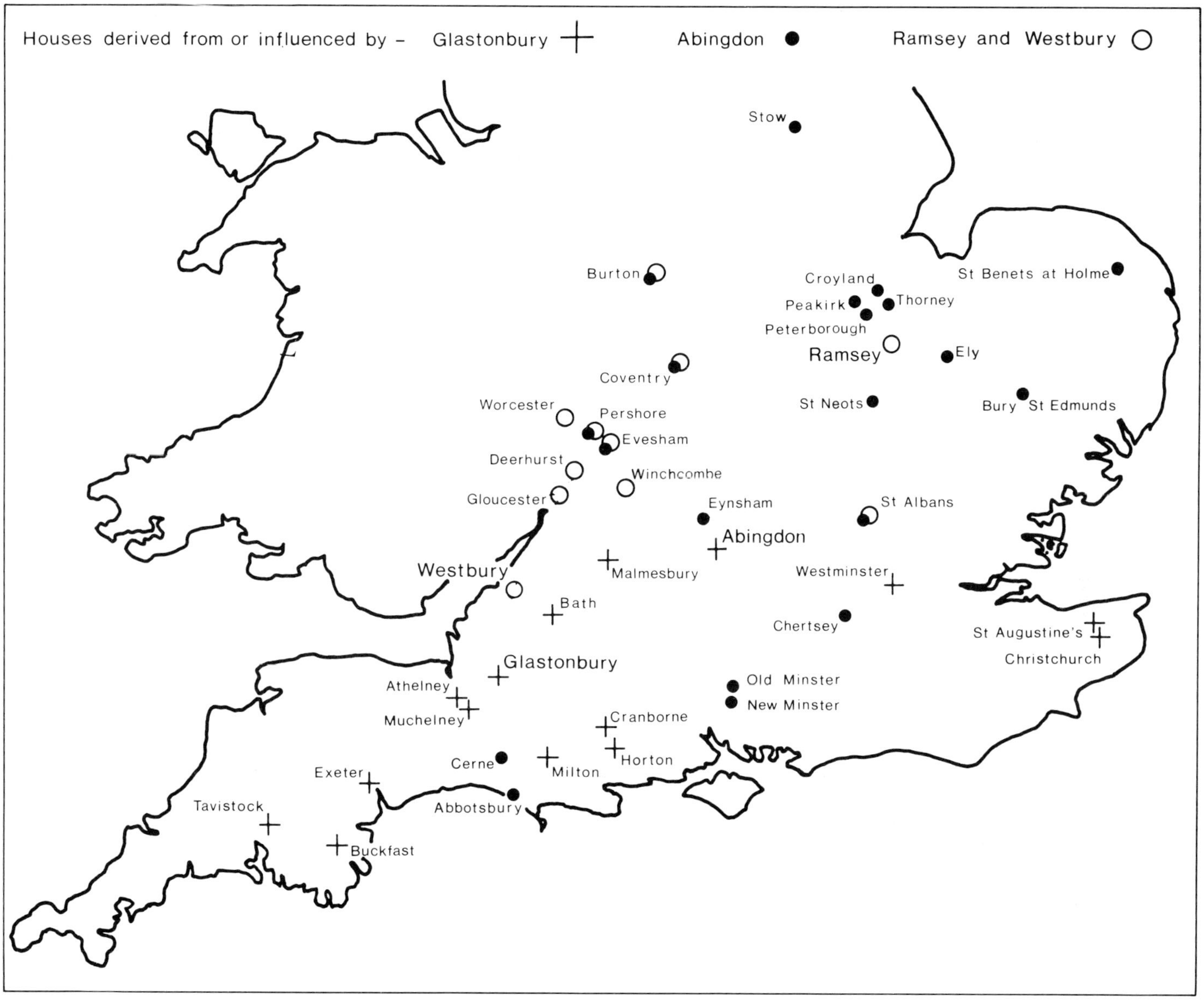

243 The Monastic Revival in late Anglo-Saxon England (Loyn 1962)

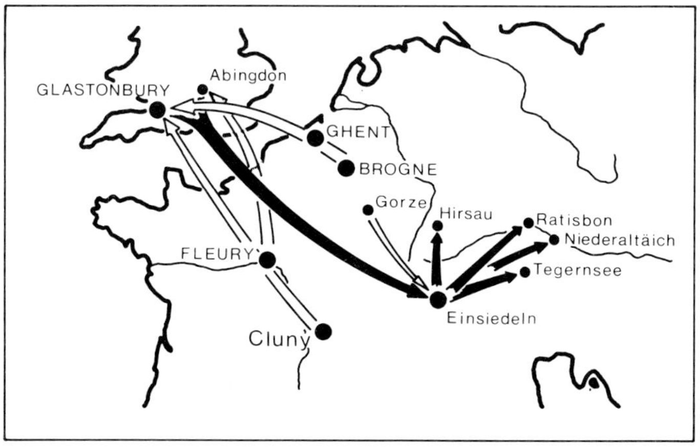

244 The interrelation of monastic rules in the tenth century

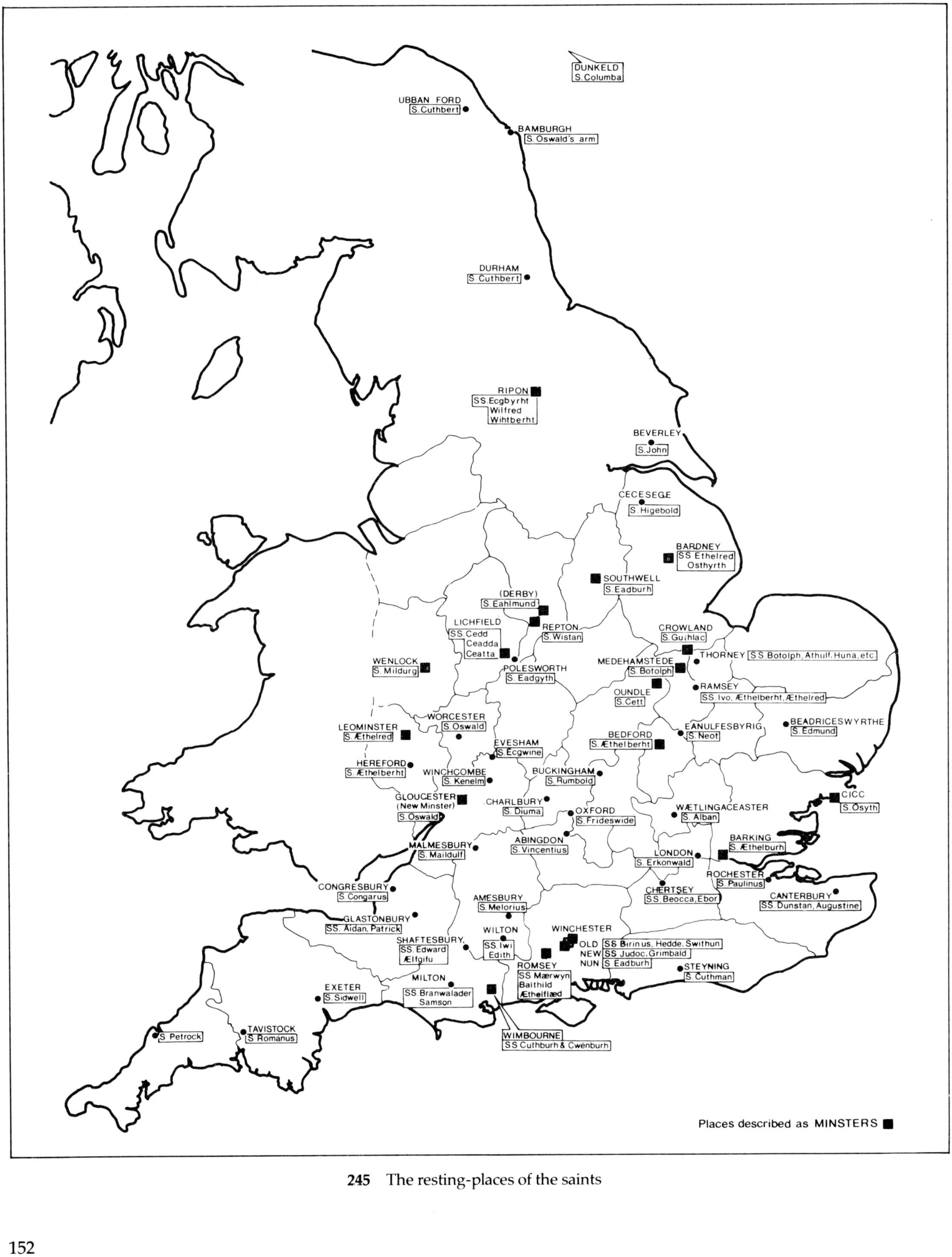

245 The resting-places of the saints

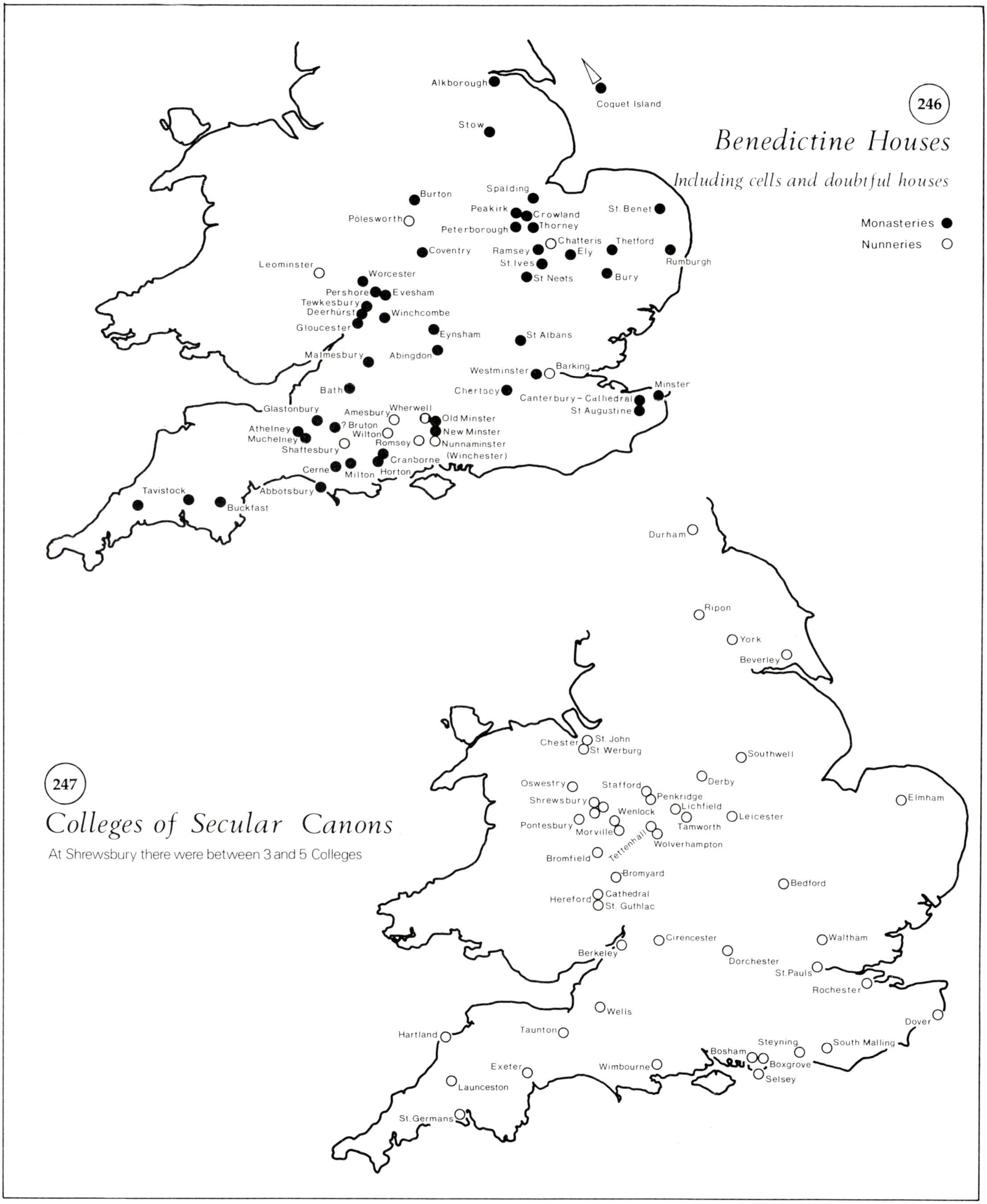

246–247 Benedictine houses and colleges of secular canons c.1060 (after Godfrey 1962)

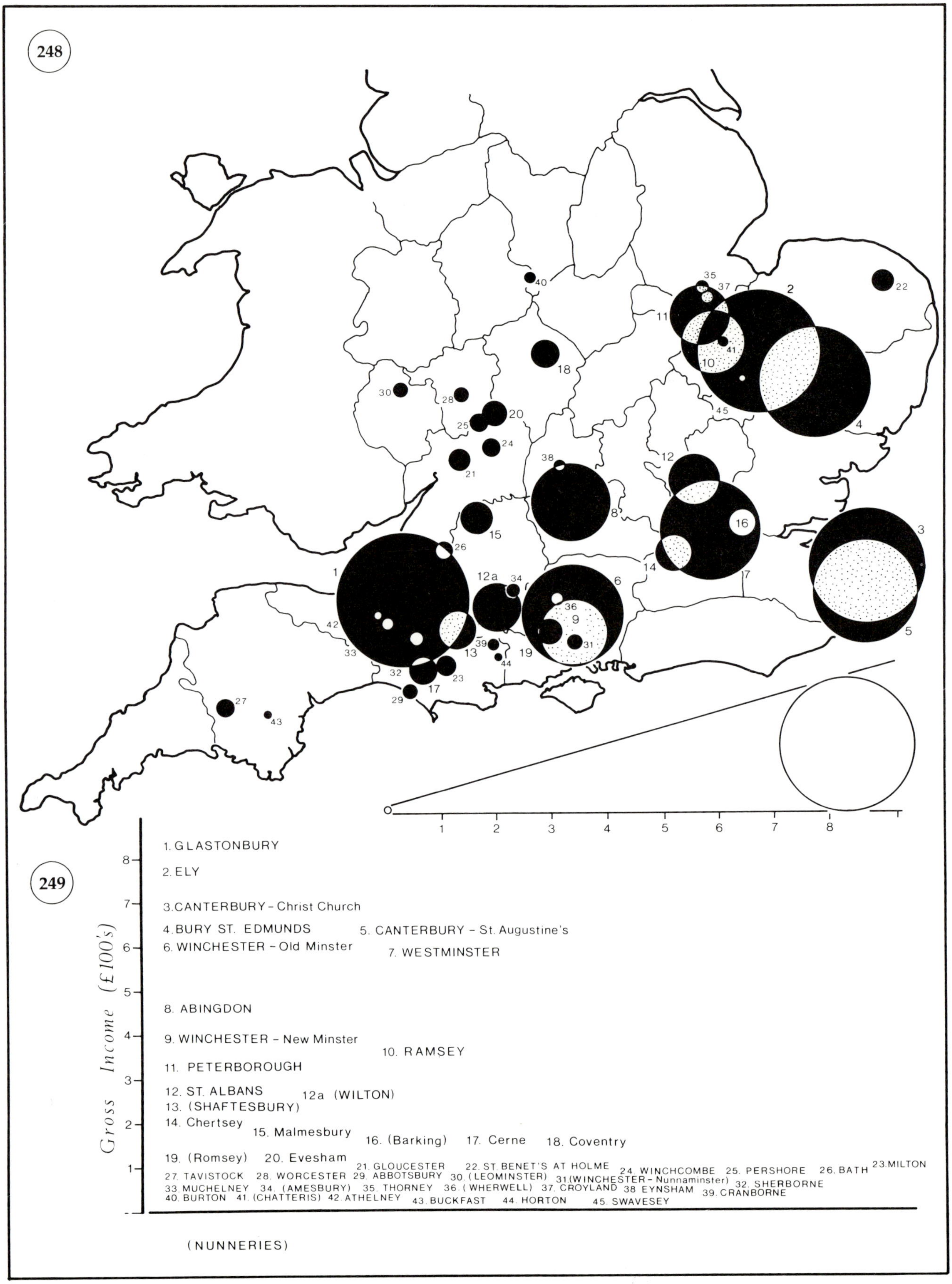

248–249 The Domesday valuation of monasteries and nunneries (£100s)

The Church and its Bishops (250–260)

Maps **250–258** are a palimpsest of the various periods and classes of information available to us. The diocesan boundaries are of the end of the Anglo-Saxon period, the monasteries are of all periods, as are bishop's seats. All churches which survive as architectural remains (Taylor and Taylor 1965) or as important archaeological remains have been included. The problem of the 'selected crosses and sculpture' is a major one; quite simply, there is no useful handlist available — even an interim one would be invaluable — as much of the work that has been done in the last few years has yet to be made more widely known. It is envisaged that these maps will need constant up-dating in view of the architectural, archaeological and monumental work now being carried out.

The chronologies in **259** and **260** enable one to establish contemporaneous bishops, but it is mainly intended to give some simplified view of the increase in dioceses to 870, the disruption of the Danish invasion period, the recovery, the increase in southern sees and their final amalgamation.

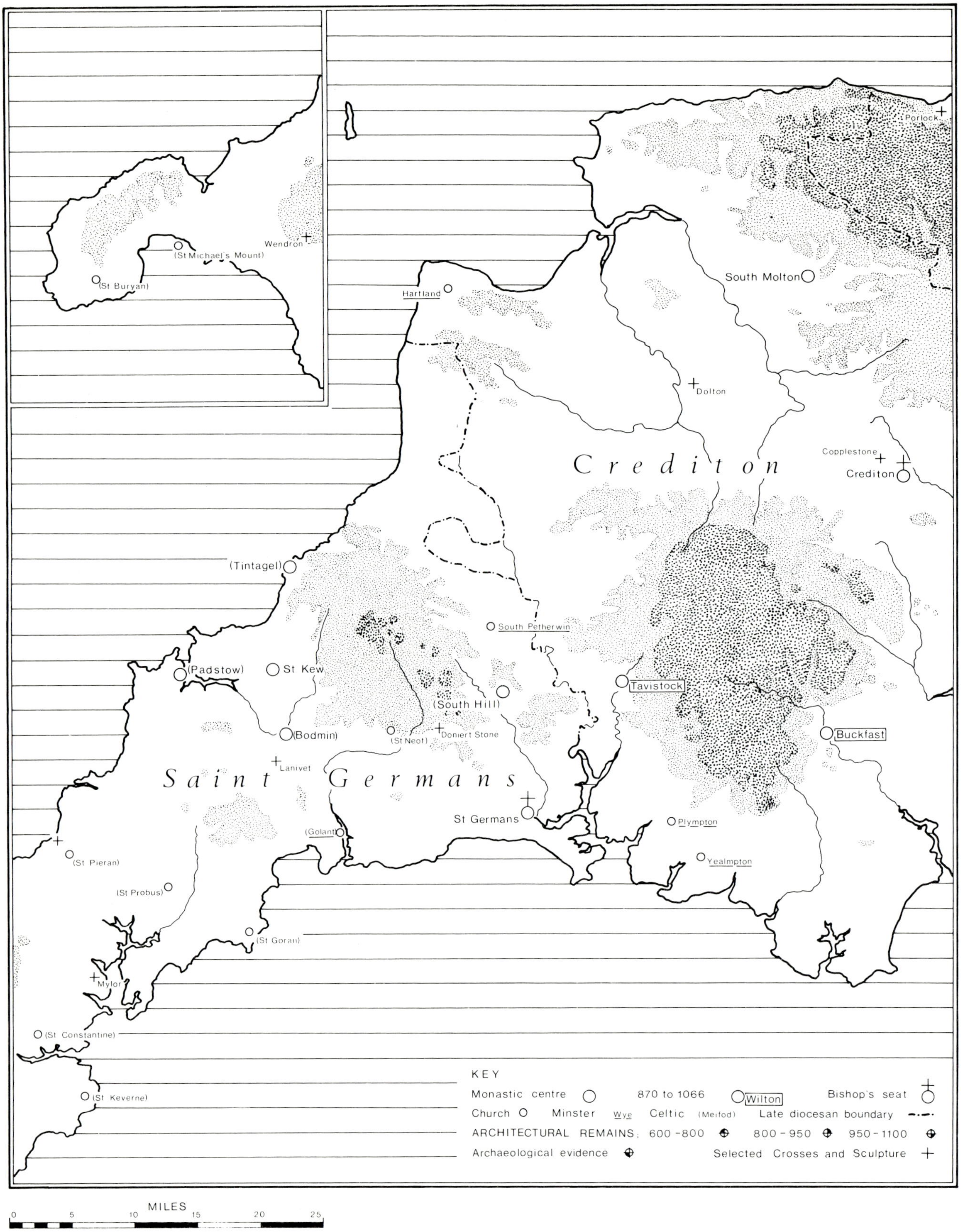

250 The Church in the south-west

251 The Church in Somerset and Dorset

252 The Church in the south

253 The Church in the south-east

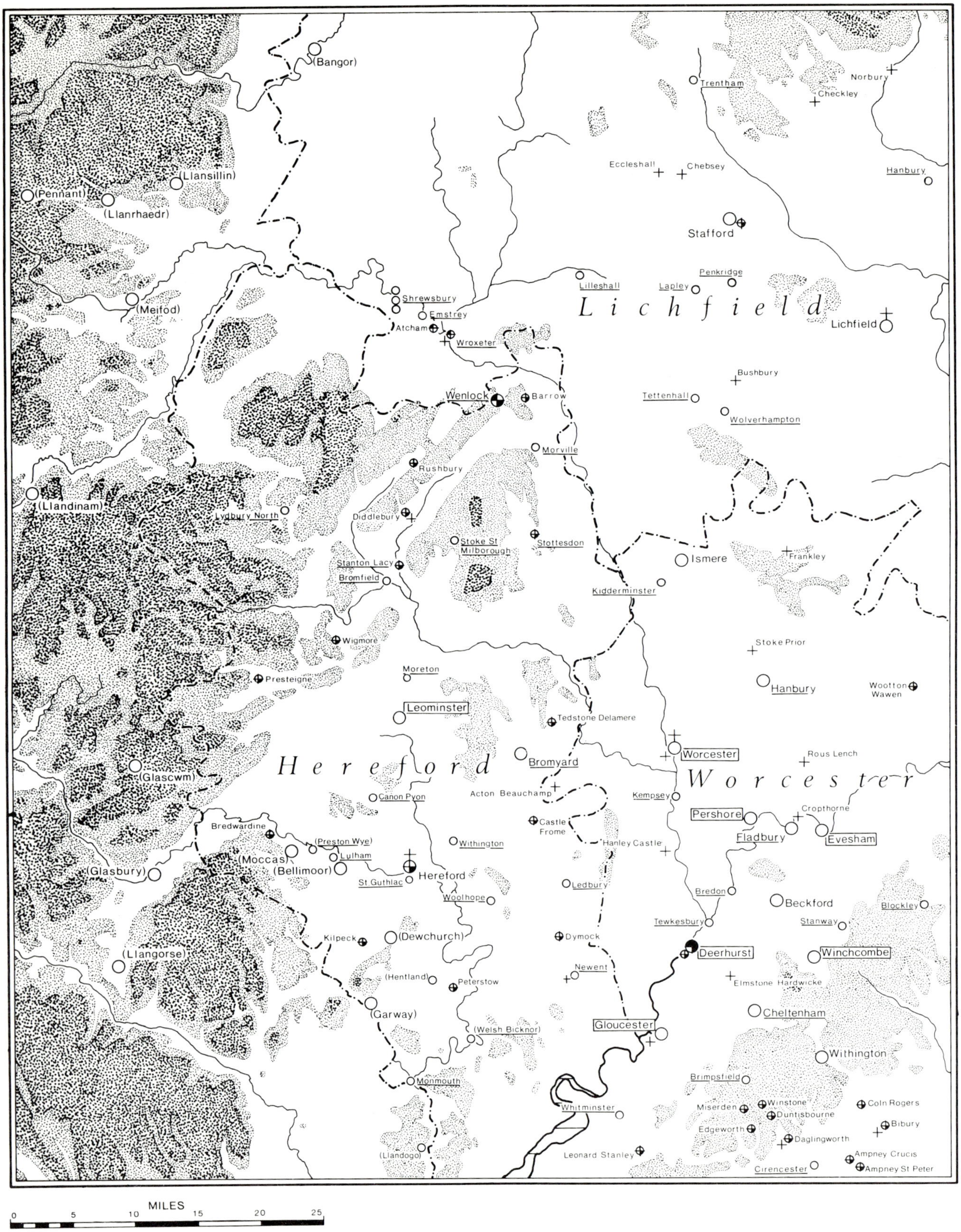

254 The Church in the west Midlands

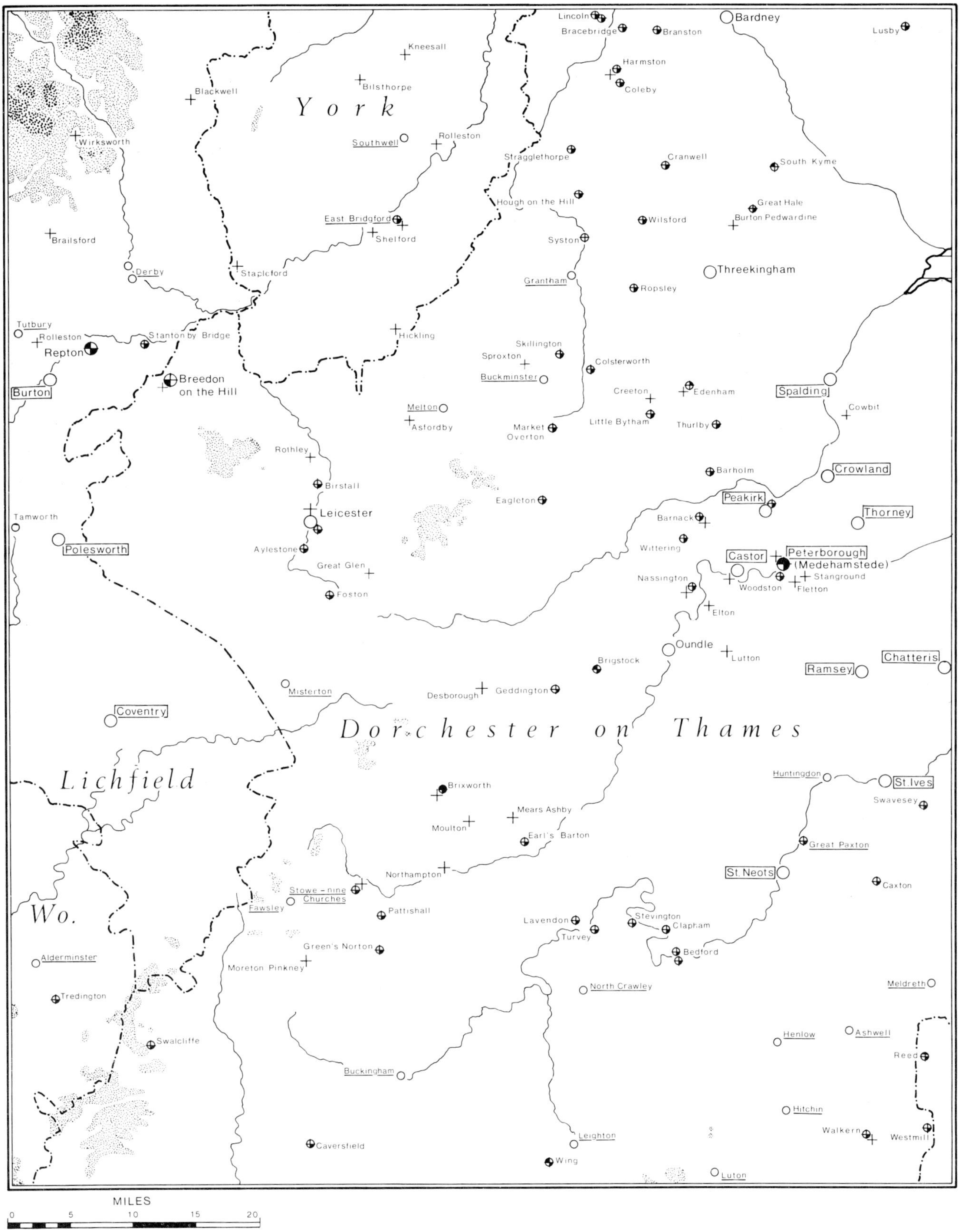

255 The Church in the east Midlands

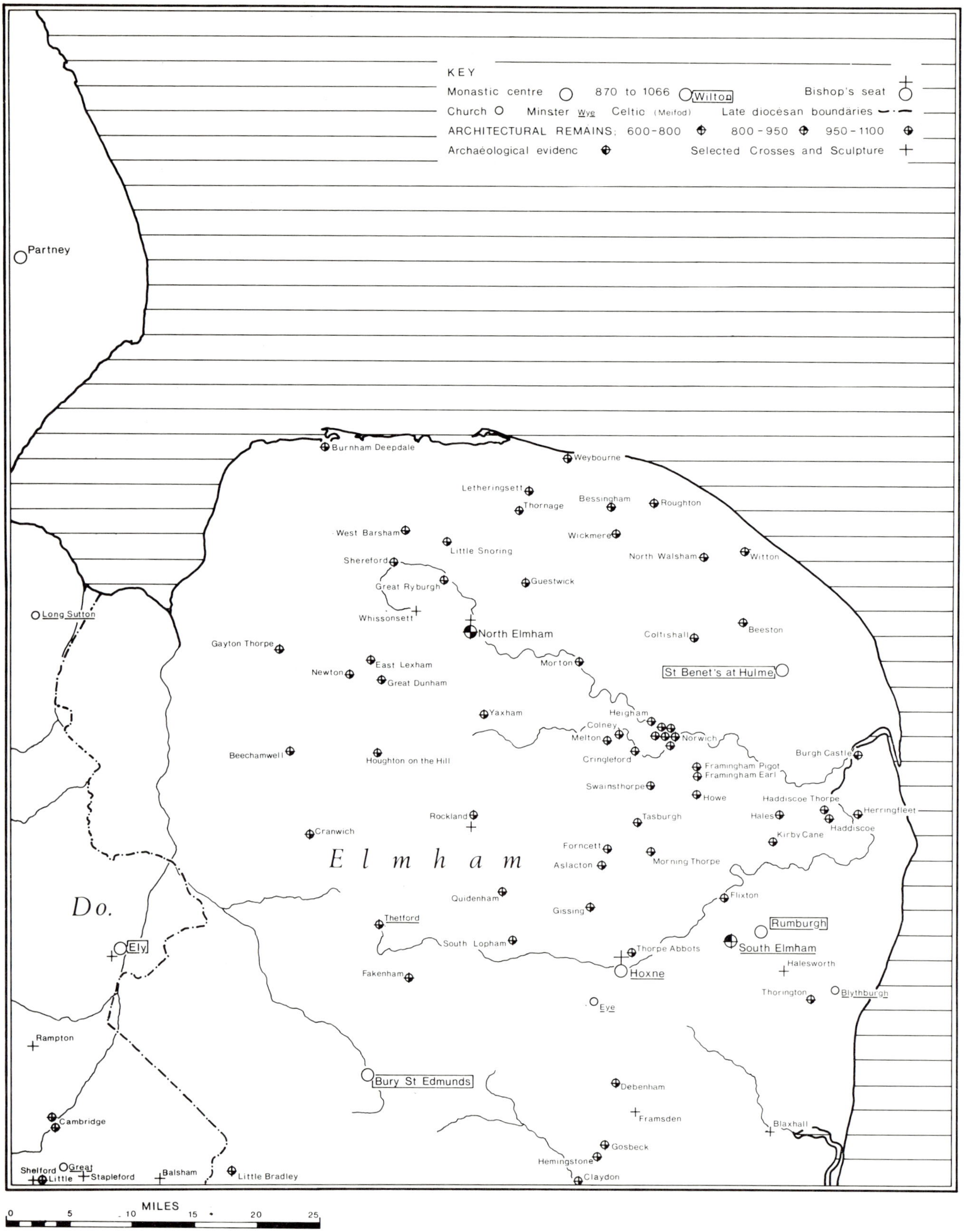

256 The Church in East Anglia

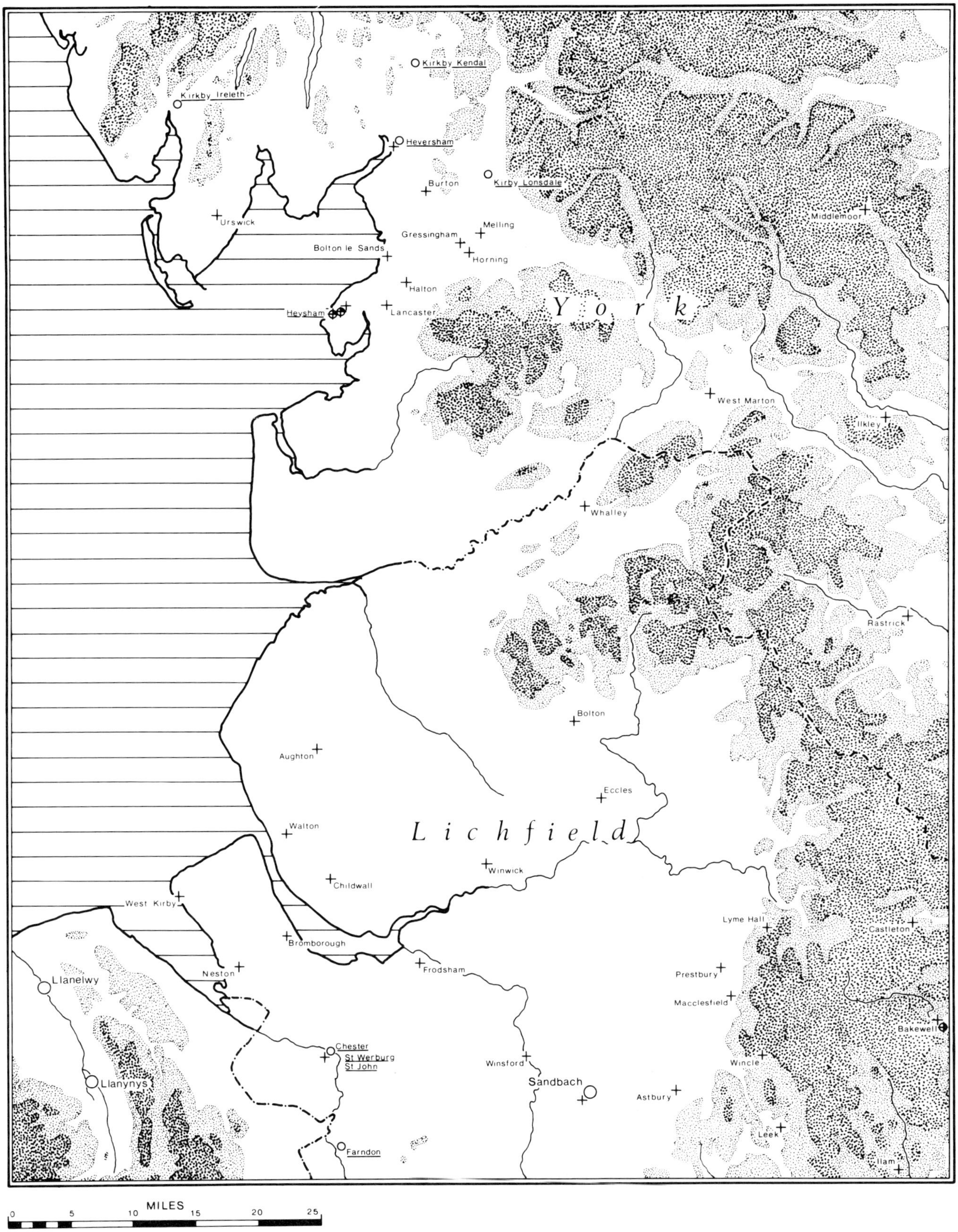

257 The Church in the north-west

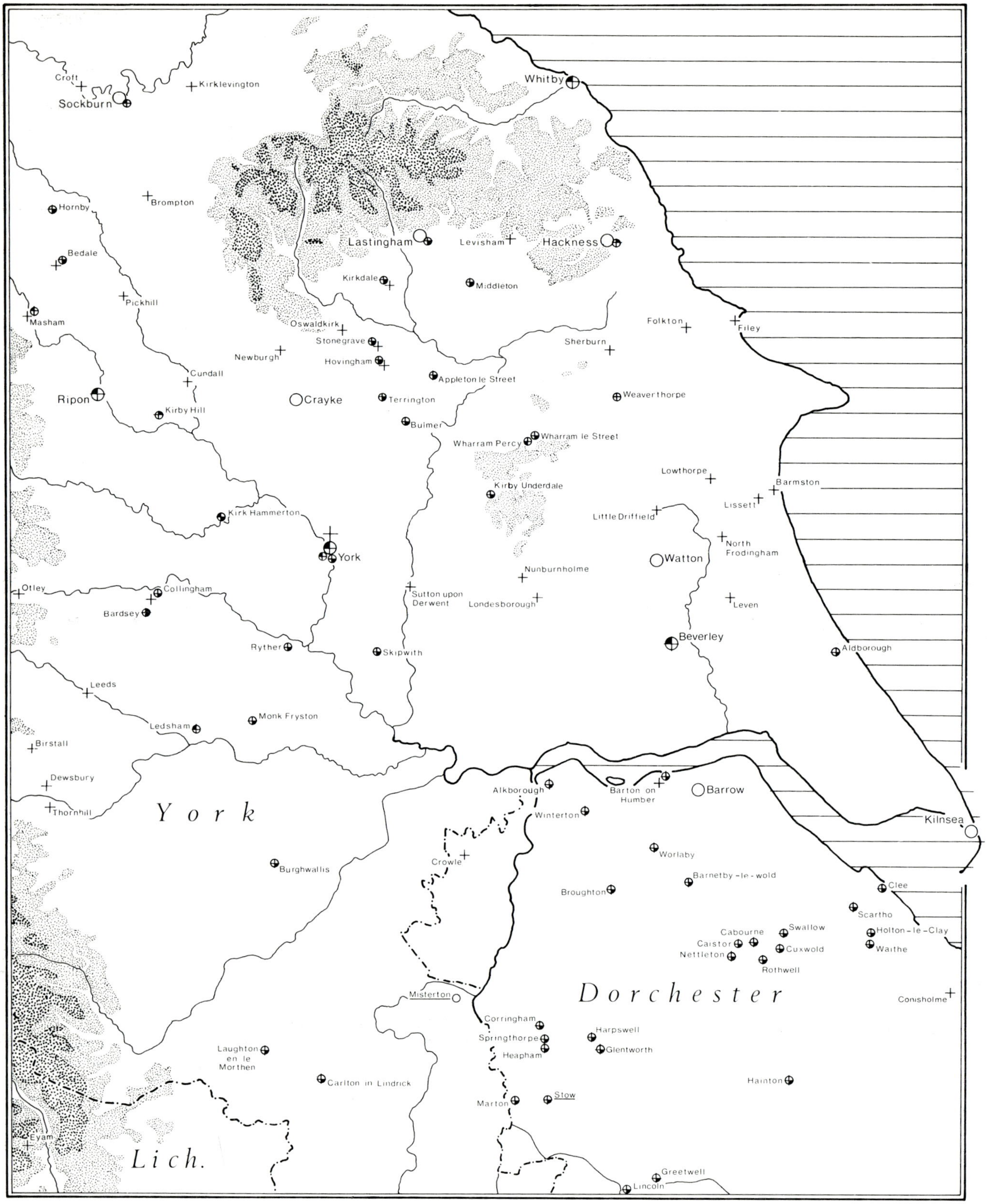

258 The Church in the north Midlands and Yorkshire

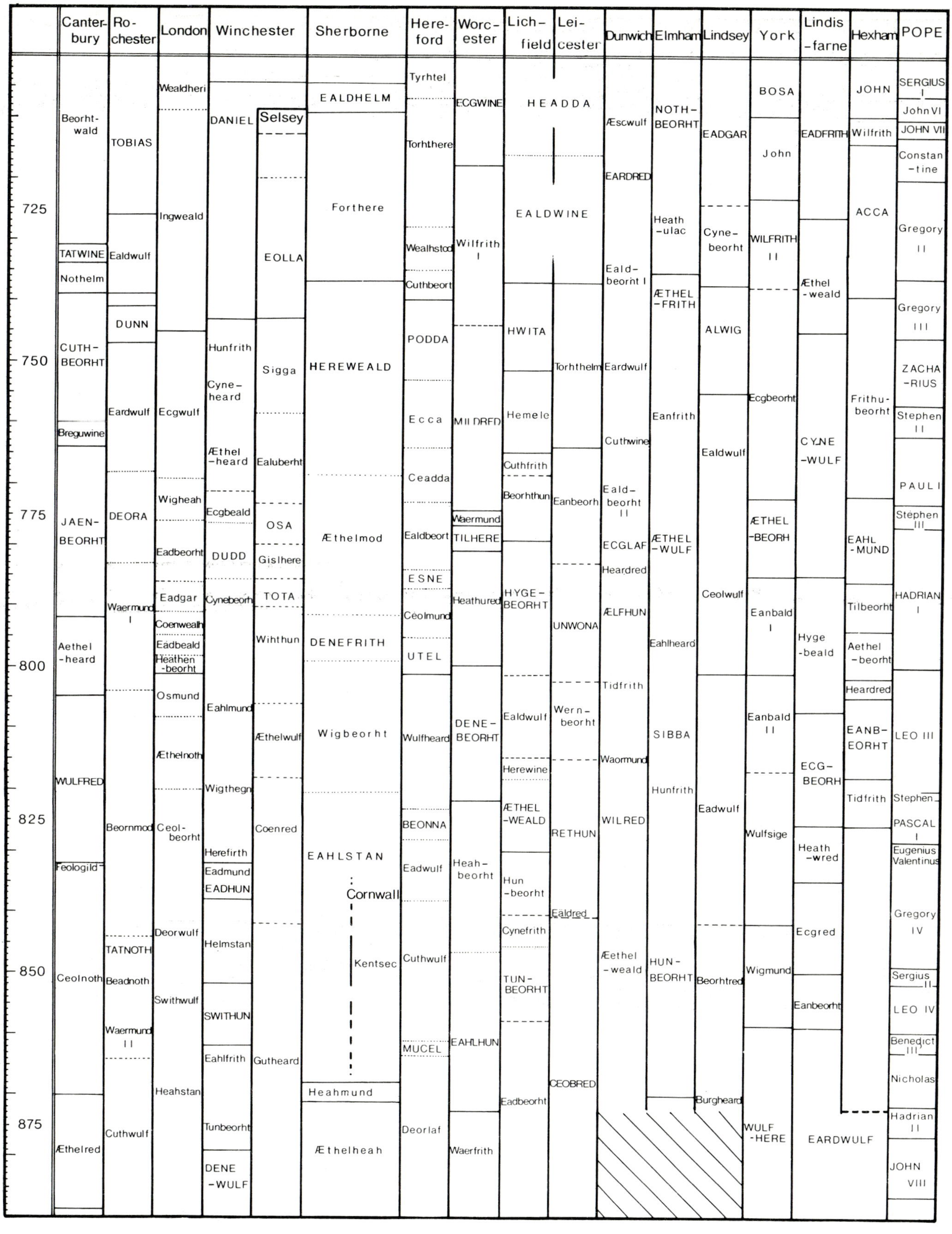

259 Bishops: chronology 700–880

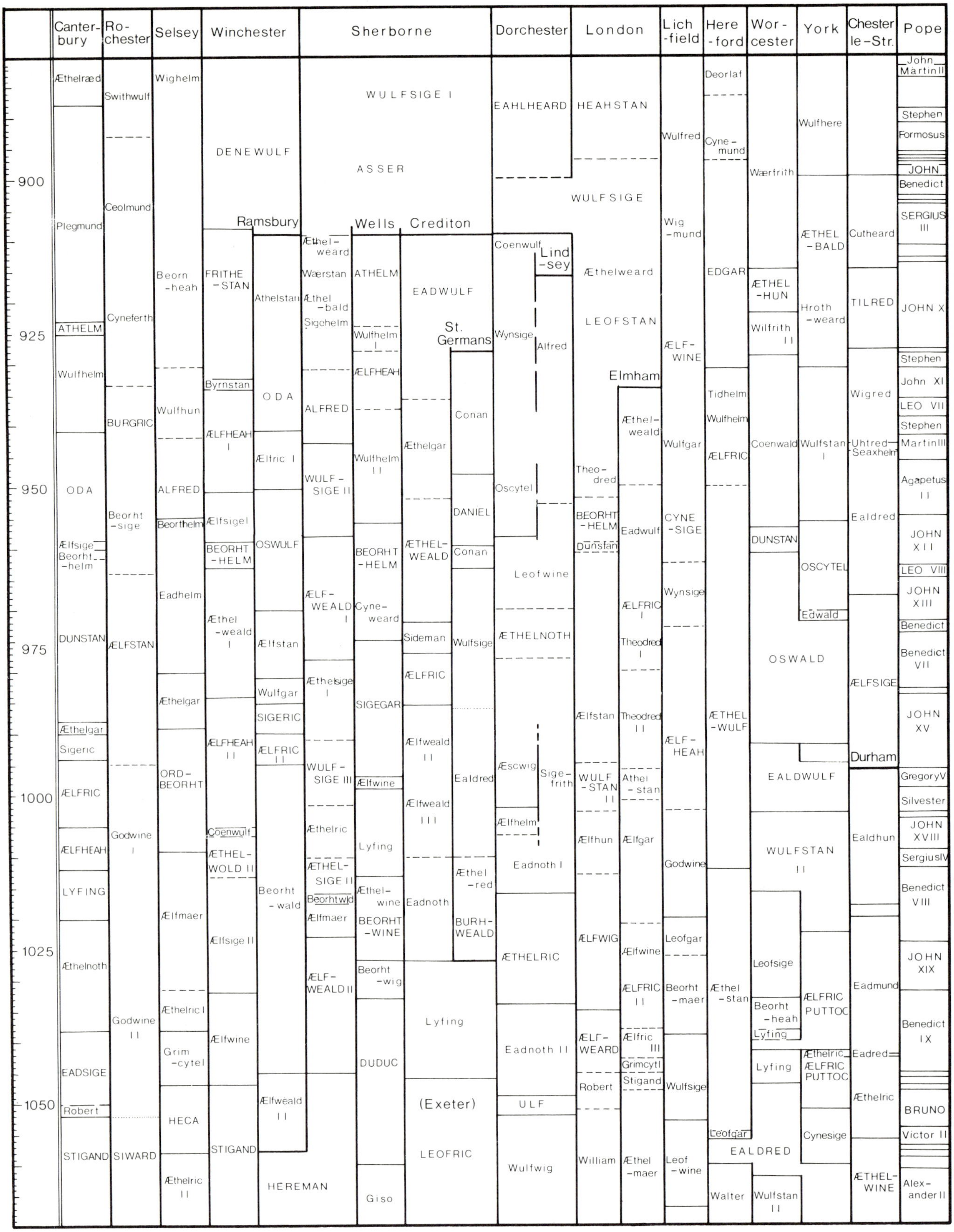

260 Bishops: chronology 880–1066

Bibliography

BARLOW, F. 1970: *Edward the Confessor*, London.

BIDDLE, M. 1976: 'Towns' in D. M. Wilson (ed.), *The Archaeology of Anglo-Saxon England*, London.

BRØNDSTED, J. 1965: *The Vikings*, London.

BROOKS, N. 1964: 'The unidentified forts of the Burghal hidage', *Med. Archaeol.* 74–90.

BRUCE-MITFORD, R. L. S. 1975: *The Sutton Hoo Ship Burial*, London.

CAMPBELL, J. 1979: in P. H. Sawyer, (ed.), *Names, Words and Graves*, Leeds.

COLGRAVE, B. 1956: *Felix of Crowland's Life of St Guthlac*, Cambridge.

DARBY, H. C. 1969: *The Domesday Geographies of England*, Cambridge.

DAVIES, W. 1978: *An Early Welsh Microcosm: Studies in the Llandaff Charters*, London.

DAVIES, W. and VIERCK, H. 1974: 'The contexts of tribal hidage: Social aggregate and settlement patterns', *Frühmitteralterliche Studien* 8.

DAVISON, B. K. 1972: 'The Burghal hidage fort of Eorpeburnan: a suggested identification', *Med. Archaeol.* 16, 123–7.

DOLLEY, R. H. M. 1966: *The Hiberno-Norse Coins in the British Museum*, London.

ELLIS, S. E. 1969: 'The petrography and provenance of Anglo-Saxon and Medieval English honestones, with notes on some other hones', *Bull. Brit. Museum (Natur. Hist.): Mineralogy* 2 (3), 133–87.

FAIRBRIDGE, R. W. 1966a: 'The changing level of the sea', *Scientific American* 202 (5).

FAIRBRIDGE, R. W. 1966b: 'Mean sea level changes, long term, eustatic and other', *Encyclopaedia of Oceanography*, New York.

FINBERG, H. P. R. 1961: *The Early Charters of the West Midlands*, Leicester.

FORD, W. J. 1976: 'Some settlement patterns in the central region of the Warwickshire Avon' in P. H. Sawyer (ed.), *Medieval Settlement, Continuity and Change*, London.

FOWLER, P. J. 1972: *Archaeology and the Landscape*, London.

FREEMAN, E. A. 1869–75: *The History of the Norman Conquest of England*, London.

GODFREY, J. 1962: *The Church in Anglo-Saxon England*, Cambridge.

GRAHAM-CAMPBELL, J. 1977: 'British antiquity – Western British, Irish and later Anglo-Saxon', *Archaeol. J.* 134.

HART, C. R. 1971: 'The tribal hidage', *TRHS* 5th series, 21.

HILL, D. H. 1969: 'The Burghal hidage – the establishment of a text', *Med. Archaeol.* 13.

HURST, J. G. 1976: 'The pottery' in D. M. Wilson (ed.), *The Archaeology of Anglo-Saxon England*, London.

JOPE, E. M. 1964: 'The Saxon building stone industry in southern and midland England', *Med. Archaeol.* 8.

KER, N. R. 1957: *Catalogue of Manuscripts containing Anglo-Saxon*, Oxford.

KNOWLES, D. 1963: *The Monastic Order in England*, Cambridge.

KNOWLES, D. 1965: *The Venerable Bede: The Ecclesiastical History of the English Nation*, London.

LAMB, H. H. 1978: *Climate, Present, Past and the Future*, London.

LEVISON, W. 1946: *England and the Continent in the Eighth Century*, Oxford.

LIEBERMANN, F. 1889: *Die Heiligen Englands*, Hanover.

LOYN, H. R. 1962: *Anglo-Saxon England and the Norman Conquest*, London.

LOYN, H. R. 1971: 'Towns in late Anglo-Saxon England : the evidence and some possible lines of enquiry' in P. Clemoes and K. Hughes (eds.), *England before the Conquest*, Cambridge

LOYN, H. R. 1977: *The Vikings in Britain*, London.

McNEILL, P. and NICHOLSON, R. 1975: *An Historical Atlas of Scotland*, St Andrews.

METCALF, D. M. 1978: 'The ranking of boroughs: numismatic evidence from the reign of Ethelred II', in D. HILL (ed.), *Ethelred the Unready*, BAR 59.

NORTH, J. J. 1963: *English Hammered Coinage*, London.

ORDNANCE SURVEY, 1935: *Britain in the Dark Ages*, 1st edn, Chessington.

ORDNANCE SURVEY, 1966: *Britain in the Dark Ages*, 2nd edn, Chessington.

ORDNANCE SURVEY, 1973: *Britain before the Norman Conquest*, Southampton.

OXENSTIERNA, E. 1976: 'The Vikings' in B. M. Fagan, *Avenues to Antiquity*, San Francisco.

RAHTZ, P. and BULLOUGH, D. 1977: 'The parts of an Anglo-Saxon mill', *Anglo-Saxon England* 6.

ROBERTSON, A. J. 1939: *Anglo-Saxon Charters*, Cambridge.

ROLLASON, D. W. 1978: 'Lists of saints' resting-places in Anglo-Saxon England', *Anglo-Saxon England* 7, 61–94.

SAWYER, P. H. 1968: *Anglo-Saxon Charters*, London.

SAWYER, P. H. 1971: *The Age of the Vikings*, 2nd edn, London.

SAWYER, P. H. 1978: *From Roman Britain to Norman England*, London.

SKEAT, W. W. 1881: *Aelfric's Lives of Saints*, Oxford.

SMITH, A. H. 1965: *The Place-names of Gloucestershire*, Cambridge.

SMYTH, A. P. 1975: *Scandinavian York and Dublin*, Dublin.

SMYTH, A. P. 1977: *Scandinavian Kings in the British Isles 850–880*, Oxford.

STENTON, F. M. 1970: *Preparatory to Anglo-Saxon England*, Oxford.

STENTON, F. M. 1971: *Anglo-Saxon England*, 3rd edn, Oxford.

TAYLOR, H. M. and TAYLOR, J. 1965: *Anglo-Saxon Architecture*, Cambridge.

TYLECOTE, R. F. 1962: *Metallurgy in Archaeology*, London.

WHITELOCK, D. 1955: *English Historical Documents c. 500–1042*, London.

WHITELOCK, D. 1965: *The Anglo-Saxon Chronicles: A Revised Translation*, London.

WILLIAMSON, J. A. 1959: *The English Channel*, London.

WILSON, D. M. 1976: *The Archaeology of Anglo-Saxon England*, London.

WILSON, M. 1968: 'The Hwicce', *Trans. Worcs. Archaeol. Soc. 3rd Series* 2.

Index

This is an Index Locorum only, as befits an Atlas. Map numbers are used throughout. The English place names are placed within traditional counties rather than ephemeral local government units. These counties are identified by the English Placename Society abbreviations.